SEARCH THESE THINGS
DILIGENTLY

SEARCH THESE THINGS
DILIGENTLY

A PERSONAL STUDY GUIDE TO THE

BOOK OF MORMON

BRIAN D. GARNER

DESERET
BOOK
SALT LAKE CITY, UTAH

Library of Congress Cataloging-in-Publication Data

Garner, Brian D.
   Search these things diligently / Brian D. Garner.
     p.   cm.
   Includes bibliographical references.
   ISBN 1-57008-951-5 (pbk.)
    1. Book of Mormon—Miscellanea.   2. Book of Mormon—Criticism, interpretation, etc.
I. Title.

BX8627. G37 2003
289.3'22—dc21   2003010814

Printed in the United States of America   18961-7075
R. R. Donnelley and Sons, Crawfordsville, IN

10 9   8   7   6   5   4   3   2   1

From almost every page of the
book [of Mormon], there will come . . .
a moving testimony that Jesus is indeed
the Christ, the Son of the Living God,
our Redeemer and Savior.

—MARION G. ROMNEY
(Conference Report, Apr. 1960, 112)

"No member of this Church can
stand approved in the presence of God
who has not seriously and carefully
read the Book of Mormon"

—JOSEPH FIELDING SMITH
(Conference Report, Oct. 1961, 18)

CONTENTS

PREFACE

As a teacher and student of the gospel for more than twenty years, I have noticed that students of the Book of Mormon seem to ask similar gospel questions again and again as they study. *Search These Things Diligently* focuses on those common questions and is arranged to accompany your scripture study and answer your questions. Because "all scripture is not of equal value" (*Teachings of Ezra Taft Benson*, 64), I have worked to emphasize the teachings of the Book of Mormon that focus on Jesus Christ and the foundational doctrines of His gospel.

Peter taught, "No prophecy of the scripture is of any private interpretation" (2 Peter 1:20). Therefore, I have included only a few of my own insights. My efforts have instead focused on the gleaning of multiple commentaries, talks, speeches, and teachings of prophets and other general authorities and scholars of the Church in order to not only help explain the scriptures but also to do so accurately.

Great efforts were made to give valuable information to the reader in a user-friendly manner. The book is outlined by chapter and verse, with a running scripture reference at the top of each page for easy access. Many charts, lists, and graphs have been included to show important patterns that emerge from the text. While the overall text is short, the reader should know that it is more comprehensive than it looks. Nearly all the statements compiled from general authorities and scholars have been weighed in such a way that only the core of their idea has been included to provide space for as many insights as possible. Where an important gospel principle is treated lightly, it is cross referenced to another place in the book where the same principle is elaborated on. Scriptural cross-references that shed additional light on a topic are also included. All sources are given so readers can more fully explore topics in other forums.

I take full responsibility for the statements of principle or doctrine given herein. While great efforts were made to achieve complete orthodoxy, the principles and doctrines do not represent official policy for The Church of Jesus Christ of Latter-day Saints. If statements by those quoted in this work were taken out of context or misrepresented in any way, I humbly seek forgiveness. My only intent is to assist the lay member of the Church in better understanding this sacred book of scripture.

I gratefully acknowledge the countless hours and efforts of my father, David H. Garner, and thank him for his careful, capable, and insightful review and critique of the manuscript. His years of experience and study, as well as his love and encouragement, have been of immense assistance. I also thank the competent and skillful team of editors and designers at Deseret Book for not only making the plain look great but also making up for my own grammatical inabilities. No one has sacrificed more in the making of this book than my wife, Ann, and our children. To them I express thanks and love and hope that this will be a valuable help for them in understanding the gospel and coming to know the Savior through the Book of Mormon. Finally and most important, I acknowledge and express my love and gratitude to my Heavenly Father, His divine Son, and the Holy Ghost for the marvelous work and wonder of the Book of Mormon and for the quiet moments of insights and teachings that have come from my personal searchings of this sacred book.

THE FIRST BOOK OF
NEPHI

1 NEPHI 1

I NEPHI I:I

How important is it to be good parents?

"Parents have a sacred duty to rear their children in love and righteousness, to provide for their physical and spiritual needs, to teach them to love and serve one another, to observe the commandments of God" ("The Family: A Proclamation to the World," *Ensign*, November 1995, 102). *See also 1 Nephi 8:36–38; insights for Enos 1:1; Mosiah 4:14–15.*

I NEPHI I:I, 17

How do we keep a journal?

"Your story should be written now while it is fresh and while the true details are available. . . .

"Get a notebook, . . . a journal that will last through all time. . . . Begin today and write in it your goings and comings, your deepest thoughts, your achievements and your failures, your associations and your triumphs, your impressions and your testimonies" (Spencer W. Kimball, *Teachings*, 351).

Why keep a journal?

"Those who keep a book of remembrance are more likely to keep the Lord in remembrance in their daily lives. Journals are a way of counting our blessings" (Spencer W. Kimball, *Ensign*, May 1978, 77).

I NEPHI I:2

What evidence of Egyptian influence is there in ancient America?

Two Egyptian statuettes were discovered on the Pacific coast of the border of El Salvador and Guatemala, three meters below the surface. They "clearly belong to a class of ancient Egyptian funerary statuettes known as *ushabti*. Both are incised with hieroglyphic Egyptian texts" (John W. Welch, ed., *Reexploring the Book of Mormon*, 18–20).

What is the "learning of the Jews and the language of the Egyptians"?

There were three basic writing systems for ancient Egyptian: (1) hiero-glyphs that included nearly four hundred picture characters; (2) hieratic; and (3) demotic. Both the hieratic and demotic writing systems were used in Lehi's time and can properly be termed "reformed Egyptian." An example of this might include the papyrus writing of Psalm 20:2–6 written in demotic and discovered in Thebes. The letters were clearly Egyptian, but the words they formed did not make sense in Egyptian. In 1944 it was discovered that the script was Egyptian, but the words the letters spelled were Aramaic. In addition to this, a piece of pottery was found with writing on it dating back to the time of Lehi. The text was determined to be a combination of Egyptian hieratic and Hebrew characters. Scholars concluded that "the scribe who wrote the text knew both Hebrew and Egyptian writing systems and commingled them in a single text" (John W. Welch and Melvin J. Thorne, *Pressing Forward with the Book of Mormon*, 241). *See also Mormon 9:32–33.*

What did the characters on the plates look like?

(Image courtesy Community of Christ Archives, Independence, Missouri. Used with permission.)

I NEPHI 1:4

Why is the phrase "it came to pass" repeated so often in the Book of Mormon?

"Instead of punctuation, the original manuscript of the Book of Mormon divides up its phrases by introducing each by an 'and,' 'behold,' 'now,' or 'It came to pass. . . .' Simply outrageous—as English literature, but it is standard Egyptian practice. . . . In Egyptian these expressions were not merely adornments, . . . they are a grammatical necessity and may not be omitted" (Hugh Nibley, *Collected Works*, 7:150).

Who was Zedekiah?

"Zedekiah reigned between 597 and 586 B.C. . . . Zedekiah revolted [against

Babylonian oppression]. Then, in 587 B.C., Nebuchadnezzar came and besieged Jerusalem. . . . Zedekiah was captured, as he fled toward Jericho. His sons, who fell into the hands of the Babylonians, were slain" (George Reynolds and Janne M. Sjodahl, *Commentary on the Book of Mormon,* 1:7–8) except one, named Mulek, who was led by the Lord to the Americas. He founded the city of Zarahemla, and later his people joined with the Nephites between 279 and 130 B.C. *See also Omni 1:19; Mosiah 25:2; Helaman 6:10; 8:21.*

Who were the "many prophets" that testified with Lehi?

"Among the prophets testifying to Jerusalem were Jeremiah, Lehi, Zephaniah, Obadiah, Habakkuk" (Joseph Fielding McConkie and Robert L. Millet, *Doctrinal Commentary,* 1:19).

I NEPHI 1:7

How does it feel to be "overcome with the Spirit" as Lehi was?

"The presence of God withdrew from Moses . . . as he was left unto himself, he fell unto the earth. . . . it was for the space of many hours before Moses did again receive his natural strength like unto man; and he said unto himself: . . . for this . . . I know that man is nothing . . . I should have withered and died in his presence; but his glory was upon me; and . . . I was transfigured" (Moses 1:9–11).

Describing the reaction of Joseph Smith and Sidney Rigdon to the vision of the three degrees of glory, Philo Dibble said, "Joseph sat firmly and calmly all the time in the midst of a magnificent glory, but Sidney sat limp and pale, apparently as limber as a rag, observing which, Joseph remarked, smilingly, 'Sidney is not used to it as I am'" (Philo Dibble, "Recollections," *Juvenile Instructor* 27 [1892], 303). *See also 1 Nephi 17:47; Moses 1:10; JS—H 1:20.*

I NEPHI 1:8

How is this verse textual evidence of the authenticity of the Book of Mormon?

In Alma 36:22 we read, "methought I saw, even as our father Lehi saw, God sitting upon his throne, surrounded with numberless concourses of angels, in the attitude of singing and praising their God." These words are a twenty-one word quote from 1 Nephi 1:8. The impressive thing about these verses is that they are separated by hundreds of pages and several weeks of translating time. (See *Church History in the Fulness of Times,* 58–59).

"Given the fact that Joseph dictated as he went, the record's consistency points to an inspired source for the translation's accuracy. After all, can you quote the twenty-one words of Lehi [after just having read them] . . . without looking?" (John W. Welch, ed., *Reexploring the Book of Mormon,* 23).

I NEPHI 1:12

Reading the word of the Lord fills us "with the Spirit of the Lord."

"I find that when I get casual in my relationships with divinity and when it seems that no divine ear is listening and no divine voice is speaking, that I am far, far away. If I immerse myself in the scriptures the distance narrows and the spirituality returns" (Spencer W. Kimball, *Teachings*, 135). *See also 1 Nephi 5:10, 17; Alma 17:2.*

I NEPHI 1:13, 15, 18

Seers see the future; prophets tell about the future.

"A seer can know of things which are past, and also of things which are to come" (Mosiah 8:17).

"God hath sent his holy prophets among all the children of men, to declare these things" (Mosiah 3:13).

I NEPHI 1:20

Who are the Jews?

"The term *Jew* often refers to a descendant from the tribe of Judah. However, the Book of Mormon also uses the term *Jew* to refer to any Israelite from the land or kingdom of Judah. . . . In addition, the Book of Mormon uses the term *Jew* sometimes to refer to the entire house of Israel" (Thomas R. Valletta, ed., *Book of Mormon for Latter-day Saint Families*, 3).

1 Nephi 2

I NEPHI 2:1

Can a dream be considered a vision?

"An inspired dream is a vision given to a person while he sleeps. . . . All inspired dreams are visions" (Bruce R. McConkie, *Mormon Doctrine*, 208).

I NEPHI 2:4

How does understanding what Lehi left and what he took with him help us better prioritize in our own lives?

What Lehi left behind	What Lehi took with him
House	Family
Land	Provisions
Gold and silver	Tents
Precious things	Scriptures (see 1 Nephi 3:3)

Where did Lehi travel when he left Jerusalem?

"Lehi's colony first traveled south from Jerusalem until they met the Red Sea (1 Nephi 2:4–6), then south-southeast until after they had stayed at Shazer and Nahom (1 Nephi 16:9–14, 33–34), and then 'nearly eastward from that time forth' until they arrived at the sea (1 Nephi 17:1–6)" (Daniel H. Ludlow, *Companion*, 92).

How important is it to thank the Lord?

"It is clear to me . . . that to 'thank the Lord thy God in all things' (D&C 59:7) is more than a social courtesy; it is a binding commandment" (James E. Faust, *Ensign*, December 1996, 2).

"And I believe that one of the greatest sins of which the inhabitants of the earth are guilty today is the sin of ingratitude" (Joseph F. Smith, *Gospel Doctrine*, 270). *See also insights for Mosiah 24:21–22.*

Why did the Lord visit Nephi?

"Whenever spiritually significant things are under way, righteous desires are present" (Neal A. Maxwell, *Ensign*, November 1996, 21). *See also 1 Nephi 11:1.*

Where is the "land which is choice above all other lands"?

"The Book of Mormon informs us that the whole of America, both North and South, is a *choice land above all other lands, in other words—Zion*" (Joseph Fielding Smith, *Doctrines of Salvation*, 3:73; emphasis in original). *See also insights for 2 Nephi 1:7, 9–11, 16, 20, 31–32.*

Laman and Lemuel were later "cursed" and cut off from the Lord's presence.

See insights for 2 Nephi 5:20–21.

Why didn't the Lord leave Laman and Lemuel in Jerusalem?

"And the Lord God said unto me: They [the Lamanites] shall be a scourge unto thy seed [the Nephites], to stir them up in remembrance of me" (2 Nephi 5:25).

1 NEPHI 3

1 NEPHI 3:5

"I have not required it of them, but it is a commandment of the Lord."

"What I the Lord have spoken . . . shall all be fulfilled, whether by mine own voice or by the voice of my servants, it is the same" (D&C 1:38).

1 NEPHI 3:7

"I will go and do."

"I made this my rule: *When the Lord commands, do it.*" (Joseph Smith, *History of the Church*, 2:170; emphasis in original).

"Obedience is a powerful spiritual medicine. It comes close to being a cure-all" (Boyd K. Packer, *"That All May Be Edified,"* 67).

"Obedience is the first law of heaven. . . . There is nothing in all eternity more important than to keep the commandments of God" (Bruce R. McConkie, *Promised Messiah*, 126).

The Lord will always prepare a way for us to keep his commandments.

"When my feeling of incompetence wholly overwhelmed me, I remembered the words of Nephi. . . . I rely upon that promise of the Lord that he will strengthen and empower me that I may be able to do this work to which I have been called" (Spencer W. Kimball, in Conference Report, October 1943, 18). *See also 1 Corinthians 10:13.*

1 NEPHI 3:11

What was "casting lots"?

"Casting lots was a means used to settle disputed questions. . . . This ancient equivalent of 'flipping a coin' resolved the matter quickly and decisively. Though the means might appear arbitrary, participants fully believed God was involved. . . . God could certainly have directed the results of any such process. [He wouldn't] use a lottery to pick an apostle" (*Quest Study Bible*, 890).

1 NEPHI 3:15

"As the Lord liveth, and as we live . . ."

See insights for 1 Nephi 4:32–37.

1 NEPHI 3:19–20

Why did the Lord want Nephi and his brothers to obtain the plates of brass?

To "preserve . . . the[ir] language" (1 Nephi 3:20)

To "preserve . . . the words . . . of all the holy prophets" [to have scripture]
(1 Nephi 3:20)

To keep a nation from dwindling in unbelief (see 1 Nephi 4:13)

To perhaps save the plates from being destroyed along with the rest of Jerusalem

I NEPHI 3:25

"Laban saw our property . . . [and] did lust after it."

"Cain said he was 'tempted because of [his] brother's flocks.' After killing Abel, he declared, 'I am free,' realizing that his brother's flocks were now his. Coveting preceded murdering" (Neal A. Maxwell, *Wonderful Flood of Light*, 101).

I NEPHI 3:29-31

Do miracles, such as seeing an angel as Laman and Lemuel did, bring testimony or conversion?

"Many men say: 'If I could only see an angel, if I could only hear an angel proclaim something, that would cause me to be faithful all the days of my life!' It had no effect upon these men [Laman and Lemuel] that were not serving the Lord, and it would have no effect today" (Heber J. Grant, in Conference Report, April 1924, 159). *See also Luke 16:30–31.*

1 NEPHI 4

I NEPHI 4:1-3, 15

How did Nephi's knowledge of scriptures assist him and his brothers in making the right choice?

"There is a power in the book [of Mormon] which will begin to flow into your lives the moment you begin a serious study of the book. You will find greater power to resist temptation. You will find the power to avoid deception. You will find the power to stay on the strait and narrow path" (Ezra Taft Benson, *Ensign*, November 1986, 7).

I NEPHI 4:6

Are we sometimes expected to accomplish things without knowing how?

Giving counsel to Elder Boyd K. Packer on one occasion, Elder Harold B. Lee said that one problem we often have is that we want to see the end from the beginning. He then counseled: "You must learn to walk to the edge of the light, and perhaps a few steps into the darkness, and you will find that the light will appear and move ahead of you" (Boyd K. Packer, *Holy Temple*, 184). *See also D&C 100:6.*

I NEPHI 4:10, 18

Are commandments ever given that run contrary to existing commandments?

"That which is wrong under one circumstance, may be, and often is, right under another. . . . Whatever God requires is right, no matter what it is" (Joseph Smith, *Teachings*, 256).

"When there is to be anything different from that which the Lord has told us already, He will reveal it to His prophet and no one else" (Harold B. Lee, *Stand Ye in Holy Places*, 159).

I NEPHI 4:11–12

Was there legal justification to kill Laban?

The penalty in the Law of Moses for attempted murder was death (see 1 Nephi 3:25–26; Exodus 21:14).

The penalty in the Law of Moses for stealing could be death (see 1 Nephi 3:13; Exodus 22:2; Deuteronomy 24:7).

After four offenses against a person, the "Law of Retaliation" (see D&C 98:23–32) was justified. In 1 Nephi 3:13 Laban had (1) tried to "slay" Laman. In 1 Nephi 4:11 he had (2) "sought to" kill Nephi. (3) "He would not hearken unto the . . . Lord"; and (4) he "had taken away our property." Therefore, "the Lord ha[d] delivered him into" the hands of Nephi (1 Nephi 4:12; D&C 98:29).

I NEPHI 4:13–15

How valuable are the scriptures to a nation?

"People as well as nations perish without scriptures. The scriptures are spiritual food for our spirit, which is just as important as physical food for our body. It was so important for Lehi to have the scriptures and records which were engraven on the brass plates that the Lord commanded Nephi to slay Laban in order to obtain them" (L. Lionel Kendrick, *Ensign*, May 1993, 14).

I NEPHI 4:20

Can the Lord change a person's voice to suit his purposes?

"As Brigham Young rose in that assembly, his face was that of Joseph Smith—the mantle of Joseph had fallen upon him, the power of God that was upon Joseph Smith was upon him, he had the voice of Joseph. . . . There was a reason for this in the mind of God; it convinced the people" (Wilford Woodruff, *Discourses*, 92–93).

I NEPHI 4:22

Who were the elders Nephi and Zoram spoke of?

"The word 'elders' has been understood to mean the heads of the most influential families of a city" (Hugh Nibley, *Collected Works*, 6:96).

I NEPHI 4:32–37

How serious is an oath, or our word of honor?

"A young man came to me not long ago and said, 'I made an agreement with a man that requires me to make certain payments each year. I am in arrears, and I can't make those payments, for if I do, it is going to cause me to lose my home. What shall I do?'

"I looked at him and said, 'Keep your agreement.'

"'Even if it costs me my home?'

"I said, 'I am not talking about your home. I am talking about your agreement; and I think your wife would rather have a husband who would keep his word, meet his obligations, keep his pledges or his covenants, and have to rent a home than to have a home with a husband who will not keep his covenants and his pledges'" (N. Eldon Tanner, in *Conference Report*, October 1966, 99). *See also Alma 44:8, 11, 15, 19–20; 53:11, 13–16.*

1 NEPHI 5

I NEPHI 5:1–4

How can we best resolve our differences in marriage without complaining?

"Don't be too critical of each other's faults. Recognize that none of us is perfect. . . .

". . . We don't need frequent reminders. Few people have ever changed for the better as a result of constant criticism or nagging. . . .

"When differences do arise, being able to discuss and resolve them is important, but there are instances when it is best to take a time-out. . . . Even letting the sun go down on your wrath can help bring you back to the problem in the morning more rested, calm, and with a better chance for resolution. . . .

". . . Any intelligent couple will have differences of opinion" (Joe J. Christensen, *Ensign*, May 1995, 64–65).

I NEPHI 5:2–3, 8

We never see Sariah complain against Lehi again.

"With the return of her sons, she knew of a certainty that the Lord had commanded her husband to flee into the wilderness. . . . Their circumstances did not change; they still slept in tents. But she had joy and comfort in the knowledge that the Lord was guiding them" (Barbara B. Smith, *Ensign*, November 1982, 85). *See also 1 Nephi 16:20.*

I NEPHI 5:7, 9–10

Why is it important to give thanks to the Lord?

"Because he knows an absence of appreciation on the part of anyone causes personal stagnation" (Marvin J. Ashton, *What Is Your Destination?* 99). *See also Alma 24:7–10; Ether 6:9, 12.*

I NEPHI 5:10–14

What did the "plates of brass" contain?

"An account of the creation of the world" (v. 11)

An account of "Adam and Eve" (v. 11)

"A record of the Jews . . . to . . . Zedekiah" (v. 12)

Prophecies of the "holy prophets" down to Jeremiah (v. 13)

A "genealogy of [Lehi's] fathers" (v. 14)

I NEPHI 5:17–18

Who used the plates of brass?

"From prophet to prophet and generation to generation the Brass Plates were handed down and preserved by the Nephites" (Bruce R. McConkie, *Mormon Doctrine*, 103). *See also Mosiah 1:16; 28:20; 3 Nephi 1:2.*

"The Indians, at a period long antecedent to the arrival of the Spaniards in America, were acquainted with a portion at least of the Old Testament" (B. H. Roberts, *New Witnesses for God*, 2:473).

I NEPHI 5:18

Who else will have the plates of brass?

"At some future date the Lord has promised to bring them forth, . . . and the scriptural accounts recorded on them are to 'go forth unto every nation'" (Bruce R. McConkie, *Mormon Doctrine*, 103).

1 NEPHI 6

I NEPHI 6:3–6

One purpose of the Book of Mormon is to "persuade men to come unto" Christ.

"Let us turn again to the Book of Mormon, . . . to learn some principles about coming unto Christ, being committed to Him, centered in Him, and consumed in Him" (Ezra Taft Benson, *Ensign*, November 1987, 84). *See also Jacob 1:7; Moroni 10:30.*

1 NEPHI 7

I NEPHI 7:1–5
Why did the Lord command that Nephi and his brothers return for this particular family?

"God said, [It is] not good that the man should be alone" (Genesis 2:18). *See also 1 Nephi 16:7.*

Lehi refers to Ishmael's sons as his sons or sons-in-law: "My sons who are the sons of Ishmael" (2 Nephi 1:1, 28).

"Lehi learned by searching the records of his fathers . . . that he was of the lineage of Manasseh. The Prophet Joseph informed us that . . . Ishmael was of the lineage of Ephraim, and that his sons married into Lehi's family, and Lehi's sons married Ishmael's daughters, thus fulfilling the words of Jacob upon Ephraim and Manasseh in the 48th chapter of Genesis" (Erastus Snow, *Journal of Discourses*, 23:184).

"Some students of the Book of Mormon have wondered how descendants of Joseph were still living in Jerusalem in 600 B.C. when most members of the tribes of Ephraim and Manasseh [Northern Kingdom] were taken into captivity by the Assyrians about 721 B.C. A scripture in 2 Chronicles may provide a clue to this problem. This account mentions that in about 941 B.C. Asa, the king of the land, gathered together at Jerusalem all of Judah and Benjamin 'and the strangers with them out of Ephraim and Manasseh' (2 Chronicles 15:9)" (Daniel H. Ludlow, *Companion*, 199).

I NEPHI 7:17
"I prayed . . . according to my faith."

"Believe in prayer and the power of prayer. Pray to the Lord with the expectation of answers" (Gordon B. Hinckley, *Teachings*, 469).

I NEPHI 7:20–21
Why should we forgive one another?

"Ye ought to forgive one another; for he that forgiveth not his brother his trespasses standeth condemned before the Lord; for there remaineth in him the greater sin" (D&C 64:9). *See also Matthew 6:14–15.*

"If we have been wronged or injured, forgiveness means to blot it completely from our minds. To forgive and forget is an ageless counsel. 'To be wronged or robbed,' said the Chinese philosopher Confucius, 'is nothing unless you continue to remember it'" (Spencer W. Kimball, *Ensign*, November 1977, 48).

1 NEPHI 8

I NEPHI 8:2

Does the Lord communicate to us through our dreams?

"I fear that in this age of sophistication there are those of us who are prone to rule out all dreams as of no purpose, and of no moment. And yet all through the scriptures there were recorded incidents where the Lord, by dreams, has directed His people" (Harold B. Lee, *Stand Ye in Holy Places*, 142).

I NEPHI 8:7-26; 11-12

What is the meaning of the vision of the tree of life?

ELEMENTS	INTERPRETATION
Dark and dreary waste (1 Nephi 8:7)	The world (1 Nephi 8:20)
Large and spacious field (1 Nephi 8:9)	The world (1 Nephi 8:20)
A tree (1 Nephi 8:10)	The love of God (1 Nephi 11:21–22)
White fruit (1 Nephi 8:10–11)	The fruit of God's love is the gift of his Son (John 3:16)
River of water (1 Nephi 8:13)	The living waters are the love of God (1 Nephi 11:25)
	The filthy waters (or tree of life) are the depths of hell (1 Nephi 12:16)
Rod of iron (1 Nephi 8:19)	The word of God (1 Nephi 11:25)
Strait and narrow path (1 Nephi 8:20)	The difficult way to the tree (Matthew 7:14)
Mist of darkness (1 Nephi 8:23)	The temptations of the devil (1 Nephi 12:17)
Great and spacious building (1 Nephi 8:26)	The pride of the world (1 Nephi 11:35–36)

I NEPHI 8:21

The same four kinds of people are described in this dream and in the parable of the sower in Matthew 13:4–8.

TREE OF LIFE DREAM	SIMILARITY	PARABLE OF THE SOWER
1 Nephi 8:21–23 Some people lose their way in the mists of darkness	Some obstacles keep people from their potential	**Matthew 13:7** Thorns choke out the seed
1 Nephi 8:24–28 Some eat the fruit but are ashamed and leave the tree	Some people begin strong but later weaken and don't endure to the end	**Matthew 13:5–6** Some seed springs up quickly but dies in the sun
1 Nephi 8:30 Some eat the fruit and fall down or stay with the tree	Some people begin and end strong	**Matthew 13:8** Some seed produces fruit
1 Nephi 8:31–33 Some people go directly to the great and spacious building	Some people don't even try	**Matthew 13:4** Some seed is eaten by birds

1 NEPHI 9

I NEPHI 9:1–5

What do the phrases "these plates" and "the other plates" refer to?

"'These plates' [found in verses 1, 2, 3, 4, 5] refers to the small plates of Nephi. 'Upon these [small] plates were recorded the more sacred matters pertaining to the ministry'" (Sidney B. Sperry, *Book of Mormon Compendium*, 16).

"The plates" or "other plates" [found in verses 2, 4] refers to the large plates of Nephi. The large plates include a record of the "secular . . . events among the descendants of Lehi, but later they contained the religious record as well" (Thomas R. Valletta, ed., *Book of Mormon for Latter-day Saint Families*, 23). *See also insights for 1 Nephi 19:1–4.*

I NEPHI 9:5

Does the Lord sometimes ask us to act on pure faith?

"[God] gave unto them commandments, that they should . . . offer the firstlings of their flocks. . . . Adam was obedient unto the commandments of the Lord. And after many days an angel of the Lord appeared unto Adam, saying: Why dost thou offer sacrifices unto the Lord? And Adam said unto him: I know not, save the Lord commanded me" (Moses 5:5–6).

1 NEPHI 9:6
How does God know "all things"?

"Angels . . . [reside], on a globe like a sea of glass and fire, where all things for their glory are manifest, past, present, and future, and are continually before the Lord. The place where God resides is a great Urim and Thummim" (D&C 130:6–8). *See also D&C 38:1–2; 88:41; insights for 2 Nephi 9:20.*

"God's omniscience is *not* solely a function of prolonged and discerning familiarity with us—but of the stunning reality that the past and present and future are part of an 'eternal now' with God!" (Neal A. Maxwell, *All These Things Shall Give Thee Experience*, 8; emphasis in original).

1 NEPHI 10

1 NEPHI 10:4–6, 11
What was the role of the Messiah?

"It . . . became necessary for the Father to send his Only Begotten Son, who was free from sin, to atone for our sins as well as for Adam's transgression, which justice demanded should be done. He accordingly offered himself a sacrifice for sins, . . . thereby redeeming us from the fall, and from our sins, on condition of repentance" (Joseph Fielding Smith, *Doctrines of Salvation*, 1:126).

1 NEPHI 10:7–10
Who is the "prophet who should come before the Messiah"?

"Jesus [taught]—'Among those that are born of women there is not a greater prophet than John the Baptist. . . .' How is it that John was considered one of the greatest prophets? . . .

"First. He was entrusted with a divine mission of preparing the way before the face of the Lord. . . .

"Secondly. He was entrusted with the important mission . . . to baptize the Son of Man . . .

"Thirdly. John, at that time, was the only legal administrator in the affairs of the kingdom there was then on the earth, and holding the keys of power" (Joseph Smith, *Teachings*, 275–76). *See also Matthew 3:1–3.*

I NEPHI 10:11

How often does the Book of Mormon teach about Christ's resurrection?

"Lehi . . . provid[ed] the first of more than eighty references in the Book of Mormon to the Resurrection" (Jeffrey R. Holland, *Christ and the New Covenant*, 37).

I NEPHI 10:17

Why would people want to "know of these things" for themselves?

"You will then know for yourselves and not for another. You will not then be dependent on man for the knowledge of God" (Joseph Smith, *Teachings*, 11).

I NEPHI 10:18

Why is it important to know that God "is the same yesterday, to-day, and forever"?

"An acquaintance with these attributes in the divine character, is essentially necessary, in order that the faith of any rational being can center in him for life and salvation . . . so that in this respect their faith can be without wavering" (Joseph Smith, *Lectures on Faith*, 3:19).

1 NEPHI 11

I NEPHI 11:1-36

How important is the vision of the tree of life?

"This vision is the central message of the Book of Mormon" (Boyd K. Packer, *Things of the Soul*, 7).

I NEPHI 11:1

What part does pondering play in receiving revelation?

"By pondering, we give the Spirit an opportunity to impress and direct. Pondering is a powerful link between the heart and the mind. As we read the scriptures, our hearts and minds are touched. If we use the gift to ponder, we can take these eternal truths and realize how we can incorporate them into our daily actions" (Marvin J. Ashton, *Ensign*, November 1987, 20). *See also D&C 76:15–19; 138:1–2, 11; JS—H 1:12–14; 3 Nephi 17:3.*

Who else has been "caught away . . . into an exceedingly high mountain"?

See Ezekiel 3:14; Moses 1:1; Matthew 17:1.

I NEPHI 11:1, 4-6

How important is believing in receiving personal revelation?

"Whoso believeth in Christ, doubting nothing, whatsoever he shall ask the Father in the name of Christ it shall be granted him" (Mormon 9:21). *See also Ether 12:6.*

I NEPHI 11:7–14:26

Nephi's vision of the tree of life was a vision about the Son of God.

Thirteen times in the vision Nephi is told to *look*; each time he learns something new about the Lord:

"Look" Reference	What is learned about Jesus Christ
Look # 1 1 Nephi 11:8–10	The white fruit of the tree is "precious above all."
Look # 2 1 Nephi 11:12–18	In Nazareth is the most beautiful virgin of all. She is the mother of "the Son of God."
Look # 3 1 Nephi 11:19–23	The woman is still called a "virgin" after the birth of the child. The child is the "Lamb of God," the "Son of the Eternal Father." Through Jesus Christ the Father offers his love, which is "most desirable above all" and brings much joy.
Look # 4 1 Nephi 11:24–25	The Son of God lived among men. Many believed and worshiped him.
Look # 5 1 Nephi 11:26–29	The Son of God is the Redeemer of the world. John the Baptist was a prophet who prepared the way for Jesus and baptized him. Afterward Jesus ministered to the people with "power and great glory." The people eventually rejected him. He called twelve apostles to assist him in his work.
Look # 6 1 Nephi 11:30	The ministering of angels assisted in the ministry of the Savior.
Look # 7 1 Nephi 11:31	The Savior healed the sick and cast out devils.
Look # 8 1 Nephi 11:32–36	Jesus was judged by the world. He was crucified and "slain for the sins of the world."
Look # 9 1 Nephi 12:1, 6–8	Jesus visited the Nephites after his resurrection and organized his Church among them.
Look # 10 1 Nephi 12:11	The righteous are forgiven of their sins through the blood of Jesus Christ.

Look # 11
1 Nephi 13:1, 34–36

The Nephite writings of the visit of Jesus would help facilitate the restoration of the Lamb's true Church.

Look # 12
1 Nephi 14:9, 12

The true Church of the Lamb would start small and grow to cover "all the face of the earth" in spite of great wickedness. The Lord will fulfill "his covenants" with Israel.

Look # 13
1 Nephi 14:18–19, 21–22, 24

At the end of the world Jesus Christ will come again.

I NEPHI 11:9-25

How do the elements of the vision of the tree of life represent Jesus Christ?

VISION OF THE TREE	VISION OF THE SAVIOR
The tree is "precious above all" (1 Nephi 11:9).	"God's . . . most precious of all gifts . . . [is] the gift of His Son Jesus Christ" (Melvin J. Ballard, Conference Report, October 1910, 82).
People "fell down" to partake of the fruit (1 Nephi 8:30).	People "fall down" before the Lord and "worship him" (1 Nephi 11:24).
The tree represents the love of God (1 Nephi 11:22).	Jesus Christ is God's love manifest to us (John 3:16).
The "rod of iron" is the "word of God" (1 Nephi 11:25).	Jesus Christ is the "Word of God" (Revelation 19:13).
"The tree of life" is the "living waters" (1 Nephi 11:25).	Jesus is called the "living water" (John 4:10; 7:37).
The path is the way to the tree (1 Nephi 8:20).	Jesus is the only "way" to "life" (John 14:6).

I NEPHI 11:11

Is the Holy Ghost a spirit "man"?

"The Holy Ghost . . . is not tabernacled in a body of flesh and bones, but is a personage of spirit; yet we know that the Spirit has manifested Himself in the form of a man" (James E. Talmage, *Articles of Faith*, 38).

I NEPHI 11:15

What do we know of this "virgin, most beautiful and fair above all other virgins"?

"Can we speak too highly of her whom the Lord has blessed above all women? There was only one Christ, and there is only one Mary. Each was noble and great. . . . We cannot but think that the Father would choose the greatest female spirit to be the mother of his Son" (Bruce R. McConkie, *Mortal Messiah*, 1:326–27, n. 4).

I NEPHI 11:16

How did Heavenly Father condescend?

"The condescension of God [the Father] lies in the fact that he, an exalted Being, steps down from his eternal throne to become the Father of a mortal Son, a Son born 'after the manner of the flesh'" (Bruce R. McConkie, *Mortal Messiah*, 1:314).

I NEPHI 11:18

Why was it necessary for Jesus to have a mortal mother?

"From his mother he inherited mortality, the power to lay down his life, to die, to permit body and spirit to separate. From his Father he inherited the power of immortality [and life]" (Bruce R. McConkie, *Mormon Doctrine*, 64).

I NEPHI 11:20

Mary was a virgin both before and after Jesus' birth

"[Jesus'] mortal mother, Mary, was called a virgin, both before and after she gave birth" (Ezra Taft Benson, *Teachings*, 7).

I NEPHI 11:22

What is "most desirable above all things"?

"The tree laden with fruit was a representation of the love of God which he sheds forth among all the children of men. The Master himself, later in his earthly ministry, explained to Nicodemus how that great love was manifested. Said he: 'For God so loved the world, that he gave his only begotten Son' . . . (John 3:16–17)" (Harold B. Lee, *Ensign*, June 1971, 6). *See also Moroni 7:44, 46.*

I NEPHI 11:26

How did the Son condescend?

Jesus Christ condescended below all things in several notable ways:

In birth:

"The Saviour . . . descended below all things. . . . There never was a child born on this earth with any less capacity than dwelt in the child that was born in a manger of his mother Mary. . . . There never was a child that descended lower in capacity, or that knew less" (Brigham Young, *Journal of Discourses*, 7:286).

In baptism:

The place of Jesus' baptism was at Bethabara, near the place where the Jordan River empties into the Dead Sea. When a person stands in these waters he is standing at the lowest point on earth, about 1,300 feet below sea level. Therefore, at his baptism, when Jesus was lowered in the waters of Jordan, he physically descended below all living things on the earth.

In life:

"As a God, He descended below all things, and made Himself subject to man in man's fallen condition; as a man, He grappled with all the circumstances incident to His sufferings in the world" (John Taylor, *Mediation and Atonement*, 151).

In the Atonement:

"The Almighty must descend below all things. . . .

". . . To suffer both body and spirit, bleeding from every pore, as he takes upon himself the sins of all men" (Bruce R. McConkie, *Millennial Messiah*, 16).

In death:

"[Jesus] submitted to all the trials of mortality, suffering 'temptations, and pain of body, hunger, thirst, and fatigue, even more than man can suffer, except it be unto death' (Mosiah 3:5–8), finally being put to death in a most ignominious manner" (Bruce R. McConkie, *Mormon Doctrine*, 155). *See also Isaiah 53:12.*

I NEPHI 11:27

How does the Holy Ghost appear "in the form of a dove"?

"The sign of the dove was instituted before the creation of the world, a witness for the Holy Ghost. . . . The Holy Ghost is a personage, and is in the form of a personage. It does not confine itself to the *form* of the dove, but in *sign* of the dove. The Holy Ghost cannot be transformed into a dove; . . . the dove is an emblem or token of truth and innocence" (Joseph Smith, *Teachings*, 276; emphasis in original). *See also LDS Bible Dictionary, s.v. "Dove, sign of."*

I NEPHI 11:32

"The Son of the everlasting God was judged of the world."

"What a bitter irony this was! He to whom all judgement has been committed (John 5:28) . . . would be judged and condemned by a wicked people" (Joseph Fielding McConkie and Robert L. Millet, *Doctrinal Commentary*, 1:83).

I NEPHI 11:33

Jesus was "slain for the sins of the world."

"Crucifixion was an indescribably cruel and loathsome mode of death. . . . It was always preceded by scourging, which reduced the naked body to a bleeding, quivering mass, and when the victim, after this unnecessary cruelty, was tied, or nailed, to the cross, where he suffered . . . burning fever, thirst, the sting of insects, utter helplessness . . . the spectacle presented was one of extreme horror" (George Reynolds and Janne M. Sjodahl, *Commentary on the Book of Mormon,* 1:90). *See also D&C 19:16, 18.*

1 NEPHI 12

I NEPHI 12:6–14:24

What future events does Nephi see and prophesy of?

REFERENCES	EVENT
1 Nephi 12:6	Christ's coming to the Americas after His resurrection
1 Nephi 12:11–12	Three to four righteous generations live after Christ's visit
1 Nephi 12:15, 19	The Lamanites destroy the Nephites because of wickedness
1 Nephi 12:20–23	The Lamanites live for many generations in unbelief and idleness
1 Nephi 13:1–10	Among the "Gentiles," or Europeans, a "great and abominable church" is organized
1 Nephi 13:12	The days of Columbus
1 Nephi 13:13	The days of the Pilgrims
1 Nephi 13:14–19	The American expansion of North America and the Revolutionary War
1 Nephi 13:20–25	The coming forth of the Bible
1 Nephi 13:34–36	The restoration of the gospel and coming forth of the Book of Mormon
1 Nephi 14:10–16	A day of great conflict between good and evil
1 Nephi 14:22, 24	The end of the world

I NEPHI 12:7–10

On what three occasions did the Lord establish his Church with twelve apostles?

During his mortal ministry in Jerusalem (Matthew 10:1–6)

During his ministry among the Nephites (3 Nephi 19:4–6)

In this dispensation (D&C 107:23)

1 NEPHI 13

I NEPHI 13:3

Who are the Gentiles Nephi saw in vision?

"Nephi . . . had a vision of the discovery and colonization of America by Europeans. He also saw the record of the Jews (the Bible) come forth" (Franklin D. Richards and James A. Little, *Compendium of the Doctrines of the Gospel*, 107).

I NEPHI 13:4–9, 26–28; 14:10–11

What is the "great and abominable church"?

"The titles *church of the devil* and *great and abominable church* are used to identify all churches or organizations . . . which are designed to take men on a course that leads away from God" (Bruce R. McConkie, *Mormon Doctrine*, 137).

I NEPHI 13:7–9

What are the goals of priestcraft?

"Priestcrafts are that men preach and set themselves up for a light unto the world, that they may get gain and praise of the world" (2 Nephi 26:29).

I NEPHI 13:10

What are the "many waters"?

"The Spirit of God inspired the great Columbus . . . to cross the many waters, the great Atlantic ocean, which separated him from the seed of Nephi's brethren" (Rulon S. Wells, in Conference Report, October 1919, 206).

I NEPHI 13:12

Who is the "man among the Gentiles"?

"That man, of course, was Christopher Columbus, who testified that he was inspired in what he did.

"'Our Lord,' said Columbus, 'unlocked my mind, sent me upon the sea, and gave me fire for the deed. Those who heard of my enterprise called it foolish, mocked me, and laughed. But who can doubt but that the Holy Ghost inspired me?' (Jacob Wasserman, Columbus, *Don Quixote of the Seas*, 19–20)" (Ezra Taft Benson, *Teachings*, 577).

I NEPHI 13:13

Who are the other Gentiles mentioned in this verse?

"[The Gentiles] refers to Christopher Columbus and the Pilgrim Fathers. It was the Lord that inspired that little band of people who . . . desired to worship him" (George Albert Smith, in Conference Report, October 1922, 95).

What captivity did the Gentiles escape?

"When it is realized how despotic the European kings were at this period, it is easily understood that the colonists did indeed flee from captivity and oppression. [The kings were] the supreme dictator[s] . . . in government, in economics . . . and in the state of religion" (Mark E. Petersen, *Great Prologue*, 33).

I NEPHI 13:14–15

Who was "scattered before the Gentiles"?

"[Nephi] saw also that the posterity of his brethren, subsequently known as the Lamanites, would . . . become subject to the Gentiles, and . . . be scattered before them" (James E. Talmage, *Articles of Faith*, 289–90).

I NEPHI 13:17–19

"Their mother Gentiles were gathered . . . to battle against them."

"Washington, during the . . . Revolutionary War . . . expressed himself repeatedly . . . That the American armies by themselves were altogether too weak to bring about this independence . . . but that independence came as a gift of God to these American colonies" (Mark E. Petersen, BYU *Speeches of the Year*, February 20, 1968).

I NEPHI 13:23–24

How valuable is the Bible to the world?

"The Bible is the book of books. . . . There is no way to overstate the worth and blessing of the Bible for mankind" (Bruce R. McConkie, *New Witness for the Articles of Faith*, 393).

I NEPHI 13:26–28

What has the "great and abominable church" done to the truth, and why?

"They have taken away from the gospel . . . many parts which are plain and most precious" (v. 26).

"Many covenants of the Lord have they taken away" (v. 26).

"There are many plain and precious things taken away from the book [the Bible]" (v. 28).

"And all this have they done that they might pervert the right ways of the Lord" (v. 27).

"An exceedingly great many do stumble, . . . Satan hath great power over them" (v. 29).

"The devil wages war against the scriptures. He hates them, perverts their plain meanings, and destroys them when he can. He entices those who heed his temptings to delete and discard, to change and corrupt, to alter and amend" (Bruce R. McConkie, *Doctrinal New Testament Commentary*, 1:624). *See also 2 Timothy 3:15–17; insights for 1 Nephi 19:10.*

1 NEPHI 13:39
What are the "other books" that confirm the truthfulness of the Bible?

"These last records which were to come forth to bear witness of the . . . Bible, are the Book of Mormon, the Doctrine and Covenants, and the revelations of the Lord to Joseph Smith" (Joseph Fielding Smith, *Man, His Origin and Destiny*, 411–12).

1 NEPHI 14

1 NEPHI 14:10
How are there "two churches only"?

"The church of the devil is the world; it is all the carnality and evil to which fallen man is heir; it is every unholy and wicked practice; it is every false religion, every supposed system of salvation which does not actually save and exalt man in the highest heaven of the celestial world. It is every church except the true church, whether parading under a Christian or a pagan banner" (Bruce R. McConkie, *Doctrinal New Testament Commentary*, 3:551). *See also D&C 1:30.*

1 NEPHI 14:13–16
How have the powers of the devil fought against the powers of the Lord?

"We saw mobbings and murders and martyrdom as the foundations of the work were laid in the United States. These same things, with greater intensity, shall yet fall upon the faithful in all nations" (Bruce R. McConkie, *Millennial Messiah*, 55).

The best preparation is to be "armed with righteousness."

"I hope that every young man . . . will resolve tonight, 'I am going to keep myself clean. I am going to serve the Lord. I am going to prepare every way I can for future service, because I want to be prepared when the final battle shall come'" (Hugh B. Brown, in Conference Report, October 1967, 115).

I NEPHI 14:21–27

What is the book that John wrote about the last days?

"His mission as the writer of the Gospel and of the Book of Revelation was assigned to him hundreds of years before he was born. This knowledge was revealed to Nephi nearly six hundred years before the birth of Christ" (Joseph Fielding Smith, *Man, His Origin and Destiny*, 527).

I NEPHI 14:28

Why was Nephi permitted to write "but a small part" of what he saw?

"I could explain a hundred fold more than I ever have of the glories of the kingdoms manifested to me in the vision, were I permitted, and were the people prepared to receive them" (Joseph Smith, *Teachings*, 304).

1 NEPHI 15

I NEPHI 15:8, 11

"Have ye inquired of the Lord?"

"No message appears in scripture more times, in more ways, than 'Ask, and ye shall receive'" (Boyd K. Packer, *Things of the Soul*, 89). *See also insight for Enos 1:15.*

I NEPHI 15:11

How does keeping the commandments affect our receiving answers to prayer?

"And if ye are purified and cleansed from all sin, ye shall ask whatsoever you will in the name of Jesus and it shall be done" (D&C 50:29).

I NEPHI 15:12–13, 16

What is the meaning of Lehi's words about the house of Israel?

Lehi spoke of these things to his sons in 1 Nephi 10:14.

SYMBOL	MEANING
The olive tree	The house of Israel
The branch of the olive tree	Nephites and Lamanites
Grafting of the natural branches of the olive tree	The Lamanites receive the gospel in the latter days

I NEPHI 15:16, 18

When will the Lamanites unite with the Abrahamic covenant?

"The Lamanites must rise again in dignity and strength to fully join their brethren and sisters of the household of God in carrying forth his work in preparation for that day when the Lord Jesus Christ will return to lead his people, when the millennium will be ushered in" (Spencer W. Kimball, *Ensign*, December 1975, 7).

I NEPHI 15:18

What was the covenant the Lord made with Abraham?

The following scriptures help to see four parts to the Abrahamic covenant.

SCRIPTURE	WHAT THE LORD TOLD ABRAHAM	HOW IT COULD RELATE TO US
Genesis 12:1	"Get thee . . unto a land that I will shew thee"	Our promised land can be exaltation
Genesis 12:2	"Make of thee a great nation"	We may have seed forever
Genesis 12:2	"Make thy name great"	We take upon us the name of Christ
Genesis 12:3	"In thee shall all the families of the earth be blessed"	We may help take the gospel to all

I NEPHI 15:23–24

How does holding fast to the rod of iron bring power over Satan?

"Not only will the word of God lead us to the fruit which is desirable above all others, but in the word of God and through it we can find the power to resist temptation, the power to thwart the work of Satan. . . .

"The word of God . . . has the power to fortify the Saints and arm them with the Spirit so they can resist evil" (Ezra Taft Benson, *Ensign*, May 1986, 80).

I NEPHI 15:29–32

The wicked will experience an "awful hell," both in this life and the next.

"Latter-day scriptures teach that there are at least three meanings for the term *hell*. It can describe our suffering here on earth (see Alma 36:18). It can refer to a part of the spirit world where those who have not repented suffer for their sins (see Alma 40:13–14). It is also used to describe the final condition of those who completely turn away from God (see D&C 29:38)" (Thomas R. Valletta, ed., *Book of Mormon for Latter-day Saint Families*, 43).

1 NEPHI 16

1 NEPHI 16:1–3

"The guilty taketh the truth to be hard, for it cutteth them to the very center."

"How we respond to the words of a living prophet when he tells us what we need to know, but would rather not hear, is [the real] test of our faithfulness" (Ezra Taft Benson, *Teachings*, 140). *See also 2 Nephi 9:40; 33:4–5; Helaman 14:10.*

1 NEPHI 16:7

Lehi's sons married Ishmael's daughters, and Ishmael's sons married Lehi's daughters.

See insights for 1 Nephi 7:1–5.

1 NEPHI 16:10

What do we know about the "round ball of curious workmanship"?

It had two spindles (v. 10).

One spindle pointed the way they should go (vv. 10, 16).

"The other was perhaps fixed on some known . . . direction" (Jeffrey R. Holland, *Christ and the New Covenant*, 176).

It operated according to their faith (v. 28).

It sometimes had messages written on it (vv. 26–27, 29).

It was called "Liahona" (see Alma 37:38).

What has the Lord given us that acts like a personal Liahona?

"Wouldn't you like to have that kind of ball? . . . The Lord gave to . . . every person, a conscience which tells him every time he starts to go on the wrong path" (Spencer W. Kimball, *Ensign*, November 1976, 79).

"The same Lord who provided a Liahona for Lehi provides for you and for me today a rare and valuable gift to give direction to our lives, . . . a patriarchal blessing" (Thomas S. Monson, *Live the Good Life*, 36–37).

"I like to think that the Book of Mormon is truly like the Liahona of old" (Robert E. Wells, in *Doctrines of the Book of Mormon*, 13).

1 NEPHI 16:20, 22, 25, 35–36

What value is there in murmuring?

"What a joy it is to see someone of good cheer, who, when others because of an unpleasant happening or development live in angry silence or vocal disgust, meets the situation with cheerful endurance and good spirits" (Marvin J. Ashton, *Ensign*, May 1986, 66). *See also Alma 62:41.*

Gratitude is the opposite of complaining. President John Taylor experienced many challenges in his life that he could have murmured or complained about. At Carthage Jail, John Taylor reports: "I was struck by a ball from the door about midway of my thigh. . . . I crawled under the bed. . . . While on my way and under the bed, I was wounded in three other places. . . . My wounds were painful" (John Taylor, *Gospel Kingdom*, 361). Later John Taylor spent much of his life in exile and died in hiding in Kaysville. On a plaque at the home where he died are inscribed his last six words: "I feel to thank the Lord."

Knowing this small part of President Taylor's life, consider what he taught about murmuring. "Do not be troubled about anything. I should be ashamed of telling any body I was troubled . . . ; talk about peace and the principles of eternal life; about God, angels. . . . I am surprised to hear any body talk about troubles, poor creatures; you have a little soul. I never had much trouble myself. . . . When trouble comes upon you I would recommend the course Bunyan took in the Pilgrim's Progress; he put his fingers in his ears, and cried life, life, eternal life. So when you hear any one talk about their troubles, put your finger in you ears, and cry life, life, eternal life." (John Taylor, *Times and Seasons* 6 [January 15, 1845]: 1102–3).

I NEPHI 16:23, 30–31
What can we do instead of complaining?

NEPHI'S PATTERN FOR SUCCESS	WHAT WE CAN DO FOR SUCCESS
"I, Nephi, did make . . . a bow, and . . . an arrow; . . . I did arm myself . . . with a sling and with stones" (v. 23)	Do what we can to overcome the problem, make preparations, plan for the future
"I said unto my father: Whither shall I go to obtain food?" (v. 23)	When needed, seek advice from our families and priesthood leaders
"I, Nephi, did go forth up into the top of the mountain" (v. 30)	Be willing to do what the Lord directs us to do
"I did slay wild beasts, insomuch that I did obtain food for our families" (v. 31)	When we do our part and do what the Lord asks, we are blessed with success

What can we learn from Nephi's example of supporting priesthood leaders?

"The bishop may be a humble man. Some of you may think you are superior to him, and you may be, but he is given authority direct from our Father in heaven. Recognize it. Seek his advice" (David O. McKay, in Conference Report, October 1967, 7).

"No man . . . understanding . . . authority and law of the Holy Priesthood will attempt for a moment to run before his file leader or to do anything that is not strictly in harmony with his wish" (Joseph F. Smith, *Gospel Doctrine*, 185).

I NEPHI 16:23
How is the story of Nephi's bow evidence of the truth of the Book of Mormon?

"According to the ancient Arab writers, the only bow-wood obtainable in all Arabia was the *nab* wood that grew only 'amid the inaccessible and overhanging crags' of Mount Jasum and Mount Azd, which are situated in the very region where . . . the broken bow incident occurred" (Hugh Nibley, *Collected Works*, 6:232).

I NEPHI 16:34
What archeological evidence is there for a place called "Nahom"?

"A group of Latter-day Saint researchers recently found evidence linking a site in [Marib] Yemen, on the south-west corner of the Arabian peninsula, to a name associated with Lehi's journey as recorded in the Book of Mormon.

"Warren Aston, Lynn Hilton, and Gregory Witt located a stone altar that professional archaeologists dated to at least 700 B.C. This altar contains an inscription confirming 'Nahom' as an actual place that existed in the peninsula before the time of Lehi" (*Ensign*, February 2001, 79).

Since the report in the February 2001 *Ensign*, two additional altars bearing the name of Nahom have been identified at the same temple site.

1 NEPHI 17

I NEPHI 17:2-3, 12
Sometimes the Lord will strengthen us rather than take away our trials.

"I will also ease the burdens which are put upon your shoulders. . . . And . . . the Lord did strengthen them that they could bear up their burdens with ease" (Mosiah 24:14–15).

I NEPHI 17:5
Where was the land of Bountiful?

"As Nephi described that land, it must have contained water, fruit, large trees for a ship, grass, wild honeybees, flowers or blossoms, a mountain, a shoreline, a cliff overlooking the depths of the sea, and metal ore. Incredible as it seems, the south coast of the Arabian peninsula from Perim to Sur has only one place in its entire length of 1,400 miles that meets that description. It is a tiny sickle of land curved around a little bay, about 28 miles long and only 7 miles wide, backed by the Qara Mountains. . . . This place is Salalah, in the state of Dhofar, the Sultanate of Oman. The coast in both directions stretches away in unbroken barrenness" (Lynn M. and Hope A. Hilton, *Ensign*, September 1976, 50–51).

I NEPHI 17:20–21

Would Laman and Lemuel really have been happy to have stayed in Jerusalem?

At about the same time Laman and Lemuel said this, Jerusalem and her people were being destroyed by the Babylonians (see Jeremiah 39:1–2). Jeremiah described it this way: "Jerusalem . . . will . . . fall by the sword . . . and their carcases will I give to be meat for the fowls of the heaven, and for the beasts of the earth. And I will make this city desolate . . . [the inhabitants of Jerusalem] will . . . eat the flesh of their sons and the flesh of their daughters" (Jeremiah 19:7–9).

I NEPHI 17:23

What did Nephi accomplish by acting instead of murmuring?

"[Nephi has] been an instrument in the hands of God, in bringing us forth into the land of promise; for were it not for him, we must have perished with hunger in the wilderness" (2 Nephi 1:24).

I NEPHI 17:23–51

Nephi used miracles of the past to show that miracles of the present are possible.

The Lord led the children of Israel out of Egyptian bondage (vv. 23–25).

He divided the Red Sea for them to escape (v. 26).

He drowned the Egyptians in the Red Sea (v. 27).

He fed the children of Israel on manna (v. 28).

He gave them water from a rock (v. 29).

He helped them defeat their enemies and inhabit the land (v. 32).

He provided a way to heal those bitten by the fiery flying serpents (v. 41).

If God can do all that then he can help Nephi build a ship (v. 51).

I NEPHI 17:30–31, 35, 37, 40

Is God's love conditional?

"The Lord loveth the righteous, but the wicked, . . . his soul hateth" (JST, Psalm 11:5).

"The people of Nephi hath he loved . . . But behold my brethren, the Lamanites hath he hated because their deeds have been evil continually" (Helaman 15:3–4).

"Renegade 'Mormon' dissenters are running through the world and spreading various foul and libelous reports against us. . . . Such characters God hates; we cannot love them. The world hates them, and we sometimes think that the devil ought to be ashamed of them" (Joseph Smith, *Teachings*, 126–27).

"While divine love can be called perfect, infinite, enduring, and universal, it cannot correctly be characterized as unconditional. The word does not appear in the scriptures. On the other hand, many verses affirm that the higher levels of love the Father and the Son feel for each of us . . . are conditional. . . . Understanding that divine love and blessings are not truly 'unconditional' can defend us against common fallacies such as these: 'Since God's love is unconditional, He will love me regardless . . .'" (Russell M. Nelson, *Ensign*, February 2003, 20–23). *See also 2 Nephi 7:1; 9:42; D&C 95:12; 124:15; John 15:10.*

I NEPHI 17:35

What will the Lord do before destroying a wicked people?

Before the floods of Noah's day, the Lord said, "'I will first send them my word, offering them deliverance from sin, and warning them of my justice, which shall certainly overtake them if they reject it, and I will destroy them'" (John Taylor, *Journal of Discourses*, 19:158).

I NEPHI 17:44

What difference does it make what we think in our hearts?

See insights for Mosiah 4:30.

I NEPHI 17:45, 55

How does the Lord most commonly communicate to us?

"I have come to know that inspiration comes more as a feeling than as a sound" (Boyd K. Packer, *That All May Be Edified*, 11).

"That which is received of [the Holy Ghost] has a more powerful effect upon the soul than anything else received in any other way" (Keith B. McMullin, *Ensign*, May 1996, 9). *See also 1 Corinthians 12:3; insight for Moroni 10:5, 7.*

I NEPHI 17:47

Why do mighty spiritual experiences leave people weak?
    See insights for 1 Nephi 1:7.

I NEPHI 17:50

What is possible with God's help?
    See 1 Nephi 9:6; insights for 2 Nephi 9:20.

1 NEPHI 18

I NEPHI 18:3

How does the Lord bless us when we go to him often?
    "Thus saith the Lord God: I will give unto the children of men line upon line, precept upon precept, here a little and there a little" (2 Nephi 28:30).

I NEPHI 18:9

Is it a sin "to make . . . merry, . . . to dance, and . . . to sing"?
    This scripture implies that dancing, singing, and laughing are sins (see also D&C 59:15–16; 88:69). However, some laughter, dancing, and singing are ways to praise God. "If thou art merry, praise the Lord with singing, with music, with dancing, and with a prayer of praise and thanksgiving" (D&C 136:28). *See also Psalm 149:1–4.*

    "Music is an important and powerful part of life. It can be an influence for good that helps you draw closer to Heavenly Father. However, it can also be used for wicked purposes. . . .
    "Choose carefully the music you listen to. . . .
    "Dancing can be fun and can provide an opportunity to meet new people. However, it too can be misused" (*For the Strength of Youth,* 20–21).

I NEPHI 18:10–23

How are the events of 1 Nephi 18 a type of the Savior's ministry?
    "All things which have been given of God . . . are the typifying of [Christ]" (2 Nephi 11:4).

NEPHI	CHRIST
Laman and Lemuel said, "We will not that our . . . brother shall be a ruler over us" (1 Nephi 18:10)	The wicked "do not desire that the Lord their God [their older brother] should rule and reign over them" (Helaman 12:6)

"Laman and Lemuel did take me and bind me with cords" (1 Nephi 18:11)

"Laman and Lemuel . . . did treat me with much harshness" (1 Nephi 18:11)

"The band and the captain and officers of the Jews took Jesus, and bound him" (John 18:12)

"The men that held Jesus mocked him, and smote [him]. And when they had blindfolded him, they struck him on the face" (Luke 22:63–64)

"The Lord did suffer [allow] it" (1 Nephi 18:11)

"They scourge him, and he suffereth it; and they smite him, and he suffereth it. Yea, they spit upon him, and he suffereth it" (1 Nephi 19:9)

"The compass, which had been prepared of the Lord, did cease to work" (1 Nephi 18:12)

"Jesus cried with a loud voice, and gave up the ghost" (Mark 15:37)

"There arose a great storm, yea, a great and terrible tempest" (1 Nephi 18:13)

At Christ's death "there arose a great storm" (3 Nephi 8:5)

"For the space of three days" (1 Nephi 18:13)

At the time of Christ's death there was darkness "for the space of three days" (3 Nephi 8:20–23)

Nephi's bands were loosed (1 Nephi 18:15)

"Christ shall loose the bands of . . . death" (Alma 11:42)

Nephi's "wrists, and . . . ankles were much swollen, and great was the soreness thereof" (1 Nephi 18:15)

"The multitude . . . did feel the prints of the nails in his hands and in his feet" (3 Nephi 11:15)

"I did look unto my God, and I did praise him . . . and I did not murmur against the Lord" (1 Nephi 18:16)

"Glory be to the Father, and I partook and finished my preparations unto the children of men" (D&C 19:19)

"My parents . . . suffered much grief because of their children" (1 Nephi 18:17)

"Remembering unto the Father my body which was laid down for you, and my blood which was shed for the remission of your sins" (D&C 27:2)

"I took the compass, and it did work . . . there was a great calm . . . I, Nephi, did guide the ship, that we sailed again towards the

"Be it known unto you all . . . that . . . Jesus Christ . . . is the stone . . . which is become the head of the corner. Neither is

promised land . . . and . . . we did arrive at the promised land" (1 Nephi 18:21–22)

there salvation in any other: for there is none other name under heaven given among men, whereby we must be saved" (Acts 4:10–12)

I NEPHI 18:11

Does the Lord always save the righteous from suffering?

Situation	The Lord removes suffering	The Lord allows suffering
Nephi is tied up by his enemy	**1 Nephi 7:18** "The bands were loosed from off my hands and feet"	**1 Nephi 18:11** "Laman and Lemuel did . . . bind me with cords, and they did treat me with much harshness; nevertheless, the Lord did suffer it"
The wicked try to kill the prophet	**Helaman 16:2** Samuel is protected when the wicked try to kill him	**Mosiah 17:20** Abinadi is killed by wicked king Noah
Good people refuse to worship false gods	**Daniel 3:17–27** Shadrach, Meshach and Abednego's lives are miraculously spared	**Abraham 1:11** Three virgins are killed because they would not worship a false god

See insights for Alma 14:11 to read about why bad things sometimes happen to good people.

I NEPHI 18:13–15, 20

What does it usually take for us to remember the Lord?

"Except the Lord doth chasten his people with many afflictions, . . . they will not remember him" (Helaman 12:3).

I NEPHI 18:16

Did Nephi ever murmur and complain?

"We find here a man [Nephi] of faith; a man who submits to affliction without murmuring. In all his history we find that he followed the commandments of the Lord" (Heber J. Grant, in Conference Report, October 1899, 19).

I NEPHI 18:21

Why did the storm stop when Nephi prayed?

"The effectual fervent prayer of a righteous man availeth much" (James 5:16).

I NEPHI 18:25

Were there horses in America before Columbus?

See insights for Alma 18:9.

1 NEPHI 19

I NEPHI 19:1–4

Which are "those first plates" and which are "these plates"?

"When the family of Lehi reached the western hemisphere, Nephi was commanded of God to make a set of plates ['those first plates'] upon which the history of his people was to be kept. He did so, recounting their journey in the wilderness and prophecies. . . . This record is known to us as the large plates. . . . Some twenty years later (ca. 570 B.C.) Nephi was commanded to make another set of plates ['these plates'] known to us as the small plates . . . (see 2 Nephi 5:28–31), in which he recorded only that which was sacred" (Joseph Fielding McConkie and Robert L. Millet, *Doctrinal Commentary*, 1:145). *See also insights for 1 Nephi 9:1–5.*

I NEPHI 19:10

Who is the God of the Old Testament?

"Christ is Jehovah, the God of the Old Testament, as well as Jesus, the Savior of the New Testament" (Jeffrey R. Holland, *Christ and the New Covenant*, 42).

What plain and precious things have been taken from the Bible?

"There is . . . very little in the Old Testament about baptism for the remission of sins or the laying on of hands for the receipt of the Holy Ghost. . . . A knowledge of them and of our Lord's divine Sonship have been restored in . . . the Pearl of Great Price" (Bruce R. McConkie, *Promised Messiah*, 142). *See also insights for 1 Nephi 13:26–28.*

Who are the prophets Zenock, Neum, and Zenos?

"Outside of what is written in the Book of Mormon, we have no record of . . . these ancient prophets. . . . Their writings must have been recorded on the [brass] plates" (Joseph Fielding Smith, *Answers to Gospel Questions*, 4:138).

"Next to Isaiah himself . . . there was not a greater prophet in all Israel than Zenos" (Bruce R. McConkie, in Monte S. Nyman and Robert L. Millet, eds., *Joseph Smith Translation*, 17).

I NEPHI 19:11

How is the voice of the Lord heard differently among the wicked and the righteous?

The Lord speaks to the righteous and they "hear my voice, . . . and they follow me" (John 10:27). To the wicked the Lord preaches sermons "with fire and sword, tempests, earthquakes, hail, rain, thunders and lightnings, and fearful destruction" (Brigham Young, *Discourses*, 111). *See also D&C 88:89–90.*

I NEPHI 19:13–14

Why have the Jews become "a hiss and a byword, . . . hated among all nations"?

"Because of the displeasure of the Father which came upon them [the Jews] for rejection of their Redeemer, . . . they brought upon themselves the hatred of all people" (Joseph Fielding Smith, *Way to Perfection*, 133).

I NEPHI 19:16

From where will the Lord gather the ten lost tribes of Israel?

"And as surely as the Lord liveth, will he gather in from the four quarters of the earth all the remnant of the seed of Jacob, who are scattered abroad upon all the face of the earth" (3 Nephi 5:24).

I NEPHI 19:17

Who will see the Second Coming?

"The glory of the Lord shall be revealed, and all flesh shall see it together" (Isaiah 40:5). *See also D&C 101:23.*

I NEPHI 19:21–24

What blessings come from reading and studying the scriptures?

"I find that when I get casual in my relationships with divinity and when it seems that no divine ear is listening and no divine voice is speaking, that I am far, far away. If I immerse myself in the scriptures the distance narrows and the spirituality returns" (Spencer W. Kimball, *Teachings*, 135).

"I think that people who study the scriptures get a dimension to their life that nobody else gets and that can't be gained in any way except by studying the scriptures. There's an increase in faith and a desire to do what's right and a feeling of inspiration and understanding that comes to people . . . that can't come in any other way" (Bruce R. McConkie, *Church News*, January 24, 1976, 4). *See also insights for 2 Nephi 32:3.*

I NEPHI 19:23

What is the specific strength of the writings of Isaiah?

"Isaiah is by every standard *the* messianic prophet of the Old Testament and . . . is the most penetrating prophetic voice in that record. He, more than any other, . . . prophesied of the Savior's coming" (Jeffrey R. Holland, *Christ and the New Covenant*, 75; emphasis in original).

1 NEPHI 19:23–24

Why should we "liken all scriptures unto us"?

"The Book of Mormon was written for us today. . . . God, who knows the end from the beginning, told [Mormon] what to include in his abridgement that we would need for our day" (Ezra Taft Benson, *Ensign*, May 1975, 63).

1 NEPHI 20

1 NEPHI 20–22

Nephi quotes Isaiah and Deuteronomy about the latter-day restoration.

"Nephi quoted two full chapters [1 Nephi 20 and 21] of Isaiah that underscore the ministry of the Savior. Then [1 Nephi 22] he made an important (and unique) commentary on a . . . verse from the book of Deuteronomy" (Jeffrey R. Holland, *Christ and the New Covenant*, 44). *See also Deuteronomy 18:15; 1 Nephi 22:21, 24–25.*

1 NEPHI 20:2

The Lord of Hosts refers to the Lord's leadership over a vast army.

"With us is the Lord our God to help us, and to fight our battles" (2 Chronicles 32:8). *See also Exodus 15:3.*

1 NEPHI 20:12

How is Jesus Christ both the first and the last?

FIRST	LAST
He was the first spirit born to our Heavenly parents (Joseph Fielding Smith, *Restoration of All Things*, 250).	He was the last sacrifice of the Law of Moses (Alma 34:14).
He was the first and only mortal begotten by our Heavenly Father (Luke 1:32, 35).	He will be the last and final judge of all (John 5:22).
He was the first and only mortal born to a virgin (1 Nephi 11:20).	His second coming will be at "the last day" (D&C 52:44).
He was the first and only mortal to live a perfect life (1 Peter 1:19).	In his second coming he will appear last to the Jews (1 Nephi 13:42).

He was the first to be resurrected
(Acts 26:23).

First he came to the Jews (1 Nephi
13:42).

The overall message of Christ being the first and the last is that he stands unique in so many ways as the one and only. He is "the way" (John 14:6) and "there is none other way nor name given under heaven whereby man can be saved" (2 Nephi 31:21). It also implies that Jesus experienced the greatest extremes, he descended below all things and will ascend above all things.

I NEPHI 20:14-17

Who is the one the Lord "loved," "called," "prosper[ed]," and "sent"?

One of Isaiah's most predominant themes is the gathering of Israel, which is accomplished primarily through the restoration of the gospel and Israel joining that restored gospel through baptism (see 1 Nephi 20:1). Several scholars disagree about who the Lord "loved," "called," "prosper[ed]," and "sent" in verses 14–17. Brother Monte Nyman suggests it is "Israel" (see *Great Are the Words of Isaiah*, 171). This seems most correct and yet too general to be completely clear. Will Israel gather Israel? That seems a bit confusing. We know in the last days that the Lord will use Ephraim—one of the tribes of Israel—to gather the rest of Israel and the Gentiles (see D&C 113:3–6; 133:30–33). Thus the best answer to this question seems to be the tribe of Ephraim.

I NEPHI 20:17-21

What are the benefits of keeping the commandments?

Profit, or prosperity (v. 17)

God's guidance (v. 17)

Peace (v. 18)

Many offspring (v. 19)

Deliverance from enemies (v. 20)

Basic necessities will be met (v. 21)

I NEPHI 20; 21

The Big Picture (adapted from *Book of Mormon Teacher Resource Manual*, 45).

The Covenant—1 Nephi 20

1. *Preface* (1 Nephi 20:1–2). Israel is to hearken, be baptized, and covenant with the Lord.

2. *Current Events* (1 Nephi 20:3–8). The Lord foretells Israel's present afflictions.

3. *The Covenant* (1 Nephi 20:9–11, 14–15). The Lord promises to defer his anger and redeem Israel.

4. *Witnesses* (1 Nephi 20:12–14, 16). All are called to witness what God has done and will do.

5. *Results* (1 Nephi 20:17–22). The Lord compares Israel's wicked and righteous acts.

The Trial—1 Nephi 21

1. *The Summons* (1 Nephi 21:1–6). God's servant says "My judgment is with the Lord."

2. *The Charge* (1 Nephi 21:7–13). The Lord declares that he has kept and will keep his promises.

3. *The Plea* (1 Nephi 21:14, 21, 24). Israel offers excuses for her lack of faith in the Lord's promises.

4. *The Verdict* (1 Nephi 21:15–20, 22–23, 25–26). The Lord assures Israel she will be redeemed.

1 NEPHI 21

I NEPHI 21:1–26

When will the prophecies of this chapter be fulfilled?

"The 49th chapter of Isaiah [or 1 Nephi 21] is having its fulfillment, as are the sayings of the Patriarchs and Prophets. . . . And they will be rapid in their fulfillment" (Wilford Woodruff, in *Collected Discourses*, 5:187).

I NEPHI 21:1

What are the isles referred to in this verse?

"Isles . . . refers not only to islands but also to the continents of the earth" (Donald W. Parry, Jay A. Parry, and Tina M. Peterson, *Understanding Isaiah*, 425). *See also 2 Nephi 10:20.*

What does it mean to be "called . . . from the womb"?

"Every man who has a calling to minister to the inhabitants of the world was ordained to that very purpose in the Grand Council of heaven before this world was" (Joseph Smith, *Teachings*, 36). *See also insights Alma 13:3, 5, 7.*

I NEPHI 21:2

How do we become "a polished shaft"?

"I am like a huge, rough stone rolling down from a high mountain; and the only polishing I get is when some corner gets rubbed off by coming in contact with something else . . . knocking off a corner here and a corner there. Thus I will become a smooth and polished shaft" (Joseph Smith, *Teachings*, 304).

I NEPHI 21:5-17

What will it take for the Lord to gather Israel?

The Lord will restore Israel (v. 6).

The Lord will preserve Israel (v. 8).

Israel will inherit her lands (v. 8).

Israel will be freed (v. 9).

There will be no more suffering (v. 10).

The Lord will show his mercy to them (v. 10).

Israel will prosper (v. 11).

They will come from the north (v. 12).

They will be beaten no more (v. 13).

God will not forget Israel (vv. 14–16).

Israel's enemies will leave (v. 17).

I NEPHI 21:9

Who are the prisoners that were let free?

"Christ brought freedom to mortal beings imprisoned by ignorance, sin, apostasy, and death. He also brought deliverance to those on the other side of the veil who had not heard the gospel but would receive it in their spirit prison" (Jeffrey R. Holland, *Christ and the New Covenant*, 82).

I NEPHI 21:15–16

How has the Lord "graven [us] upon the palms of [his] hands"?

"Christ will not forget the children he has redeemed. . . . The painful reminders . . . are the marks of the Roman nails graven upon the palms of his hands" (Jeffrey R. Holland, *Christ and the New Covenant*, 84).

I NEPHI 21:19–26

The modern state of Israel could be a partial fulfilment of the gathering.

PROPHECY	MODERN FULFILLMENT
"The land of . . . destruction, shall . . . be too narrow by reason of the inhabitants" (v. 19)	The post-1948 state of Israel was a narrow strip of land—from 15 to 20 miles wide—because of the Palestinians, who already lived there.
"The children whom thou shalt have, after thou hast lost the first, shall . . . say: The place is too strait [or narrow] . . . give place to me that I may dwell" (v. 20)	The lost children could be the six million killed in the holocaust. The new children need more room to live. Israel's borders were enlarged in 1967 after the Six Day War.
Israel will lament being "desolate, a captive, and removing to and fro" (v. 21)	The Jews for centuries (see insight for 1 Nephi 19:13–14) have been desolate—without a place to stay, moving from place to place.
"The Gentiles . . . shall bring" them and "be [their] nursing fathers, and . . . nursing mothers" (vv. 22–23)	It was only with the help of the United Nations, Great Britain, and the Balfour Declaration that a state of Israel was formed.

1 NEPHI 22

I NEPHI 22:2

By what power "are all things made known"?

"The Holy Ghost . . . will show unto you all things what ye should do" (2 Nephi 32:5).

I NEPHI 22:3, 12

How is the scattering and gathering of Israel "both temporal and spiritual"?

See insights for 3 Nephi 20:13, 29; 21:24–26, 28, 33.

I NEPHI 22:3, 25

Where was Israel scattered and from where will they be gathered?

Israel was "scattered upon all the face of the earth" (Ezekiel 34:6; see also 1 Nephi 10:13).

"The scattered remnants of Israel, who have been driven to the ends of the earth, come to a knowledge of the truth" (D&C 109:67).

I NEPHI 22:5

Why was Israel scattered in the first place?

"Why was Israel scattered? . . . Because they rejected the gospel, defiled the priesthood, forsook the church, and . . . turned from the Lord. . . . They forsook the Abrahamic covenant" (Bruce R. McConkie, *New Witness for the Articles of Faith*, 515).

I NEPHI 22:7

Who is the "mighty nation among the Gentiles"?

"It was from this American land, and from the great nation raised up to the Gentiles upon it, that the doctrine of the 'voice of the people' has been proclaimed with such power . . . [and] felt in all the world" (Joseph Fielding Smith, *Progress of Man*, 463).

I NEPHI 22:8

What is the "marvelous work among the Gentiles"?

"The marvelous work spoken of is the restoration of the gospel, including the coming forth of the Book of Mormon" (Bruce R. McConkie, *New Witness for the Articles of Faith*, 560).

I NEPHI 22:13

Who is the "great and abominable church"?

See insights for 1 Nephi 13:4–9, 26–28; 14:10–11.

I NEPHI 22:13–15

How will the "great and abominable church . . . tumble to the dust and . . . fall"?

"[It] will be destroyed, simply because every corruptible thing will be consumed at the Second Coming. In that day the Lord will truly fight the battles of his saints" (Bruce R. McConkie, *New Witness for the Articles of Faith*, 562–63).

I NEPHI 22:16-22

Who will endure the calamities preceding the Second Coming?

"Vengeance cometh speedily upon the ungodly as the whirlwind; and who shall escape it? . . . Zion shall escape if she observe to do all things whatsoever I have commanded her" (D&C 97:22, 25).

"The priesthood of God who honor their priesthood, and who are worthy of their blessings are the only ones who shall have this safety. . . . No other people have a right to be shielded from these judgments. . . . Not even this people will escape them entirely" (Wilford Woodruff, in *Collected Discourses*, 4:229–30).

"We do not say that all of the Saints will be spared and saved from the coming day of desolation. But we do say there is no promise of safety and no promise of security except for those who love the Lord and who are seeking to do all that he commands" (Bruce R. McConkie, *Ensign*, May 1979, 93).

"I explained concerning the coming of the Son of Man; also that it is a false idea that the Saints will escape all the judgments, whilst the wicked suffer; for all flesh is subject to suffer, and 'the righteous shall hardly escape;' still many of the Saints will escape" (Joseph Smith, *Teachings*, 162). *See also insights for Mormon 8:3.*

I NEPHI 22:17

How are the righteous saved "by fire"?

Because the wicked will be destroyed by fire at the Second Coming, this verse might seem better worded if it said that the righteous will be saved *from* fire, not *by* fire. Another verse of scripture lends understanding. At the time of the flood, Noah and his family were saved not *from* the water but *by* the water (see 1 Peter 3:20). At the time of both events the world was and will be completely cleansed of wickedness—once by water and once by fire. At the first cleansing the earth experienced a baptism of water; the second cleansing will be a confirmation of spirit by fire. If the waters that saved the family of Noah and condemned the wicked were the waters of baptism, then those saved by the fire at the Second Coming must be saved by the fire of the Holy Ghost.

I NEPHI 22:18

How will the "vapor of smoke" come?

"It may be . . . that nothing except the power of faith and the authority of the priesthood can save individuals and congregations from the atomic holocausts that surely shall be" (Bruce R. McConkie, *Ensign*, May 1979, 93).

I NEPHI 22:19

What will happen to those "who fight against Zion"?

"The New Jerusalem, a land of peace, a city of refuge, a place of safety for the saints of the Most High God. . . . The wicked will not come unto it, and it shall be called Zion . . . the only people that shall not be at war one with another. . . . It shall be said among the wicked: Let us not go up to battle against Zion, for the inhabitants of Zion are terrible; wherefore we cannot stand" (D&C 45:66–70).

I NEPHI 22:24

How will Jesus "reign in dominion, and might, and power, and great glory"?

"Christ and the resurrected Saints will reign over the earth during the thousand years. They will not probably dwell upon the earth, but will visit it when they please, or when it is necessary" (Joseph Smith, *Teachings*, 268).

I NEPHI 22:26

What will cause Satan to have no power during the millennium?

"Satan will be bound by the power of God; but he will be bound also by the determination of the people of God not to listen to him" (George Q. Cannon, Conference Report, October 1897, 65). An angel has the key and specific assignment to seal up Satan for 1,000 years (see Revelation 20:1–3; D&C 88:110).

"We need not become paralyzed with fear of Satan's power. He can have no power over us unless we permit it. He is really a coward, and if we stand firm, he will retreat. The Apostle James counseled: 'Submit yourselves . . . to God. Resist the devil, and he will flee from you' (James 4:7)" (James E. Faust, *Ensign*, September 1995, 6).

THE SECOND BOOK OF
NEPHI

The First Book of Nephi was written by Nephi, son of Lehi, with the exception of 1 Nephi 8 (the account of Lehi's vision) and 1 Nephi 20–21 (quotes from Isaiah). The authorship of the Second Book of Nephi was even more shared. Though Nephi was the chief scribe and writer, he authored only ten of the thirty-three chapters. Lehi, Nephi's father, is quoted in chapters 1–4; Jacob, Nephi's brother, was responsible for chapters 6 and 9–10; Isaiah was the source of chapters 7–8, 12–24, and 27; and Nephi wrote chapters 5, 11, 25–26, and 28–33.

The Second Book of Nephi's major focus is Jesus Christ. In fact, the words "Jesus Christ" are not found in 1 Nephi, while they are collectively mentioned sixty-two times in 2 Nephi. Nephi even justifies using Isaiah and Jacob as part of his material because they knew Jesus Christ (see 2 Nephi 11:3). We know that Lehi is also an eyewitness of the Savior (see 1 Nephi 1:8; 2 Nephi 1:15). Thus, 2 Nephi is a record of four witnesses—Lehi, Nephi, Isaiah and Jacob—all bearing testimony of the reality of Jesus Christ.

2 NEPHI 1

2 NEPHI 1:5

"The Lord hath covenanted this land unto me, and to my children forever."

"Different portions of the earth have been pointed out by the Almighty, from time to time, to His children, as their everlasting inheritance. . . . The meek among the Jaredites, together with a remnant of the tribe of Joseph, were promised the great western continent" (Orson Pratt, *Journal of Discourses*, 1:332).

2 NEPHI 1:6

What people are "brought by the hand of the Lord" to this land?

"Other nations were to come, not as nations, but as members of nations; and they have come and are coming and shall come, led hither by the hand of the Lord" (James E. Talmage, in Conference Report, October 1919, 98).

2 NEPHI 1:7, 9–11, 16, 20, 31–32

What are the conditions of America's liberty?

"Because our nation is a creation of heaven, and because it has a divine destiny, we Americans must learn that it can continue to exist only as it aligns itself with the powers of heaven. . . . Our first President, George Washington . . . warned that if we are to survive as a free and independent nation, we must obey the Almighty God who brought us into being" (Mark E. Petersen, in Conference Report, April 1968, 59).

"Even this nation will be on the verge of crumbling to pieces and tumbling to the ground, and when the Constitution is upon the brink of ruin, this people will be the Staff upon which the Nation shall lean, and they shall bear the Constitution away from the very verge of destruction" (Joseph Smith, *Discourses of the Prophet Joseph Smith*, 304).

2 NEPHI 1:13–14, 21, 23

How can we "awake," "shake off the awful chains," and "arise"?

"What makes a man a man? Let's turn to the Book of Mormon . . . for an answer. . . .

"The challenge to '*arise from the dust*' means to overcome evil behaviors that destroy character and ruin lives. Physical appetites must be controlled.

"'*Awake from a deep sleep,* . . . even from the sleep of hell' suggests a process of learning and becoming aware of God's holy purposes. No sleep is deeper or more deadly than the sleep of ignorance.

"'*Shake off the awful chains by which ye are bound*' indicates the need to overcome bad habits, even the seemingly little habits that grow into strong 'chains of hell.' (See 2 Ne. 26:22; Alma 5:7.)

"'*Be determined in one mind and in one heart, united in all things*' requires full commitment to righteousness and a singleness of purpose so that one's will is made compatible with the will of God.

"'*Put on the armor of righteousness*' reminds us of the need to wear the helmet of salvation, pick up the sword of truth, use the shield of faith, and accept the full protective coverings of the Lord" (Carlos E. Asay, *Ensign*, May 1992, 40–41).

2 NEPHI 1:26

Nephi taught "the truth . . . which he could not restrain."

"His word was in mine heart as a burning fire shut up in my bones, and I was weary with forbearing, and I could not stay" (Jeremiah 20:9). *See also Moroni 9:6.*

2 NEPHI 1:28

In what way were Ishmael's sons also Lehi's sons?

See insights for 1 Nephi 7:1–5.

2 NEPHI 1:30–31

How can our actions affect our posterity?

"The Prophet Joseph Smith declared . . . that the eternal sealings of faithful parents and the divine promises made to them for valiant service in the Cause of Truth, would save not only themselves, but likewise their posterity. Though some of the sheep may wander, the eye of the Shepherd is upon them, and sooner or later they will feel the tentacles of Divine Providence reaching out after them and drawing them back to the fold. Either in this life or the life to come, they will return. They will have to pay their debt to justice; they will suffer for their sins; and may tread a thorny path; but if it leads them at last . . . to a loving and forgiving father's heart and home, the painful experience will not have been in vain" (Orson F. Whitney, in Conference Report, April 1929, 110).

Why would Zoram's seed be blessed with Nephi's seed?

"He that receiveth a prophet . . . shall receive a prophet's reward" (Matthew 10:41).

2 NEPHI 2

2 NEPHI 2:1–30

Where can we learn the most about the Atonement?

"Our most explicit teachings on the atonement of Christ are in 2 Nephi 2 and 9 and Alma 34" (Bruce R. McConkie, *Promised Messiah*, 421).

2 NEPHI 2:2

What advantages can come from our afflictions?

See insights for Alma 14:11.

2 NEPHI 2:4

Who else has "beheld in [their] youth" the glory of the Lord?

SAMUEL	MORMON	JOSEPH SMITH
"The Lord had called the child . . . the Lord came, and stood, and called as at other times, Samuel, Samuel.	"And I, being fifteen years of age and being somewhat of a sober mind, therefore I was visited of the Lord, and tasted and knew of the	"I was at this time in my fifteenth year. . . . I saw two Personages. . . . One of them spake . . . calling me by name and said,

Then Samuel answered, Speak; for thy servant heareth" (1 Samuel 3:8, 10). goodness of Jesus" (Mormon 1:15). pointing to the other—*This is My Beloved Son. Hear Him!*" (JS—H 1:7, 17).

2 NEPHI 2:4, 7

How is salvation free and how is it not free?

"*Unconditional or general salvation*, that which comes by grace alone without obedience to gospel law, consists in the mere fact of being resurrected.

" . . . *Conditional or individual salvation*, that which comes by grace coupled with gospel obedience, consists in receiving an inheritance in the celestial kingdom of God" (Bruce R. McConkie, *Mormon Doctrine*, 669).

2 NEPHI 2:5

How do people "know good from evil"?

See insights for Moroni 7:12–13, 16–17.

Why is "no flesh . . . justified" by the law?

"Men . . . would be cut off temporally because they do not keep the law perfectly; and they would be cut off spiritually because . . . 'no unclean thing can dwell . . . in [God's] presence' (Moses 6:57)." (Gerald N. Lund, *Jesus Christ, Key to the Plan of Salvation*, 88).

2 NEPHI 2:9–10, 26

Did Jesus Christ redeem all men from the effects of the Fall?

"We believe that through the sufferings, death, and atonement of Jesus Christ all mankind, without one exception, are to be completely and fully redeemed, both body and spirit, from the endless banishment and curse to which they were consigned by Adam's transgression; and that this universal salvation and redemption of the whole human family from the endless penalty of the original sin, is effected without any conditions whatever on their part; that is . . . whether they keep the commandments or break them, whether they are righteous or unrighteous, it will make no difference in relation to their redemption . . . from the penalty of Adam's transgression" (Orson Pratt, cited in James E. Talmage, *Articles of Faith*, 430). *See also D&C 19:16.*

What is the meaning of the word Atonement?

"In the English language, the components are *at-one-ment*, suggesting that a person is at one with another. . . .

" . . . In Hebrew, the basic word for atonement is *kaphar*, a verb that means 'to cover' or 'to forgive.' Closely related is the Aramaic and Arabic word *kafat*, meaning 'a close embrace'" (Russell M. Nelson, *Perfection Pending*, 165–66).

2 NEPHI 2:11–15

Why is "opposition in all things" necessary?

"Notice the major points . . . as to why there must be opposition before a man can be truly free and . . . experience real joy: (1) Every law has both a punishment and a blessing attached to it. (2) Disobedience to law requires a punishment which results in misery. (3) Obedience to law provides a blessing which results in happiness (joy). (4) Without law there can be neither punishment nor blessing, neither misery nor happiness. . . . (5) Thus happiness (or joy) can exist only where the possibility of [the] opposite . . . also exists. (6) In order to exercise free agency a person must have the possibility (and the freedom) of choice." (Daniel H. Ludlow, *Companion*, 125).

2 NEPHI 2:14, 26

What does it mean to "be acted upon"?

"Each of us must take the responsibility for the moral decisions we make. . . . Being acted upon means somebody else is pulling the strings. . . . Many want to avoid the responsibility for their acts" (James E. Faust, *Ensign*, November 1995, 46).

2 NEPHI 2:17–18

Why did an "angel of God" become the devil?

"O Lucifer, son of the morning! how art thou cut down to the ground, which didst weaken the nations! For thou hast said . . . I will ascend into heaven, I will exalt my throne above the stars of God: . . . I will ascend above the heights . . . I will be like the most High" (Isaiah 14:12–14).

2 NEPHI 2:18, 27

What similarity do Satan and Heavenly Father have?

They both want us to be like them. Jesus explains, "What manner of men ought ye to be? Verily I say unto you, even as I am" (3 Nephi 27:27). "The devil . . . seeketh that all men might be miserable like unto himself" (2 Nephi 2:27).

"The Lord wants us to have a fulness of joy like His, while the devil wants all men to be miserable like unto himself" (Ezra Taft Benson, *Teachings*, 382).

2 NEPHI 2:19, 25

What were the effects of the fall of Adam?

(see Daniel H. Ludlow, *Companion*, 127.)

STATUS OF ADAM AND EVE BEFORE THE FALL	STATUS OF ADAM AND EVE AFTER THE FALL
1. They were in the presence of God.	1. They were cast out of the presence of God—that is, they suffered a spiritual death.
2. They were not mortal—that is, they were not subject to physical death).	2. They became mortal (subject to physical death (2 Nephi 2:22).
3. They were in a state of innocence—that is, they did not know the difference between good and evil. (2 Nephi 2:23.)	3. They knew good from evil.
4. They "would have had no children" (2 Nephi 2:23).	4. They had children.

2 NEPHI 2:20–21

Why are we here on Earth?

"Why are you here on planet earth?

"One of the most important reasons is to receive a mortal body. Another is to be tested—to experience mortality—to determine what you will do with life's challenging opportunities" (Russell M. Nelson, *Ensign*, November 1990, 74). *See Abraham 3:24–25.*

2 NEPHI 2:22

How long would Adam and Eve have lived in the Garden of Eden had they not fallen?

"There was no blood in Adam's body before the fall. He was not then 'flesh' as we know it, that is in the sense of mortality. In that state Adam could have remained in the Garden of Eden forever" (Joseph Fielding Smith, *Doctrines of Salvation*, 1:92).

Did Adam sin by partaking of the forbidden fruit?

"Adam and Eve therefore did the very thing that the Lord intended them to do. . . .

". . . The Lord said to Adam that if he wished to remain as he was in the garden, then he was not to eat the fruit, but if he desired to eat it and partake of death he was at liberty to do so. So really it was not in the true sense a transgression of a divine commandment. . . .

"It was the divine plan from the very beginning" (Joseph Fielding Smith, *Answers to Gospel Questions*, 4:80). *See also 2 Nephi 9:6.*

2 NEPHI 2:25

"Men are, that they might have joy."

"Happiness is the object and design of our existence; and will be the end thereof, if we pursue the path that leads to it; and this path is . . . keeping all the commandments of God" (Joseph Smith, *Teachings*, 255). *See also Mosiah 2:41.*

2 NEPHI 2:27

What principles are necessary for agency to exist?

"Four great principles must be in force if there is to be agency: 1. Laws must exist, laws ordained by an Omnipotent power, laws which can be obeyed or disobeyed; 2. Opposites must exist—good and evil, virtue and vice, right and wrong—that is, there must be an opposition, one force pulling one way and another pulling the other; 3. A knowledge of good and evil must be had by those who are to enjoy the agency, that is, they must know the difference between the opposites; and 4. An unfettered power of choice must prevail" (Bruce R. McConkie, *Mormon Doctrine*, 26). *See also 2 Nephi 2:5, 16.*

Whose fault is it if I am happy or sad?

"We can choose our reactions to difficulties and challenges. . . .

". . . Self-pity and discouragement do not come from the teachings of the gospel of Jesus Christ. . . . It is up to us to choose whether we want to reflect the voices of gloom or gladness" (Marvin J. Ashton, *Ensign*, May 1991, 20). *See also insights for Helaman 14:30–31.*

2 NEPHI 2:29

What "give[s] the spirit of the devil power to captivate"?

"All beings who have bodies have power over those who have not. The devil has no power over us only as we permit him. The moment we revolt at anything which comes from God, the devil takes power" (Joseph Smith, *Teachings*, 181).

2 NEPHI 3

2 NEPHI 3:1–25

Which Joseph is which?

Joseph son of Lehi: Verses 1, 3, 22, 23, 25

Joseph of Egypt: Verses 4–7, 14–16, 22

Joseph Smith Jr. (also referred to as "a choice seer"): Verses 6–11, 13–15, 18

Joseph Smith Sr.: Verse 15

"The etymology of the name *Joseph* is usually given as 'the Lord addeth.' . . . Though appropriate, such renderings have veiled a richer meaning associated with the name. In Genesis 30:24, . . . the Hebrew text reads *Asaph*, which means 'he who gathers,' 'he who causes to return.' . . . Thus the great prophet of the Restoration was given the name that . . . describes his divine calling" (Joseph Fielding McConkie and Robert L. Millet, *Doctrinal Commentary*, 1:209).

2 NEPHI 3:3, 23

How did Joseph's seed survive the destruction of the Nephites at the end of the Book of Mormon?

They could have been among Hagoth's people that went "northward" (see Alma 63:5).

Many Nephites dissented and joined the Lamanites (see Alma 43:13; 47:35; Moroni 9:24).

There were some periods of history when Lamanites and Nephites had peaceful interaction with each other (see Helaman 6:7). During this time there could have been intermarriage.

Joseph Smith found the remains of a "white Lamanite" (see Joseph Fielding Smith, *Doctrines of Salvation*, 3:238).

2 NEPHI 3:5, 7–8, 11, 15

Who is identified as an instrument in the latter-day restoration?

In his patriarchal blessing, Joseph Smith Jr. was told: "I bless thee with . . . the blessings of thy father Joseph, the son of Jacob. Behold he looked after his posterity in the last days; . . . he sought diligently to know from whence the son should come who should bring forth the word of the Lord, by which they might be enlightened and brought back to the true fold, and his eyes beheld thee, my son; his heart rejoiced and his soul was satisfied" (Archibald F. Bennett, *Saviors on Mount Zion*, 68).

"It was decreed in the counsels of eternity, long before the foundations of the earth were laid, that he, Joseph Smith, should be the man, in the last dispensation of this world, to bring forth the word of God to the people, and receive the fulness of the keys and power of the Priesthood" (Brigham Young, *Discourses*, 108).

2 NEPHI 3:6–7, 9

How is Joseph Smith "like unto Moses"?

JOSEPH SMITH JR.	MOSES
In 1830 members of the Church suffered persecutions in the New York State area. Joseph told them that the Lord would deliver them from their enemies and lead them to a "land of promise, a land flowing with milk and honey" (D&C 38:18).	In about 1300 B.C. the children of Israel were suffering bondage to the Egyptians. Moses told them the Lord would deliver them from their enemies and lead them to "a land flowing with milk and honey" (Exodus 3:8).
Once the Saints arrived in the state of Ohio, the Lord told Joseph, "I will give unto you my law" (D&C 38:32).	After the children of Israel left Egypt and gathered in the wilderness of Sinai, Moses was given the "law" (Exodus 24:12).
Ohio was not the ultimate destination of Zion, but many important things happened there (D&C 57:1–3).	The wilderness of Sinai was not the ultimate destination of the children of Israel, but many important things happened there (Exodus 13).
The Lord made a "spokesman" (Sidney Rigdon) for Joseph (2 Nephi 3:18).	The Lord made a "spokesman" (Aaron) for Moses (Exodus 4:14–16).
Joseph received many of the ten commandments as part of the law (D&C 42:18–29).	While in the wilderness of Sinai, Moses received the ten commandments as part of the law (Exodus 20:3–17).
In Ohio, Joseph oversaw the construction of the first temple in this dispensation (D&C 109 and 110).	In the wilderness of Sinai, Moses constructed the tabernacle, a portable temple (Exodus 25–31).
Joseph sent men to the promised land of Missouri, whose capital was to be the New Jerusalem (D&C 57:1–3).	Moses sent men to the promised land of Canaan, whose capital was to be Jerusalem (Numbers 13).
Zion was not fully established in	Zion was not established in the

the promised land of Missouri
in the days of Joseph (D&C 58:4, 44).

promised land of Canaan in the
days of Moses (Deuteronomy 34:4–5).

The New Jerusalem will be built
and become a co-capital during the
Millennium (Isaiah 2:3).

Jerusalem will be rebuilt and
become a co-capital during the
Millennium (Isaiah 2:3).

2 NEPHI 3:12

How did the writings of Judah and the writings of Joseph "grow together"?

"The stick or record of Judah—the Old Testament and the New Testament—and the stick or record of Ephraim—the Book of Mormon, which is another testament of Jesus Christ—are now woven together in such a way that as you pore over one you are drawn to the other; as you learn from one you are enlightened by the other. They are indeed one in our hands. Ezekiel's prophecy now stands fulfilled" (Boyd K. Packer, *Let Not Your Heart Be Troubled*, 8–9). *See also Ezekiel 37:16–17, 19.*

2 NEPHI 3:18

Who are the people spoken of in this verse?

"Someone of the seed of Joseph . . . would write the Lord's law, and yet another, a spokesman, would declare it. . . .

". . . With this in mind, note these words of the Lord: '. . . I will give unto him [Mormon] that he shall write the writing of the fruit of thy loins [the Nephites], unto the fruit of thy loins [the Lamanites]; and the spokesman of thy loins [Joseph Smith] shall declare it.' That is, Mormon wrote the Book of Mormon, but what he wrote was taken from the writings of the Nephite prophets; and these writings, compiled into one book, were translated by Joseph Smith and sent forth by him unto the Lamanites" (Bruce R. McConkie, *New Witness for the Articles of Faith*, 426).

2 NEPHI 4

2 NEPHI 4:1–2

What happened to the prophecies of Joseph?

"The record of Abraham translated by the Prophet was subsequently printed. . . . However, the translation of the book of Joseph has not yet been published. Evidently the record of Joseph was translated by the Prophet, but . . . was not published" (Daniel H. Ludlow, *Companion*, 131).

2 NEPHI 4:3-11

Lehi's blessings to his posterity

"The children of Laman" (vv. 3–7)
Keep the commandments and prosper.
Your posterity will not all die.

"The sons and daughters of Lemuel" (vv. 8–9)
Same as the blessing to the children of Laman.

"The sons of Ishmael" (v. 10)
These blessings were not enumerated.

"Sam" (v. 11)
Inherit the land.
His seed to be numbered with Nephi's seed.

2 NEPHI 4:5

When are parents not responsible for their children's misbehavior?

"The measure of our success as parents . . . will not rest solely on how our children turn out. . . .

"It is not uncommon for responsible parents to lose one of their children, for a time, to influences over which they have no control" (Boyd K. Packer, *Ensign*, May 1992, 68). *See insights for 2 Nephi 1:30–31.*

When are parents responsible for their children's misbehavior?

"There are parents who say: We will let our children grow to manhood and womanhood and choose for themselves. In taking this attitude parents fail in the discharging of a parental responsibility. . . . The Father of all mankind expects parents . . . to assist him in shaping and guiding human lives" (David O. McKay, in Conference Report, April 1955, 27).

2 NEPHI 4:9

How is the Lord blessing the seed of Lehi?

"I saw it in South America as I looked into the faces of missionaries. . . . I was nearly overwhelmed with the confirmation that these children of Father Lehi and of Sariah were there in the Lord's service because our Heavenly Father honors his promises to families. To nearly his last breath, Lehi taught and testified and tried to bless his children. . . . In the eyes and faces of those missionaries I felt confirmation that God has kept his promises to reach out to Lehi's covenant children" (Henry B. Eyring, *Ensign*, May 1996, 64).

2 NEPHI 4:15-35

Why are these verses referred to as "Nephi's Psalm"?

"This is a true psalm in both form and idea. Its rhythm is comparable to the noble cadence of David's poems. It not only praises God, but lays bare to us the very depths of Nephi's soul" (Sidney B. Sperry, *Our Book of Mormon*, 111).

2 NEPHI 4:15-16

"My soul delighteth in the scriptures."

"During the war in Vietnam, some of our men were taken prisoner and kept in nearly total isolation. Permitted no access to the scriptures, they later told how they hungered for the words of truth, more than for food, more than for freedom itself. What they would have given for a mere fragment of the Bible or the Book of Mormon that lay so idly on our shelves!" (Spencer W. Kimball, *Ensign*, July 1985, 4).

2 NEPHI 4:17-19, 26-29

What kind of sins was Nephi guilty of?

"Nephi's references to personal sins should not be taken to imply any serious moral transgression on his part. No man could have seen and known God as he did who was not pure in heart.

"Rather, he is almost surely alluding to the . . . anger, impatience, and frustration he must have felt at times" (Rodney Turner, in Monte S. Nyman and Charles D. Tate Jr., eds., *First Nephi*, 93).

2 NEPHI 4:19-34

What promised blessings come to those who trust in the Lord?

God will support them (v. 20).

He will lead them through their afflictions (v. 20).

He will preserve them (v. 20).

He will fill them with love (v. 21).

He will confound their enemies (v. 22).

He will hear their prayers (v. 23).

He will give them knowledge (v. 23).

Angels could administer to them (v. 24).

He can bless them with visions (v. 25).

2 NEPHI 4:27–29

Who struggles to overcome sin?

"The most noble of souls, the greatest of prophets, need heaven's help to endure in faith to the end. Joseph Fielding Smith, even in his ninety-fifth year, . . . frequently said, 'I pray that I may be true and faithful to the end'" (Joseph Fielding McConkie and Robert L. Millet, *Doctrinal Commentary*, 1:219). *See also 1 John 1:8; insights for Mosiah 5:2.*

2 NEPHI 5

2 NEPHI 5:10–25

What were the differences in the actions (and results of those actions) of these two peoples?

NEPHITE ACTIVITIES	LAMANITE ACTIVITIES
The Nephites kept "the commandments" (v. 10).	The Lamanites did "not hearken" unto the Lord, and were guilty of "iniquity" (vv. 20–21).
The Nephites planted grains and raised "flocks and herds" (v. 11).	The Lamanites "did seek in the wilderness for beasts of prey" (v. 24).
The Nephites learned to "labor with their hands" (v. 17).	The Lamanites became "an idle people" (v. 24).
The Nephites "did prosper exceedingly" (vv. 11, 13).	The Lamanites became a loathsome people (v. 22).
The Nephites lived in happiness (v. 27).	The Lamanites experienced a "sore cursing" (v. 21).

2 NEPHI 5:15

How is the phrase "to build buildings" evidence of Book of Mormon authenticity?

To "build buildings" (Mosiah 9:8; 11:13; 23:5), to have "dreamed a dream" (1 Nephi 3:2; 8:2), and to "vow a vow" (Numbers 30:2) are all examples of a Hebrew literary construction called "cognate accusative." Though English syntax avoids using such a construction, "Hebrew and other Semitic languages . . . encourage it. . . .

". . . Therefore, in using the phrase 'to build a building,' the Book of Mormon adheres to a Hebrew and Semitic practice that is not common in English" (Paul Y. Hoskisson, in Monte S. Nyman and Charles D. Tate, Jr., eds., *First Nephi*, 288).

2 NEPHI 5:16

Why did Nephi build a temple?

"All of our efforts in proclaiming the gospel, perfecting the Saints, and redeeming the dead lead to the holy temple. This is because the temple ordinances are absolutely crucial; we cannot return to God's presence without them. I encourage everyone to worthily attend the temple or to work toward the day when you can enter that holy house to receive your ordinances and covenants" (Howard W. Hunter, *Ensign*, November 1994, 88). *See also D&C 128:15.*

2 NEPHI 5:17, 24

Why are we commanded to be industrious and not idle?

"The spirit of the Gospel of the Lord Jesus Christ is opposed to idleness. We do not believe that a man who has that spirit can rest content if he is not busily employed" (in James R. Clark, comp., *Messages of the First Presidency*, 3:113).

"If we want to keep the Spirit, we must work. There is no greater exhilaration or satisfaction than to know, after a hard day of work, that we have done our best" (Ezra Taft Benson, *Teachings*, 483).

2 NEPHI 5:18

Why was Nephi opposed to having a king?

See insights for Mosiah 29:13, 16.

2 NEPHI 5:20–21

How are the wicked "cut off from the presence of the Lord"?

"The Spirit of the Lord will not argue with men, nor abide in them, except they yield obedience to the Lord's commandments.

". . . The Spirit of the Lord cannot dwell in unclean tabernacles. . . . There are members of the Church who take no time to inform themselves by study and faith. . . . When this is the case, those who are guilty are easily deceived and are in danger of turning away to false doctrines and theories of men" (Joseph Fielding Smith, *Answers to Gospel Questions*, 3:29).

2 NEPHI 5:20–24

What was the curse that was placed upon the Lamanites?

"The dark skin was placed upon the Lamanites so that they could be distinguished from the Nephites and to keep the two peoples from mixing. The dark skin was the sign of the curse [But not the curse itself]. The curse was the withdrawal of the Spirit of the Lord. . . .

"The dark skin of those who have come into the Church is no longer to be considered a sign of the curse. Many of these converts are delightsome and have the Spirit of the Lord" (Joseph Fielding Smith, *Answers to Gospel Questions*, 3:122–23). *See also Alma 3:6–14; 3 Nephi 2:15.*

2 NEPHI 5:21

Why were certain groups of people cursed?

"The Amlicites . . . had come out in open rebellion against God; therefore it was expedient that the curse should fall upon them . . . they brought upon themselves the curse; and even so doth every man that is cursed bring upon himself his own condemnation" (Alma 3:18–19).

2 NEPHI 5:26

Were Jacob and Joseph ordained to offices in the Aaronic priesthood?

"The Nephites officiated by virtue of the Melchizedek Priesthood from the days of Lehi to the days of the appearance of our Savior among them. It is true that Nephi 'consecrated Jacob and Joseph' that they should be priests and teachers over the land of the Nephites, but the fact that plural terms *priests and teachers* were used indicates that this was not a reference to the definite office in the [Aaronic] priesthood in either case, but it was a general assignment to teach, direct, and admonish the people" (Joseph Fielding Smith, *Answers to Gospel Questions*, 1:124).

2 NEPHI 5:28–32

When were Nephi's plates made?

"It is quite clear from 2 Nephi 5:28–33 that the small plates were not prepared until thirty years after Lehi left Jerusalem, or approximately 570 B.C." (Daniel H. Ludlow, *Companion*, 134).

2 NEPHI 6

2 NEPHI 6:1

"The words of Jacob, the brother of Nephi."

"Apparently Nephi was so impressed with his younger brother's sermons on these subjects [atonement and witness of Christ] that he asked him to speak for the record" (Jeffrey R. Holland, *Christ and the New Covenant*, 65).

2 NEPHI 6:2

What is the phrase "holy order" a reference to?

"Why the first is called the Melchizedek Priesthood is because Melchizedek was such a great high priest. Before his day it was called the Holy Priesthood, after the Order of the Son of God" (D&C 107:2–3). *See also Alma 13:8.*

2 NEPHI 6:6

What is the "standard" that is to be set up among the "Gentiles"?

"This Church is the standard which Isaiah said the Lord would set up for the people in the latter days" (Marion G. Romney, in Conference Report, April 1961, 119).

2 NEPHI 6:8–9

When were the Jews "carried away captive," and when were they to return?

"Bible scholars recognize two great deportations. The first took place in the year 596 B.C. . . .

"The second deportation took place in the year 586 B.C. . . .

"They did return under Zerubbabel in 537 B.C." (George Reynolds and Janne M. Sjodahl, *Commentary on the Book of Mormon*, 1:282).

2 NEPHI 6:8–18

What did Jacob teach us about the first and second comings of Jesus Christ?

The First Coming of Jesus Christ

Jesus would be born as a mortal (v. 9).

He would be born among the Jews (v. 9).

He would be born in the land of Jerusalem (v. 8).

The Jews would harden their hearts against the Holy One of Israel (v. 10).

He would be scourged (v. 9).

He would be crucified (v. 9).

The Second Coming of Jesus Christ

The Jews will gather before the Second Coming (v. 11).

The Second Coming will be in "power and great glory" (v. 14).

The wicked will be destroyed at the Second Coming (v. 14).

The faithful will not be destroyed at the Second Coming (v. 14).

Fire, tempests, earthquakes, bloodsheds, famine, and pestilence will accompany the Second Coming (v. 15).

The Lord will deliver his covenant people at the Second Coming (v. 17).

All flesh will know that Jesus is the "Mighty One of Jacob" at the Second Coming (v. 18).

2 NEPHI 6:9

How torturous was death by crucifixion?

"Death by crucifixion was at once the most lingering and most painful of all forms of execution. The victim lived in ever increasing torture, generally for many hours, sometimes for days. The spikes so cruelly driven through hands and feet penetrated and crushed sensitive nerves and quivering tendons, yet inflicted no mortal wound. The welcome relief of death came through the exhaustion caused by intense and unremitting pain, through localized inflammation and congestion of organs incident to the strained and unnatural posture of the body" (James E. Talmage, *Jesus the Christ*, 608).

2 NEPHI 6:11

When will the Jews be gathered to the lands of their inheritance?

"Not many of the Jews . . . will believe in Christ before he comes. The Book of Mormon tells us that they shall *begin* to believe in him. They are now *beginning* to believe in him. The Jews today look upon Christ as a great Rabbi. . . .

". . . But the great body of the Jews who are there assembled will not receive Christ as their Redeemer until he comes himself and makes himself manifest unto them" (Joseph Fielding Smith, *Doctrines of Salvation*, 3:9; emphasis in original).

2 NEPHI 6:16-17

When will the "Mighty God . . . deliver his covenant people"?

"The nations will gather and lay siege to Jerusalem. Part of the city will fall, with dire consequences to its inhabitants, when a great earthquake will come, the Mount of Olives will cleave in twain, and the persecuted people will flee into this valley for safety. At that particular time will the Savior come as their Deliverer" (Joseph Fielding Smith, *Doctrines of Salvation*, 3:47). *See also D&C 45:51–52.*

2 NEPHI 6:18

How will the wicked eat their "own flesh" and "be drunken with their own blood"?

"Their own Flesh . . . their own Blood. [This] signifies internal wars" (George Reynolds and Janne M. Sjodahl, *Commentary on the Book of Mormon*, 1:284).

2 Nephi 7

2 NEPHI 7-8, 12-24, 27

Why do Jacob and Nephi quote so much of Isaiah?

See insights for 2 Nephi 11:2.

2 NEPHI 7:1

What does the law of divorce have to do with being separated from God?

"Under this law [the law of divorce], if a wife was found unfaithful (unclean) her husband could dissolve the marriage by giving her a 'bill of divorcement.' Even though Israel had been unfaithful to her husband—the Lord—He had never given her such a document. . . .

". . . It appears that ancient 'mother Israel' left her Husband (put herself away)" (Hoyt W. Brewster Jr., *Isaiah Plain & Simple*, 206, 208).

2 NEPHI 7:2

Christ asks, "Have I no power to deliver?"

"Save for the exception of the very few who defect to perdition, there is no habit, no addiction, no rebellion, no transgression, no apostasy, no crime exempted from the promise of complete forgiveness. That is the promise of the atonement of Christ" (Boyd K. Packer, *Ensign*, November 1995, 20).

2 NEPHI 7:6

"I gave . . . my cheeks to them that plucked off the hair."

"Plucking the hair of a man's face or beard was looked upon as a shameful way of degrading him. (See 2 Samuel 10:1–4.) . . . It is descriptive of the rude way in which [Christ] was treated by the Jews and the Romans during His final hours" (Hoyt W. Brewster Jr., *Isaiah Plain & Simple*, 211). *See also Matthew 26:67.*

2 NEPHI 7:11

What happens to those who walk in their own light instead of the Lord's?

"Those who kindle fires and gird themselves with firebrands—that is, those who conspire evil and plan the destruction of the faithful or who walk by their own lights—shall be trapped by their own snares. They shall come to a sorrowful end" (Sidney B. Sperry, *Book of Mormon Compendium*, 158). *See also D&C 133:71.*

2 NEPHI 8

2 NEPHI 8:1, 14

What are the "rock" and the "hole"?

"Our rock and [hole] are Abraham and Sarah, from whom we descend. Ultimately . . . the rock we come from is . . . Christ, who is called the Rock at least thirty-four times in the scriptures" (Donald W. Parry, Jay A. Parry, and Tina M. Peterson, *Understanding Isaiah*, 450).

2 NEPHI 8:6

How will the heavens "vanish away" and the earth "wax old"?

"The passing away of an earth simply means that it will . . . become a celestial body" (Joseph Fielding Smith, *Doctrines of Salvation*, 1:72). *See also D&C 130:9.*

2 NEPHI 8:7

How can God's law be written in our hearts?

"Through the Holy Ghost the truth is woven into the very fibre and sinews of the body so that it cannot be forgotten" (Joseph Fielding Smith, *Doctrines of Salvation*, 1:48). *See also Jeremiah 20:9; insights for Alma 5:14, 26.*

2 NEPHI 8:9

Who are Rahab and the dragon?

Footnote *c* for this verse takes us to Isaiah 27:1, which states that Rahab is "leviathan the piercing serpent, even leviathan that crooked serpent . . . the dragon that [is] in the sea."

"The great dragon was cast out, that old serpent, called the Devil, and Satan" (Revelation 12:9; 20:2).

2 NEPHI 8:17–20

Who are the "two sons . . . full of the fury of the Lord"?

"They are two prophets that are to be raised up to the Jewish nation in the last days, at the time of the restoration, and to prophesy to the Jews after they are gathered" (D&C 77:15).

"These two shall be followers of that humble man, Joseph Smith. . . . No doubt they will be members of the Council of the Twelve or of the First Presidency of the Church" (Bruce R. McConkie, *Doctrinal New Testament Commentary*, 3:509).

2 NEPHI 8:24

What does it mean to put on "strength" and "beautiful garments"?

"To put on her strength is to put on the authority of the priesthood" (D&C 113:8).

"What are those garments? Those garments are the garments of righteousness, the garments of devotion to the truth—the gospel in action" (Ezra Taft Benson, *Teachings*, 347).

Who are the "uncircumcised and unclean"?

"Circumcision was . . . a symbol of the covenant entered into between the Father of the Faithful and . . . the Hebrew people" (Sidney B. Sperry, *Paul's Life and Letters*, 56). Therefore, the "uncircumcised" are those who have not made covenants with the Lord.

2 NEPHI 9

2 NEPHI 9:1-54

How significant is this chapter?

"This is a wonderfully explicit sermon . . . on Christ and his eternal covenant with the human family" (Jeffrey R. Holland, *Christ and the New Covenant*, 69).

"Our most explicit teachings on the atonement of Christ are in 2 Nephi 2 and 9 and Alma 34" (Bruce R. McConkie, *Promised Messiah*, 421).

2 NEPHI 9:6

"The fall came by reason of transgression."

"I never speak of the part Eve took in this fall as a sin, nor do I accuse Adam of a sin. . . . This was a transgression of the law, but not a sin" (Joseph Fielding Smith, *Doctrines of Salvation*, 1:114, 115). *See also 2 Nephi 2:22.*

2 NEPHI 9:6-10

What are the two deaths that were introduced to mankind because of the fall of Adam?

"Death entered the world by means of Adam's fall—death of two kinds, temporal and spiritual. Temporal death passes upon all men when they depart this mortal life. . . . Spiritual death passes upon all men when they become accountable for their sins. . . . They die spiritually; . . . they are cast out of the presence of God" (Bruce R. McConkie, *Promised Messiah*, 349–50).

2 NEPHI 9:7, 11-12

How did the "infinite atonement" overcome temporal and spiritual death?

"Jesus did come into the world to ransom it. Through his atonement we were bought from death and hell. Death and hell were paid—paid in full— and Christ was the only one who could pay that debt" (Joseph Fielding Smith, *Doctrines of Salvation*, 1:125).

Can we overcome spiritual death while in mortality?

"All the world today, I am sorry to say, with the exception of a handful of people who have obeyed the new and everlasting covenant, are suffering this spiritual death. . . . In order that they may be redeemed and saved from the spiritual death . . . they must repent of their sins" (Joseph F. Smith, *Gospel Doctrine*, 433).

2 NEPHI 9:13

What makes a resurrected body "incorruptible, and immortal"?

"Concerning the resurrection, I will merely say that all men will come from the grave . . . all will be raised by the power of God, having spirit in their bodies, and not blood" (Joseph Smith, *Teachings*, 199–200).

2 NEPHI 9:13-14

When will our "knowledge . . . be perfect"?

"Eventually a man will . . . understand all truth. Things are taught in a fragmentary way now, but we will know them in full . . . after the resurrection" (Joseph Fielding Smith, in Conference Report, April 1928, 66).

2 NEPHI 9:20

Why is it important to believe in a God who knows all things?

"If it were not for the idea existing in the minds of men that God had all knowledge it would be impossible for them to exercise faith in Him" (Joseph Smith, *Lectures on Faith*, 43). *See also D&C 130:7; 2 Nephi 2:24; Alma 26:35; Mormon 8:17; Moroni 7:22*

2 NEPHI 9:21

How difficult was it for the Savior to suffer the "pains of every living creature"?

See insights for Mosiah 3:7; Alma 7:11–13.

Even though Jesus suffered for all, his suffering is futile if we don't repent.

"Christ's sacrifice is fully effective only for the repentant. He suffered and died for us, yet if we do not repent, all his anguish and pain on our account are futile" (Spencer W. Kimball, *Teachings*, 70). *See also D&C 19:16–19.*

2 NEPHI 9:25-26

Who are those with "no law" that will be delivered?

"When no moral law applies (as with little children, the mentally impaired, those ignorant of the gospel until they are taught it, and so forth), the power of the Atonement 'satisfieth the demands of . . . justice'" (Jeffrey R. Holland, *Christ and the New Covenant*, 68).

2 NEPHI 9:28-29

When is learning appropriate and when is it foolish?

"You should not be hesitant to pursue knowledge. . . . Study to your heart's content any worthy field of inquiry, just remember that all knowledge is not equal in value" (Boyd K. Packer, in Monte S. Nyman and Charles D. Tate Jr., eds., *Jacob through Words of Mormon*, 10).

"Increasingly, the Latter-day Saints must choose between the reasoning of men and the revelations of God. . . . [some] with their worldly wisdom, are leading some of the members astray" (Ezra Taft Benson, *Teachings*, 354).

2 NEPHI 9:30–38

Jacob gives nine warnings.

SCRIPTURE	THE WARNING	THE PUNISHMENT
Verse 30; 1 Timothy 6:10	The rich who "despise the poor"	They shall perish
Verse 31	The deaf that "will not hear"	They shall perish
Verse 32	The blind that "will not see"	They shall perish
Verse 33	Those who refuse to covenant with God	A "knowledge of their iniquities shall smite them at the last day"
Verse 34; Proverbs 6:16–19	The liar	He shall be "thrust down to hell"
Verse 35; D&C 42:79	The murderer	He shall die
Verse 36; Alma 39:5	People guilty of immorality	Shall be "thrust down to hell"
Verse 37	Those who "worship idols"	Devil delights in them
Verse 38; Alma 34:32–34	Those who die in their sins	They will return to God in their sins

2 NEPHI 9:34

How serious is the sin of lying?

"In the telestial world . . . are they who are liars, . . . and adulterers" (D&C 76:98, 103).

"These six things doth the Lord hate: yea, seven are an abomination unto him: a proud look, a lying tongue, and hands that shed innocent blood, an heart that deviseth wicked imaginations, feet that be swift in running to mischief, a false witness that speaketh lies, and he that soweth discord among brethren" (Proverbs 6:16–19). In a list of seven things God hates, lying is listed twice.

2 NEPHI 9:39

What difference do our thoughts make?

"Each of us, with discipline and effort, has the capacity to control our thoughts. . . . This is part of the process of developing spiritual, physical, and emotional maturity" (Gordon B. Hinckley, *Teachings*, 579). *See also insights for Mosiah 4:30.*

2 NEPHI 9:41

Why is this an unusual rendering of "narrow" and "straight"?

In the many times the phrase "strait and narrow" is used in scripture, "strait" means *narrow* (see Matthew 7:14). However, 2 Nephi 9:41 is the only place in scripture where the word is spelled "straight." This gives the additional insight that the path of God is not only narrow but also undeviating and not crooked.

"The Holy One of Israel . . . employeth no servant there."

"We have the agency to make choices, but ultimately we will be accountable for each choice we make. We may deceive others, but there is One we will never deceive" (James E. Faust, *Ensign*, November 1996, 42).

2 NEPHI 9:44–45, 47–48

"I shook your iniquities from my soul."

"It was an ancient practice for the Lord's prophets to take off their garments and shake them as a sign that they were rid of the blood and sins of those to whom they had been sent to testify. (2 Ne. 9:44; Jac. 1:19; 2:2; Mosiah 2:28; Morm. 9:35.) Similar symbolism is used in latter-day revelation: 'Cleanse your hearts and your garments, lest the blood of this generation be required at your hands' . . . (D&C 112:33; 88:85; 135:5)" (Bruce R. McConkie, *Mormon Doctrine*, 304). *See also insights for Jacob 1:19.*

2 NEPHI 9:45–48

Is it better to repent or to not sin in the first place?

"If a person has determined that sin can easily be wiped out, . . . with an idea in his mind that repentance will . . . place him on a level with his fellow who has kept in virtue the commandments, from the beginning—time will wake him up to his serious and great mistake. He may and will be forgiven, if he repent; the blood of Christ will make him free . . . but all this will not return to him any loss sustained, nor place him on an equal footing with his neighbor who has kept the commandments of the better law. Nor will it place him in the position where he would have been, had he not committed wrong" (Joseph F. Smith, *Gospel Doctrine*, 374).

"I am convinced that we must impress you young people with the awfulness of sin rather than to content ourselves with merely teaching the way of repentance" (Harold B. Lee, *Decisions for Successful Living*, 88).

2 NEPHI 9:49–50

"My heart delighteth in righteousness."

"There is no better evidence for the goodness of man than his desire to learn the principles of the gospel of Jesus Christ. He delights in being instructed from the scriptures" (Boyd K. Packer, *Teach Ye Diligently*, 153).

2 NEPHI 9:52

"Pray . . . by day and give thanks . . . by night."

See insights for Alma 37:37.

2 NEPHI 10

2 NEPHI 10:2, 15, 17

"I will fulfill my promises."

See insights for 2 Nephi 9:1, 53.

2 NEPHI 10:3

This is the first time the word Christ appears in the Book of Mormon. What is the meaning of the name Jesus Christ?

HEBREW	GREEK	ENGLISH
Messiah	Christ	Anointed one (see LDS Bible Dictionary, 633)
Joshua	Jesus	Savior (see LDS Bible Dictionary, 713; 2 Nephi 25:19)

2 NEPHI 10:5–6

What is the cause of "destructions, famines, pestilences, and bloodshed"?

"Anguish and wrath and tribulation and the withdrawing of the Spirit of God from the earth await this generation, until they are visited with utter desolation. [Because] this generation is . . . corrupt" (Joseph Smith, *Teachings*, 328).

2 NEPHI 10:6–8

How are the Jews scattered and gathered?

See insights for 1 Nephi 21:19–26; 2 Nephi 6:11.

2 NEPHI 10:10–14

What are the conditions of sustained liberty in America?

"Ye shall have no king nor ruler, for I will be your king and watch over you. Wherefore, hear my voice and follow me, and you shall be a free people" (D&C 38:21–22).

2 NEPHI 10:16

"They who are not for me are against me."

"Before you joined this Church you stood on neutral ground. When the gospel was preached good and evil were set before you. You could choose either or neither. There were two opposite masters inviting you to serve them. When you joined this Church you enlisted to serve God. When you did that you left the neutral gound, and you never can get back . . . to it. Should you forsake the master you enlisted to serve it will be by the instigation of the evil one, and you will follow his dictation and be his servant" (Joseph Smith, quoted in *Juvenile Instructor*, 27:492). *See also insights for 3 Nephi 13:24.*

2 NEPHI 10:18

How will the Gentiles be "numbered among the house of Israel"?

"While the tribes of Israel were specially favored, . . . the Lord . . . took means to include the nations of the Gentiles within the pale of these blessings given to Abraham, by the scattering of his children, thus sprinkling his blood among the Gentiles entitling them to the privileges of the sacred covenants which were conferred upon Israel, but, of course, on their worthiness. Moreover, the Lord provided in the blessing to Abraham that the pure Gentiles who had none of the blood of Abraham in their veins, should also partake of the blessings of Abraham through obedience by the principle of adoption" (Joseph Fielding Smith, *Restoration of All Things*, 159).

2 NEPHI 11

2 NEPHI 11:2

How important are the words of Isaiah?

"He [Isaiah] is quoted more often in the New Testament, Book of Mormon, Doctrine and Covenants, and contemporary documents such as the Dead Sea Scrolls than any other Old World prophet" (Jeffrey R. Holland, *Christ and the New Covenant*, 75–76).

If the Isaiah verses in the Book of Mormon were removed from their present position and collected into one book, that book would contain 592 verses—more verses than are found in twelve of the fifteen books in the Book of Mormon. The accompanying graph lists the number of verses left in each book in the Book of Mormon after the Isaiah verses have been removed.

Books are listed in order of their size, demonstrating that a book of Isaiah verses only would be the fourth largest in the Book of Mormon.

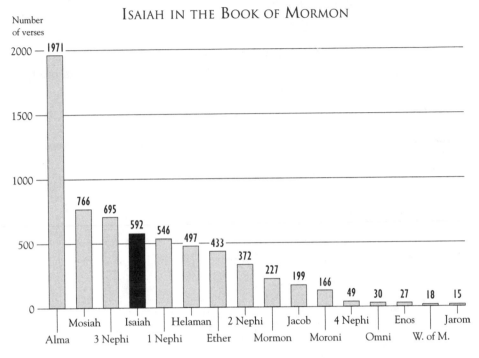

ISAIAH IN THE BOOK OF MORMON

2 NEPHI 11:2–3

Seeing the Redeemer qualifies prophets.

ISAIAH	NEPHI	JACOB
Isaiah 6:1: "I saw also the Lord sitting upon a throne, high and lifted up"	**1 Nephi 2:16:** "I, Nephi . . . did cry unto the Lord; and behold he did visit me"	**2 Nephi 2:1–4:** "Jacob . . . thou art redeemed, because of thy Redeemer . . . thou hast beheld in thy youth his glory"

2 NEPHI 11:3

God will establish his word "by the words of three."

"Nephi, Jacob, and Isaiah are three early types and shadows of Oliver Cowdery, David Whitmer, and Martin Harris—witnesses positioned right at the front of the book where Oliver, David, and Martin . . . would later be positioned. But Nephi, Jacob, and Isaiah bore a very special witness— they testified of the divinity of Jesus Christ, the Son of God" (Jeffrey R. Holland, *Ensign*, January 1996, 14). *See also Matthew 18:16.*

2 NEPHI 11:4

How many things created by God are types of Christ?

"All things have their likeness, and all things are created and made to bear record of me, both things which are temporal, and things which are spiritual; . . . all things bear record of me" (Moses 6:63). *See also insights for 1 Nephi 18:10–23.*

2 NEPHI 11:8

What are some helps in understanding Isaiah?

Ten keys to understanding Isaiah:

1. Gain an overall knowledge of the plan of salvation

2. Learn the position and destiny of the house of Israel

3. Know the chief doctrines about which Isaiah chose to write

4. Use the Book of Mormon

5. Use latter-day revelation

6. Learn how the New Testament interprets Isaiah

7. Study Isaiah in its Old Testament context

8. Learn the manner of prophesying used among the Jews in Isaiah's day

9. Have the Spirit

10. Devote yourself to hard, conscientious study (Taken from Bruce R. McConkie, *Ensign*, October 1973, 80–83). *See also insights for 2 Nephi 25:1–7.*

2 NEPHI 12

2 NEPHI 12–24

A summary of the Isaiah chapters Nephi quoted:

2 NEPHI	ISAIAH	MESSAGE
12	2	Establishment of Zion, restoration of gospel, including temple blessings
13	3	Judah to be scattered, including the Nephites
14	4	Latter-day contrasts: The world vs. Zion

2 NEPHI 12:2

"The Lord's house shall be established in the top of the mountains."

"[Second Nephi 12:2] has specific reference to the Salt Lake Temple and to the other temples built in the top of the Rocky Mountains, and it has a general reference to the temple yet to be built in the New Jerusalem in Jackson County, Missouri" (Bruce R. McConkie, *New Witness for the Articles of Faith*, 539–40).

2 NEPHI 12:3

How will the law go out from Zion and the "word of the Lord from Jerusalem"?

"Years ago I went with the brethren to the Idaho Falls Temple, and I heard in that inspired prayer of the First Presidency a definition of the meaning of that term 'out of Zion shall go forth the law.' Note what they said: 'We thank thee that thou hast revealed to us that those who gave us our constitutional form of government were men wise in thy sight and that thou didst raise them up for the very purpose of putting forth that sacred document . . . to fulfill the ancient prophecy of Isaiah and Micah that ". . . out of Zion shall go forth the law"'" (Harold B. Lee, *Ensign*, November 1971, 15).

2 NEPHI 12:4

When will people not "learn war any more"?

"The millennial day . . . that promised time when 'they shall beat their swords into plowshares, and their spears into pruninghooks: nation shall not lift up sword against nation, neither shall they learn war any more . . . [but shall] walk in the light of the Lord' (Isa. 2:4–5)" (Howard W. Hunter, *Ensign*, November 1994, 88).

2 NEPHI 12:10, 19

What causes the wicked to want to hide from the Lord?

"I did remember all my sins and iniquities, for which I was tormented with the pains of hell . . . Oh, thought I, that I could be banished and become extinct both soul and body, that I might not be brought to stand in the presence of my God" (Alma 36:13, 15). *See also Luke 23:30.*

2 NEPHI 12:13

What is the meaning of "the cedars of Lebanon" and "the oaks of Bashan"?

"[These high or valuable groves are] used in the way of metaphor and allegory for kings, princes, potentates of the highest rank" (Adam Clarke, *Holy Bible*, 31).

2 NEPHI 12:19, 21

How will the glory of the Lord destroy the wicked at his coming?

"For the presence of the Lord shall be as the melting fire that burneth, and as the fire which causeth the waters to boil" (D&C 133:41). *See also D&C 5:19.*

2 NEPHI 12:20

Why will the wicked cast their gold and silver "to the moles and to the bats"?

"The imagery of verse 20 is striking: the people will throw their gold and silver idols to moles and bats, animals who are blind. . . . The irony of this is that people who understood the material value of the precious metals, and should also have seen the spiritual impotence of the idols, will throw these precious items to animals who will not be able to see them at all" (Victor L. Ludlow, *Isaiah: Prophet, Seer, and Poet*, 92).

2 NEPHI 13

2 NEPHI 13:1

What does it mean to "take away . . . the stay and the staff"?

"Life is supported by bread and water . . . so that 'breaking the staff of bread' . . . is equivalent to physical destruction" (C. F. Keil and F. Delitzsch, *Commentary on the Old Testament*, 7:129).

2 NEPHI 13:4

Who are the "babes" that "shall rule over them"?

The Hebrew term for *babes* is *ta' a luw lim* which means "caprice" or a "tyrant." So in other words, they will have *rulers that are childish*, cruel, weak—where anarchy and mob-rule prevail (see C. F. Keil and F. Delitzsch, *Commentary on the Old Testament*, 7:132–33).

2 NEPHI 13:5

What will be the general relationship between the youth and the elderly?

"In these days, it may be typical for children to show neither deference nor honor to their elders" (Donald W. Parry, Jay A. Parry, and Tina M. Peterson, *Understanding Isaiah*, 39).

2 NEPHI 13:9

How do people's countenances "witness against them, and . . . declare their sin"?

"Every person who lives in this world wields an influence, whether for good or for evil. It is not what he says alone, it is not alone what he does. It is what he is. Every man, every person radiates what he or she is . . . It is what we are and what we radiate that affects . . . people" (David O. McKay, in Conference Report, April 1963, 129).

2 NEPHI 13:12

How will Satan disrupt family roles?

"Today the undermining of the home and family is on the increase, with the devil anxiously working to displace the father as the head of the home and create rebellion among the children" (Ezra Taft Benson, *Teachings*, 541).

2 NEPHI 13:14

What is the "vineyard"?

"For the vineyard of the Lord of hosts is the house of Israel, and the men of Judah his pleasant plant" (Isaiah 5:7).

2 NEPHI 13:16–23

Who are the "daughters of Zion" described in these verses?

There are at least two interpretations for who the "daughters of Zion" represent. First, these verses are a physical description of members in the last days. "It is, . . . a sad reflection on the 'daughters of Zion' when they dress immodestly. Moreover, this remark pertains to the men as well as to the women" (Joseph Fielding Smith, *Answers to Gospel Questions*, 5:174). Second, these "daughters of Zion" could represent those members of the Church that have accepted the baptimal covenant and later forsake their vows and turn to the gods of men.

What is the meaning of the descriptions of the "daughters of Zion"?

DESCRIPTION	MEANING
"Walk with stretched forth necks" (v. 16)	Acting with pride
With "wanton eyes" (v. 16)	Seductive eyes that focus on carnality
"Mincing as they go" (v. 16)	Short, rapid steps to draw attention to them
"Making a tinkling with their feet" (v. 16)	Ornaments and bells on their ankles
"Smite with a scab" (v. 17)	An itchy rash that lessens their beauty
"Discover their secret parts" (v. 17)	To put them to open shame
"Cauls" (v. 18)	Hair nets or head bands
"Round tires" (v. 18)	Crescent shaped ornaments
"Chains" (v. 19)	Pendants, necklaces, and earrings
"Mufflers" (v. 19)	Veils
"Bonnets" (v. 20)	Headdresses
"Ornaments of the legs" (v. 20)	Ankle chains and sashes
"Changeable suits of apparel" (v. 22)	Various pairs of expensive robes and garments
"Hoods" (v. 23)	Women's turbans

(Adapted from Hoyt W. Brewster Jr., *Isaiah Plain & Simple*, 31–32.)

2 NEPHI 13:24

What is the meaning of "baldness" in this verse?

"Self-imposed baldness, . . . sitting on the ground, . . . and sackcloth . . . are all symbols of mourning, . . . mourning caused by God's judgments on

Judah and Jerusalem as well as upon the world in the last days" (Donald W. Parry, Jay A. Parry, and Tina M. Peterson, *Understanding Isaiah*, 44).

2 NEPHI 13:24–26

How are these verses descriptive of the results of war?

DESCRIPTION	MEANING
"There shall be stink" (v. 24)	The stench of dead bodies will sicken the air
"A rent" (v. 24)	Clothing ripped or torn, like rags
"Baldness" (v. 24)	Shaving heads and beards was a symbol of captivity
"Sackcloth" (v. 24)	A coarse, dark cloth made of goat or camel hair
"Burning" (v. 24)	Branding, another symbol of captivity
"Sit upon the ground" (v. 26)	A posture of mourning

(Adapted from Hoyt W. Brewster Jr., *Isaiah Plain & Simple*, 33–34.)

2 NEPHI 14

2 NEPHI 14:1

How does the Joseph Smith Translation help us understand this verse?

The Joseph Smith Translation moves this verse to be the last verse of the previous chapter. It is the natural result of the wars spoken of there.

Why will "seven women . . . take hold of one man"?

"'In that day,' (14:1) when the judgments will have removed so many men that there is a great scarcity of them, 'seven women' . . . will request a man's hand in marriage. . . . Having a good knowledge of the importance of marriage, they request a man to take away their reproach. In Isaiah's day . . . it was . . . a disgrace to remain unmarried" (Sidney B. Sperry, *Book of Mormon Compendium*, 183–84). *See also Genesis 30:22.*

2 NEPHI 14:2

What is the "branch"?

"The days come, saith the Lord, that I will raise unto David a righteous Branch [LDS Bible footnote *b* says "Jesus Christ"], and a King shall reign and prosper" (Jeremiah 23:5).

2 NEPHI 14:5

"A cloud and smoke by day and the shining of a flaming fire by night."

The fire by night and the cloud by day are symbols of the presence of the Lord. "When the New Jerusalem is built on this land, Jesus will visit that city, his glory will be upon its dwelling places" (Orson Pratt, *Journal of Discourses*, 14:334). *See also insights for 2 Nephi 16:4.*

2 NEPHI 14:5–6

"Zion shall be a defence . . . a place of refuge."

"The time is soon coming, when no man will have any peace but in Zion" (Joseph Smith, *Teachings*, 161). *See also D&C 45:66–70.*

2 NEPHI 15

2 NEPHI 15:1

What effect can good music have in our lives?

"Some of the greatest sermons are preached by the singing of hymns. Hymns move us to repentance and good works, build testimony and faith, comfort the weary, console the mourning, and inspire us to endure to the end" (*Hymns of The Church of Jesus Christ of Latter-day Saints*, ix).

2 NEPHI 15:1–6

What are the symbols of this parable?

SYMBOL	MEANING
Vineyard (vv. 1, 3)	House of Israel (v. 7)
Well beloved (v. 1)	Jesus Christ (Mormon 5:14)
Fruitful hill (v. 1)	The vineyard was planted in a choice area
Fenced it (v. 2)	The Lord's protections given to safeguard Israel (Hoyt W. Brewster Jr., *Isaiah Plain & Simple*, 43)
Choicest vine (v. 2)	The tribe of Judah (v. 7)
Tower (v. 2)	The temple of Solomon (Nyman, *Great Are the Words of Isaiah*, 42)
Wine-press (v. 2)	High expectations of the Lord (Hoyt W. Brewster Jr., *Isaiah Plain & Simple*, 42)

Grapes (vv. 2, 4)	Righteous people (Thomas R. Valletta, ed., *Book of Mormon for Latter-day Saint Families*, 108)
Wild grapes (vv. 2, 4)	Wicked people who "regard not the work of the Lord" (v. 12), "cast away the law of the Lord . . . and [despise] his word" (v. 24)
Lay it waste (v. 6)	Houses will be desolate, cities without inhabitants (v. 9), Israel will be in captivity (v. 13), the Lord smote the wicked (v. 25)
Briers and thorns (v. 6)	Non-Israelite Gentiles to inhabit the lands

2 NEPHI 15:8

What sin is it to join "house to house"?

"Property acquired for selfish purposes is not a blessing. Greed is never satisfied" (George Reynolds and Janne M. Sjodahl, *Commentary on the Book of Mormon*, 1:334).

2 NEPHI 15:12

How does evil music have an influence in the world?

"Some music is spiritually very destructive. . . . The tempo, the sounds, and the lifestyle of those who perform it repel the Spirit. . . . It can smother your spiritual senses" (Boyd K. Packer, *Ensign*, November 1994, 61).

2 NEPHI 15:13

What are the detriments of not having knowledge?

"A man is saved no faster than he gets knowledge, for if he does not get knowledge, he will be brought into captivity. . . . [We need] revelation to assist us, and give us knowledge of the things of God" (Joseph Smith, *Teachings*, 217).

2 NEPHI 15:14

What is the "hell" spoken of in this verse?

"Hades, the Greek, or Sheol, the Hebrew, these two significations mean a world of spirits. Hades, Sheol, paradise, spirits in prison, are all one: it is a world of spirits" (Joseph Smith, *Teachings*, 310).

2 NEPHI 15:18

What is the "cart rope"?

"They are tied to their sins like beasts to their burdens [or oxen to their carts]" (LDS Bible, Isaiah 5:18, footnote c).

2 NEPHI 15:23

Who are those who "justify the wicked for reward"?

"This refers to those who take bribes. . . . One wonders if Isaiah saw those well-known figures . . . who accept payment for endorsing harmful products such as alcohol" (Hoyt W. Brewster Jr., *Isaiah Plain & Simple*, 50).

2 NEPHI 15:26

What is the "ensign" to be lifted up "to the nations"?

"This Church is the standard which Isaiah said the Lord would set up. . . . This Church is the ensign" (Marion G. Romney, in Conference Report, April 1961, 119).

2 NEPHI 15:26–27

How will they move "swiftly" without being "weary"?

"Isaiah seemed to indicate that the gathering should take place in the day of the train and the airplane. . . . He seems to have described them in unmistakable words" (LeGrand Richards, *Marvelous Work and a Wonder*, 229–30).

2 NEPHI 16

2 NEPHI 16:1

Temples are likely places to see visions of the Lord.

"Inasmuch as my people build a house unto me in the name of the Lord, and do not suffer any unclean thing to come into it . . . my presence shall be there, for I will come into it, and all the pure in heart that shall come into it shall see God" (D&C 97:15–16). *See also Ezekiel 1:26; Revelation 4:2–4.*

What is the meaning of long robes, or a "train"?

"The Hebrew term [for coat of many colours] may indicate simply a long coat with sleeves" (LDS Bible, Genesis 37:3, footnote c).

"This speaks of the Lord's flowing temple robes. . . . The image of the hems of God's robe filling the temple is used to symbolize the purity, righteousness, and power of the Lord that filled the temple" (Donald W. Parry, Jay A. Parry, and Tina M. Peterson, *Understanding Isaiah*, 64–65).

2 NEPHI 16:2

What are the "seraphim" with six wings?

"Seraphs are angels who reside in the presence of God. . . .

"In Hebrew the plural of seraph is *seraphim*. . . . The fact that these holy beings were shown to him as having wings was simply to symbolize their 'power, to move, to act, etc.' as was the case also in visions others had received. (D. & C. 77:4)" (Bruce R. McConkie, *Mormon Doctrine*, 702–3).

2 NEPHI 16:4

Why was the house "filled with smoke"?

Smoke has often symbolized the presence of the Lord. "Mount Sinai was altogether on a smoke, because the Lord descended upon it in fire" (Exodus 19:18). "The temple was filled with smoke from the glory of God, and from his power" (Revelation 15:8). In ancient Israel at the altar of incense, the officiating priest would burn incense and the smoke would rise, symbolizing their prayers ascending to heaven. This act of prayer was also the last act prior to the priest entering the holy place and the "presence of God."

2 NEPHI 16:6-7

How was his "iniquity . . . taken away, and . . . sin purged"?

Isaiah's "iniquity" was removed by a "live coal." Nephi taught, "A remission of your sins [comes] by fire and by the Holy Ghost" (2 Nephi 31:17). The altar of burnt offerings represented the Lord Jesus Christ and his final sacrifice of the Atonement. The fire is the purifying agent of the sacrifice.

2 NEPHI 16:8

Who else said "Here am I; send me"?

The premortal Savior used language very similar to Isaiah's: "Whom shall I send? And one answered like unto the Son of Man: Here am I, send me" (Abraham 3:27).

2 NEPHI 16:9-10

Why could they hear but not understand?

Some people's spiritual sensitivity is so poor they simply cannot understand spiritual things. *See also Matthew 13:15; John 12:37–41; Acts 28:25–27.*

2 NEPHI 17

2 NEPHI 17:1-12

Who are Syria and Israel, who were to combine forces against Judah?

"The southern kingdom of Judah was threatened by an alliance of the northern kingdom of Israel with Syria. . . .

". . . Isaiah prophesies that . . . these two countries will be the ones that will be destroyed" (Hoyt W. Brewster Jr., *Isaiah Plain & Simple*, 62).

2 NEPHI 17:3

Who was "Shearjashub"?

"Isaiah [took] his son Shear-jashub with him to meet Ahaz. . . . the meaning of his son's name [is] 'The remnant shall return.' . . . The son's presence

. . . may have been to remind Ahaz of the prophecy that Judah would not be utterly destroyed" (Monte S. Nyman, *Great Are the Words of Isaiah*, 54).

2 NEPHI 17:13–17

"A virgin shall conceive, and shall bear a son, and shall call his name Immanuel."

"There are plural or parallel elements to this prophecy, as with so much of Isaiah's writing. The most immediate meaning was probably focused on Isaiah's wife, a pure and good woman who brought forth a son about this time, the child becoming a type and shadow of the greater, later fulfillment of the prophecy that would be realized in the birth of Jesus Christ. . . . His title *Immanuel* would be carried forward to the latter days, being applied to the Savior" (Jeffrey R. Holland, *Christ and the New Covenant*, 79). *See also Matthew 1:22–23.*

Nephi's motivation to include so much of Isaiah's writing was to "persuade [everyone] to believe in the Lord their Redeemer" (1 Nephi 19:23). Consider what Isaiah says about the Savior.

REFERENCE	WHAT WE LEARN ABOUT JESUS CHRIST FROM ISAIAH
2 Nephi 17:14	His mother would be a virgin and he would be called "Immanuel."
2 Nephi 17:15	He would choose goodness and righteousness.
2 Nephi 18:6	He would be rejected by most people at his first coming.
2 Nephi 18:7–8	His second coming would be in power and glory.
2 Nephi 18:9–12, 14–15	Those who oppose him will fail, but those who seek him will be blessed.
2 Nephi 18:13, 16–17	We prepare for Christ's second coming by heeding scriptures and words of the prophets.
2 Nephi 19:5; see also 20:16–18	At the Second Coming the wicked will be destroyed by fire.
2 Nephi 19:6	Christ will rule politically in the world during the Millennium.
2 Nephi 19:7	His power and control will be limitless and have no end.
2 Nephi 21:1–2	He will have the spirit of wisdom, might, understanding, and knowledge.
2 Nephi 21:3–5	He will righteously judge, and he will slay the wicked.

| 2 Nephi 23:10 | The sun, moon, and stars will not shine at the Second Coming. |
| 2 Nephi 23:13 | Earthquakes will accompany his return. |

2 NEPHI 17:16

"Before the child shall know to refuse the evil and choose the good . . ."

"Before . . . the age of accountability, which is eight years old (D&C 68:25), the kingdoms of Syria and Israel (Northern Kingdom) will be laid waste. This prophecy was fulfilled" (Donald W. Parry, Jay A. Parry, and Tina M. Peterson, *Understanding Isaiah*, 76).

2 NEPHI 17:18–25

"The Lord shall hiss for the fly . . . and for the bee."

Israel's wickedness would prompt the Lord to punish them, from Egypt in the south to Assyria in the north—the two ends of the known world. Israel's enemies are compared to flies and bees, pests that won't leave their victims alone.

2 NEPHI 17:20

Why would the Assyrians "shave with a razor" the captives?

"The Assyrians cut off all the hair from their captives for three reasons: humiliation, sanitation . . . and separation (if any slaves escaped . . . they could not blend in with other peoples)" (Victor L. Ludlow, *Isaiah: Prophet, Seer, and Poet*, 145).

2 NEPHI 18

2 NEPHI 18:1–2

What are the "roll" and "witnesses"?

"Isaiah is told to write . . . on a large scroll or tablet. . . .

". . . In keeping with the law of witnesses, . . . Isaiah has two witnesses on hand to record and testify of what was being said" (Hoyt W. Brewster Jr., *Isaiah Plain & Simple*, 75, 76).

2 NEPHI 18:3–8

How is the "Immanuel" prophecy of 2 Nephi 17 and 18 dualistic in nature?

THEME	CHRIST— 2 NEPHI 17:14–17	ISAIAH— 2 NEPHI 18:3–7
Mother	Virgin (v. 14)	Prophetess (v. 3)

Conception	Shall conceive (v. 14)	She conceived (v. 3)
Child is a son	Bear a son (v. 14)	Bare a son (v. 3)
Naming a son	Call his name Immanuel (v. 14)	Call his name Maher-shalal-hash-baz (v. 3)
Child shall have knowledge	Before the child shall know (v. 16)	Before the child shall have knowledge (v. 4)
Child before eight years	To refuse the evil and choose the good (v. 16)	To cry, My father, and my mother (v. 4)
Land	Land . . . shall be forsaken (v. 16)	Damascus and Samaria shall be taken away (v. 4)
Kings	Both her kings (v. 16)	King of Assyria (v. 4)
Role of the Lord	Lord shall bring upon thee (v. 17)	Lord bringeth up upon them (v. 7)
Assyrian King	King of Assyria (v. 17)	King of Assyria (v. 7)

(Donald W. Parry, Jay A. Parry, and Tina M. Peterson, *Understanding Isaiah*, 73.)

2 NEPHI 18:6–8

What were "the waters of Shiloah" and "the waters of the river"?

"The waters of Shiloah" refers to a pool in the southern part of Jerusalem that anciently was the city's main water source. These waters "also represent the continuous tender care that the Lord provided for his people as he sought to lead them with gentle promptings of the Spirit. The Judean leaders rejected the Lord's advice offered through Isaiah, who foretold how the raging floodwaters of the Euphrates River would replace the waters of Shiloah. Instead of gentle water around their knees, the raging torrent of the Assyrian army would gather around their necks" (Victor L. Ludlow, *Isaiah: Prophet, Seer, and Poet*, 145).

2 NEPHI 18:16, 20

Truth is found in the "law" (scriptures) and the "testimony" (words of the prophets).

"When people request revelation . . . [their] sources are to be tested according to the law (of Moses) and the testimony (of the prophets)" (Monte S. Nyman, *Great Are the Words of Isaiah*, 65). *See also insights for Jacob 7:10–12.*

2 NEPHI 18:17–19

"I will wait upon the Lord, . . . and I will look for him."

"I would commend you to *seek this Jesus* of whom the prophets and apostles have written" (Ether 12:41; emphasis added). *See also Hebrews 9:28.*

2 NEPHI 18:18

How were Isaiah and his children "signs" for Israel?

"Maher-shalal-hash-baz is Hebrew for 'in making speed to the spoil, he hasteneth the prey.' The name describes the events spoken of in 2 Nephi 18:4. . . . Shearjashub means 'the remnant will return,' a reference to the day when Israel will be gathered from her scattered condition" (*Book of Mormon Student Manual Religion 121–122* [1982], 93–94).

2 NEPHI 19

2 NEPHI 19:1

Where is the land of Zebulun and Naphtali?

"Zebulun and Naphtali . . . formed the northern border of Israel. . . . [It] was the first area captured by the Assyrians in the time of Isaiah (see 2 Kings 15:29)" (Monte S. Nyman, *Great Are the Words of Isaiah*, 67).

2 NEPHI 19:1–2

"The people that walked in darkness have seen a great light."

"The 'dimness' and 'darkness' were apostasy and captivity (Isa. 8:20–22); the 'great light' is Christ (Isa. 9:6–7)" (LDS Bible, Isaiah 9:2, footnote *a*).

2 NEPHI 19:3

How is Isaiah clearer in the Book of Mormon than in the Bible?

"In the Bible the first part of the verse reads, 'Thou hast multiplied the nation, and not increased the joy,' but Nephi excludes the word *not*. The version that Nephi is quoting makes the verse clearer, showing that Jesus Christ will bring gladness and joy" (Thomas R. Valletta, ed., *Book of Mormon for Latter-day Saint Families*, 117).

2 NEPHI 19:4

What is the meaning of the "yoke," the "staff," and the "rod"?

"These three items—the yoke, staff, and rod—signify forms of oppression" (Donald W. Parry, Jay A. Parry, and Tina M. Peterson, *Understanding Isaiah*, 95).

2 NEPHI 19:5

"This shall be with burning and fuel of fire."

During the Millennium "the material and equipment needed for war will be destroyed" (Sidney B. Sperry, *Book of Mormon Compendium*, 207). *See also 2 Nephi 12:4.*

2 NEPHI 19:9–20:4

What are the problems of being obsessed with self?

SCRIPTURE	TEMPTATION	MANIFESTATION OF SIN
2 Nephi 19:9–13	Pride	Focus on self
2 Nephi 19:14–16	Power	Promotes self
2 Nephi 19:17–21	Passion	Gratifies self
2 Nephi 20:1–4	Exploit the poor	Destroys self

2 NEPHI 19:12

How are "the Syrians before and the Philistines behind"?

"Israel . . . would be attacked on the east by the Syrians and on the west by the Philistines" (Hoyt W. Brewster Jr., *Isaiah Plain & Simple*, 91).

2 NEPHI 19:12, 17, 21; 20:4

What does it mean that the Lord's "hand is stretched out still"?

"The phrase 'his hand is stretched out still' can be understood in at least two ways: (1) The punishment of the Lord is still forthcoming if His people don't repent, and (2) 'in spite of all, the Lord is available if they will turn to him' (LDS edition of the King James Bible, Isaiah 9:12, note d)" (Thomas R. Valletta, ed., *Book of Mormon for Latter-day Saint Families*, 118).

2 NEPHI 19:14–15

What is the "head and tail, branch and rush" that will be cut off by the Lord?

"*Head* represents the elders and old men . . . and *tail* symbolizes false prophets.

". . . The branch is a palm branch, . . . representing society's leaders; the bulrush stem, located near the ground, represents the common people" (Donald W. Parry, Jay A. Parry, and Tina M. Peterson, *Understanding Isaiah*, 100).

2 NEPHI 19:17

Why would the Lord "have no joy"?

"The Lord takes no pleasure in dispensing divine punishment upon the wicked" (Hoyt W. Brewster Jr., *Isaiah Plain & Simple*, 93).

2 NEPHI 19:21

Ephraim and Manasseh "shall be against Judah."

"The Jerusalem Bible reads 'Manasseh devours Ephraim, Ephraim [devours] Manasseh,' meaning that tribes, families, and even brothers will contend against one another" (Donald W. Parry, Jay A. Parry, and Tina M. Peterson, *Understanding Isaiah*, 101).

2 NEPHI 20

2 NEPHI 20:5-6

Does the Lord use one evil nation to destroy another?

"The Assyrian king would be . . . used for the correction of an erring people" (George Reynolds and Janne M. Sjodahl, *Commentary on the Book of Mormon*, 1:352). *See also Mormon 4:5.*

2 NEPHI 20:9

What are Calno, Carchemish, Hamath, Arpad, Samaria, and Damascus?

This was a list of the cities conquered by Assyria, listed in geographical order from Assyria to Jerusalem.

2 NEPHI 20:12, 24-25

How would Assyria be punished?

"The Lord will punish the king of Assyria for his 'stout heart' and 'high looks' (arrogance, pride, and boasting). This prophecy was fulfilled when a desolating sickness was sent into the Assyrian camps, causing many deaths, and the king was later slain by his own sons (2 Kings 19:32–37)" (Hoyt W. Brewster Jr., *Isaiah Plain & Simple*, 100).

2 NEPHI 20:16, 25

How long will the wicked enjoy their success?

"The works of men, or . . . the works of the devil . . . they have joy in their works for a season, and by and by the end cometh, and they are hewn down and cast into the fire" (3 Nephi 27:11).

2 NEPHI 20:26

What was "the slaughter of Midian"?

The "slaughter of Midian" refers to the victory of Gideon over the Midianites in Judges 7. Isaiah's point is that the Lord, not Israel's strength, destroyed the Midianites.

2 NEPHI 20:27

Who was anointed that would take away their burdens?

"Oil . . . may refer to the Messiah (Hebrew 'anointed one'), who was anointed with olive oil and the Holy Ghost (Acts 10:38)" (Donald W. Parry, Jay A. Parry, and Tina M. Peterson, *Understanding Isaiah*, 112).

2 NEPHI 20:28-32

The Assyrian army advances from Aiath to Jerusalem.

"The Assyrians did later invade Judah and came almost into Jerusalem. (Isaiah 36–37.) However, the invasion Isaiah foretells may also be eschatological [millennial] and refer to the future attack upon Jerusalem. . . . (See Zech. 14:2; Rev. 11:1–13; JST Matt. 24). Another reason for looking at the end of chapter [20] from a latter-day context is that chapter [21] is . . . to be fulfilled after 1823, for Moroni told Joseph Smith in September of that year 'that it was about to be fulfilled' (JS—H 1:40)" (Victor L. Ludlow, *Isaiah: Prophet, Seer, and Poet*, 165).

2 NEPHI 21

2 NEPHI 21:1-16

How important is Isaiah chapter 11?

Isaiah chapter eleven is "one of the most important chapters in all scripture. Not only does Jacob quote it here, . . . but on September 21, 1823, the resurrected angel Moroni quoted this chapter to Joseph Smith and said it was about to be fulfilled. Also, . . . (section 113) is devoted primarily to an explanation of this chapter" (Daniel H. Ludlow, *Companion*, 143).

2 NEPHI 21:1

What is the meaning of the "rod," the "stem," "Jesse," and "branch"?

NAME	MEANING
Rod	Joseph Smith Jr. (D&C 113:3–4; Sidney B. Sperry, *Book of Mormon Compendium*, 223)
Stem	Jesus Christ (D&C 113:1–2)
Jesse	The father of David (Ruth 4:17), Jesse represents the royal lineage of King David's kingdom (Bruce R. McConkie, *Promised Messiah*, 192–93)
Branch	Jesus Christ (Jeremiah 23:3–6; Bruce R. McConkie, *Promised Messiah*, 192–93)

2 NEPHI 21:2-5

Who do the pronouns "him," "his," and "he" refer to?

"The principal character in this passage is Jesus Christ" (Jeffrey R. Holland, *Christ and the New Covenant*, 86).

2 NEPHI 21:6-9

When will "the wolf . . . dwell with the lamb, and the leopard . . . lie down with the kid"?

"Men must become harmless before the brute creation, and when men lose their vicious dispositions and cease to destroy the animal race, the lion and the lamb can dwell together" (Joseph Smith, *Teachings*, 71).

2 NEPHI 21:7

What is the meaning of the comment that "the lion shall eat straw"?

"[Isaiah's] prophecy that the lion will pasture like the ox suggests that there will be no shedding of blood during the Millennium by man or beast" (Donald W. Parry, Jay A. Parry, and Tina M. Peterson, *Understanding Isaiah*, 119–20). *See also D&C 101:26.*

2 NEPHI 21:8

What are the "asp" and the "cockatrice"?

An asp is "a kind of poisonous serpent (Deut. 32:33)" and a cockatrice is another "venomous snake" (LDS Bible Dictionary, s.v. "Asp," "Cockatrice").

2 NEPHI 21:9

"The earth shall be full of the knowledge of the Lord."

"All things . . . will be revealed anew, in order to fulfill that passage. . . . Things of all former dispensations will be made manifest and revealed anew." (Orson Pratt, *Journal of Discourses*, 16:47).

2 NEPHI 21:10

Who is the "root of Jesse"?

"The prophet here mentioned is Joseph Smith, to whom the priesthood came, who received the keys of the kingdom" (Bruce R. McConkie, *Millennial Messiah*, 339–40). *See also D&C 110:16; 113:5–6.*

2 NEPHI 21:11-12

When is the first and the second time that the Lord will recover his people?

"The first time was when the Lord led Israel out of Egyptian bondage and captivity. When did the Lord set his hand the 'second time' to recover the remnant of his people? . . . He shall gather together the dispersed of Judah from the four corners of the earth" (LeGrand Richards, *Marvelous Work and a Wonder*, 202).

2 NEPHI 21:13

"Ephraim shall not envy Judah, and Judah shall not vex Ephraim."

"Tensions and hostilities . . . existed between Ephraim (the Northern

Kingdom) and Judah (the Southern Kingdom). . . . God's latter-day gathering will result in the uniting of the kingdoms of Judah and Israel, made possible because [of] the gospel. . . . The Book of Mormon also plays a prominent role in reuniting Ephraim and Judah (Ezek. 37:15–28)" (Donald W. Parry, Jay A. Parry, and Tina M. Peterson, *Understanding Isaiah*, 124).

2 NEPHI 21:14–15

United Israel and Judah "shall lay their hand upon Edom and Moab" and Egypt.

These verses have a double meaning. In addition to latter-day Israel having physical power over their enemies, some of these countries and cities often carry a symbolic meaning.

Assyria	=	World's power
Moab	=	World's pride (see also Isaiah 16:6)
Egypt	=	World's glory and abundance
Damascus	=	World's gods, idols of men
Jerusalem	=	Worldly or false piety
Babylon	=	World wickedness
Edom	=	Fallen world

The added symbolic meaning teaches that Israel and Judah in the last days will conquer or overcome worldy pride (Moab), fallen nature (Edom), and worldly glories and riches (Egypt).

What is "the tongue of the Egyptian sea"?

"The tongue of the Egyptian sea" is a reference to Israel's crossing the Red Sea. Isaiah uses the miracle of ancient Israel's physical deliverance to typify the Lord's spiritual gathering of latter-day Israel (see Jeremiah 16:14–15).

2 NEPHI 21:16

"There shall be a highway for the remnant of his people."

"It appears that a way will be provided to assemble the outcasts of Israel again in their promised land. The safe and secure physical arrangements, whatever they may be, will, in fact, be but symbolical of the way of holiness whereon only the righteous can find footing" (Bruce R. McConkie, *Millennial Messiah*, 327).

2 NEPHI 22

2 NEPHI 22:2

What do we know of the name "Jehovah"?

This original name of God was highly reverenced and so rarely spoken that the "original pronunciation of the name may be unknown to mortal man.

When reading orally, the Israelites substituted the name *Adonai*, meaning literally, *my Lord*. Elder James E. Talmage tells us that '*Jehovah* is the Anglicized rendering of the Hebrew, *Yahveh* or *Jahveh*, signifying the *Self-existent One*, or *The Eternal*. . . . (Talmage, p. 36; see also DCE, 276)" (Hoyt W. Brewster Jr., *Isaiah Plain & Simple*, 121).

2 NEPHI 22:3
What are the "wells of salvation" that will bring joy?

"[This phrase] has reference to the feast of tabernacles, or tents, celebrated by the Jews at the close of the year in grateful remembrance of . . . abundant harvests. . . . The observance lasted for seven days. A libation [offering of drink] was an important part of the services every day. It was at the close of such a festival that our Lord stood on the temple ground and invited the people to come unto him. . . . Jesus cried with a loud voice: 'If any man thirst, let him come unto me, and drink. He that believeth on me, as the scripture hath said, out of his innermost parts shall flow rivers of living water.' You need not thirst, because you cannot always stay by this stream (John 7:37, 38)" (George Reynolds and Janne M. Sjodahl, *Commentary on the Book of Mormon*, 1:360).

2 NEPHI 22:6
When will Jesus be physically "in the midst" of his people?

"Christ . . . will reign personally upon the earth during a thousand years of peace known as the millennium" (Hugh B. Brown, *Abundant Life*, 320). *See also Articles of Faith 1:10.*

2 NEPHI 23

2 NEPHI 23:1
What is "the burden of Babylon"?

"[The] 'burden' as used in Isaiah is a message of doom 'lifted up' against a people. . . . The historic destruction of wicked Babylon, prophesied in Isa. 13 and 14, is made typical of the ultimate destruction of the whole wicked world" (LDS Bible, Isaiah 13:1, footnotes *b* and *c*).

2 NEPHI 23:4–5, 15
Who will be involved in the final world war?

"At the very moment of the Second Coming of our Lord, 'all nations' shall be gathered 'against Jerusalem to battle' (Zech. 11; 12; 13; 14). . . . As John expressed it, 'the kings of the earth and of the whole world' will be gathered" (Bruce R. McConkie, *Mormon Doctrine*, 74). *See also Revelation 16:14–16.*

2 NEPHI 23:5-22

How does the past destruction of the Babylonians apply to the last days?

Just as the Medes conquered the Babylonians, so will the wicked be destroyed at the Second Coming. "Thus the past becomes the key that unlocks the future. As history has its cycles, so prophecies have multiple fulfillments and repeated applications. Isaiah's prophecies of events now past foretell events yet future. The past is the stage upon which the future is portrayed" (Joseph Fielding McConkie and Robert L. Millet, *Doctrinal Commentary*, 1:282). *See also Moses 7:60–61, 64.*

2 NEPHI 23:12

What is "fine gold" and the "golden wedge of Ophir"?

"*Fine* gold . . . is a grade of a higher quality than metal simply referred to as *gold*, and the gold of Ophir . . . was prized in the ancient Near East because it was a grade of gold of the highest quality" (Donald W. Parry, Jay A. Parry, and Tina M. Peterson, *Understanding Isaiah*, 136).

2 NEPHI 23:13

When and how has the earth been "remove[d] out of her place"?

"When the earth was framed and brought into existence and man was placed upon it, it was near the throne of our Father in heaven. . . . But when man fell, the earth fell into space, and took up its abode in this planetary system, and the sun became our light. . . . When [the earth] is glorified it will return again unto the presence of the Father, and it will dwell there" (Brigham Young, *Journal of Discourses*, 17:144). *See also Abraham 5:13.*

2 NEPHI 23:17-22

Who were the Medes and what happened to Babylon?

The Medes came from Persia and conquered the city of Babylon "by means of strategy. After a long siege, apparently without effect, Cyrus, who led the besieging Medes and Persians, decided to turn the Euphrates out of its course and enter on the dry river bed. That was a gigantic undertaking. The river was 1,500 feet wide and 12 feet deep. However, the undertaking was successful. The invaders entered [under the city walls] from two sides, the former inflow and outflow of the river, and so quietly did they take possession that most of the people did not know what was happening till it was too late to make resistance. Aristotle had been informed that some of the inhabitants did not know until three days afterwards that the city had fallen" (George Reynolds and Janne M. Sjodahl, *Commentary on the Book of Mormon*, 1:364).

2 NEPHI 24

2 NEPHI 24:1-3

When will "Israel . . . return to their lands"?

There are at least three times when this prophecy could be fulfilled. First, when Cyrus the Great of Persia issued an order allowing the Jews to return from Babylon in about 538 B.C. Second, the modern-day return of the Jews to the Holy Land. And third, at "the second coming of Christ, when the Jews will accept him as their Savior" (Victor L. Ludlow, *Isaiah: Prophet, Seer, and Poet*, 186).

2 NEPHI 24:4-8

How will the whole earth be "at rest, and . . . quiet"?

"Not only will civil strife come to an end, but evidently 'the voice of thunderings, and the voice of lightnings, and the voice of tempests, and the voice of waves of the sea heaving themselves beyond their bounds' (D&C 88:89–91), and 'earthquakes . . . in divers places' (Matthew 24:7) shall cease" (Hoyt W. Brewster Jr., *Isaiah Plain & Simple*, 138).

2 NEPHI 24:8

"No feller is come."

"The word *feller* as it is used . . . refers to a person who fells or cuts down trees" (Daniel H. Ludlow, *Companion*, 145).

2 NEPHI 24:12

What is the meaning of "son of the morning"?

"Isaiah's reference to Satan as a 'son of the morning' is usually interpreted to mean that he was one of the early spirits born of our Father in Heaven" (Monte S. Nyman, *Great Are the Words of Isaiah*, 85).

2 NEPHI 24:13-14

What did Lucifer think he could do?

"The enemy was not satisfied, nor had he quit the field, but by new methods he would seek to destroy this work. . . . He is vain enough to think, and he believes it confidently, that in the end he will be victorious and become king of this world" (Melvin J. Ballard, *New Era*, March 1984, 35).

2 NEPHI 24:23

What are "bittern" and "besom"?

"'Bittern' is a species of heron, a bird with long feathers on the breast and neck, and a strong, pointed bill" (George Reynolds and Janne M. Sjodahl, *Commentary on the Book of Mormon*, 1:367).

A besom is a "broom" (Hoyt W. Brewster Jr., *Isaiah Plain & Simple*, 144).

2 NEPHI 24:28–31

Why did the Lord tell Palestina to "rejoice not"?

"Isaiah seems to be telling Philistia not to rejoice over his predictions of the ruin and downfall of Judah, her traditional enemy. For whereas the kingdom of Judah will fall, there will come a glorious day when the people of Israel will rise above their troubles, secure from the attacks of their enemies" (Sidney B. Sperry, *Book of Mormon Compendium*, 244).

2 NEPHI 24:29

What is the progressive relationship of these prophesied events?

"Philistia shall see the death of one or more enemies as the means of deliverance from oppression, yet worse dangers (out of the serpent's root) are to come. Sidney Sperry points out the serpent's root, cockatrice (venomous viper), and fiery flying serpent are 'all symbolic of evil to come upon her [Philistia].' (Book of Mormon Compendium, 245.) Each of these represents a more deadly threat than the previous one" (Hoyt W. Brewster Jr., *Isaiah Plain & Simple*, 148–49).

2 NEPHI 25

2 NEPHI 25:1–7

How can we better understand Isaiah?

1. Listen to the words of modern prophets (v. 4).

2. Seek for the "spirit of prophecy" (v. 4).

3. Understand the manners and customs of the Jews (v. 5).

4. Know the geography (v. 6). *See also insights for 2 Nephi 11:8.*

2 NEPHI 25:9–10

The wicked are never destroyed by God until they have been warned by prophets.

"When . . . ancient kingdoms and peoples became wicked and corrupt, . . . the Lord raised up prophets to warn them; and these prophets . . . warned these nations and cities of the judgments that would overtake them" (Wilford Woodruff, in *Collected Discourses*, 1:242).

2 NEPHI 25:10–19

What events did Nephi prophesy about?

Destruction of Jerusalem by Babylon (v. 10)

Jews carried away captive (v. 10)

Some Jews return from Babylon to Jerusalem (v. 11)

Christ will be born among the Jews (v. 12)

He will be rejected by the Jews (v. 12)

They will crucify Jesus (v. 13)

After three days he will be resurrected (v. 13)

Jerusalem will be destroyed again (v. 14)

The Jews will then be scattered among all nations (v. 15)

The Jews will be scourged by many nations for many generations (v. 16)

They will be scourged until they believe in Christ (v. 16)

Then the Lord will gather them (v. 17)

They shall have his scriptures (v. 18)

The scriptures will convince them that Jesus is the Christ (v. 18)

2 NEPHI 25:13

How would Christ rise "with healing in his wings"?

"He . . . came with healing in his wings, to bear the sorrows and sickness of the people" (Bruce R. McConkie, *Mortal Messiah*, 2:301).

2 NEPHI 25:18, 22, 28

What role will the Book of Mormon play in our judgment?

"For me there could be no more impelling reason for reading the Book of Mormon than this statement of the Lord that we shall be judged by what is written in it" (Marion G. Romney, in Conference Report, April 1960, 110).

2 NEPHI 25:23

How do grace and works combine to qualify someone for salvation?

"Christians have often disputed as to whether what leads the Christian home is good actions or Faith in Christ. I have no right really to speak on such a difficult question, but it does seem to me like asking which blade in a pair of scissors is most necessary" (C. S. Lewis, *Mere Christianity*, 129).

Stephen E. Robinson tells the "parable of the bicycle," illustrating how *grace* and *works* function in concert to qualify one for salvation. His little daughter wanted a bicycle. He told her that if she saved all her money she would someday have enough to buy a bike. After several weeks she had saved sixty-one cents and wanted to go to the store. At the bike shop she saw the price of the bike she wanted and realized with great disappointment that she might not ever have enough money.

Her father told her, "'You give me everything you've got, the whole sixty-one cents, and a hug and a kiss, and this bike is yours.'

". . . She gave me a big hug and a kiss and handed over the sixty-one cents. . . . It occurred to me that this was a parable for the atonement of Christ.

". . . We want the kingdom of God. . . . But the horrible price—perfect performance—is hopelessly beyond our means. . . . At some point . . . we realize what the full price of admission into that kingdom is . . . and then we despair.

"But . . . when we finally realize our inability to perfect and save ourselves . . . the Savior steps in and says, 'So you've done all you can do, but it's not enough. Well, don't despair. . . . You give me . . . all you can do, and I will provide the rest'" (Stephen E. Robinson, *Believing Christ*, 32–33). *See also insights for Ether 2:23, 25.*

2 NEPHI 25:26–28

"We talk of Christ, we rejoice in Christ, we preach of Christ . . ."

"To 'believe in Christ' . . . is the ultimate purpose of the entire book [of Mormon]" (Jeffrey R. Holland, *Christ and the New Covenant*, 322).

"Let us . . . be convinced that Jesus is the Christ. Let us continually reread the Book of Mormon so that we might more fully come to Christ, be committed to Him, centered in Him, and consumed in Him" (Ezra Taft Benson, *Teachings*, 11).

2 NEPHI 26

2 NEPHI 26:1

What law did Christ change when he came to the Book of Mormon people?

"They did not walk any more after the performances and ordinances of the law of Moses; but they did walk after the commandments which they had received from their Lord" (4 Nephi 1:12).

2 NEPHI 26:7, 10

Sometimes all we can do is trust that God's "ways are just."

"Without the idea of the existence of the attribute justice in the Deity, men could not have confidence sufficient to place themselves under his guidance and direction; for they would be filled with fear and doubt lest the judge of all the earth would not do right" (Joseph Smith, *Lectures on Faith*, 4:13). *See also Mormon 6:17.*

2 NEPHI 26:8

"The righteous . . . shall not perish."

See 3 Nephi 10:12; insights for 1 Nephi 22:16–22.

2 NEPHI 26:11

What happens when "the Spirit ceaseth to strive with man"?

"One of the most tragic experiences that can come to individuals [is] to have the Lord withdraw His Spirit from us. . . . When withdrawn, it becomes difficult for us to pray, to have direction and guidance, to withstand evil" (Harold B. Lee, *Stand Ye in Holy Places*, 117–18).

2 NEPHI 26:13

What role does the Holy Ghost have in our knowing Christ?

"One who receives the witness of the Holy Ghost has a sure knowledge that . . . Jesus Christ is our Elder Brother in the spirit and the Only Begotten of the Father in the flesh, our Savior and Redeemer" (Marion G. Romney, in Conference Report, October 1967, 137).

2 NEPHI 26:16–17

How do Book of Mormon peoples speak "out of the ground" with a "familiar spirit"?

"Obviously, the only way a dead people could speak 'out of the ground' or 'low out of the dust' would be by the written word, and this the people did through the Book of Mormon. Truly it has a familiar spirit, for it contains the words of the prophets of the God of Israel" (LeGrand Richards, *Marvelous Work and a Wonder*, 67–68).

2 NEPHI 26:22

Satan will patiently and carefully lead people to hell.

"Lucifer . . . will use his logic to confuse and his rationalizations to destroy. He will shade meanings, open doors an inch at a time, and lead from purest white through all the shades of gray to . . . black" (Spencer W. Kimball, *Teachings*, 151–52).

What is a "flaxen cord"?

"The flaxen cord, a lightweight rope, precedes the 'chains of hell'" (Thomas R. Valletta, ed., *Book of Mormon for Latter-day Saint Families*, 134).

2 NEPHI 26:24

What does the Lord do "for the benefit of the world"?

"Why should Christ have volunteered to make this sacrifice? What was the motive that inspired and sustained him from the time of that council in heaven until the moment of his agonized cry 'It is finished'? (John 19:30.)

". . . His supernal and all-embracing love for mankind" (Hugh B. Brown, in Conference Report, April 1962, 108).

2 NEPHI 26:27

What salvation is "free for all men"?

See insights for 2 Nephi 2:4, 7.

2 NEPHI 26:28, 33

Is one race more privileged than the others?

"I hope we can all overcome any differences of culture, race, and language. . . . In my experience, no race or class seems superior to any other in spirituality and faithfulness" (James E. Faust, *Ensign*, May 1995, 61).

2 NEPHI 26:29

What are "priestcrafts"?

"There is a difference between priestcraft and Priesthood. Priestcraft builds up itself, it is not authorized of God. Priestcraft oppresses the people; but the Priesthood of God emancipates men" (George Q. Cannon, *Journal of Discourses*, 13:55).

2 NEPHI 27

2 NEPHI 27:1

When are "the days of the Gentiles"?

"We are living in the days of the Gentiles when this prediction was to be fulfilled" (Joseph Fielding Smith, in Conference Report, April 1952, 27).

2 NEPHI 27:7, 10

What is the sealed book containing the revelations of God from beginning to end?

"The sealed portion of the Book of Mormon . . . will give an account of life in the pre-existence; of the creation of all things; of the Fall and the Atonement and the Second Coming; . . . of life in the spirit world . . . ; of the kingdoms of glory" (Bruce R. McConkie, *Sermons and Writings of Bruce R. McConkie*, 277).

2 NEPHI 27:8, 10–11

When will the sealed book be "delivered," or published?

"When we ourselves, members of the Church, are willing to keep the commandments . . . then the Lord is ready to bring forth the other record and give it to us, but we are not ready now to receive it. Why? Because we have not lived up to the requirements . . . in the reading of the record which had been given to us" (Joseph Fielding Smith, in Conference Report, October 1961, 20).

2 NEPHI 27:12

Who were the "three witnesses" that would see the book?

"These men were Oliver Cowdery, David Whitmer, and Martin Harris. They left the Church, but to the day of their death they maintained their testimony regarding the . . . divinity of this book" (Heber J. Grant, *Gospel Standards*, 27). *See also D&C 17.*

2 NEPHI 27:13

Who were the few others that would see the plates?

"Joseph Smith himself exhibited the plates to eight other persons, viz: Christian, Jacob, Peter and John Whitmer; Hiram Page, Joseph Smith, Sen., Hyrum Smith and Samuel H. Smith. . . . They had seen, and handled the plates from which the Book of Mormon had been translated" (B. H. Roberts, *New Witnesses for God*, 1:192).

2 NEPHI 27:15-20

Who are the people referred to as "him," "another," and "the learned"?

"Joseph Smith was commanded of the Lord to send another, Martin Harris to New York.

". . . Charles Anthon was indeed a learned man by the world's standards: he was a professor of classics—Greek and Latin—at Columbia University in New York" (Joseph Fielding McConkie and Robert L. Millet, *Doctrinal Commentary*, 1:322). *For more details of this story see JS—H 1:61–65.*

2 NEPHI 27:20

How did Joseph Smith read what the Lord gave him?

"The Prophet did see . . . through the Urim and Thummim the translation of each sentence from the plates into the English language" (B. H. Roberts, *Defense of the Faith and the Saints*, 1:301).

2 NEPHI 27:22

What did Joseph do with the book when he was finished?

"It is not even now in the possession of mortals; it was returned by Joseph Smith to Moroni, its divinely appointed custodian. . . . For the present, the book is kept from us" (Bruce R. McConkie, *New Witness for the Articles of Faith*, 443).

2 NEPHI 27:26

What is the "marvelous work and a wonder" that the Lord would do among his people?

"This marvelous work is the restoration of the Church and the Gospel" (Joseph Fielding Smith, *Church History and Modern Revelation*, 1:33).

2 NEPHI 27:28

The land of Israel "shall be turned into a fruitful field."

"Isaiah describes a nation which would be destroyed suddenly, but which would speak in modern times, literally from the grave, by means of a book.

". . . Palestine is now the fruitful field he envisioned, and the book has been published" (Mark E. Petersen, *Ensign*, November 1977, 12).

2 NEPHI 27:31

Who is "the terrible one"?

"The terrible ones in verse 5 were Jerusalem's enemies; here the *terrible one* may refer to Satan himself" (Donald W. Parry, Jay A. Parry, and Tina M. Peterson, *Understanding Isaiah*, 273).

2 NEPHI 27:33

Why will Jacob's face not "wax pale"?

"The house of Jacob has been made ashamed, and his face has waxed pale, ever since he was driven away from . . . Canaan, but the Lord has now brought forth out of the ground a book which shall, accompanied by His power, restore the tribes of Jacob . . . in the land of Palestine" (Orson Pratt, *Orson Pratt's Works*, 278).

2 NEPHI 28

2 NEPHI 28:1

"I have spoken unto you, according as the Spirit hath constrained me."

The only appropriate way to teach the gospel is by the Spirit (*see D&C* 50:14, 18).

2 NEPHI 28:3

Why are the many churches in the world only forgeries of the truth?

"The Church, we may say, is his, only if he [Jesus Christ] is the founder of it. No painter, no matter how much of an artist he is, can make a genuine Rembrandt" (George Reynolds and Janne M. Sjodahl, *Commentary on the Book of Mormon*, 1:403).

2 NEPHI 28:3-31

What are Satan's tools, teachings, and tactics?

Builds up false churches (v. 3)

Creates contention (v. 4)

Relies on learning, not on the Spirit (v. 4)

Denies the power and existence of God (v. 5)

Denies miracles (v. 6)

Teaches that there is life beyond mortality (v. 7)

Says God will allow some sin (v. 8)

Says God will save everyone (v. 8)

Tempts people to sin now, repent later (v. 8)

Encourages pride (vv. 9, 12)

Robs the poor (v. 13)

Persecutes the meek (v. 13)

Promotes whoredoms, immorality (v. 14)

Emphasizes riches (v. 15)

Twists the truth (v. 15)

Hates that which is good (v. 16)

Promotes anger (v. 19)

Pacifies people, everything is fine (v. 21)

Uses flattery (v. 22)

Teaches that there is no hell nor devil (v. 22)

Says there is no need for more scripture (v. 29)

Says to trust in man, not in God (v. 31)

2 NEPHI 28:4, 14, 22

Are "learning," "whoredoms," and "flatter[y]" a problem today?

"There are at least three dangers that threaten the Church within. . . . As I see these, they are flattery of prominent men in the world, false educational ideas, and sexual impurity" (Joseph F. Smith, *Gospel Doctrine*, 312).

2 NEPHI 28:5, 22

What danger lies in believing that there is no devil?

"A corollary to the pernicious falsehood that God is dead is the equally pernicious doctrine that there is no devil. Satan himself is the father of both of these lies. To believe them . . . will continue to lead men to destruction" (Marion G. Romney, *Ensign*, June 1971, 35).

2 NEPHI 28:7-8

Would the Lord "justify in committing a little sin"?

"Our heavenly Father is . . . more terrible to the workers of iniquity, more awful in the executions of His punishments, and more ready to detect every false way, than we are apt to suppose Him to be" (Joseph Smith, *Teachings*, 257).

2 NEPHI 28:16, 20

How does Satan lead us to "revile . . . rage . . . anger"?

"It should come as no surprise that one of the adversary's tactics in the latter days is stirring up hatred among the children of men. He loves to see us criticize each other, make fun or take advantage" (Marvin J. Ashton, *Ensign*, May 1992, 19).

2 NEPHI 28:17, 19, 32

Who is repentance offered to?

"God never forgets us, even those who turn away from or deny Him. If they repent and come unto Him, He will be merciful to them, 'for [His] arm is lengthened out all the day long' (2 Nephi 28:32)" (Neal A. Maxwell, *Wonderful Flood of Light*, 60).

2 NEPHI 28:18

Who is the "great and abominable church, the whore of all the earth"?

See insights for 1 Nephi 13:4–9, 26–28; 14:10–11.

2 NEPHI 28:21-22

Why is leading people "away carefully down to hell" such an effective method?

"It does not matter how small the sins are. . . . The safest road to Hell is the gradual one—the gentle slope, soft underfoot, without sudden turnings, without milestones, without signposts" (C.S. Lewis, *Screwtape Letters*, 64–65).

2 NEPHI 28:24-25

What is the problem with being "at ease in Zion"?

"[Some] people . . . are basically unrepentant because they are not 'doing the commandments.' They are Church members who are steeped in lethargy. They neither drink nor commit the sexual sins. They do not gamble nor rob nor kill. They are good citizens and splendid neighbors, but spiritually speaking they seem to be in a long, deep sleep. They are doing nothing seriously wrong except in their failures to do the right things to earn their exaltation" (Spencer W. Kimball, *Miracle of Forgiveness*, 211–12).

2 NEPHI 28:29

Some will say "we need no more of the word of God."

"Some of our friends . . . are bold to say that we have everything written in the Bible which God ever spoke to man since the world began. . . . It is nowhere said in [the Bible] by the mouth of God, that He would not, after giving what is there contained, speak again" (Joseph Smith, *Teachings*, 61).

2 NEPHI 28:30

Why does the Lord "give line upon line"?

"It is not wisdom that we should have all knowledge at once presented before us; but that we should have a little at a time; then we can comprehend it" (Joseph Smith, *Teachings*, 297).

2 NEPHI 29

2 NEPHI 29:3, 6

"A Bible! A Bible! We have got a Bible, and there cannot be any more Bible."

"Strange as it may seem to present day enemies of the truth, their very opposition to the receipt of more of the word of the Lord by way of the Book of Mormon is one of the signs of the times" (Bruce R. McConkie, *Mormon Doctrine*, 719).

2 NEPHI 29:7, 11–12

"I shall also speak unto all nations of the earth and they shall write it."

"As Latter-day Saints we have accepted the Bible, the Book of Mormon, the Doctrine and Covenants, and the Pearl of Great Price. . . . But we also acknowledge our obligation to accept truth from whatever source it comes. All the sacred writings will some day be gathered together" (George Reynolds and Janne M. Sjodahl, *Commentary on the Book of Mormon*, 1:413).

2 NEPHI 29:8

How does "the testimony of two" reinforce a single witness?

"The Bible sits on the pulpit of hundreds of different religious sects. The Book of Mormon, the record of Joseph, verifies and clarifies the Bible. It removes stumbling blocks, it restores many plain and precious things. We testify that when used together, the Bible and the Book of Mormon confound false doctrines, lay down contentions, and establish peace (see 2 Nephi 3:12)" (Ezra Taft Benson, *Teachings*, 63).

2 NEPHI 29:9

"Because . . . I have spoken one word ye need not suppose that I cannot speak another."

"Does God love us less than those led by the ancient prophets? Do we need his guidance and instruction less? Reason suggests that this cannot be. Does he not care? Has he lost his voice? Has he gone on a permanent vacation? Does he sleep? The unreasonableness of each of these proposals is self-evident" (James E. Faust, *Ensign*, May 1980, 13).

2 NEPHI 29:10

Does the Bible contain all the words of the Lord?

"Lost books are among the treasures yet to come forth. Over twenty of these are mentioned in the existing scriptures. Perhaps most startling and voluminous will be the records of the lost tribes of Israel" (Neal A. Maxwell, *Ensign*, November 1986, 52). *See also 2 Nephi 29:13; 1 Chronicles 29:29; 2 Chronicles 9:29; 12:15; Galatians 3:8; Ephesians 3:3; Colossians 4:16; Jude 1:14.*

2 NEPHI 29:13

When will we have the words of the Jews, the Nephites, and the lost tribes?

"Now the Lord has placed us on probation as members of the Church. He has given us the Book of Mormon, which is the lesser part. . . . Then the Lord is ready to bring forth the other record and give it to us, but we are not ready now to receive it. Why? Because we have not lived up to the requirements in this probationary state in the reading of the record which had been given" (Joseph Fielding Smith, in Conference Report, October 1961, 20).

2 NEPHI 30

2 NEPHI 30:2

Which is more important, the way we live or our nationality?

"Jews and Gentiles are on a level of equality before God, for Gentiles who repent, thereby join the covenant people and share its privileges and prerogatives. . . . 'There is no difference between the Jew and the Greek'—Gentile—'for the same Lord over all is rich unto all that call upon him' (Rom. 10:12)" (George Reynolds and Janne M. Sjodahl, *Commentary on the Book of Mormon*, 1:418).

2 NEPHI 30:4

How were the Nephites "descendants of the Jews"?

"It is true that Lehi and his family were descendants of Joseph through the lineage of Manasseh (Alma 10:3), and Ishmael was a descendant of

Ephraim, according to the statement of the Prophet Joseph Smith. . . . The Nephites were of the Jews, not so much by descent as by citizenship. . . .

". . . Lehi was a citizen of Jerusalem, in the kingdom of Judah. . . . All of the inhabitants of the kingdom of Judah, no matter which tribe they had descended through, were known as Jews" (Joseph Fielding Smith, Answers to Gospel Questions, 1:142).

2 NEPHI 30:6

Why did "pure and . . . delightsome" replace "white and . . . delightsome" in the 1981 edition?

"Except the 1840 edition of the Book of Mormon, in all editions prior to 1981 this verse read 'a white and delightsome people.' The 1981 change was made in conformity with the 1840 edition (the only one personally revised by Joseph Smith). . . . Robert J. Matthews wrote: '. . . This correction does not negate the concept that future generations of Lamanites will become white, but it removes the concept that one has to be white to be delightsome to the Lord'" (Rodney Turner, in Monte S. Nyman and Charles D. Tate Jr., eds., Second Nephi, 156 n. 8).

2 NEPHI 30:9-10

How will the Lord "cause a great division among the people"?

See insights for 2 Nephi 10:16.

2 NEPHI 30:11

What are the "girdle" and "reins"?

"A 'girdle' is a belt or sash that wraps around the waist. The 'loins' and 'reins' stand for a man's moral character. Christ will be completely wrapped in righteousness and faithfulness" (Thomas R. Valletta, ed., Book of Mormon for Latter-day Saint Families, 145).

2 NEPHI 30:12-15

What conditions will exist during the Millennium?

See insights for 2 Nephi 21:6-9.

2 NEPHI 30:16-18

How much more will "be made known" in that day?

"For the future, there is to be new revelation that will dwarf into comparative insignificance all the knowledge now revealed from heaven. When the sealed portion of the Book of Mormon comes forth it will 'reveal all things from the foundation of the world unto the end thereof'" (Bruce R. McConkie, Mormon Doctrine, 649).

2 NEPHI 30:18

"Satan shall have power . . . no more, for a long time."
See insights for 1 Nephi 22:26.

2 NEPHI 31

2 NEPHI 31:1–21

Where can we read about "baptism by water, and . . . by the Holy Ghost"?

"The greatest sermon we have on baptism and the receipt of the Holy Ghost is 2 Nephi 31" (Bruce R. McConkie, *Promised Messiah*, 421).

2 NEPHI 31:2–21

What is "the doctrine of Christ"?

"The 'doctrine of Christ' as taught by Nephi . . . focuses on faith in the Lord Jesus Christ, repentance, baptism by immersion, receiving the gift of the Holy Ghost, and enduring to the end. . . . 'The doctrine of Christ' is simple and direct. It focuses on the first principles of the gospel exclusively. . . . It is in the clarity and simplicity of 'the doctrine of Christ' that its impact is found" (Jeffrey R. Holland, *Christ and the New Covenant*, 49–50). *See also 3 Nephi 11:32–35; 27:13–21.*

2 NEPHI 31:3

How does the Lord speak to men?

"When conversing with men, God and his angels speak according to the language and understanding of those they have chosen to address" (Joseph Fielding McConkie and Robert L. Millet, *Doctrinal Commentary*, 1:359).

2 NEPHI 31:5–9

Why would Jesus need to be baptized?

"Christ did fulfill all righteousness in being baptized in that: 1. He humbled himself before the Father; 2. He covenanted to be obedient and keep the Father's commandments; 3. He had to be baptized to gain admission to the celestial kingdom; and 4. He set an example for all men to follow. (2 Ne. 31:4–11)" (Bruce R. McConkie, *Mormon Doctrine*, 71).

2 NEPHI 31:7–10, 12–13, 16

How should we follow the example of Jesus Christ?

"Perfect worship is emulation. We honor those whom we imitate. The most perfect way of worship is to be holy as Jehovah is holy" (Bruce R. McConkie, *Promised Messiah*, 568). *See also insights for Alma 39:2, 11; 3 Nephi 18:16, 24; 27:27.*

2 NEPHI 31:11, 15

"I heard a voice from the Father."

"This doctrine of repentance [and baptism] is so crucial that the Father himself made a declaration on this point. . . .

". . . For the most part, the voice of the Father has usually been limited in scripture to introducing his Beloved Son" (Jeffrey R. Holland, *Christ and the New Covenant*, 51). *See also insights for 3 Nephi 11:7.*

2 NEPHI 31:12–14, 17–18

How important is it to receive the gift of the Holy Ghost?

"You might as well baptize a bag of sand as a man, if not done in view of the remission of sins and getting of the Holy Ghost. Baptism by water is but half a baptism, and is good for nothing without the other half—that is, the baptism of the Holy Ghost" (Joseph Smith, *Teachings*, 314).

2 NEPHI 31:13

How serious is the sin of hypocrisy?

"The one sin that the Savior condemned as much as any other was the sin of hypocrisy—the living of the double life, the life we let our friends . . . believe, and the life we actually live" (J. Reuben Clark Jr., *Behold the Lamb of God*, 294).

2 NEPHI 31:17

Was the ordinance of baptism commonly practiced before the days of Christ?

"This scripture indicates clearly that baptism was practiced, at least among the Nephites, hundreds of years before the Savior was born.

". . . The *Jewish Encyclopedia* indicates that baptism was a common practice in ancient Israel . . . (Vol. 2, p. 499)" (Daniel H. Ludlow, *Companion*, 154).

Where does remission of sins come from?

"This baptism of fire and of the Holy Ghost here spoken of by Nephi . . . cleanses, heals, and purifies the soul. It is the sealing and sign of forgiveness" (Marion G. Romney, *Learning for the Eternities*, 133).

2 NEPHI 31:17–21

What must we do after faith, repentance, baptism, and the gift of the Holy Ghost?

"Keeping God's commandments is a challenge to the faith and willpower of the most resolute soul.

"Doing the Lord's commandments . . . is an effort extending through the balance of life" (Spencer W. Kimball, *Miracle of Forgiveness*, 202).

2 NEPHI 31:18

What is one important role of the Holy Ghost?

"No man can know that Jesus is the Christ, but by the Holy Ghost" (Joseph Smith, *Teachings*, 243).

2 NEPHI 31:20

When can we have the promise of eternal life?

"After a person has faith in Christ, repents of his sins, and is baptized for the remission of his sins and receives the Holy Ghost, (by the laying on of hands), which is the first Comforter, then let him continue . . . living by every word of God, and the Lord will soon say unto him, Son, thou shalt be exalted. When the Lord has thoroughly proved him, and finds that the man is determined to serve Him at all hazards, then the man will find his calling and his election made sure" (Joseph Smith, *Teachings*, 150).

2 NEPHI 31:21

How are the Father, the Son, and the Holy Ghost "one God"?

See insights for Mosiah 15:2–5.

2 NEPHI 32

2 NEPHI 32:2

What does it mean to "speak with the tongue of angels"?

"Of all the best gifts, perhaps none is to be sought more earnestly than the ability to speak with the tongue of angels. Success in many callings depends in large measure upon the convincing power of voice and word. Without the tongue of angels, the servants of God are just ordinary men and women; but, armed with the Spirit and the words of Christ, they become "like unto angels" and teach persuasively and powerfully" (Carlos E. Asay, *In the Lord's Service*, 172).

2 NEPHI 32:3

What blessings come from "feast[ing] upon the words of Christ"?

"If [you] are acquainted with the revelations, there is no question—personal or social or political or occupational—that need go unanswered. Therein is contained the fulness of the everlasting gospel. Therein we find principles of truth that will resolve every confusion and every problem and every dilemma that will face the human family or any individual in it" (Boyd K. Packer, "Teach the Scriptures," 5).

2 NEPHI 32:5

What can the Holy Ghost teach us?

"[Joseph said,] Tell the brethren to be humble and faithful and be sure to keep the Spirit of the Lord, that it will lead them aright. Be careful and not turn away the still, small voice; it will teach them what to do and where to go" (Marion G. Romney, in Conference Report, April 1944, 141).

2 NEPHI 32:6

What changed when Jesus came to visit the Book of Mormon people?

"They did not walk any more after the performances and ordinances of the law of Moses; but they did walk after the commandments which they had received from their Lord and their God" (4 Nephi 1:12).

2 NEPHI 32:7

Why would the Spirit stop Nephi from saying more?

See insights for Alma 12:9.

2 NEPHI 32:8–9

"The Spirit teacheth a man to pray."

"Pray over, and for your families, your cattle, your flocks, your herds, your corn, and all things that you possess; ask the blessing of God upon all your labors, and everything that you engage in" (Joseph Smith, *Teachings*, 247). *See also insights for 1 Nephi 15:8, 11; Alma 34:17–27; 37:37.*

2 NEPHI 33

2 NEPHI 33:1

How can a message be delivered to the hearts of men?

"The Twelve have the right . . . to teach the people by the spirit of revelation, by the spirit of prophecy and the power of God. . . .

"God has made that promise . . . unto those who go out to preach the Gospel . . . by the spirit of revelation. It is then carried to the hearts of the people" (George Q. Cannon, *Journal of Discourses*, 23:365–66).

2 NEPHI 33:4

How has the Lord made the words of the Book of Mormon "strong"?

"[The Book of Mormon] is the book that will save the world and prepare the sons of men for joy and peace here and now and everlasting life in eternity" (Bruce R. McConkie, *Ensign*, November 1983, 74).

2 NEPHI 33:5

Who is it that becomes angry with scripture?

"Many are angry with the Book of Mormon. . . . The book marks the path by which we return to God, and there is but one spirit that opposes such a journey" (Joseph Fielding McConkie and Robert L. Millet, *Doctrinal Commentary*, 1:373).

2 NEPHI 33:7-9

What importance does the Book of Mormon give to the characteristic of charity?

Both the first and the last writers of the Book of Mormon, Nephi and Moroni, conclude their writings with discussions of charity, the most important Christlike attribute to emulate. *See also Moroni 7:46.*

2 NEPHI 33:10

What is the relationship between doctrines taught in the Bible and in the Book of Mormon?

"All scripture comes from God; all scripture is true; and every divine word accords with every other word from the same heavenly source. The Bible bears witness of the Book of Mormon, and the Book of Mormon testifies of the Bible. . . . Those who believe one believe the other" (Bruce R. McConkie, *New Witness for the Articles of Faith*, 394).

2 NEPHI 33:11, 15

What role will the scriptures have in our judgment?

"Though men may reject the teachings of the apostles and prophets concerning Jesus Christ and his gospel, yet those very teachings shall rise to condemn the unbelievers in the day of judgment" (Bruce R. McConkie, *Doctrinal New Testament Commentary*, 1:330).

2 NEPHI 33:15

"Amen" is another title of Jesus Christ.

"Christ is called 'the Amen, the faithful and true witness'" (LDS Bible Dictionary, s.v. "Amen"). *See also 2 Corinthians 1:20; Revelation 3:14.*

THE BOOK OF
JACOB

Jacob was the younger brother of Nephi and the son of Lehi. Before he died, Nephi made Jacob, rather than one of his own sons, custodian of the plates. He explained, "These plates should be handed down . . . from one prophet to another" (1 Nephi 19:4). Nephi had already included some of Jacob's teachings in the plates (see 2 Nephi 6; 9–10). Like Nephi, Jacob was an eyewitness of the Savior (see 2 Nephi 11:2–3). Jacob's writings focus on Jesus Christ and his Atonement.

JACOB 1

JACOB 1:4, 6–8

Jacob was to focus on Christ in his writings.

"The 'anxiety' of Book of Mormon prophets finds no more eloquent expression than the invitation for all men to 'come unto Christ.' Such is the purpose of the Book of Mormon. Such is the purpose of the Restored Gospel in these latter days. Mormonism has no other purpose" (Joseph Fielding McConkie and Robert L. Millet, *Doctrinal Commentary*, 2:3).

JACOB 1:7

When were the days of provocation?

"Moses plainly taught . . . the children of Israel in the wilderness, and sought diligently to sanctify his people that they might behold the face of God; but they hardened their hearts and could not endure his presence; therefore, the Lord in his wrath, for his anger was kindled against them, swore that they should not enter into his rest while in the wilderness" (D&C 84:23–24).

JACOB 1:8

When should we "view" Christ's death?

"How many members of the Church, when partaking of the emblems of the sacrament, try to visualize the extreme suffering of the Son of God as he went through his torment in our behalf?" (Joseph Fielding Smith, *Answers to Gospel Questions*, 5:9).

How do we "suffer his cross"?

"Any great affliction or trial that comes upon the saints does in itself constitute a *cross* they must bear as part of their obligation to overcome the world.

". . . Saints are to carry the cross of service and consecration, the cross of devotion and obedience" (Bruce R. McConkie, *Mormon Doctrine*, 173).

What is it to "bear the shame of the world"?

"For a man to lay down his all, his character and reputation, his honor, and applause, his good name among men, his houses, his lands, his brothers and sisters, his wife and children, and even his own life also—counting all things but filth and dross for the excellency of the knowledge of Jesus Christ—requires more than mere belief" (Joseph Smith, *Lectures on Faith*, 6:5).

JACOB 1:13

How were the terms "Lamanites" and "Nephites" used in the Book of Mormon?

"The Book of Mormon is careful to specify that the terms Lamanite and Nephite are used in a loose and general sense to designate not racial but political (e.g., Mormon 1:9), military (Alma 43:4), religious (4 Nephi 1:38), and cultural (Alma 53:10, 15; 3:10–11) divisions and groupings of people. The Lamanite and Nephite division was tribal rather than racial . . . (Alma 43:13; 4 Nephi 1:36–37)" (Hugh Nibley, *Collected Works*, 7:216).

JACOB 1:17

How do men obtain their "errand from the Lord"?

"There are those who claim authority from some secret ordinations of the past. Even now some claim special revealed authority to lead or to teach the people. . . .

"The Lord has never operated in that way. These things were not done in a corner (see Acts 26:26); there is light on every official call and every authorized ordination, and it has always been that way" (Boyd K. Packer, *Let Not Your Heart Be Troubled*, 133). *See also Articles of Faith 1:5.*

JACOB 1:18

In what way were Jacob and Joseph "consecrated priests and teachers"?

See insights for 2 Nephi 5:26.

JACOB 1:19

When can other people's sins come "upon our own heads"?

"If you do not magnify your callings, God will hold you responsible for those whom you might have saved had you done your duty" (John Taylor, *Journal of Discourses*, 20:23–24). *See also Ezekiel 3:18, 21; Moroni 9:6; insights for 2 Nephi 9:44–45, 47–48.*

JACOB 2

JACOB 2:5

Who can tell our thoughts?

"Men's thoughts are secret and cannot be pried into by other men, or for that matter by devils . . .

"However, the Lord can and does on occasion reveal to his prophets the thoughts and intents of the hearts of men" (Bruce R. McConkie, *Mormon Doctrine*, 777).

JACOB 2:6–10

Why did it grieve the soul of Jacob to speak of these things?

"[Jacob's] soul seemed to be—wounded by the transgression of others, wounded by the daggers of sorrow and suffering that wounded the Savior himself" (Jeffrey R. Holland, *Christ and the New Covenant*, 71).

JACOB 2:7, 33, 35

Why should we be careful of our actions toward those who are "tender" and "delicate"?

"Whoso shall offend one of these little ones which believe in me, it were better for him that a millstone were hanged about his neck, and that he were drowned in the depth of the sea" (Matthew 18:6).

JACOB 2:12–13

What is wrong with searching for "many riches"?

President Brigham Young said, "The worst fear I have about this people is that they will get rich in this country, forget God and his people, wax fat, and kick themselves out of the Church and go to hell. This people will stand mobbing, robbing, poverty, and all manner of persecution, and be true. But my greater fear for them is that they cannot stand wealth" (Brigham Young, cited in Preston Nibley, *Brigham Young*, 127–28). *See also 1 Timothy 6:10.*

JACOB 2:13-17, 20-22

How does pride get in the way of loving our neighbors?

"Someone has said, 'Pride gets no pleasure out of having something, only out of having more of it than the next man'" (Ezra Taft Benson, *Teachings*, 436). *See insights for Helaman 11:37.*

JACOB 2:18-19

Before all else, "seek ye for the kingdom of God."

"When we put God first, all other things fall into their proper place or drop out of our lives. Our love of the Lord will govern the claims for our affection, the demands on our time, the interests we pursue, and the order of our priorities" (Ezra Taft Benson, *Ensign*, May 1988, 4). *See also Matthew 22:36–38.*

JACOB 2:23

Which was the worst sin of those discussed by Jacob?

"The doctrine of this Church is that sexual sin—the illicit sexual relations of men and women—stands, in its enormity, next to murder" (in James R. Clark, comp., *Messages of the First Presidency*, 6:176).

"No more loathsome cancer disfigures the body and soul of society today than the frightful affliction of sexual sin" (Joseph Fielding Smith, *Restoration of All Things*, 261).

JACOB 2:24, 27

"David and Solomon truly had many wives, . . . which thing was abominable."

"From modern revelation we understand why Jacob condemned David and Solomon for having married many wives and concubines without the Lord's approval. It is a sin to take plural wives when God has not specifically commanded it. Abraham, for example, had plural wives and was not condemned because God had commanded it (see D&C 132:37–39)" (Thomas R. Valletta, ed., *Book of Mormon for Latter-day Saint Families*, 156).

"There shall not any man among you have save it be one wife."

"Plural marriage is not essential to salvation or exaltation. Nephi and his people were denied the power to have more than one wife and yet they could gain every blessing in eternity that the Lord ever offered to any people. In our day, the Lord summarized by revelation the whole doctrine of exaltation and predicated it upon the marriage of one man to one woman. (D. & C. 132:1–28)" (Bruce R. McConkie, *Mormon Doctrine*, 578).

JACOB 2:28

How does the Lord feel about "the chastity of women"?

"A beautiful, modest, gracious woman is creation's masterpiece" (David O. McKay, *Gospel Ideals*, 449). *See also Proverbs 31:10.*

JACOB 2:30

What is the Lord's purpose for plural marriage?

"Jacob indicates that if the Lord commands people to practice polygamy in order to 'raise up seed' unto himself, then the people should practice polygamy" (Daniel H. Ludlow, *Companion*, 159).

JACOB 2:34

How serious is it to know the commandments and break them?

"For of him unto whom much is given much is required; and he who sins against the greater light shall receive the greater condemnation" (D&C 82:3).

JACOB 3

JACOB 3:1

How does knowing that God will "send down justice" affect our relationship with him?

See insights for 2 Nephi 26:7, 10.

JACOB 3:1-2

How can the "pure in heart" be consoled in their afflictions?

"The Holy Spirit speaks peace to the hearts of . . . disconsolate mortals, he is called the Comforter. He brings peace and solace, love and quiet enjoyment, the joy of redemption and the hope of eternal life" (Bruce R. McConkie, *New Witness for the Articles of Faith*, 268).

JACOB 3:3-4, 8, 11

What promise is given to those who truly repent?

"There is forgiveness for the sinner who truly repents. God's mercy is just as boundless as his justice" (J. Reuben Clark Jr., in Conference Report, October 1938, 138).

JACOB 3:5-6

What promises are given to the Lamanites?

"There are many promises which are extended to the Lamanites; for it is because of the traditions of their fathers that caused them to remain in their state of ignorance; therefore the Lord will be merciful unto them and prolong their existence in the land. And at some period of time they will be brought to believe in his word" (Alma 9:16–17).

JACOB 3:7, 9–10

How do the mistakes of fathers affect their children?

"Consider this sobering forecast: 'About 40 percent of U.S. children will go to sleep in homes in which their fathers do not live'" (David Blankenhorn, 'Life without Father,' *USA Weekend*, 26 Feb. 1995, 6–7).

"Some estimate this will rise to 60 percent. This same commentator has written, 'Fatherlessness is the engine driving our most urgent social problems, from crime to adolescent pregnancy to domestic violence'" (Neal A. Maxwell, *Ensign*, May 1995, 67). *See also D&C 68:25.*

JACOB 3:11

Who become "angels to the devil" and experience "the second death"?

"The only persons who will be completely overcome by this dreadful fate are the sons of perdition, who go with the devil and his angels into 'outer darkness.' . . .

". . . Those who have had the testimony of the Holy Ghost and who have known the truth and then have rejected it and put Christ to open shame" (Joseph Fielding Smith, *Answers to Gospel Questions*, 1:76, 78).

JACOB 4

JACOB 4:1, 3

How did the "difficulty of engraving" affect the writers of the gold plates?

"Because of the toil of etching their messages upon the plates, . . . the record keepers would weigh their words carefully, would labor to record those things which were of greatest worth" (Joseph Fielding McConkie and Robert L. Millet, *Doctrinal Commentary*, 2:32).

JACOB 4:4–5

What is the primary purpose of the scriptures?

"When we come to understand really the scriptures, we discover that every single purpose therein is to testify that Jesus Christ was to come, is the Son of God, and was to work out a redemption for us" (Antoine R. Ivins, in Conference Report, October 1956, 49).

JACOB 4:5

What was the purpose of keeping the law of Moses?

"Just as our conformity to gospel standards, while dwelling as lowly mortals apart from our Maker, prepares us to return to his presence, . . . so the Mosaic standards prepared the chosen of Israel to believe and obey that gospel by conformity to which eternal life is won" (Bruce R. McConkie, *Promised Messiah*, 416).

What can we learn from Abraham's offering of Isaac?

"I think as I read the story of Abraham's sacrifices of his son Isaac that our Father is trying to tell us what it cost him to give his Son as a gift to the world. . . .

"Our Father in heaven went through all that and more, for in his case the hand was not stayed" (Melvin J. Ballard, in Bryant S. Hinckley, *Sermons and Missionary Services*, 152–53).

JACOB 4:6

Searching the scriptures brings hope and faith.

"Faith comes by hearing the word of God" (Joseph Smith, *Teachings*, 148). *See also Romans 10:17.*

JACOB 4:7

What power can the Lord bless us with in spite of our weakness?

"I know that I am nothing; as to my strength I am weak; therefore I will not boast of myself, but I will boast of my God, for in his strength I can do all things" (Alma 26:12).

JACOB 4:8–10

How does knowing of God's power affect our trust in him?

"Unless God had power over all things, . . . men could not be saved. But with the idea of the existence of this attribute planted in the mind, men feel as though they had nothing to fear" (Joseph Smith, *Lectures on Faith*, 4:11).

JACOB 4:11–12

What role does Christ's atonement play in our being reconciled to our Father?

"Salvation in the kingdom of God is predicated on the atonement of Christ and that man of himself could not bring it to pass. . . . Only 'by the blood of Christ' can man be reconciled unto God" (Bruce R. McConkie, *Mormon Doctrine*, 672).

"Why not speak of the atonement of Christ?"

"'Why not speak of the atonement of Christ?'" (Jacob 4:12). Brothers and sisters, given man's true self-interest, why should we really speak much of anything else?" (Neal A. Maxwell, *Ensign*, November 1986, 53).

JACOB 4:14

What is the "mark," and how do we sometimes look beyond it?

"My fellowmen, it matters so very much how we regard and view Jesus

Christ. Some seek to substitute Caesars for Christ. Others are blinded because they are 'looking beyond the mark' (Jacob 4:14) when the mark is Christ" (Neal A. Maxwell, *Ensign*, May 1976, 26).

"Sometimes we focus too much of our attention and energy upon our temporal wants, not only to entertain ourselves and gratify our physical appetites, but also to gain recognition, position, and power. We can become so consumed by the pursuit of these things that we sacrifice the sweetness and enduring peace of mind that are found in spiritual well-being" (Dean L. Larsen, *Ensign*, November 1987, 12).

JACOB 4:15–17
What is the stone that the Jews rejected?

"The head of their corner. The Jews having rejected the cornerstone, which is Christ, the question is, 'How can they ever build upon that sure and firm foundation?' Jacob, being led by the spirit of prophecy promises to unfold that *mystery*. . . . He then proceeds to explain this mystery by quoting the Prophet Zenos" (George Reynolds and Janne M. Sjodahl, *Commentary on the Book of Mormon*, 1:471–72; emphasis in original).

JACOB 5

JACOB 5:1–77
What is an allegory?

"An allegory is the description of one thing under the image of another" (Daniel H. Ludlow, *Companion*, 160).

Who was Zenos?

Zenos was a prophet in ancient Israel, living before 600 B.C. He is quoted often in the Book of Mormon (see 1 Nephi 19:10–17; Alma 33:3–15; Helaman 15:11; 3 Nephi 10:16). Zenos was killed because he testified boldly of Jesus Christ (see Helaman 8:19). Elder Bruce R. McConkie said, "I do not think I overstate the matter, . . . when I say that next to Isaiah himself . . . there was not a greater prophet in all Israel than Zenos" (cited in Monte S. Nyman and Charles D. Tate Jr., eds., *Second Nephi*, 210–11).

What strength is there in the allegory of Zenos?

"We have something in the Book of Mormon that, if we did not have any other truth expressed in it, would be sufficient evidence of the divinity of this book. I have reference to the fifth chapter of Jacob. . . . I think this is one of the greatest passages in the Book of Mormon. . . . No greater parable was ever recorded" (Joseph Fielding Smith, *Answers to Gospel Questions*, 4:203).

What is the primary message of the allegory of Zenos?

"Even as the Lord of the vineyard and his workers strive to bolster, prune, purify, and otherwise make productive their trees in what amounts to a one-chapter historical sketch of the scattering and gathering of Israel, the deeper meaning of the Atonement undergirds and overarches their labors. In spite of cuttings and graftings and nourishings that mix and mingle trees in virtually all parts of the vineyard, it is bringing them back to their source that is the principal theme of this allegory. Returning, repenting, reuniting—at-one-ment—this is the message throughout" (Jeffrey R. Holland, *Christ and the New Covenant*, 165).

Understanding the symbols of the allegory:

Symbol	Meaning of the Symbol
The vineyard (v. 3)	The world
Master or Lord of the vineyard (v. 4)	The Lord Jesus Christ
Servants (v. 7)	Prophets
Tame olive tree (v. 3)	The house of Israel
Wild olive tree (v. 7, 10)	Gentiles, or non-Israelites (later in the allegory the wild branches are apostate Israel)
Branches (v. 6)	Groups of people
Roots of the tame olive tree (v. 8)	The covenants the Lord makes with his children, a constant source of strength and life to the faithful
The fruit (v. 13)	The lives or works of men
Digging, pruning, fertilizing (vv. 4–5)	The work the Lord does through his servants for his children to help them be obedient and fruitful
Nourish the tree (v. 12)	Strengthen the people according to the Lord's "words" (v. 12)
Transplanting the branches (vv. 7–8)	Scattering groups of people throughout the world, or restoring them to where they came from
Nethermost part of the vineyard (v. 13)	Different places in the world far away from Israel

A good spot of ground, choice above all others (v. 43)	Lehi's promised land of the Americas was described as "a land . . . choice above all other lands" (1 Nephi 2:20)
Grafting (v. 8)	The joining of one group of people to another; and to "come to the knowledge of the true Messiah" (1 Nephi 10:14)
Decaying branches (vv. 3–4)	People dying spiritually from sin and apostasy
Casting branches into the fire (v. 7)	God's judgments

The story of the allegory is an account of four visits of the Lord to his people.

1. The Lord's first visit (Jacob 5:4–14): Assyrian and Babylonian period, 722 B.C. to 586 B.C.

"Now in that parable the olive tree is the House of Israel. . . . In its native land it began to die. So the Lord took branches like the Nephites, like the lost tribes, and like others that the Lord led off . . . to other parts of the earth. He planted them all over his vineyard, which is the world" (Joseph Fielding Smith, *Answers to Gospel Questions*, 4:204).

2. The Lord's second visit (Jacob 5:15–28): From the Babylonian captivity to the time of Christ

After many years many of the Gentiles in Abraham's land were living righteously. Scattered Israel in many poor parts of the world had also become righteous. The last group of scattered Israel was placed in a very favorable place. Of this last group only a part of the people were righteous.

3. The Lord's third visit (Jacob 5:29–74): From the Apostasy to the Restoration

After many more years the Gentiles in Israel became wicked. Scattered Israel had also become wicked in all parts of the world. The Lord will remove the wicked living in Israel and gather Israel back to their homeland. Prophets begin to have success and a few of the people begin to live righteously.

4. The Lord's fourth visit (Jacob 5:75–77): The last days, Millennium, and post-Millennium

There begins to be righteousness again. For a long time (1,000 years) the Lord lays up good fruit. Then wickedness comes again, the righteous and wicked are gathered, and the wicked are destroyed.

JACOB 5:8

Why did the Lord scatter Israel "whithersoever" he would?

"The scattering of Israel throughout the world sprinkled the blood that believes, so that many nations may now partake of the gospel plan" (James E. Faust, *Ensign*, November 1982, 87).

JACOB 5:44

Who lived in the Americas before Lehi's family?

"Reference here is to the destruction of the Jaredite nation. See Ether 15; Moroni 9:23" (Joseph Fielding McConkie and Robert L. Millet, *Doctrinal Commentary*, 2:62).

JACOB 5:72

"The Lord of the vineyard labored also with them."

"I can't leave this conference without saying to you that I have a conviction that the Master hasn't been absent from us on these occasions. This is his church. Where else would he rather be than right here at the headquarters of his church? He isn't an absentee master" (Harold B. Lee, *Ensign*, January 1973, 134).

JACOB 6

JACOB 6:4

Which characteristic of God seems most dominant in the allegory?

"In his concluding commentary on the allegory, Jacob [said] . . . 'How merciful is our God unto us'" (Jeffrey R. Holland, *Christ and the New Covenant*, 166).

What is it to be "a gainsaying people"?

"To say that Israel is 'a gainsaying people' is to say that they are quick to object, to oppose, resist, contradict, or speak against that which comes from God" (Joseph Fielding McConkie and Robert L. Millet, *Doctrinal Commentary*, 2:78).

JACOB 6:4-8

"As many as will not harden their hearts shall be saved."

"It is necessary that men should have the broken heart, the tender and soft heart, and the contrite spirit. . . . I cannot afford to be hard-hearted, . . . to be stubborn, . . . to be haughty and high-minded" (Francis M. Lyman, in Conference Report, October 1897, 16).

JACOB 6:7

How can members be "nourished by the good word of God"?

"That is what our members really want when they gather in a meeting or come into a classroom anyway. . . . They come seeking a spiritual experience. They want peace. They want their faith fortified and their hope renewed.

They want, in short, to be nourished by the good word of God" (Jeffrey R. Holland, *Ensign*, May 1998, 26).

JACOB 6:9

Why was there a need for Christ to bring "redemption and . . . resurrection"?

"Adam became mortal; spiritual death came to him; and mortal death came to him. . . .

"In order for him to get back to the place whence he began, it was necessary that there should be an atonement. . . .

". . . [Christ] alone could make the sacrifice which would enable us to have our bodies and our spirits reunited in the due time of the Lord and then go back to the Father" (J. Reuben Clark Jr., in Conference Report, October 1955, 23).

JACOB 6:10

What is "endless torment"?

"I am endless, and the punishment which is given from my hand is endless punishment, for Endless is my name. Wherefore—. . . Endless punishment is God's punishment" (D&C 19:10, 12).

"Eternal punishment, or endless punishment, does not mean that those who partake of it must endure it forever" (Joseph Fielding Smith, *Doctrines of Salvation*, 2:228).

JACOB 7

JACOB 7:2, 4

What is the danger of "flattering" words?

"When the Devil cannot overcome an individual through temptation to commit wickedness, . . . he will adopt a course of flattery.

"When a man is proud and arrogant, flattery fills him with vanity" (Brigham Young, *Discourses*, 81, 228).

What is an antichrist?

See insights for Alma 30:6.

JACOB 7:4

Why do some people have problems when they are "learned"?

See insights for 2 Nephi 9:28–29.

JACOB 7:6–7

Were the "doctrine of Christ" and "the law of Moses" mutually exclusive?

"The dishonest Sherem knew that Moses and the other prophets had spoken of Christ and that their teachings were not only consistent with the gospel but also pointed people toward its future fulness" (Jeffrey R. Holland, *Christ and the New Covenant*, 148).

JACOB 7:10–12

How can the combined force of the scriptures, the prophets, and the Holy Ghost help us?

"May I suggest three short tests to avoid being deceived. . . .

"1. What do the standard works have to say about it? . . .

"2. The second guide is: what do the latter-day Presidents of the Church have to say on the subject—particularly the living President? . . .

"3. The third and final test is the Holy Ghost—the test of the Spirit" (Ezra Taft Benson, in Conference Report, October 1963, 16–18).

JACOB 7:11

Why does every prophet speak "concerning this Christ"?

"The preeminent duty of a prophet is to bear witness of Jesus Christ" (Joseph Fielding McConkie and Robert L. Millet, *Doctrinal Commentary*, 2:86).

"This is the great basic purpose of the restoration of the gospel . . . to declare the living reality of God. . . . Jesus Christ is his firstborn, the Only Begotten in the flesh, who condescended to come to earth; who . . . taught the way of salvation; who offered Himself a sacrifice for all. . . . Through Him, and by Him, and of Him, all are assured salvation from death and are offered the opportunity of eternal life" (Gordon B. Hinckley, *Ensign*, May 1986, 47).

JACOB 7:12

What would have happened had there been "no atonement made"?

"The atonement of the Master is the central point of world history. Without it, the whole purpose for the creation of earth and our living upon it would fail" (Marion G. Romney, in Conference Report, October 1953, 34).

JACOB 7:23

How can we receive the blessings of peace and love?

"Learn of me, and listen to my words; . . . and you shall have peace in me" (D&C 19:23).

"Whoso keepeth his word, in him verily is the love of God perfected" (1 John 2:5).

JACOB 7:26

How do our lives pass away "like as it were unto us a dream"?

"How poetic and descriptive Jacob is in describing the fleeting moments and hours of our mortal probation! Moments blend into hours, hours into days, days into years, years into decades. . . . Because the day of probation is over in an instant, . . . the prophets continually plead for the people of the earth to guard their time, to improve their time, and to make wise use of their time" (Joseph Fielding McConkie and Robert L. Millet, *Doctrinal Commentary*, 2:92).

JACOB 7:27

Why does the French word "adieu" appear in the Book of Mormon?

"Some anti-LDS critics of the Book of Mormon have raised the question as to how Jacob could possibly have used such a word as *adieu*. . . . Joseph Smith felt free in his translation to use any words familiar to himself and his readers that would best convey the meaning of the original author. . . . Would it be unreasonable to remind these critics that *none of the words* contained in the English translation of the book of Jacob were used by Jacob himself?" (Daniel H. Ludlow, *Companion*, 163; emphasis in original).

THE BOOK OF
ENOS

ENOS 1:1

How important is a parent's role to teach, nurture, and admonish the family?

"'The greatest of the Lord's work you brethren will ever do as fathers will be within the walls of your own home.' Don't neglect your wives, you brethren. Don't neglect your children. Take time for family home evening. . . . Teach them, guide them, and guard them" (Harold B. Lee, *Ensign*, July 1973, 98–99). *See also insights for 1 Nephi 1:1.*

ENOS 1:2

Is a "wrestle" before the Lord required to receive a remission of sins?

See insights for Alma 36:11–13.

ENOS 1:3

"The words . . . I had often heard my father speak . . . sunk deep into my heart."

"By pondering, we give the Spirit an opportunity to impress and direct. Pondering is a powerful link between the heart and the mind. . . . If we . . . ponder, we can take these eternal truths and realize how we can incorporate them into our daily actions" (Marvin J. Ashton, *Ensign*, November 1987, 20). *See also insights for 1 Nephi 11:1.*

ENOS 1:4

"I cried unto him in mighty prayer."

"We should live so as to deem it [prayer] one of the greatest privileges accorded to us. . . .

"It matters not whether you or I feel like praying. . . . If we do not feel like it, we should pray till we do" (Brigham Young, *Discourses*, 43, 44).

ENOS 1:4–7

Is the miraculous prayer and forgiveness of Enos common?

"The scriptures record remarkable accounts of men whose lives changed dramatically, in an instant, as it were. . . .

"But we must be cautious as we discuss these remarkable examples. Though they are real and powerful, they are the exception more than the rule.

For every Paul, for every Enos, and for every King Lamoni, there are hundreds and thousands of people who find the process of repentance much more subtle, much more imperceptible. Day by day they move closer to the Lord, little realizing they are building a godlike life" (Ezra Taft Benson, *Ensign*, October 1989, 5).

ENOS 1:4, 9, 11

Why did Enos desire the welfare of others after he himself had repented?

"You cannot lift another soul until you are standing on higher ground than he is. You must be sure, if you would rescue the man, that you yourself are setting the example of what you would have him be. You cannot light a fire in another soul unless it is burning in your own soul" (Harold B. Lee, *Ensign*, July 1973, 123).

ENOS 1:8

How can we know Christ without seeing him?

"The impressions on the soul that come from the Holy Ghost are far more significant than a vision. . . . Every member of the Church should have the impressions on his soul made by the Holy Ghost that Jesus is the Son of God indelibly pictured so that they cannot be forgotten" (Joseph Fielding Smith, *Seek Ye Earnestly*, 214). *See also insights for Moroni 10:5, 7.*

Why is faith in Christ necessary to receive forgiveness of sins?

See insights for 2 Nephi 7:2.

ENOS 1:10

When can the Lord visit us?

"It isn't the Lord who withholds himself from us. It is we who withhold ourselves from him because of our failure to keep his commandments" (Harold B. Lee, in Conference Report, October 1966, 117).

ENOS 1:12

"After I had prayed and labored with all diligence, the Lord said . . . I will grant unto thee . . . thy desires."

"Pray as though everything depends on the Lord, then work as though everything depends on you" (Gene R. Cook, *Receiving Answers to Our Prayers*, 56). *See also insights for Ether 2:23, 25.*

ENOS 1:15

What is required for us to receive "whatsoever thing" we pray for?

"And, if they (the saints) will exercise their faith aright, there is no good thing, which they can desire, that will be withheld from them" (George Q. Cannon, *Millennial Star*, 25:74).

ENOS 1:21

Did the Nephites have horses?

See insights for Alma 18:9.

ENOS 1:23

What seems necessary for people to remain righteous?

"Thus we see that except the Lord doth chasten his people with many afflictions, . . . they will not remember him" (Helaman 12:3).

ENOS 1:26–27

What allows someone to look forward to meeting their Redeemer "with pleasure"?

"Peace in this world always comes after the receiver has done the works of righteousness. Enos . . . had . . . demonstrated, by good works . . . faith in Christ before the reward came. This is the way peace comes in this world. It can be obtained in no other way. The promised peace . . . emanates from Christ. He is the source of it. His spirit is the essence of it" (Hugh B. Brown, in Conference Report, April 1967, 82).

THE BOOK OF
JAROM

JAROM 1:2

How valuable is the information recorded on the plates thus far?

As we come to the close of the records of the small plates of Nephi, we remember that Mormon was prompted to include them for a "wise purpose" (Words of Mormon 1:7) Jarom here explains that these small plates included the whole "plan of salvation." It is no wonder that an all-knowing Lord placed this powerful teaching at the beginning of the Book of Mormon, knowing that many who would never finish the whole book would read and re-read the first books. In D&C 10:45 the Lord explains that the small plates "do throw greater views upon my gospel." "We do know that . . . on the small plates was the personal declarations of three great witnesses, [Nephi, Jacob, and Isaiah], . . . testifying that Jesus is the Christ." (Jeffrey R. Holland, *Ensign*, January 1996, 12).

JAROM 1:3

How merciful is our God?

See insights for Mosiah 26:30.

JAROM 1:5

How can we better keep the sabbath day holy?

"What fits the purpose of the Sabbath? Here are a few suggestions: Activities that contribute to greater spirituality; essential Church meetings in the house of prayer; acquisition of spiritual knowledge—reading the scriptures, Church history and biographies; . . . building family unity; visiting the sick and aged shut-ins; singing the songs of Zion and listening to inspired music; paying devotions to the Most High—personal and family prayer; fasting, administrations, father's blessings; preparing food with singleness of heart—simple meals prepared largely on Saturday" (Ezra Taft Benson, *Teachings*, 439). *See also insights for Mosiah 13:16–19.*

JAROM 1:9

"Inasmuch as ye will keep my commandments ye shall prosper in the land."

See insights for 1 Nephi 2:20.

126

THE BOOK OF
OMNI

OMNI 1:7

How sure is the prophecy that the Lord will "spare the righteous"?

See insights for 1 Nephi 22:16–22.

OMNI 1:12

Who were the people of Zarahemla?

"The Bible states that the sons of Zedekiah were slain before his eyes, and then the Babylonians put out his eyes and carried him in fetters into Babylon. Mulek, son of Zedekiah, was spared by the power of the Lord and with other fugitives was directed across the "great waters" to this land. . . . [The] Mulekites were later discovered by the Nephites and the two people became one, the Mulekites being known henceforth as Nephites" (Joseph Fielding Smith, *Doctrines of Salvation*, 3:322–23).

OMNI 1:12, 14, 15, 21

Who are the peoples of Mosiah, Zarahemla, Zedekiah, and Coriantumr?

	THE PEOPLE OF MOSIAH	THE PEOPLE OF ZARAHEMLA	THE PEOPLE OF ZEDEKIAH	THE PEOPLE OF CORIANTUMR
Common name of people	Nephites and Lamanites	Mulekites	Jews	Jaredites
Where they came from	Left Jerusalem in about 600 B.C.	Left Jerusalem in about 589 B.C.	One of the tribes of Israel, carried away captive by the Babylonians in 589 B.C.	Left the tower of Babel in about 2290 B.C.
Where they lived	Americas, south of the Mulekites in the land	Americas, north of the Nephites in the land	Jerusalem and scattered throughout the world	Americas, north of the Mulekites in the land

	called Nephi	called Zarahemla		called Desolation
Where to read about their history	History recorded throughout the Book of Mormon	Did not keep their own history but merged with the Nephites in about 130 B.C.	History is recorded in the Bible	History recorded in the book of Ether, in the Book of Mormon

OMNI 1:17

What happens to those who either have no scriptures or refuse to study what they have?

"The Mulekites . . . failed to bring with them any sacred scriptures or records. Omni recorded the condition of a nation without scriptures.

". . . They did not know the Savior. The pattern is the same for individuals as it is for nations. Without searching the scriptures, they cease to know the Savior" (L. Lionel Kendrick, *Ensign*, May 1993, 14).

OMNI 1:25

"There is nothing which is good save it comes from the Lord: and that which is evil cometh from the devil."

See insights for Moroni 7:12–13, 16–17.

OMNI 1:26

What must we be willing to give to effectively "come unto Christ"?

"Let us here observe, that a religion that does not require the sacrifice of all things never has power sufficient to produce the faith necessary unto life and salvation; . . . salvation never could be obtained without the sacrifice of all earthly things" (Joseph Smith, *Lectures on Faith*, 6:58).

"I went before [the Lord] and in essence said, 'I'm not neutral, and You can do with me what You want. If You need my vote, it's there. I don't care what You do with me, and You don't have to take anything from me because I give it to You—everything, all I own, all I am'" (Boyd K. Packer, *That All May Be Edified*, 272).

THE WORDS OF
MORMON

What is the purpose of "The Words of Mormon"?

"The two pages comprising The Words of Mormon are approximately five hundred years out of context. . . .

"The Words of Mormon were apparently written near the end of Mormon's life for the purpose of connecting two major records [the small plates and the large plates of Nephi]" (Daniel H. Ludlow, *Companion*, 171).

Are we ever expected to obey commandments without knowing why?

"After Mormon had completed his abridgment of five hundred years of Nephite history, he . . . was prompted to include the small plates with his abridgment, without really knowing why. (See verse 7.) He apparently did not know what would happen to his records after they would come into the hands of Joseph Smith.

". . . After the loss of these [116] pages by Martin Harris, the Lord commanded the Prophet to translate further in the plates of Mormon without retranslating the first portion. However, since the small plates contained a more spiritual account of the same time period, the teachings of greatest value were not lost for the readers of the Book of Mormon" (Victor L. Ludlow, in Kent P. Jackson, ed., *Studies in Scripture, 7: 1 Nephi to Alma 29*, 203).

Will we be judged by the "word of God" in the Book of Mormon?

See insights for 2 Nephi 25:18, 22, 28.

Where does our "peace in the land" come from?

"In obedience there is joy and peace . . . and as God has designed our happiness . . . he never has—He never will institute an ordinance or give a commandment to His people that is not calculated in its nature to promote that happiness" (Joseph Smith, *Teachings*, 256). *See also insights for Mosiah 2:41.*

The Book of

MOSIAH

MOSIAH 1

MOSIAH 1:1-2

"King Benjamin . . . had three sons. . . . And he caused that they should be taught."

See insights for Enos 1:1.

MOSIAH 1:2

"And it came to pass that he had three sons."

"Note that the main story in the book of Mosiah is told in the third person rather than in the first person as was the custom in the earlier books [small plates of Nephi] of the Book of Mormon. The reason for this is that someone else is now telling the story, and that 'someone else' is Mormon. With the beginning of the book of Mosiah we start our study of Mormon's abridgment of various books that had been written on the large plates of Nephi. (3 Nephi 5:8–12)" (Daniel H. Ludlow, *Companion*, 173).

MOSIAH 1:3-7

How would people have suffered had they not had the scriptures?

Consider these blessings that come from searching the scriptures (see also insights for Omni 1:17):

Avoid ignorance (v. 3)

Remember all that the Lord wants us to know (v. 4)

Fulfill the commandments (v. 4)

Understand the mysteries of God (v. 5)

Keep the commandments always before us (v. 5)

Avoid unbelief and strengthen faith (v. 5)

Identify incorrect traditions (v. 5)

Know the truth (v. 6)

MOSIAH 1:11–12

What name did King Benjamin want to give the people?

"Take upon you the name of Christ . . . this is the name that I said I should give unto you that never should be blotted out, except it be through transgression" (Mosiah 5:8, 11).

MOSIAH 1:16

What were the plates of brass, sword of Laban, and "ball or director" used for?

"The brass plates and the sword of Laban [and Liahona] were . . . things that reminded King Benjamin's people of the faithfulness of their ancestors and of the many blessings that God had given them" (Thomas R. Valletta, ed., *Book of Mormon for Latter-day Saint Families*, 188).

MOSIAH 2

MOSIAH 2:11–21, 27

What is the value of righteous service?

"We lose our life by serving and lifting others. By so doing we experience the only true and lasting happiness. Service is not something we endure on this earth so we can earn the right to live in the celestial kingdom. Service is the very fiber of which an exalted life in the celestial kingdom is made.

". . . We are truly happy only when we are engaged in unselfish service. Let us use the freedom which comes from self-reliance in giving and serving" (Marion G. Romney, *Ensign*, November 1982, 93).

MOSIAH 2:17

"When ye are in the service of your fellow beings ye are only in the service of your God."

"In this statement Benjamin includes the essence of the two great commandments that were later enunciated by the Savior: (1) that we should love God with all our heart, soul, and mind, and (2) that we should love our neighbors as ourselves. . . .

"If we truly love God and keep his commandments, we will serve our brothers because he has commanded us to love them" (Daniel H. Ludlow, *Companion*, 174). *See also Matthew 22:38–40; Matthew 25:40.*

MOSIAH 2:28

How can we avoid sharing in the guilt of others' sins?

See insights for Jacob 1:19.

MOSIAH 2:34

How can we render unto our Heavenly Father "all that [we] have and are"?

See insights for Omni 1:26.

MOSIAH 2:36-37

How do we withdraw ourselves from the Spirit of the Lord?

See insights for Helaman 4:24–25; 6:35.

MOSIAH 2:36-39

Who does mercy have no claim on?

"'Mercy hath no claim' on any man unless and until he repents and turns to the Lord. (Mosiah 2:38–39.) . . .

"Mercy is thus for the repentant, the faithful, the obedient, those who love and serve God. All others fail to escape the clutches of justice" (Bruce R. McConkie, *Mormon Doctrine*, 485).

MOSIAH 2:41

"Consider on the blessed and happy state of those that keep the commandments."

"Happiness is the object and design of our existence; and will be the end thereof, if we pursue the path that leads to it; and this path is virtue, uprightness, faithfulness, holiness, and keeping all the commandments of God" (Joseph Smith, *Teachings*, 255–56).

MOSIAH 3

MOSIAH 3:2

Where did King Benjamin get the information for his speech?

"An angel from heaven recited to King Benjamin what well may be the greatest sermon ever delivered on the atonement of Christ the Lord (Mosiah 3)" (Bruce R. McConkie, *Promised Messiah*, 232).

MOSIAH 3:3-5

How is the message of Jesus Christ one of "glad tidings of great joy"?

"The Messiah comes in power; he is anointed, commissioned from on high; he comes in his Father's name, to do his Father's will. . . . And his glorious message . . . is the everlasting gospel, the plan of salvation; it is the glad tidings of great joy that salvation is in Christ, that man shall gain the victory over the grave, that he has power to gain eternal life" (Bruce R. McConkie, *Mortal Messiah*, 2:21–22).

MOSIAH 3:5, 17, 21

Why is it important to know that Christ is omnipotent?

See insights for 2 Nephi 9:20.

MOSIAH 3:7

How were temptation, pain, hunger, thirst, and fatigue all part of the Atonement?

"Christ's agony in the garden is unfathomable by the finite mind, both as to intensity and cause. . . . He struggled and groaned under a burden such as no other being who has lived on earth might even conceive as possible. It was not physical pain, nor mental anguish alone, that caused Him to suffer such torture as to produce an extrusion of blood from every pore; but a spiritual agony of soul such as only God was capable of experiencing. No other man, however great his powers of physical or mental endurance, could have suffered so; for his human organism would have succumbed, and syncope would have produced unconsciousness and welcome oblivion. In that hour of anguish Christ met and overcame all the horrors that Satan, 'the prince of this world' could inflict" (James E. Talmage, *Jesus the Christ*, 568–69).

"In Gethsemane, the suffering Jesus began to be 'sore amazed' (Mark 14:33), or, in the Greek, 'awestruck' and 'astonished.'

"Imagine, Jehovah, the Creator of this and other worlds, 'astonished'! Jesus knew cognitively what He must do, but not experientially. He had never personally known the exquisite and exacting process of an atonement before. Thus, when the agony came in its fulness, it was so much, much worse than even He with his unique intellect had ever imagined! . . .

"The cumulative weight of all mortal sins—past, present, and future—pressed upon that perfect, sinless, and sensitive Soul! All our infirmities and sicknesses were somehow, too, a part of the awful arithmetic of the Atonement. (See Alma 7:11–12; Isa. 53:3–5; Matt. 8:17.) The anguished Jesus not only pled with the Father that the hour and cup might pass from Him, but with this relevant citation. 'And he said, Abba, Father, all things are possible unto thee; take away this cup from me.' (Mark 14:35–36.)

"Had not Jesus, as Jehovah, said to Abraham, 'Is any thing too hard for the Lord?' (Gen. 18:14.) . . .

"Jesus' request was not theater! . . .

"The wondrous and glorious Atonement was the central act in all of human history. It was the hinge on which all else that finally matters turned" (Neal A. Maxwell, *Ensign*, May 1985, 72–73).

MOSIAH 3:8

How is Jesus "the Father"?

See insights for Mosiah 15:2–5.

MOSIAH 3:16

Christ atones for the sins of little children.

"Little children are not capable of sinning, King Benjamin taught, but they suffer the effects of the fall of Adam. . . . Nevertheless, Christ atones for that fall" (Jeffrey R. Holland, *Christ and the New Covenant*, 100–101).

MOSIAH 3:19

What is the natural man?

"The 'natural man' is the 'earthy man' who has allowed rude animal passions to overshadow his spiritual inclinations" (Spencer W. Kimball, *Ensign*, January 1984, 4).

What is a saint, and how do we become one?

"The word *saint* is tied to the Hebrew root *kadosh*, which means to separate, to be apart from, and to become sacred and holy (Brown, Driver, Briggs, *Hebrew and English Lexicon*, p. 872). . . . They are a people who have separated themselves from that which is worldly" (Joseph Fielding McConkie and Robert L. Millet, *Doctrinal Commentary*, 2:153).

MOSIAH 3:20

When will "the knowledge of a Savior . . . spread throughout every nation"?

"In the full and complete sense, the fulfillment of this promise is millennial, a time when 'the earth shall be full of the knowledge of the Lord, as the waters cover the sea' (Isaiah 11:9; 2 Nephi 21:9)" (Joseph Fielding McConkie and Robert L. Millet, *Doctrinal Commentary*, 2:154).

MOSIAH 3:25-26

Will the evil go to a place "from whence they can no more return"?

"After a person has been assigned to his place in the kingdom, either in the telestial, the terrestrial, or the celestial, or to his exaltation, he will never advance from his assigned glory to another glory. That is eternal!" (Spencer W. Kimball, *Teachings*, 50).

MOSIAH 4

MOSIAH 4:2

How do we "apply the atoning blood of Christ that we may receive forgiveness"?

"When you have done all that you can to repent of your sins, . . . and have made amends and restitution to the best of your ability, . . . if you seek for and you find that peace of conscience, by that token you may know that the Lord has accepted of your repentance" (Harold B. Lee, *Ensign*, July 1973, 122–23). *See also insight for Enos 1:8.*

MOSIAH 4:2, 5, 11

Why are we "less than the dust of the earth"?

See Moses 1:9–10; insights for Helaman 12:7–18.

MOSIAH 4:6-8

How can salvation come to us?

"Benjamin told them they (1) must believe in the goodness of God and in the atonement of Jesus Christ, (2) must repent of their sins and forsake them, and (3) must humble themselves before God and ask in sincerity of heart for forgiveness" (Daniel H. Ludlow, *Companion*, 180).

MOSIAH 4:9-10

"Believe in God."

"Belief, humble belief, is the foundation of all righteousness and the beginning of spiritual progression. It goes before good works, opens the door to . . . truth, and charts the course to eternal life" (Bruce R. McConkie, *New Witness for the Articles of Faith*, 21).

MOSIAH 4:6, 11-12, 26

How do we stand "steadfastly in the faith"?

"To be steadfast is to be fixed, firm, or unwavering. . . . To be constant and consistent in living by faith. No word in the scriptures better describes spiritual maturity than does *steadfast*" (Joseph Fielding McConkie and Robert L. Millet, *Doctrinal Commentary*, 2:162; emphasis in original).

MOSIAH 4:14-15

What responsibilities do parents have with their children?

"Parents have a sacred duty to rear their children in love and righteousness, to provide for their physical and spiritual needs, to teach them to love and serve one another, to observe the commandments. . . . Husbands and wives—mothers and fathers—will be held accountable before God for the discharge of these obligations" ("The Family: A Proclamation to the World," *Ensign*, November 1995, 102). *See also D&C 68:25; 83:4.*

MOSIAH 4:16-26

Why do we administer of our "substance unto him that standeth in need"?

"If each individual in all the world fasted from two meals once a month, the money thus saved could provide ample means to care for all the poor in all the world. Let us maintain that standard the Lord has given, so that the world may see the beauty of this thing" (Melvin J. Ballard, in Conference Report, April 1912, 88).

MOSIAH 4:19

In what way are we all beggars?

See insights for Moroni 7:18.

MOSIAH 4:21

"God . . . doth grant unto you whatsoever ye ask that is right, in faith."

See insights for 3 Nephi 18:20.

MOSIAH 4:24

What if "I give not because I have not"?

"[You] who have been denied the blessings . . . in this life—who say in their heart, if I could have done, I would have done, or I would give if I had, but I cannot, for I have not—the Lord will bless you as though you had done" (Harold B. Lee, *Ye Are the Light of the World*, 292).

MOSIAH 4:27

Why should we do all things "in wisdom and order"?

"When we run faster than we are able, we get both inefficient and tired. . . .

"I have on my office wall a wise and useful reminder by Anne Morrow Lindbergh concerning one of the realities of life. She wrote, 'My life cannot implement in action the demands of all the people to whom my heart responds.' That's good counsel for us all, not as an excuse to forgo duty, but as a sage point about pace and the need for quality in relationships" (Neal A. Maxwell, *Deposition of a Disciple*, 58).

MOSIAH 4:30

Will we be judged by our thoughts as well as by our words and deeds?

"Think clean thoughts. Those who think clean thoughts do not do filthy deeds. . . . You sow thoughts and you reap acts, you sow acts and you reap habits, you sow habits and you reap a character, and your character determines your eternal destiny. 'As [a man] thinketh in his heart, so is he' (Proverbs 23:7)" (Ezra Taft Benson, *Teachings*, 445–46). *See also 2 Nephi 9:39; Alma 12:14.*

MOSIAH 5

MOSIAH 5:2

Why should we sustain our priesthood leaders?

"[A] person is not truly converted unless he sees the power of God resting upon the leaders of this church and it goes down into his heart like fire" (Harold B. Lee, *Teachings*, 520).

What does it mean to have "a mighty change in us"?

"No one can be born again without baptism, but the immersion in water and the laying on of hands to confer the Holy Ghost do not of themselves guarantee that a person has been or will be born again. The new birth takes place only for those who actually enjoy the . . . Holy Ghost, only for those who are fully converted, who have given themselves without restraint to the Lord" (Bruce R. McConkie, *Mormon Doctrine*, 101).

How do we get to the point that we have "no more disposition to do evil"?

"The nearer man approaches perfection, the clearer are his views, and the greater his enjoyments, till he has overcome the evils of his life and lost every desire for sin" (Joseph Smith, *Teachings*, 51).

MOSIAH 5:3–4

What are the results of having the Spirit?

"The Holy Ghost . . . shows them things past, present, and to come. It opens the vision of the mind, unlocks . . . wisdom, and they begin to understand the things of God" (Brigham Young, *Journal of Discourses* 1:241). *See also D&C 50:24.*

MOSIAH 5:5, 8, 11–12

What are three covenants of baptism?

"That they may . . . witness . . . that they are willing to take upon them the name of thy Son, and always remember him, and keep his commandments" (Moroni 4:3).

1. "Take upon you the name of Christ."

"We are willing to take upon ourselves the name of the Son. In so doing we choose him as our leader and our ideal; and he is the one perfect character in all the world" (David O. McKay, *Gospel Ideals*, 146).

2. "Remember to retain the name [of Christ] written always in your hearts."

"How we treat our family members, our neighbors, business associates, and all we meet will reveal if we have taken His name upon us and do always remember Him. How we conduct our lives, all we do and all we say, reflects on how we remember Him" (Robert D. Hales, *Ensign*, November 1997, 25). *See also insights for Helaman 5:5–14.*

3. "Be obedient to his commandments."

"Through baptism we . . . promise to do the things that He would do, including obeying God's commandments" (M. Russell Ballard, *Our Search for Happiness*, 90).

MOSIAH 5:7

Those who accept the covenants of baptism become "the children of Christ."

"Christ . . . is the Father of redeemed, restored, spiritual life. . . . The faithful are born again—of Christ and by Christ and through Christ—when this mighty change wrought by him comes into their hearts" (Jeffrey R. Holland, *Christ and the New Covenant*, 102–3).

MOSIAH 5:9–10, 12

What is the difference between the "right hand" and the "left hand of God"?

"The right hand or side is called the dexter and the left the sinister. Dexter connotes something favorable; sinister, something unfavorable or unfortunate" (Joseph Fielding Smith, *Answers to Gospel Questions*, 1:158). *See also Matthew 25:41; Alma 5:58.*

MOSIAH 5:15

"Always abounding in good works . . ."

"Men should be anxiously engaged in a good cause, and do many things of their own free will" (D&C 58:27). *See also Matthew 7:21–23.*

MOSIAH 6

MOSIAH 6:1, 3

Why did King Benjamin list "those who had entered into a covenant"?

"After they had been received unto baptism, . . . their names were taken, that they might be remembered and nourished by the good word of God, to keep them in the right way, to keep them continually watchful unto prayer" (Moroni 6:4).

MOSIAH 6:7

What is the value in sustaining ourselves?

"Learn to like your work. . . . God has blessed us with the privilege of working. When he said, "Earn thy bread by the sweat of thy brow," he gave us a blessing. . . . Too much leisure is dangerous. Work is a divine gift" (David O. McKay, *Gospel Ideals*, 497).

"Work brings happiness, self-esteem, and prosperity. It is the means of all accomplishment; it is the opposite of idleness. We are commanded to work. (See Gen. 3:19.) Attempts to obtain our temporal, social, emotional, or spiritual well-being by means of a dole violate the divine mandate that we should work for what we receive" (Spencer W. Kimball, *Ensign*, November 1977, 77). *See also insights for Mosiah 9:12; Mosiah 23:5.*

MOSIAH 7

MOSIAH 7:2–18

Ammon was a type of Christ.

Many ancient prophets are types of Christ. *See insights for 1 Nephi 18:10–23.*

AMMON	JESUS CHRIST	PARALLEL
Mosiah 7:2	John 5:36	Both Ammon and Jesus were sent to help a lost people.
Mosiah 7:3	Psalm 24:8	Both are described as mighty and strong.
Mosiah 7:4, 16	Matthew 4:1–2	Both experienced forty days of hunger, thirst, and fatigue.
Mosiah 7:6	Matthew 26:37	Both took three others with them and went a little further.
Mosiah 7:7	John 18:12	Both were arrested, bound, and taken away.
Mosiah 7:8	Luke 23:7	Both were brought before kings and questioned.
Mosiah 7:18; 22:11	D&C 138:23	Ammon led the people out of physical bondage. Jesus delivers the people from death and hell.

(Adapted from *Book of Mormon Teacher Resource Manual*, 108.)

MOSIAH 7:9

Who were Limhi, Noah, and Zeniff?

Limhi, Noah, and Zeniff were three generations of kings ruling the Nephite people who left Zarahemla and removed to the land of Nephi-Lehi.

They reigned about the same time as Kings Mosiah I, Benjamin, and Mosiah II, who ruled in Zarahemla.

MOSIAH 7:26-28

Many prophets are killed for teaching that Christ is "God, the Father."

"One Book of Mormon prophet—Abinadi—was put to death for teaching . . . that Christ could appropriately be called both the Father and the Son" (Jeffrey R. Holland, *Christ and the New Covenant*, 189). *To read about other prophets who experienced the same fate, see 1 Nephi 1:19–20; Alma 33:15–17; Helaman 8:17–19; 3 Nephi 6:23; 10:15; Luke 22:70–71.*

MOSIAH 8

MOSIAH 8:13

What were these "interpreters"?

"Reference is here made to . . . the Urim and Thummim. The Urim and Thummim consists of two special stones, or as Ammon refers to them, 'interpreters.' The Hebrew words urim and thummim (both plural) may be associated with the words *lights* and *perfections*" (Joseph Fielding McConkie and Robert L. Millet, *Doctrinal Commentary*, 2:190; emphasis in original). *See also JS—H 1:35.*

MOSIAH 8:13-17

What is a "seer"?

"A seer is one who sees with spiritual eyes. He perceives the meaning of that which seems obscure to others; therefore he is an interpreter and clarifier of eternal truth. He foresees the future from the past and the present. This he does by the power of the Lord operating through him directly, or indirectly with the aid of divine instruments such as the Urim and Thummim. In short, he is one who sees" (John A. Widtsoe, *Evidences and Reconciliations*, 258).

MOSIAH 8:20

Who does "she" refer to?

"The antecedent of *she* in this sentence is wisdom. Joseph Smith's translation of this verse as 'she should rule' rather than 'it should rule' is in harmony with the Semitic world view. In Hebrew and other languages of the ancient Near East *wisdom* is a feminine noun" (Joseph Fielding McConkie and Robert L. Millet, *Doctrinal Commentary*, 2:192; emphasis in original).

MOSIAH 9

MOSIAH 9:12

What are the dangers in being "a lazy and an idolatrous people"?

"Neither temporal nor spiritual salvation can be gained without work, and idleness is a grievous sin. Idlers—those who waste time in doing nothing, who are lazy, indolent, slothful—'shall be had in remembrance before the Lord.' (D. & C. 68:30–31.) . . . Idleness and abominable practices always go together. . . . Idleness breeds idolatry. (Alma 1:32)" (Bruce R. McConkie, *Mormon Doctrine*, 372). *See also insights for Mosiah 6:7.*

MOSIAH 9:17–19

"In the strength of the Lord did we go forth to battle."

In virtually every case in the Book of Mormon, the righteous win the battle. In this battle the casualty rate of righteous compared to wicked was better than one righteous death to every ten deaths of the enemy. Even so, often some righteous perish in the fight. *See insights for 1 Nephi 22:16–22.*

MOSIAH 10

MOSIAH 10:4–5

"I did cause that the men . . . [and] the women should . . . work."

See insights for Mosiah 6:7.

MOSIAH 11

MOSIAH 11–17

How was Abinadi a type of Christ?

ABINADI	JESUS CHRIST	SIMILARITIES
Mosiah 11:20–25; 12:9	Matthew 4:17; Luke 4:28	Both called the people to repentance; the people became angry at their preaching.
Mosiah 11:26	Luke 4:29–30	The people they taught tried to kill them, but they were delivered.
Mosiah 12:9	John 18:12; Luke 23:7	Both were bound and taken before the king.
Mosiah 12:17–18	Matthew 26:57	Both were judged by a council of priests.

Mosiah 12:19	Mark 14:55–59; Luke 20:19–20	The judges tried to catch them in their words.
Mosiah 12:26	Matthew 23:13–26	Both rebuked the religious leaders.
Mosiah 13:1	John 10:20	Both were accused of being crazy.
Mosiah 14; 17:1	Luke 4:16–21, 28–30	Abinadi quoted from Isaiah's prophecies of the Savior, and then Noah had him killed. Jesus quoted from Isaiah's prophecies of the Savior, and then the people of Nazareth tried to kill him.
Mosiah 17:5–6	Acts 10:40; 1 Peter 3:18–19	Abinadi spent three days in prison. Jesus spent three days in the tomb, during which time he preached to the spirits in prison.
Mosiah 17:7–8	Matthew 26:63–66	Both taught that Christ was God.
Mosiah 17:9	John 18:1–8	Both allowed themselves to be arrested.
Mosiah 17:9–10	John 10:17–18	Both willingly suffered death.
Mosiah 17:10	Matthew 27:22–24	Both were innocent of wrongdoing.
Mosiah 17:11	Matthew 27:15–18	In both cases the political leader was willing to release them.
Mosiah 17:12	Luke 23:2	Both were accused of treason.
Mosiah 17:13	John 19:1	Both were scourged.
Mosiah 17:19	Luke 23:46	Both died while praying for the reception of their soul.
Mosiah 17:20	John 19:30; see also Hebrews 9:15–16	Both sealed their testimony with their blood.

(Adapted from Jeffrey R. Holland, *Christ and the New Covenant*, 171–72.)

MOSIAH 11:2

What are some of the dangers of walking "after the desires of" our own hearts?

"Prophets frequently warn about the dangers of [selfishness]. The distance between constant self-pleasing and self-worship is shorter than we think. Stubborn selfishness is actually rebellion against God, because, warned Samuel, 'stubbornness is as . . . idolatry' (1 Samuel 15:23).

"Selfishness is much more than an ordinary problem, because it activates all the cardinal sins. It is the detonator in the breaking of the Ten Commandments" (Neal A. Maxwell, *Men and Women of Christ*, 8).

MOSIAH 11:7

"They were deceived by the vain and flattering words of the king."
See insights for Jacob 7:2, 4.

MOSIAH 11:14

Why should we avoid placing our hearts upon riches?
"The love of money is the root of all evil" (1 Timothy 6:10). *See also insights for Alma 11:20, 24.*

MOSIAH 11:19

What recent counsel was forgotten by those who "were lifted up" in pride?
See insights for Helaman 12:7–18.

MOSIAH 11:26

Why were the people "wroth" with Abinadi?
"I knew that I had spoken hard things against the wicked, according to the truth; . . . wherefore, the guilty taketh the truth to be hard, for it cutteth them to the very center" (1 Nephi 16:2).

MOSIAH 11:26–29

What is the relationship between anger and murder?
"Ye have heard that it hath been said by them of old time that, Thou shalt not kill; and whosoever shall kill, shall be in danger of the judgment of God. But I say unto you that whosoever is angry with his brother, shall be in danger of his judgment" (JST, Matthew 5:23 24). *See also insights for Alma 2:8–10.*

MOSIAH 12

MOSIAH 12:3

When was Abinadi's prophecy about king Noah fulfilled?
"They were angry with the king [Noah], and caused that he should suffer, even unto death by fire" (Mosiah 19:20).

MOSIAH 12:13–14

"What great sins have thy people committed? . . . We are guiltless."

"Woe unto them that call evil good, and good evil" (Isaiah 5:20).

MOSIAH 12:27–29

What difference does it make where our hearts are?

Where our hearts are determines what we worship. "For where your treasure is, there will your heart be also" (Matthew 6:21). The Lord told the Prophet Joseph Smith "'They draw near to me with their lips, but their hearts are far from me'" (JS—H 1:19).

MOSIAH 13

MOSIAH 13:2–3

"Touch me not . . . for I have not delivered the message."

"Hold on thy way . . . for their [the enemy's] bounds are set, they cannot pass. Thy days are known, and thy years shall not be numbered less" (D&C 122:9).

"And may I say for the consolation of those who mourn, and for the comfort and guidance of all of us, that no righteous man is ever taken before his time" (Joseph Fielding Smith, *Ensign*, December 1971, 10).

MOSIAH 13:4, 7

The truth cuts the wicked to their hearts.

See insights for 1 Nephi 16:1–3.

MOSIAH 13:10

How was Abinadi "a type and a shadow of things which are to come"?

The phrase "type and shadow" carries at least two meanings. First, there would be similarities in the deaths of Abinadi and Noah—they both suffered death by fire (see Mosiah 19:20). Second, there would be similarities between the ministry of Abinadi and the ministry of Jesus Christ. *See also insights for Mosiah 11–17.*

MOSIAH 13:11

What happens when the commandments are "written in [our] hearts"?

"When we know who we are and what God expects of us—when his 'law [is] written in [our] hearts'—we are spiritually protected. We become better people" (Russell M. Nelson, *Ensign*, May 1995, 34).

MOSIAH 13:11-24

Abinadi taught them the Ten Commandments.

ABINADI	MOSES	THE TEN COMMANDMENTS
Mosiah 12:35	Exodus 20:3	1. Have no other gods before me
Mosiah 13:12	Exodus 20:4	2. Make no graven image
Mosiah 13:15	Exodus 20:7	3. Don't take the name of God in vain
Mosiah 13:16	Exodus 20:8	4. Keep the sabbath day holy
Mosiah 13:20	Exodus 20:12	5. Honor thy father and mother
Mosiah 13:21	Exodus 20:13	6. Thou shalt not kill
Mosiah 13:22	Exodus 20:14	7. Thou shalt not commit adultery
Mosiah 13:22	Exodus 20:15	8. Thou shalt not steal
Mosiah 13:23	Exodus 20:16	9. Thou shalt not bear false witness
Mosiah 13:24	Exodus 20:17	10. Thou shalt not covet

MOSIAH 13:12-13

What "graven image[s]" do people worship today?

"Whatever thing a man sets his heart and his trust in most is his god; and if his god doesn't also happen to be the true and living God of Israel, that man is laboring in idolatry" (Spencer W. Kimball, *Ensign*, June 1976, 4).

"Modern idols or false gods can take such forms as clothes, homes, businesses, machines, automobiles, pleasure boats, and numerous other material deflectors from the path of godhood" (Spencer W. Kimball, *Teachings*, 244).

MOSIAH 13:15

How do people today take the name of the Lord in vain?

"1. We may take the name of God in vain by profane speech.

"2. We take it in vain when we swear falsely, not being true to our oaths covenants and promises.

"3. We take it in vain in a blasphemous sense when we presume to speak in that name without authority.

"4. And we take his name in vain whenever we wilfully do aught that is in defiance of his commandments, since we have taken his name upon ourselves" (James E. Talmage, in Conference Report, October 1931, 53).

MOSIAH 13:16–19

What should we do on the sabbath day "to keep it holy"?

"To observe [the Sabbath], one will be on his knees in prayer, preparing lessons, studying the gospel, meditating, visiting the ill and distressed, writing letters to missionaries, taking a nap, reading wholesome material, and attending all the meetings of that day at which he is expected" (Spencer W. Kimball, *Ensign*, January 1978, 4).

MOSIAH 13:20

"Honor thy father and thy mother."

"No one has a greater interest in your welfare, in your happiness, in your future than do your mothers and fathers. . . . Your problems are not substantially different from what theirs were. . . . Listen to them. What they ask you to do may not be to your liking. But you will be much happier if you do it" (Gordon B. Hinckley, *Teachings*, 209).

MOSIAH 13:22

"Thou shalt not commit adultery."

See insights for Alma 39:5–6.

"Thou shalt not steal."

"Dishonesty is destructive to character. The theft of pennies or . . . commodities may impoverish little the one from whom the goods are taken, but it is a shrivelling, dwarfing process to the one who steals" (Spencer W. Kimball, *Teachings*, 198).

MOSIAH 13:23

"Thou shalt not bear false witness."

See insights for 2 Nephi 9:34.

MOSIAH 13:24

"Thou shalt not covet."

"To covet is to have an eager, extreme, and ungodly desire for something. The presence of covetousness in a human soul shows that such person has not overcome the world" (Bruce R. McConkie, *Mormon Doctrine*, 168).

MOSIAH 13:28, 32

"Were it not for the atonement . . . his people . . . must unavoidably perish."

"Suppose we have the scriptures, the gospel, the priesthood, the Church, the ordinances, the organization, even the keys of the kingdom—everything . . . down to the last jot and tittle—and yet there is no atonement of Christ. What then? Can we be saved? . . .

"Most assuredly we will not. . . . We are saved by the blood of Christ (Acts 20:28; 1 Cor. 6:20)" (Bruce R. McConkie, *Sermons and Writings of Bruce R. McConkie,* 76).

MOSIAH 13:33

Prophets have prophesied about the "coming of the Messiah."
See insights for Jacob 7:11.

MOSIAH 14

MOSIAH 14:1–12

"Doth not Isaiah say . . ."

"Surely the most sublime . . . declaration of the life, death, and atoning sacrifice of the Lord Jesus Christ is that found in the 53rd chapter of Isaiah, quoted in its entirety . . . by Abinadi" (Jeffrey R. Holland, *Christ and the New Covenant,* 89).

Consider the following prophecies and fulfillments of this detailed chapter.

MESSIANIC PROPHECIES FROM MOSIAH 14 OR ISAIAH 53	FULFILLMENT OF MESSIANIC PROPHECIES
"He is despised and rejected" (v. 3)	"[Jesus] said, Therefore said I unto you, that no man can come unto me, except it were given unto him of my Father. From that time many of his disciples went back, and walked no more with him" (John 6:65–66).
"A man of sorrows, and acquainted with grief" (v. 3)	"[Jesus] suffereth the pains of all men, yea, the pains of every living creature" (2 Nephi 9:21). "He . . . began to be sorrowful and very heavy. Then saith he unto them, My soul is exceeding sorrowful, even unto death" (Matthew 26:37–38).
"We hid . . . our faces from him . . . and we esteemed him not" (v. 3)	"Then all the disciples forsook him, and fled" (Matthew 26:56).
"He has borne our griefs, and carried our sorrows; . . . he was wounded for our transgressions" (vv. 4–5)	"He shall go forth, suffering pains and afflictions and temptations of every kind. . . . And he will take upon him their infirmities . . . according to the flesh, . . . that he might take upon him the sins of his people, that he might blot out their transgressions" (Alma 7:11–13).
"With his stripes we are	"He will take upon him death, that he may

healed" (v. 5)

"Every one to his own way" (v. 6)

"He opened not his mouth" (v. 7)

"He is brought as a lamb to the slaughter. . . . He had done no evil" (vv. 7, 9)

"He was taken from prison and from judgment" (v. 8)

"He made his grave with the wicked" (v. 9)

"He made his grave . . . with the rich in his death" (v. 9)

"Neither was any deceit in his mouth" (v. 9)

"It pleased the Lord to bruise him. . . . He shall see the travail of his soul, and shall be satisfied" (vv. 10–11)

loose the bands of death which bind his people" (Alma 7:12).

"Jesus saith unto him, I am the way, the truth, and the life" (John 14:6). "They seek not the Lord to establish his righteousness, but every man walketh in his own way, and after the image of his own god" (D&C 1:16).

"When Herod saw Jesus . . . he questioned with him in many words; but he [Jesus] answered him nothing" (Luke 23:8–9; see also Matthew 27:13–14).

"The Lamb slain from the foundation of the world" (Revelation 13:8). "With the precious blood of Christ, as of a lamb without blemish and without spot" (1 Peter 1:19).

"The Lamb of God, that he was taken by the people; yea, the Son of the everlasting God was judged of the world" (1 Nephi 11:32).

"Then were there two thieves crucified with him, one on the right hand, and another on the left" (Matthew 27:38).

"There came a rich man of Arimathaea, named Joseph, who also himself was Jesus' disciple: He went to Pilate, and begged the body of Jesus. . . . When Joseph had taken the body, he wrapped it in a clean linen cloth, and laid it in his own new tomb, which he had hewn out in the rock" (Matthew 27:57–60).

"Then said Jesus, Father, forgive them; for they know not what they do" (Luke 23:34).

"Therefore doth my Father love me, because I lay down my life, that I might take it again. No man taketh it from me, but I lay it down of myself" (John 10:17–18).

MOSIAH 14:2

How was Jesus "a tender plant" and "a root out of dry ground"?

"He was 'tender' in at least two ways—he was young, pure, innocent, and particularly vulnerable to the pain of sin all around him, and he was caring, thoughtful, sensitive, and kind—in short, tender. . . . He was to anchor himself and become a mighty root" (Jeffrey R. Holland, *Christ and the New Covenant*, 90).

"He hath no form nor comeliness . . . no beauty that we should desire him."

"[The Messiah] grew up and lived as other men live, subject to the ills and troubles of mortality . . .

"There is no mystique, no dynamic appearance, no halo around his head, thunders do not roll and lightnings do not flash at his appearance. . . . He is a man among men, appearing, speaking, dressing, . . . as they are" (Bruce R. McConkie, *Promised Messiah*, 477–78).

MOSIAH 14:10

Who is the "seed" of Jesus that he will see?

"When we take upon ourselves His name and covenant to keep His commandments, it is then that we become His sons and daughters, 'the children of Christ'" (Neal A. Maxwell, *Men and Women of Christ*, 37). *See also Mosiah 5:3–7.*

MOSIAH 15

MOSIAH 15:1

Abinadi was killed after teaching that "God himself" would become a man.

See insights for Mosiah 7:26–28.

MOSIAH 15:2–5

How are the Father and Son "one God"?

1. In many ways, the Son is like the Father.

"In the exalted family of the Gods, the Father and the Son are one. They have the same character, perfections, and attributes. They think the same thoughts, speak the same words, perform the same acts, have the same desires, and do the same works. They possess the same power, have the same mind, know the same truths, live in the same light and glory. To know one is to know the other; to see one is to see the other; to hear the voice of one is to hear the voice of the other. Their unity is perfect. The Son is in the express image of his Father's person; each has a body of flesh and bones as tangible as man's" (Bruce R. McConkie, *Promised Messiah*, 9).

2. In other ways, the Son literally *is* the Father.

"[First] The Savior becomes our Father, in the sense in which . . . he offers us life, eternal life, through the atonement. . . .

"[Second] We become the children, sons and daughters of Jesus Christ, through our covenants of obedience to him [see Mosiah 5:7]. . . .

"[Third] Christ is also our Father because his Father has given him of his fulness; that is, he has received a fulness of the glory of the Father [see D&C 93:1–5, 16–17]. . . .

"[Therefore] the Father has honored Christ by placing his name upon him, so that he can minister in and through that name as though he were the Father. . . .

"[Fourth] Our Lord is also called the Father in the sense that he is the Father or Creator of the heavens and the earth and all things" (Joseph Fielding Smith, *Doctrines of Salvation*, 1:29–30). *See also insights for 3 Nephi 11:27.*

MOSIAH 15:7

What kind of sacrifice is it to let our will be "swallowed up in the will of the Father"?

"The submission of one's will is placing on God's altar the only uniquely personal thing one has to place there. The many other things we 'give' are actually the things He has already given or loaned to us. However, when we finally submit ourselves by letting our individual wills be swallowed up in God's will, we will really be giving something to Him! It is the only possession which is truly ours to give" (Neal A. Maxwell, *If Thou Endure It Well*, 54).

MOSIAH 15:9, 19

How can Christ have both mercy and justice?

"In his love and in his mercy, a gracious God seeks the salvation of all his children. But he cannot save the righteous without damning the wicked; he cannot reward the obedient without condemning the rebellious; he cannot fill the hearts of the righteous with unmeasured blessings without pouring out his wrath upon the wicked" (Bruce R. McConkie, *Millennial Messiah*, 499).

MOSIAH 15:12

Did Christ bear only the sins of the righteous?

"In Gethsemane and on the cross Jesus suffered for the sins of all men, good and bad, that they might be resurrected from the dead and have immortal life. . . . Jesus paid for the sins of every human soul who has lived or will live upon the earth" (Marion G. Romney, in Conference Report, April 1948, 77). *See also D&C 19:16.*

MOSIAH 15:21–23

Will there be order in the resurrection?

"In Christ shall all be made alive. . . . But every man in his own order: Christ the firstfruits; afterward they that are Christ's at his coming" (1 Corinthians 15:22–23).

ORDER OF THE RESURRECTION

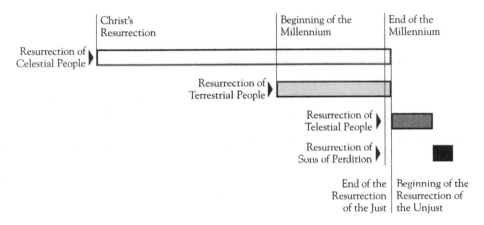

Who has part in the "first resurrection"?

"All those that have kept the commandments of God" (v. 22).

Those who die "in their ignorance, not having salvation declared unto them" (v. 24) but who "would have received it if they had" heard it (D&C 137:7).

"And little children" (v. 25). *See also insights for Moroni 8:8.*

MOSIAH 15:29

When will the Lord "bring again Zion"?

"Righteousness will I send down out of heaven . . . [at] the time of my coming. . . . The Lord said unto Enoch: Then shalt thou and all thy city meet them there, and we will receive them into our bosom, and they shall see us; and we will fall upon their necks, and they shall fall upon our necks, and we will kiss each other; . . . and it shall be Zion" (Moses 7:62–64).

MOSIAH 15:30

When will the Lord redeem Jerusalem?

See D&C 45:47–52.

MOSIAH 16

MOSIAH 16:1

Who will see the Second Coming of the Lord?

"The second advent of the Son of God is to be . . . accompanied with great power and glory, something that will not be done in a small portion of the earth like Palestine, and seen only by a few; but it will be an event that will be seen by all—all flesh shall see the glory of the Lord" (Orson Pratt, *Journal of Discourses*, 18:171).

MOSIAH 16:3

What role did the devil play in the fall of Adam and Eve?

"Adam and Eve willingly made a choice, choosing the path toward growth and godhood. . . . With the enticement of Lucifer, . . . as Abinadi phrased it, they consciously chose" (Jeffrey R. Holland, *Christ and the New Covenant*, 203).

MOSIAH 16:6–7

"If Christ had not come . . . there could have been no redemption" and *"no resurrection."*

See insights for 2 Nephi 9:6–10.

MOSIAH 16:9

How is Christ "the light and the life of the world"?

"Whenever the cold hand of death strikes, there shines through the gloom and the darkness of that hour the triumphant figure of the Lord Jesus Christ. . . . He is our comfort, our only true comfort, when the dark shroud of earthly night closes about us as the spirit departs the human form" (Gordon B. Hinckley, in Sheri L. Dew, *Go Forward with Faith*, 532–33).

MOSIAH 16:13

"Ought ye not to tremble and repent of your sins"?

"Despise not, and wonder not, but hearken unto the words of the Lord. . . . Come unto the Lord with all your heart, and work out your own salvation with fear and trembling before him" (Mormon 9:27).

MOSIAH 16:15

How is Christ "the very Eternal Father"?

See insights for Mosiah 15:2–5.

MOSIAH 17

MOSIAH 17:3, 8-10, 20

Abinadi said, "I will not recall [my] words."

"Be strong—in standing for the right. We live in an age of compromise and acquiescence. In situations with which we are daily confronted, we know what is right, but under pressure from our peers and the beguiling voices of those who would persuade us, we capitulate. We compromise. . . . We must cultivate the strength to follow our convictions" (Gordon B. Hinckley, *Teachings*, 135).

MOSIAH 17:8

Because Abinadi taught that "God himself should come," he was put to death.

See insights for Mosiah 7:26–28.

MOSIAH 17:17-18

When did this prophecy come true?

See Mosiah 19:20; Alma 25:7–12.

MOSIAH 17:20

"He fell, . . . having been put to death."

"Those that die in me shall not taste of death, for it shall be sweet unto them" (D&C 42:46). *See also D&C 98:13.*

"Martyrdom is . . . the supreme earthly sacrifice" (Bruce R. McConkie, *Mormon Doctrine*, 469).

MOSIAH 18

MOSIAH 18:4

What is the meaning of the word Mormon?

See insights for Mormon 1:1.

MOSIAH 18:8-10

What covenants were made between the Lord and those who were baptized?

What the People Promised to Do

Be called the people of Christ (v. 8)

Bear one another's burdens (v. 8)

Mourn with those that mourn (v. 9)

Comfort those that stand in need (v. 9)

Stand as witnesses of God at all times (v. 9)

Live these covenants until death (v. 9)

Serve God (v. 10)

Keep his commandments (v. 10)

What God Promised to Do in Return

Redeem his people (v. 9)

Allow them to take part in the first resurrection (v. 9)

Pour out his Spirit upon them (v. 10)

MOSIAH 18:13, 18

Did Alma have the authority to baptize?

"Alma was baptized and held the priesthood before the coming of Abinadi" (Joseph Fielding Smith, *Doctrines of Salvation*, 2:336–37).

What is a primary purpose of baptism?

Some people are "baptized . . . for the remission of sins" (D&C 84:64). However, since children who are baptized when they turn eight have no sins, the purpose of baptism that Alma stated—to give a testimony of their covenant with the Lord—is the primary purpose of baptism (see also 2 Nephi 31:5–9; Mosiah 21:35; 3 Nephi 7:25). The prophet Joseph Smith taught, "Baptism is a sign to God, to angels, and to heaven that we do the will of God" (Joseph Smith, *Teachings*, 198).

MOSIAH 18:13–14

Did Alma baptize himself?

"If he had authority to baptize that is evidence that he had been baptized. Therefore, when Alma baptized himself with Helaman that was not a case of Alma baptizing himself, but merely as a token to the Lord of his humility and full repentance" (Joseph Fielding Smith, *Answers to Gospel Questions*, 3:204).

They were "buried in the water."

"The mode of baptism is by immersion in water. Sprinkling or pouring did not come into vogue until two or three centuries after Christ. . . . Baptism cannot be by any other means than immersion of the entire body in water. . . . It is in the similitude of the death, burial, and resurrection of Jesus Christ, and of all others who have received the resurrection" (Joseph Fielding Smith, *Doctrines of Salvation*, 2:323).

MOSIAH 18:14

"They arose and came forth out of the water rejoicing, being filled with the Spirit."

"No sooner had I baptized Oliver Cowdery, than the Holy Ghost fell upon him, and he stood up and prophesied many things which should shortly come to pass. And again, so soon as I had been baptized by him, I also had the spirit of prophecy. . . . We were filled with the Holy Ghost, and rejoiced in the God of our salvation" (JS—H 1:73).

MOSIAH 18:28

How can I learn to faithfully give to the needy?

"Some may ask, 'How do I obtain these righteous feelings in giving? How do I overcome giving grudgingly? How do I obtain the "pure love of Christ?"' To those I would say: Faithfully live all the commandments, give of yourselves, care for your families, serve in church callings, perform missionary work, pay tithes and offerings, study the scriptures—and the list could go on. As you lose yourself in this service, the Lord will touch and soften your heart" (Marion G. Romney, *Ensign*, November 1981, 93). *See also Moroni 7:6–8.*

MOSIAH 19

MOSIAH 19–24

How do the people of Limhi compare with the people of Alma?

The prophet Alma seemed to describe Limhi's people, who were forced to remember the Lord during their Lamanite bondage, with these words: "Ye are compelled to be humble; . . . a man sometimes, if he is compelled to be humble, seeketh repentance" (Alma 32:13). Three verses later Alma seemed to describe Alma (his father) and Alma's people with these words: "Blessed are they who humble themselves without being compelled to be humble" (Alma 32:16). Consider the following details:

What were the people like?

PEOPLE OF LIMHI	PEOPLE OF ALMA
(Mosiah 19:2–20)	(Mosiah 18:3–21)
They were divided (v. 2).	They believed Alma (v. 3).
They were contentious (v. 3).	They traveled to hear the gospel (v. 4).
They fled before the Lamanites (v. 9).	They endured risk (vv. 4, 6).
They abandoned their families (v. 11).	They were taught to repent and have faith in the Lord (v. 7).
They had their daughters plead for them (v. 13).	They covenanted with God (vv. 8–11).

They killed their king (v. 20).

They were filled with grace (v. 16).

They were taught to love one another (v. 21).

What happened to them, and how did they react?

PEOPLE OF LIMHI	PEOPLE OF ALMA
(Mosiah 19:22–20:22)	**(Mosiah 23:2–37)**
They were brought into captivity and paid a 50 percent tribute (19:22).	The Lord strengthened them (v. 2).
They lived peacefully in bondage for two years (19:29).	They built a city (vv. 5, 20).
The Lamanites attacked them (20:7).	They prospered exceedingly (vv. 19–20).
They fought back (20:8–11).	The Lamanites found them (v. 25).
They accepted bondage (20:22).	They cried to the Lord (v. 28).
	They surrendered and accepted bondage (vv. 29, 36–37).

What were the conditions of their bondage?

PEOPLE OF LIMHI	PEOPLE OF ALMA
(Mosiah 21:3–6)	**(Mosiah 24:8–14)**
The Lamanites smote them on the cheeks (v. 3).	Amulon persecuted them (v. 8).
They exercised authority over them (v. 3).	He exercised authority over them and gave them taskmasters (v. 9).
They gave them heavy burdens and drove them like animals (v. 3).	Their afflictions were great (v. 10).
	They were threatened with death (v. 11).
	They had burdens on their backs (v. 14).

How did they respond to this bondage?

People of Limhi	People of Alma
(Mosiah 21:6–14, 25–26)	**(Mosiah 24:10–16)**
They began to murmur (v. 6).	They cried mightily to God (v. 10).
They went to war and were defeated three times, many were killed and there was much sorrow (vv. 7–12).	They prayed in their hearts (v. 12).
They were compelled to be humble (vv. 13–14).	They submitted cheerfully (v. 15).
They accepted their bondage and abuse (v. 13).	They showed faith and patience (v. 16).
They cried mightily to the Lord (v. 14).	
They sent for help (vv. 25–26).	

What was the result of their actions?

People of Limhi	People of Alma
(Mosiah 21:15–22:16)	**(Mosiah 24:13–25)**
The Lord was slow to hear them (21:15).	The Lord spoke to them (v. 13).
The Lord softened the hearts of their enemies, who eased their burdens (21:15).	He promised to deliver them (v. 13).
They were not delivered at first (21:15).	He eased their burdens and strengthened them (vv. 14–15).
They prospered by degrees (21:16).	He promised to deliver them "on the morrow" (v. 16).
They helped others (21:17).	He caused a deep sleep to come upon the guards (v. 19).
They covenanted to serve God (21:31).	They escaped (v. 20).
They gave wine to the Lamanite guards, who then fell sleep (22:7, 10).	
They escaped (22:11).	

MOSIAH 19:8

What are the dangers of caring only for our own life?

"As long as they have in their hearts selfishness and greed, and the desire for power and for wealth, and for all of the other things that belong to this world, and forget the things of the kingdom of God, there will be no peace, and there will be no contentment. There will be quarreling and contention, strife and war, and in the midst of all their labor, trouble will come which they could avoid" (Joseph Fielding Smith, *Doctrines of Salvation*, 3:49–50).

MOSIAH 19:20–21

"They . . . caused that he should suffer, even unto death by fire."

This was in fulfillment of prophecies made by Abinadi, found in Mosiah 12:3; 17:17–18.

MOSIAH 19:25–26; 20:14, 22, 24

How serious is it to make an oath?

See insights for 1 Nephi 4:32–37.

MOSIAH 20

MOSIAH 20:11

What can justify war?

See insights for Alma 43:9, 26, 30, 45–50; 44:5; 46:12; 48:10, 24.

MOSIAH 21

MOSIAH 21:15

What happens when we become slow to hear the word of the Lord?

When people are "slow to hearken unto the voice of the Lord their God; . . . the Lord their God is slow to hearken unto their prayers, to answer them in the day of their trouble" (D&C 101:7).

MOSIAH 21:17

How important is it that we impart to "the widows and their children"?

"Pure religion and undefiled before God and the Father is this, To visit the fatherless and widows in their affliction" (James 1:27).

MOSIAH 22

MOSIAH 22:1

Why would Ammon and King Lamoni want "the voice of the people"?

"It is not common that the voice of the people desireth anything contrary to that which is right; . . . therefore . . . do your business by the voice of the people" (Mosiah 29:26).

MOSIAH 23

MOSIAH 23:5

Why should we be industrious?

"Our primary purpose was to set up . . . a system under which the curse of idleness would be done away with, the evils of a dole abolished, and independence, industry, thrift, and self-respect be once more established amongst our people. The aim of the Church is to help the people to help themselves" (Heber J. Grant, *Gospel Standards*, 123–24). *See also insights for Mosiah 6:7.*

MOSIAH 23:7

"Ye shall not esteem one flesh above another."

"The priest, not esteeming himself above his hearers, for the preacher was no better than the hearer, neither was the teacher any better than the learner; and thus they were all equal" (Alma 1:26).

MOSIAH 23:9–10

Why does repentance require suffering?

"For those who have strayed, the Savior has provided a way back. But it is not without pain. Repentance is not easy; it takes time—painful time! You deceive yourself if you believe you can break the promises you have made with Heavenly Father and suffer no consequence" (M. Russell Ballard, *Ensign*, May 1993, 7).

MOSIAH 23:15

Why should every man "love his neighbor as himself"?

See John 13:34–35; insights for Mosiah 2:17.

MOSIAH 23:21

Why does the Lord chasten his people?

"I rejoice in afflictions, for they are necessary to humble and prove us, that we may comprehend ourselves, become acquainted with our weakness and infirmities; and I rejoice when I triumph over them, because God answers my prayers; therefore I feel to rejoice all the day long" (John Taylor, *Gospel Kingdom*, 234). *See also Hebrews 12:6; insights for Helaman 12:3.*

MOSIAH 24

MOSIAH 24:12

Who can know the thoughts of our hearts?

See D&C 6:16; insights for Jacob 2:5.

MOSIAH 24:14–15

Sometimes the Lord will ease our burdens rather than take them away.

"[The Lord] loves us and pours out His Spirit upon us and blesses us with light and understanding, upholds, comforts and strengthens us, and enables us to bear our afflictions with patience and fortitude" (George Q. Cannon, in *Collected Discourses*, 2:176). *See also 1 Nephi 17:2–3, 12.*

MOSIAH 24:21–22

"They poured out their thanks to God."

"The Prophet Joseph is reported to have said at one time that one of the greatest sins for which the Latter-day Saints would be guilty would be the sin of ingratitude. I presume most of us have not thought of that as a serious sin. . . . I feel we need to devote more of our prayers to expressions of gratitude and thanksgiving" (Ezra Taft Benson, *Teachings*, 363). *See also D&C 59:7, 21; insights for 1 Nephi 2:7.*

MOSIAH 25

MOSIAH 25:2

Who was Mulek?

See insights for Omni 1:12.

MOSIAH 25:5–11

What were the effects of scripture reading on the people of Mosiah?

They were "struck with wonder and amazement" (v. 7).

They "were filled with exceedingly great joy" (v. 8).

They felt "sorrow" for the deaths of so many (v. 9).

They recognized the "goodness of God" (v. 10).

They felt the need to "give thanks to God" (v. 10).

The sins of others "filled [them] with pain and anguish" (v. 11).

MOSIAH 25:12

What should fathers do for their children?

"Fathers, if you wish your children to be taught in the principles of the gospel, . . . if you wish them to be obedient to and united with you, love them! and prove to them that you do love them by your every word or act to them. . . . When you speak or talk to them, do it not in anger, do it not harshly. . . . Speak to them kindly. . . . Use no lash and no violence, but . . . approach them with reason, with persuasion and love unfeigned" (Joseph F. Smith, *Gospel Doctrine*, 316). *See also D&C 121:45.*

MOSIAH 25:17–18, 23

What are the requirements for those who desire to be baptized?

"There are three requirements of an applicant for baptism: (1) He must be humble, so that he asks for it as a favor. He who comes with broken heart and contrite spirit is in the proper frame of mind for that ordinance; (2) He must show before the Church that he is repentant and willing to take upon him the name of Jesus Christ. . . . (3) He must manifest by his works that he has received the Spirit. " (Hyrum M. Smith and Janne M. Sjodahl, *Doctrine and Covenants*, 105). *See also D&C 20:37.*

MOSIAH 26

MOSIAH 26:6

What are the dangers of "flattering words"?

See insights for Jacob 7:2, 4.

MOSIAH 26:13

Where can we go when we are troubled?

"If your problems be too great for human intelligence or too much for human strength, you too, if you are faithful and appeal rightly unto the source of divine power, might have standing by you in your hour of peril or great need an angel of God, whose you are and whom you serve" (Harold B. Lee, in Conference Report, October 1946, 146).

MOSIAH 26:25

What is the "second trump"?

"The 'second trump' refers to the announcement of the second resurrection or the resurrection of the unjust (see D&C 76:81–86)" (Thomas R. Valletta, ed., *Book of Mormon for Latter-day Saint Families*, 250).

MOSIAH 26:29

Why is confession necessary?

"One has not repented until he has bared his soul and admitted his intentions and weaknesses without excuses, or rationalizations. When one admits that his sin is as *big* as it really *is*, then he is ready to begin his repentance" (Spencer W. Kimball, *Teachings*, 81; emphasis in original).

Which sins should be confessed to the Lord and which to the bishop?

"We are to confess all our sins unto the Lord. For transgressions which are wholly personal, affecting none but ourselves and the Lord, such confession would seem to be sufficient.

"For misconduct which offends another, confession should also be made to the offended one, and his forgiveness sought.

"Finally, where one's transgressions are of such a nature as would, unrepented of, put in jeopardy his right to membership or fellowship [serious sins] in the Church of Jesus Christ, full and effective confession would . . . require confession by the repentant sinner to his bishop" (Marion G. Romney, in Conference Report, October 1955, 125).

MOSIAH 26:30

"As often as my people repent will I forgive them."

"I repeat, save for the exception of the very few who defect to perdition, there is no habit, no addiction, no rebellion, no transgression, no apostasy, no crime exempted from the promise of complete forgiveness. That is the promise of the atonement of Christ" (Boyd K. Packer, *Ensign*, November 1995, 20). *See also Alma 5:33.*

"I believe that our Heavenly Father wants to save every one of his children. . . .

"I believe that in his justice and mercy he will give us the maximum reward for our acts, give us all that he can give, and in the reverse, I believe that he will impose upon us the minimum penalty which it is possible for him to impose" (J. Reuben Clark Jr., in Conference Report, October 1953, 84).

MOSIAH 26:31

"Ye shall also forgive one another your trespasses."

"Remember that we must forgive even if our offender did not repent and ask forgiveness. . . . Do we follow that commandment or do we sulk in our bitterness, waiting for our offender to learn of it and to kneel to us in remorse?

"And this reconciliation suggests also forgetting. Unless you forget, have you forgiven? . . .

"No bitterness of past frictions can be held in memory if we forgive with all our hearts" (Spencer W. Kimball, in Conference Report, October 1949, 132). *See also Matthew 6:14–15; D&C 64:9–11.*

MOSIAH 26:32, 36

What does it mean to not be numbered among the church?

"The scriptures speak of Church members being 'cast out' or 'cut off,' or having their names 'blotted out.' This means excommunication. This dread action means the total severance of the individual from the Church. The person who is excommunicated loses his membership in the Church and all attendant blessings. As an excommunicant, he is in a worse situation than he was before he joined the Church. He has lost the Holy Ghost, his priesthood, his endowments, his sealings, his privileges, and his claim upon eternal life" (Spencer W. Kimball, *Teachings*, 100). *See also D&C 42:28.*

"The Lord is on your side and you must remember that numerous people are saved by excommunication. They are not *lost* by excommunication. They are *saved* through excommunication" (Spencer W. Kimball, *Teachings*, 98; emphasis in original).

MOSIAH 26:39

What is the value in giving "thanks in all things"?

See insights for Mosiah 24:21–22.

MOSIAH 27

MOSIAH 27:1–2

Why do we experience persecutions?

"There was a time when we were driven by mobs, and our faith was tried in various ways. It is necessary that there should still be trials to test the faith of this people. There are no mobs now, we do not have our houses burnt down now, or our cattle shot down. But shall we be without trials? No. . . . It is necessary you should be tried for a while in order to develop your strength" (George Q. Cannon, *Journal of Discourses*, 22:109).

MOSIAH 27:2–3

How important is freedom of religion?

"Freedom of worship is one of the basic doctrines of the gospel. Indeed, in one manner of speaking it is the most basic of all doctrines, even taking precedence over the nature and kind of being that God is, or the atoning sacrifice of the son of God" (Bruce R. McConkie, *New Witness for the Articles of Faith*, 655). *See also Articles of Faith 1:11.*

MOSIAH 27:14, 22–23

How effective are the prayers of others in our behalf?

"We learn that there is majestic, undeniable power in the love and prayer of a parent. The angel who appeared to Alma and the sons of Mosiah did not come in response to any righteousness on their part. . . . He came in response to the prayers of a faithful parent" (Jeffrey R. Holland, *However Long and Hard the Road*, 81).

MOSIAH 27:22–23

What benefits come to those who fast and pray?

"A certain kind of devil goes not out except by fasting and prayer, the scriptures tell us. (See Matt. 17:14–21.) Periodic fasting can help clear up the mind and strengthen the body and the spirit. . . . To make a fast most fruitful, it should be coupled with prayer and meditation" (Ezra Taft Benson, *Ensign*, October 1986, 4).

MOSIAH 27:24–28

What difference is there in the lives of those who are "born again"?

"No person whose soul is illuminated by the burning Spirit of God can in this world of sin and dense darkness remain passive. He is driven by an irresistible urge to fit himself to be an active agent of God in furthering righteousness" (Marion G. Romney, in Conference Report, October 1941, 89). *See also Mosiah 5:2.*

"When we have undergone this mighty change, . . . it is as though we have become a new person. . . . You have forsaken lives of sin . . . and through applying the blood of Christ in your lives, have become clean. You have no more disposition to return to your old ways. You are in reality a new person" (Ezra Taft Benson, *Teachings*, 470).

MOSIAH 27:28–29

"Wading through much tribulation, repenting nigh unto death"

See insights for Alma 36:11–13.

Does serious sin take away all opportunity for the Lord's mercy?

"If you have made a serious mistake in your life and Satan would have you believe that your opportunity for true joy and happiness is past, study the lives of Alma the younger and his companions, the sons of Mosiah. (See Mosiah 27; Alma 5:3–62.) When the process of repentance is complete, you can rejoice with a new heart and unlimited opportunity for happiness" (Richard G. Scott, *Ensign*, October 1984, 10).

MOSIAH 27:32–35

Is it necessary to "repair all . . . injuries" in order to repent?

"There are many things which a repentant soul can do to make amends.

'A broken heart and a contrite spirit' will usually find ways to restore to some extent. The true spirit of repentance demands that he who injures shall do everything in his power to right the wrong" (Spencer W. Kimball, *Miracle of Forgiveness*, 192). *See also Leviticus 6:4.*

MOSIAH 27:37

Why did the sons of Mosiah "publish good tidings"?

"After conversion comes the desire to share—not so much out of a sense of duty, even though that responsibility falls on the priesthood, but out of a sincere love and appreciation for that which has been received. When such a 'pearl of great price' comes into our lives, we cannot be content just to admire it by ourselves. It must be shared! And here is the great joy and happiness of the gift!" (L. Tom Perry, *Ensign*, May 1984, 79).

MOSIAH 28

MOSIAH 28:1-3

What is the primary purpose for sharing the gospel?

"To serve the Lord as a full-time missionary is a privilege; the primary purpose of full-time missionary service is the building up of the kingdom of God" (David B. Haight, *Ensign*, November 1993, 62).

MOSIAH 28:10

What sacrifices did the sons of Mosiah make to serve missions?

"The four missionary sons of Mosiah did not choose the easy course. Their choice was neither convenient, nor popular: They gave up the kingship. . . . They were ridiculed even by other members of the Church. . . . Their choice to serve a mission was not one of convenience" (Harold G. Hillam, *Ensign*, November 1995, 41).

MOSIAH 28:17-19

What was the account on these records?

"Limhi brought to Mosiah a record . . . which record Mosiah translated . . . and which gave an account of the Jaredites. In translating this record Mosiah kept from going forth to the people that particular part forbidden of the Lord. . . . When Moroni made his abridgment of the record of Ether, he copied on his record the vision of the brother of Jared. . . . However, Moroni also sealed up the greater things in this vision . . . [which] should not be made known even in our day" (Joseph Fielding Smith, *Answers to Gospel Questions*, 1:161–62).

MOSIAH 29

MOSIAH 29:7-36

What are the advantages of democracy over monarchy?

"A monarchy is a good system of government *if* the people can be assured they will always have good and righteous kings. (Mosiah 23:8.) However, the weakness of a monarchy is that 'ye cannot dethrone an iniquitous king save it be through much contention, and the shedding of much blood.' (Mosiah 29:21.)

". . . The value of this system of democratic government is that 'it is not common that the voice of the people desireth anything contrary to that which is right.' (Mosiah 29:26)" (Daniel H. Ludlow, *Companion*, 193).

DISADVANTAGES OF AN UNRIGHTEOUS MONARCHY	ADVANTAGES OF A DEMOCRACY
Contentions, anger, wars, shedding much blood, perverting the ways of the Lord (v. 7)	Peace (v. 10)
Much sin (v. 9)	Seek for wise leaders (v. 11)
Iniquity and great destruction (v. 17)	Choose leaders by the desires of the majority of the people (v. 25)
Bondage (v. 18)	The majority usually choose the right (v. 26)
Can't dethrone wicked king without bloodshed (v. 21)	If leaders are wicked they can be removed without bloodshed (vv. 28–29)
Destruction of righteous laws (v. 22)	The people have liberties, rights, and privileges of equality (v. 32)
Wickedness becomes the law (v. 23)	The people carry some responsibilities for the government (v. 34)
Wicked kings will answer for the wickedness of their people (v. 31)	
Inequality is the rule (v. 32)	
Stealing, plundering and whoredoms (v. 36)	

MOSIAH 29:13, 16

"Because all men are not just it is not expedient that ye should have . . . kings."

"It is the nature and disposition of almost all men, as soon as they get a little authority, as they suppose, they will immediately begin to exercise unrighteous dominion" (D&C 121:39).

MOSIAH 29:25, 39

How can we best choose our political leaders?

"We believe that . . . civil officers . . . that . . . administer the law in equity and justice should be sought for and upheld by the voice of the people" (D&C 134:3).

MOSIAH 29:27

What will happen if the "voice of the people" chooses iniquity?

"There is no power that can wreck the government that God has established in this country unless it be the people themselves" (Anthony W. Ivins, in Conference Report, October 1932, 108).

MOSIAH 29:32, 39

What caused the people in these verses to rejoice?

"A lot of us take our civil rights for granted. We were born in a free country. We think freedom could never end. But it could. . . .

"The only way we can keep our freedom is to work at it. Not some of us. All of us. Not some of the time, but all of the time. . . .

"Give it your faith, your belief, and give it your active support in civic affairs" (Spencer W. Kimball, *Teachings*, 405).

MOSIAH 29:42

What did it mean that Alma was the "first chief judge" as well as the "high priest"?

"This theocratic system, patterned after the order and system that prevailed in heaven, was the government of God. . . . He gave direction in all things both civil and ecclesiastical; there was no separation of church and state" (Bruce R. McConkie, *New Witness for the Articles of Faith*, 35).

THE BOOK OF
ALMA

ALMA 1

ALMA 1:3

Which priest or teacher should be "supported by the people"?

"From the sectarian view, the true Church has a *lay ministry*, meaning that bishops and other church officers do not receive financial compensation for their work. . . . From the Lord's view, his Church is a 'kingdom of priests' in which every worthy and qualified man is a minister" (Bruce R. McConkie, *Mormon Doctrine*, 505).

ALMA 1:3, 19–22

Do those who persecute the Church really hurt it?

"Every time they persecute . . . this people, they elevate us, . . . and strengthen the hands and arms of this people. And every time they undertake to lessen our number, they increase it. . . . Righteousness and power with God increase in this people in proportion as the Devil struggles to destroy it" (Brigham Young, *Discourses*, 351).

ALMA 1:4

Why is the idea that "all mankind should be saved" so appealing?

"Nehor's words appealed to many of the people; they were easy words because they required neither obedience nor sacrifice. As we face many decisions in life, the easy and popular messages of the world will seem appealing. But . . . it will take great courage to choose the right" (L. Tom Perry, *Living with Enthusiasm*, 108–9).

ALMA 1:6

What is wrong with wearing "costly apparel"?

"Worldly styles and fashions . . . are improper and to be avoided. Almost always the apparel so involved is excessively costly, with those who wear it being lifted up in the pride of their hearts" (Bruce R. McConkie, *Doctrinal New Testament Commentary*, 3:80).

ALMA 1:12, 16

What do riches and honor have to do with "priestcraft"?

"Priesthood and priestcraft are two opposites. . . . When [ministers'] inter-est is in gaining personal popularity and financial gain, . . . they are engaged, in a greater or lesser degree, in the practice of priestcrafts" (Bruce R. McConkie, Mormon Doctrine, 593).

ALMA 1:26

Who is considered "equal" in the Church?

"In the Lord's Church the members are a congregation of equals; . . . every man and woman may speak in the name of God the Lord . . . (see D&C 1:20). The bishop perhaps is a plumber, while his clerk is the vice president of a large corporation" (Joseph Fielding McConkie and Robert L. Millet, Doctrinal Commentary, 3: 10).

ALMA 1:27-31

What blessings come to those who are willing to "impart of their substance"?

"The scriptures contain many evidences of the Lord's willingness to pros-per his people with the riches of the earth when they demonstrate that they will use this abundance prudently, with humility and charity, always acknowl-edging the source of their blessings" (Dean L. Larsen, Ensign, November 1992, 40).

ALMA 2

ALMA 2:2-3

What are the differences between a government ruled by a king and a democracy?

See insights for Mosiah 29:7–36.

ALMA 2:8-10

What makes anger such a serious sin?

"Anger is a yielding to Satan's influence by surrendering our self-control. It is the thought-sin that leads to hostile . . . behavior. . . . Unchecked, anger can quickly trigger an explosion of cruel words and other forms of . . . abuse" (Lynn G. Robbins, Ensign, May 1998, 80–81). *See also Alma 19:21–22; 3 Nephi 12:21–22.*

ALMA 2:17, 25

When is war justified?

See insights for Alma 43:9, 26, 30, 45–50; 44:5; 46:12; 48:10, 24.

ALMA 2:18, 28, 31, 35

Where does safety come from in times of conflict?

"Where is there safety in the world today? Safety can't be won by tanks and guns and the airplanes and atomic bombs. There is only one place of safety and that is within the realm of the power of Almighty God that he gives to those who keep his commandments" (Harold B. Lee, *Ensign*, January 1974, 128).

ALMA 3

ALMA 3:4, 10, 13

Both anciently and in the modern day, the wicked have "marked themselves."

"Young women, you do not need to drape rings up and down your ears. One modest pair of earrings is sufficient. . . . A young man . . . does not need tattoos or earrings on or in his body. The First Presidency and the Quorum of the Twelve are all united in counseling against these things" (Gordon B. Hinckley, *New Era*, January 2001, 11). *See Alma 23:16; 27:27 for how the righteous also distinguish themselves.*

ALMA 3:6–14

The Lamanites were cursed and marked by the Lord.

There was a difference between the curse and the mark of dark skin placed upon the Lamanites. This difference is emphasized by the use of the conjuction "and" rather than "or" in verses 7 and 14. *See also insights for 2 Nephi 5:20–24.*

THE CURSE	THE MARK OF THE DARK SKIN
The curse was that the Lamanites were "cut off from [God's] presence" (2 Nephi 5:20).	The "skin of blackness" was given so that the Lamanites "might not be enticing" to the Nephites (2 Nephi 5:21).

ALMA 3:18–19

How and why are some people cursed?

"He had caused the cursing to come upon them . . . because of their iniquity" (2 Nephi 5:21).

ALMA 3:26–27

We "reap eternal happiness or eternal misery, according to the spirit" that we follow.

"What is this life? . . . The Latter-day Saints are living for things [on] the other side of the vail. . . . Our eternal destiny depends upon the manner in which we spend our short lives here in the flesh" (Wilford Woodruff, *Journal of Discourses*, 17:194).

ALMA 4

ALMA 4:2

Is it appropriate to feel "greatly afflicted" when we lose a loved one?

"Thou shalt live together in love, . . . thou shalt weep for the loss of them that die" (D&C 42:45).

ALMA 4:6

How can people be wealthy and remain faithful?

"Many people who remained faithful . . . while they were poor may be unable to stand when they are rich. Riches [have] a very corrupting effect upon the human heart, and it requires a very pure people to be as honest, virtuous, humble and upright when surrounded by luxury and wealth" (George Q. Cannon, *Gospel Truth*, 525).

They were "lifted up in the pride of their eyes."

See insights for Helaman 11:37.

ALMA 4:11

How important is it to be a good example?

"How much easier it is to understand and accept if the seeker after truth can also see the principles of the gospel at work in the lives of other believers. No greater service can be given to the missionary calling of this Church than to be exemplary in positive Christian virtues in our lives" (Spencer W. Kimball, *Teachings*, 555). *See also insights for 2 Nephi 31:7–10, 12–13, 16.*

ALMA 4:20

Another name for the Melchizedek Priesthood is "the holy order of God."

See insights for Alma 13:1–2, 6–11, 14.

ALMA 5

ALMA 5:1–62

"Have ye spiritually been born of God?"

"In what is without question the greatest sermon of which we have knowledge on the subject of being 'born of God,' our friend Alma reasons on this matter of being saved through the blood of Christ" (Bruce R. McConkie, *Promised Messiah*, 251).

ALMA 5:3, 44

"I, Alma, having been consecrated by my father, Alma, to be a high priest."

"We believe that a man must be called of God, by prophecy, and by the laying on of hands by those who are in authority, to preach the Gospel and administer in the ordinances thereof" (Articles of Faith 1:5).

ALMA 5:6-59

Alma's forty-two questions give a step-by-step formula for how to be born again.

"Do we frequently review the crucial questions which Alma asks the members of the Church in the fifth chapter of Alma in the Book of Mormon?" (Ezra Taft Benson, *Ensign*, May 1987, 85).

"Changes in the heart and soul occur as a result of planting and nourishing the seed. Scripture study, prayer, obedience, and service are key elements in building faith in Christ" (Merrill J. Bateman, *Ensign*, November 1992, 28).

ALMA 5:6-7

God is the one who delivers our souls from hell and changes our hearts.

"A new heart also will I give you, and a new spirit will I put within you: and I will take away the stony heart out of your flesh, and I will give you an heart of flesh" (Ezekiel 36:26).

"The Lord works from the inside out. The world works from the outside in. The world would take people out of the slums. Christ takes the slums out of people, and then they take themselves out of the slums. The world would mold men by changing their environment. Christ changes men, who then change their environment. The world would shape human behavior, but Christ can change human nature" (Ezra Taft Benson, *Ensign*, July 1989, 4).

ALMA 5:9-10

What caused them to be loosed from the "bands of death" and the "chains of hell"?

"The Atonement . . . brings an additional kind of rebirth, something of immediate renewal, help, and hope that allow us to rise above sorrows and sickness, misfortunes. . . . With his mighty arm around us and lifting us, we face life more joyfully even as we face death more triumphantly" (Jeffrey R. Holland, *Christ and the New Covenant*, 224).

ALMA 5:14, 26

What is the spiritual change of heart?

"The verb, 'convert,' means 'to turn from one belief or course to another.' That 'conversion' is 'a spiritual and moral change attending a change of belief with conviction.' As used in the scriptures, 'converted' generally implies . . . a motivating faith in [Christ] and in his gospel—a faith which works a transformation, an actual change in one's understanding of life's meaning and in his allegiance to God—in interest, in thought, and in conduct. While conversion may be accomplished in stages, one is not really converted in the full sense of the term unless and until he is at heart a new person. 'Born again' is the scriptural term" (Marion G. Romney, in Conference Report, October 1963, 23).

ALMA 5:15-18, 22

Some day we will all be judged "before the tribunal of God."

"I tell you the Lord is taking account of us. We are individually in His presence. . . . The Lord . . . will take note of us, and will record our works and our deeds. Thank God for that . . . principle of the gospel of Jesus Christ, that every one of us will have to give an account for the deeds we do in the flesh, and that every man will be rewarded according to his works, whether they be good or evil" (in James R. Clark, comp., *Messages of the First Presidency*, 5:86).

ALMA 5:26

"If ye have experienced a change of heart . . . can ye feel so now?"

"This is a call to keep our witness and our experience with the Spirit current and up to date. . . . We cannot afford to pause and homestead on spiritual plateaus. Our task is to move on, to progress" (Joseph Fielding McConkie and Robert L. Millet, *Doctrinal Commentary*, 3:32).

ALMA 5:32-33, 49-51

How integral is repentance to the message of the gospel?

"Say nothing but repentance unto this generation" (D&C 6:9).

"The mission of The Church of Jesus Christ of Latter-day Saints is to call people everywhere to repentance" (Spencer W. Kimball, *Miracle of Forgiveness*, 367).

ALMA 5:34

What is the bread and water that we can partake of freely?

"Jesus said unto them, I am the bread of life" (John 6:35).

"Saith the Lord . . . my people have committed two evils; they have forsaken me the fountain of living waters" (Jeremiah 2:9, 13).

ALMA 5:37-39, 60

Who will hear the voice of the good shepherd?

"Christ is . . . the Good Shepherd. . . . *His saints* are the sheep; his sheepfold is the Church of Jesus Christ; . . . 'and he shall feed his sheep, and in him they shall find pasture.' (1 Ne. 22:25)" (Bruce R. McConkie, *Mormon Doctrine*, 328; emphasis in original). *See also John 10:27.*

ALMA 5:40

"Whatsoever is good cometh from God, and whatsoever is evil cometh from the devil."

See insights for Moroni 7:12–13, 16–17.

ALMA 5:43

Why should we teach the gospel in plain terms?

"President Harold B. Lee, frequently challenged those who teach the gospel to do so in such a manner that their students would not only understand what they had been taught but also could not misunderstand the principles taught" (Joseph Fielding McConkie and Robert L. Millet, *Doctrinal Commentary*, 3:39).

ALMA 5:45

What does it mean to testify the gospel is true?

"To bear one's testimony is to make a solemn declaration, affirmation or attestation that personal revelation has been received certifying to the truth of those realities which comprise a testimony" (Bruce R. McConkie, *Mormon Doctrine*, 786).

ALMA 5:46

How can we gain a testimony for ourselves?

"You may *know*. You need not be in doubt. Follow the prescribed procedures, and you may have an absolute knowledge that these things are absolute truths. The necessary procedure is: study, think, pray, and do. Revelation is the key. God will make it known to you" (Spencer W. Kimball, *Teachings*, 63; emphasis in original).

ALMA 5:49

How essential is it that we be born again?

"To gain salvation in the celestial kingdom men must be born again (Alma 7:14); born of water and of the Spirit (John 3:1–13); born of God, so that they are changed, . . . becoming new creatures" (Bruce R. McConkie, *Mormon Doctrine*, 100).

ALMA 5:52

What is the meaning of "an unquenchable fire"?

See insights for Alma 41:7.

ALMA 5:58

What is the "book of life"?

"The *book of life*, or *Lamb's book of Life*, is the record kept in heaven which contains the names of the faithful and an account of their righteous covenants and deeds" (Bruce R. McConkie, *Mormon Doctrine*, 97; emphasis in original).

What difference does it really make if some speak against the Church?

"This is God's work. He is in it. He is with those who lead it. . . . The great and glorious caravan, the Church of the living God, is moving onward and forward to the accomplishment of its great purposes. And let the dogs bark. They amount to little when they fight God" (Melvin J. Ballard, in Conference Report, April 1921, 108).

ALMA 6

ALMA 6:3

What does it mean when some have "their names . . . blotted out"?

See insights for Mosiah 26:32, 36.

ALMA 6:6

"They should gather . . . together oft, and join in fasting and mighty prayer."

See insights for Moroni 6:5–6; Mosiah 27:22–23.

ALMA 6:7

What are the benefits of having organized regulations?

"Any man who is imbued with the spirit of this Gospel will understand that God has established an order in His Church, for its guidance and government" (Charles W. Penrose, in Conference Report, October 1915, 40). *See also D&C 88:119.*

ALMA 7

ALMA 7:7

The Redeemer is more important than anything else.

"The fundamental principles of our religion are the testimony of the Apostles and Prophets, concerning Jesus Christ, that He died, was buried, and rose again the third day, and ascended into heaven; and all other things which pertain to our religion are only appendages to it" (Joseph Smith, *Teachings*, 121). *See also insights for Jacob 4:11–12.*

ALMA 7:10

How important was Mary, the mother of Jesus?

See insights for 1 Nephi 11:15.

Was Jesus the son of the Father or of the Holy Ghost?

"Jesus is the Son of God, not of the Holy Ghost. . . . Alma perfectly describes our Lord's conception and birth by prophesying: Christ 'shall be born of Mary . . . who shall be overshadowed and *conceive by the power of the Holy Ghost,* and bring forth a son, yea, even *the Son of God.*' (Alma 7:10.) Nephi spoke similarly when he said that at the time of her conception, Mary 'was carried away in the Spirit'" (Bruce R. McConkie, *Doctrinal New Testament Commentary,* 1:82–83; emphasis in original).

ALMA 7:11

How did Jesus know "temptations" better than anyone else?

"C. S. Lewis also wrote: 'A silly idea is current that good people do not know what temptation means. This is an obvious lie. Only those who try to resist temptation know how strong it is. . . . You find out the strength of a wind by trying to walk against it, not by lying down'" (*Mere Christianity,* New York: Macmillan, 1960, 124; quoted in James E. Faust, *Ensign,* November 1987, 35).

ALMA 7:11–13

Jesus suffered all pains, afflictions, temptations, sicknesses, death, infirmities, and sins.

"Jesus' daily mortal experiences and His ministry, to be sure, acquainted Him by observation with a sample of human sicknesses, grief, pains, sorrows, and infirmities which are 'common to man' (1 Corinthians 10:13). But the agonies of the Atonement were infinite and first-hand! Since not all human sorrow and pain is connected to sin, the full intensiveness of the Atonement involved bearing our pains, infirmities, and sicknesses, as well as our sins. Whatever our sufferings, we can safely cast our 'care upon him; for he careth for [us]' (1 Peter 5:7)" (Neal A. Maxwell, *"Not My Will, But Thine,"* 51).

"The Savior's atonement is . . . the healing power not only for sin, but also for carelessness, inadequacy, and all mortal bitterness. The Atonement is not just for sinners" (Bruce C. Hafen, *Ensign,* April 1990, 7). *See also D&C 19:18.*

"[Jesus Christ] knows the deepest and most personal burdens we carry. He knows the most public and poignant pains we bear. He descended below all such grief in order that he might lift us above it. There is no anguish or sorrow or sadness in life that he has not suffered in our behalf" (Jeffrey R. Holland, *Christ and the New Covenant,* 224).

ALMA 7:12

How did Jesus "loose the bands of death which bind his people"?

See insights for Alma 11:43–44.

How does Jesus succor his people?

"Elder Talmage used the word *succor.* Do you know its meaning? It is used often in the scriptures to describe Christ's care for and attention to us. It means literally 'to run to.' What a magnificent way to describe the Savior's urgent effort in our behalf! . . . He is unfailingly running to help us" (Jeffrey R. Holland, *Ensign*, April 1998, 22; emphasis in original).

ALMA 7:15

"Show unto your God that ye are willing to repent of your sins."
See insights for Mosiah 5:5, 8, 11–12.

ALMA 7:17, 19–20

How valuable is the ability to perceive?
"The gift of discernment is essential to the leadership of the Church. . . .
". . . Every member in the restored Church of Christ could have this gift if he willed to do so. . . . With this gift they would be able to detect something of the disloyal, rebellious, and sinister influences" (Stephen L Richards, in Conference Report, April 1950, 163). *See insights for Alma 10:17.*

ALMA 7:20

"His course is one eternal round."
"God's course is one eternal round but it is not one monotonous round. God is never bored. . . . There is always so much to notice, so much to do, so many ways to help, so many possibilities to pursue" (Neal A. Maxwell, *A More Excellent Way*, 84–85).

ALMA 7:23

What are the attributes of a Saint?
"We are to develop certain eternal attributes. . . . A saint is one who is meek, humble, patient, full of love, and who is sufficiently submissive that he can cope with 'all things which the Lord seeth fit to inflict upon him even as a child doth submit to his father.' (Mosiah 3:19.) Parallel insights occur in Alma, who stressed our need to become humble, submissive, gentle, easy to be entreated, and patient" (Neal A. Maxwell, *We Will Prove Them Herewith*, 61).

ALMA 7:25

What are the ultimate blessings of Abraham, Isaac, and Jacob?
"Abraham . . . Isaac also and Jacob . . . have entered into their exaltation, according to the promises, and sit upon thrones, and are not angels but are gods" (D&C 132:37).

ALMA 8

ALMA 8:9, 11

Why would Satan seek to get a "great hold upon the hearts of the people"?

"I will tell you in your mind and in your heart, by the Holy Ghost, . . . which shall dwell in your heart" (D&C 8:2). Because the heart serves as the seat of our desires and the source of our communication with the Lord, it is little wonder that Satan focuses his efforts on the hearts of men. *See also insights for 4 Nephi 1:15, 28, 31, 34.*

ALMA 8:13

People typically reject missionaries more often than they accept them.

"In June 1830, Samuel Harrison Smith trudged down a country road in New York State on the first official missionary journey of the restored Church. He had been set apart by his brother, the Prophet Joseph. This first missionary traveled twenty-five miles that first day without disposing of a single copy of the new and strange book that he carried on his back. Seeking lodging for the night, faint and hungry, he was turned away, after briefly explaining his mission, with the words: 'You liar, get out of my house. You shan't stay one minute with your books.' Continuing his journey, discouraged and with heavy heart, he slept that first night under an apple tree" (Ezra Taft Benson, *Teachings*, 188).

ALMA 8:14

What is the cause of most of the sorrow described in the scriptures?

"The pain most frequently spoken of in the scriptures is the pain and anguish of the Lord and His prophets for the disobedient souls" (Robert D. Hales, *Ensign*, November 1998, 15).

It is often when we are weighed down with tribulation that the Lord is closest to us.

"Sometimes when you are going through the most severe tests, you will be nearer to God than you have any idea, for like the experience of the Master Himself in the temptation on the mount, in the Garden of Gethsemane, and on the cross at Calvary, . . . 'And, behold, angels came and ministered unto him' (Matthew 4:11). Sometimes that may happen to you in the midst of your trials" (Harold B. Lee, *Teachings*, 192).

ALMA 8:19-21

The Lord often answers our prayers through another person.

"God does notice us, and he watches over us. But it is usually through another person that he meets our needs. Therefore, it is vital that we serve each other in the kingdom. . . . Often, our acts of service consist of simple encouragement or of giving mundane help with mundane tasks, but what glorious consequences can flow from mundane acts and from small but deliberate deeds!" (Spencer W. Kimball, *Ensign*, December 1974, 5).

ALMA 8:30–31

Where does power come from?

"Your authority comes through your ordination; your power comes through obedience and worthiness" (Boyd K. Packer, *Ensign*, November 1981, 32).

ALMA 9

ALMA 9:2–3

When shall the earth pass away?

See D&C 130:9; insights for Ether 13:9.

ALMA 9:8–10, 13–14

What seems to be necessary for us not to forget God?

"Except the Lord doth chasten his people with many afflictions, yea, except he doth visit them with death and with terror, and with famine and with all manner of pestilence, they will not remember him" (Helaman 12:3). *See also insights for Helaman 5:5–14.*

ALMA 9:14

Those who do not keep the commandments are "cut off from . . . the Lord."

See insights for 2 Nephi 5:20–21.

ALMA 9:15–23

Why would it be more tolerable for wicked Lamanites than for fallen Nephites?

"Those who do not profess to know anything of the Lord are far better off than we are, unless we live our religion, for we who know the Master's will and do it not, will be beaten with many stripes; while they who do not know the master's will and do it not will be beaten with few stripes" (Brigham Young, *Journal of Discourses*, 16:111–12).

ALMA 9:16–17, 24

"There are many promises . . . extended to the Lamanites."

"At the time that the Prophet Joseph Smith translated this Book of Mormon, I suppose the impression was general, as it is to-day, that the Indians were a perishing race, that they would soon disappear from the face of the land" (George Q. Cannon, *Journal of Discourses*, 25:124). *See also Mormon 7:1–10.*

ALMA 9:28

When shall "men . . . reap a reward of their works"?

See insights for Mosiah 4:30.

ALMA 9:31-32

Why were the people upset when Alma called them stiffnecked?

"The guilty taketh the truth to be hard, for it cutteth them to the very center" (1 Nephi 16:2).

Alma 10

ALMA 10:2

What was "the writing . . . upon the wall of the temple"?

"This is the only time Aminadi is mentioned, and our present Book of Mormon gives no further details concerning the writing written by the finger of God upon the wall of the temple" (Daniel H. Ludlow, *Companion*, 198).

ALMA 10:3

"Lehi . . . was a descendant of Manasseh."

See insights for 1 Nephi 7:1–5.

ALMA 10:5-6

Why would Amulek not hear the promptings of the Lord?

"He is a classic case of an essentially good man being out of touch with the great spiritual realities; . . . because, though he was basically good, he was preoccupied with the cares of the world" (Neal A. Maxwell, *Meek and Lowly*, 12).

ALMA 10:7-10, 20

In what way do angels minister to men today?

"But the ministering of angels can also be unseen. Angelic messages can be delivered by a voice or merely by thoughts or feelings communicated to the mind. . . . Most angelic communications are felt or heard rather than seen" (Dallin H. Oaks, *Ensign*, November 1998, 39). *See also Alma 12:29.*

ALMA 10:12

"There was more than one witness who testified."

"The Lord . . . operates through a law called the law of witnesses. This law provides that in the mouth of two or three witnesses shall the truth of His word be established in all ages" (Ezra Taft Benson, *Teachings*, 50). *See also D&C 6:28; 2 Nephi 27:12–14; Matthew 18:16.*

ALMA 10:17

How could Amulek know of the people's designs and perceive their thoughts?

"The gift of discernment . . . when highly developed arises largely out of an acute sensitivity to . . . spiritual impressions . . . to read under the surface as it were, to detect hidden evil, and more importantly to find the good that may be concealed" (Stephen L Richards, in Conference Report, April 1950, 162). *See also insights for Alma 7:17, 19–20.*

ALMA 10:22-23, 27

What difference do the actions of a few righteous people make?

"Our world is now much the same as it was in the days of the Nephite prophet. . . . Of course, there are many many upright and faithful who live all the commandments and whose lives and prayers keep the world from destruction" (Spencer W. Kimball, *Ensign*, June 1971, 16).

"You are so very important. This work is so much the stronger because of you. Whenever you step over the line in an immoral act or in doing any other evil thing, the Church is that much weaker because of what you have done. When you stand true and faithful, it is that much stronger. Each one of you counts" (Gordon B. Hinckley, *Ensign*, May 1996, 94). *See also Genesis 18:23; Alma 62:40; insights for Mosiah 27:14, 22–23.*

ALMA 10:32

"The object of these lawyers was to get gain."

See insights for Alma 11:20, 24.

ALMA 11

ALMA 11:3-19

"This is the value of . . . their reckoning."

Gold	Silver	Measure of Grain
Not mentioned	Leah	⅛ measure
Not mentioned	Shiblum	¼ measure
Not mentioned	Shiblon	½ measure
Senine	Senum	1 measure
Antion	Not mentioned	1½ measure
Seon	Amnor	2 measure
Shum	Ezrom	4 measure
Limnah	Onti	7 measure

"This system of weights and measures used in Central America today is similar to the Nephite monetary system" (Thomas R. Valletta, ed., *Book of Mormon for Latter-day Saint Families*, 294).

ALMA 11:20, 24

The love of money caused the people to riot against Alma and Amulek.

"The *Wall Street Journal acknowledged*, 'Money is an article which may be used as a universal passport to everywhere except heaven, and as a universal provider of everything except happiness.' Henrik Ibsen wrote, 'Money may buy the husk of many things, but not the kernel. It brings you food, but not the appetite; medicine, but not health; acquaintances, but not friends; servants, but not faithfulness; days of joy, but not peace or happiness'" (James E. Faust, *To Reach Even Unto You*, 8; emphasis in original).

ALMA 11:28-29

In what way is there no more than one God?

"Zeezrom . . . asks whether there is more than one God. Amulek answers that there is not. Amulek is, of course, speaking entirely of the Savior, of the Lord Jehovah. . . . That same Jehovah had spoken anciently to Isaiah: 'I, even I, am the Lord; and beside me there is no saviour' (Isaiah 43:11)" (Joseph Fielding McConkie and Robert L. Millet, *Doctrinal Commentary*, 3:76).

ALMA 11:34

Jesus will not "save his people in their sins."

"Remember also the words which Amulek spake unto Zeezrom, in the city of Ammonihah; for he said unto him that the Lord surely should come to redeem his people, but that he should not come to redeem them in their sins, but to redeem them from their sins" (Helaman 5:10).

ALMA 11:37

"No unclean thing can inherit the kingdom of heaven."

"Cleanliness, it is said, is a part of godliness. No unclean thing—and I think that means cleanliness of person, cleanliness of body, as well as cleanliness of heart, and cleanliness of spirit—no unclean thing can enter into the presence of God" (Joseph F. Smith, in Conference Report, April 1914, 8).

ALMA 11:38-39

How is "the Son of God the very Eternal Father"?

See insights for Mosiah 15:2–5.

ALMA 11:39

How is Jesus "the beginning and the end, the first and the last"?

See insights for 1 Nephi 20:12.

ALMA 11:41–42, 44

Who "shall rise from the dead"?

"In the resurrection from the dead, when all shall be raised, 'every man in his order,' the spirit and the body will be joined together, and they will 'not die after;' we are there told that the resurrection will come to all mankind, the great and the small, the good and the bad, all races and tribes" (Charles W. Penrose, in Conference Report, October 1911, 49).

When will the resurrection occur?

See insights for Alma 40:4, 8–9, 16, 18–19.

ALMA 11:43–44

How perfect are resurrected bodies?

"Deformity will be removed; defects will be eliminated, and men and women shall attain to the perfection . . . that God designed in the beginning. It is his purpose that men and women, his children, . . . shall be made perfect, physically as well as spiritually" (Joseph F. Smith, *Gospel Doctrine*, 23).

ALMA 11:45

Can a resurrected body ever die again?

"After the resurrection from the dead our bodies will be spiritual bodies, but they will be bodies that are tangible, bodies that have been purified, but they will nevertheless be bodies of flesh and bones. They will not be blood bodies. They will no longer be quickened by blood but quickened by the spirit which is eternal, and they shall become immortal and shall never die" (Joseph Fielding Smith, *Doctrines of Salvation*, 2:285). *See also insights for Alma 41:2, 12.*

What form of your body will you have in the resurrection?

"The body will come forth as it is laid to rest, for there is no growth or development in the grave. As it is laid down, so will it arise, and changes to perfection will come by the law of restitution. . . . The body, after the resurrection will develop to the full stature of man" (Joseph F. Smith, in Joseph Smith, *Teachings*, 200 n. 4). *See also D&C 88:28.*

"A question may be asked—'Will mothers have their children in eternity?' Yes! Yes! Mothers, you shall have your children; for they shall have eternal life, for their debt is paid. There is no damnation awaiting them for they are in the spirit. But as the child dies, so shall it rise from the dead. . . . It will never grow [in the grave]; it will still be the child, in the same precise form [when it rises] as . . . before it died" (in James R. Clark, comp., *Messages of the First Presidency,* 1:223).

The resurrection is an ordinance.

"We are in possession of all the ordinances that can be administered in the flesh; but there are other ordinances and administrations that must be administered beyond this world. . . . We have not, neither can we receive here, the ordinance and the keys of the resurrection. They will be given to those who have passed off this stage of action . . . They will be ordained, by those who hold the keys of the resurrection, to go forth and resurrect the Saints" (Brigham Young, *Discourses,* 397).

ALMA 12

ALMA 12:3, 7

Who can know our thoughts?

See insights for Jacob 2:5; Alma 10:17.

ALMA 12:9

When is it appropriate to share sacred mysteries of God?

"I have learned that strong, impressive spiritual experiences do not come to us very frequently. And when they do, they are generally for our own edification, instruction, or correction. Unless we are called by proper authority to do so, they do not position us to counsel or to correct others" (Boyd K. Packer, *Ensign,* January 1983, 53).

"Should you receive a vision or revelation from the Almighty, one that the Lord gave you concerning yourselves, . . . you should shut it up and seal it as closed, and lock it as tight as heaven is to you, and make it as secret as the grave. The Lord has no confidence in those who reveal secrets, for he cannot safely reveal himself to such persons" (Brigham Young, *Discourses,* 40–41). *See also D&C* 63:64.

ALMA 12:14

How could "our words . . . our works . . . and our thoughts . . . condemn us"?

See insights for Mosiah 4:30.

ALMA 12:16, 32

What are the second death, spiritual death, and temporal death?

"Death entered the world by means of Adam's fall—death of two kinds, temporal and spiritual. Temporal death passes upon all men when they depart this mortal life. . . . Spiritual death passes upon all men when they . . . sin [and] die spiritually; . . . they are cast out of the presence of God" (Bruce R. McConkie, *Promised Messiah*, 349–50).

"The only persons who will be completely overcome by this dreadful fate [the second death] are the sons of perdition, who go with the devil and his angels into 'outer darkness'" (Joseph Fielding Smith, ed., *Answers to Gospel Questions*, 1:76).

ALMA 12:24

What is "a probationary state"?

"What an essential doctrine . . . of prolonged opportunity for mortal men and women in which the gospel can be taught to and accepted by them" (Jeffrey R. Holland, *Christ and the New Covenant*, 209).

ALMA 12:25-26, 30, 33-34

What is the plan of redemption?

"The gospel is the plan of salvation, the plan ordained and established by the Father to enable his spirit children to advance and progress and become like him. It is all of the laws, truths, rites, ordinances, and performances by conformity to which men can save themselves with eternal exaltation in the mansions on high. It is the system that enables the sons of God to become gods" (Bruce R. McConkie, *Mortal Messiah*, 2:8).

ALMA 12:31

"Placing themselves in a state to act . . ."

"Agency is largely a product of knowledge and understanding. Adam and Eve, in their paradisiacal condition, were naively innocent and thus unable to serve as responsible moral agents. Having partaken of the fruit of the tree of knowledge of good and evil, having gained an understanding of good and evil, . . . they were now in a position to act instead of simply being acted upon" (Joseph Fielding McConkie and Robert L. Millet, *Doctrinal Commentary*, 3:90). *See also 2 Nephi 2:13.*

ALMA 12:34-37

What is "the rest of God" that the righteous will enter?

"It means entering into the knowledge and love of God, having faith in his purpose and in his plan, to such an extent that we know we are right, and that we are not hunting for something else, we are not disturbed by every wind of doctrine" (Joseph F. Smith, *Gospel Doctrine*, 58).

ALMA 12:36-37

When and what was "the first provocation" and "the last provocation"?

"The first death, with all its attendant evils, has extended its ravages . . . since the first law was broken. If God, then, has fulfilled His word in the first provocation, to the very letter, why should any one suppose that He will not inflict the second death as a penalty of the second provocation?" (Orson Pratt, *Journal of Discourses*, 1:330).

ALMA 13

ALMA 13:1-2, 6-11, 14

What is the "holy order" God used to ordain priests?

"Before [Melchizedek's] day it was called *the Holy Priesthood, after the Order of the Son of God*. But out of respect or reverence to the name of the Supreme Being, to avoid the too frequent repetition of his name, they, the church, in ancient days, called that priesthood after Melchizedek, or the Melchizedek Priesthood" (D&C 107:3-4; emphasis in original).

ALMA 13:3

What is the "preparatory redemption"?

"They were 'called with a holy calling, yea, with that holy calling which was prepared with, and according to a preparatory redemption.' They could preach redemption; they could foretell its coming; but their work was preparatory only. Redemption itself would come through the ministry of Him of whom they were but types and shadows" (Bruce R. McConkie, *Promised Messiah*, 451-52).

"In the first place being left to choose good or evil . . ."

"God gave his children their free agency even in the spirit world, by which the individual spirits had the privilege, just as men have here, of choosing the good . . . or partaking of the evil to suffer the consequences of their sins. Because of this, some even there were more faithful than others in keeping the commandments of the Lord" (Joseph Fielding Smith, *Doctrines of Salvation*, 1:58-59).

ALMA 13:3, 5

"In the first place they were on the same standing."

"Alma says that those 'ordained unto the high priesthood of the holy order of God' were 'in the first place,' that is in pre-existence, 'on the same standing with their brethren,' meaning that initially all had equal opportunity to progress through righteousness" (Bruce R. McConkie, *Mormon Doctrine*, 477).

ALMA 13:3, 5, 7

"Being called and prepared from the foundation of the world . . ."

"Remember, in the world before we came here, faithful women were given certain assignments while faithful men were foreordained to certain priesthood tasks" (Spencer W. Kimball, *Teachings*, 316).

ALMA 13:6

What is the purpose of the priesthood?

"The Melchizedek Priesthood . . . is the channel through which all knowledge, doctrine, the plan of salvation and every important matter is revealed from heaven" (Joseph Smith, *Teachings*, 166–67).

ALMA 13:12

"They . . . could not look upon sin save it were with abhorrence."

"This passage indicates an attitude which is basic to the sanctification we should all be seeking . . . wherein there is not merely a renunciation but also a deep abhorrence of the sin" (Spencer W. Kimball, *Miracle of Forgiveness*, 354–55).

ALMA 13:14–19

How great was the prophet Melchizedek?

"[Alma] proceeded to tell more about Melchizedek than is known anywhere else in scripture. . . .

"He was king over the land of Salem (Jeru-salem).

"His people had waxed strong in iniquity and abomination, had all gone astray. . . .

"He exercised faith in spite of such opposition.

"He received the 'office of the high priesthood according to the holy order of God.'

"He preached repentance unto his people.

"He established peace and was therefore called the prince of peace.

"He reigned under his father.

"Alma noted that there were many prominent figures before and after Melchizedek, 'but none were greater. . . .'

"Surely no greater tribute or more generous adulation could be mentioned than to be so much like the Son of God that one's name could be substituted for his in the title of the most powerful force in the universe—the Holy Priesthood, after the Order of the Son of God" (Jeffrey R. Holland, *Christ and the New Covenant*, 175).

ALMA 13:15

"Abraham paid tithes of one-tenth part of all he possessed."
   See insights for 3 Nephi 24:8–12.

ALMA 13:20

What is the meaning of the word "wrest"?

   "[The Nephite] teachers and leaders had put into the Scriptures, by wrest-ing them, otherwise by twisting and turning them, meanings that were not true" (George Reynolds and Janne M. Sjodahl, *Commentary on the Book of Mormon*, 4:206).

ALMA 13:23

"In plain terms, that we may understand, that we cannot err . . ."
   See insights for Alma 5:43.

ALMA 13:27

Why should we "not procrastinate the day" of our repentance?
   See insights for Alma 34:32–35.

ALMA 13:28

"Ye may not be tempted above that which ye can bear."

   "Be sure you understand that God will not allow you to be tempted beyond your ability to resist. (See 1 Cor. 10:13.) He does not give you chal-lenges that you cannot surmount. He will not ask more than you can do, but may ask right up to your limits so you can prove yourselves" (Joseph B. Wirthlin, *Ensign*, November 1989, 75).

ALMA 14

ALMA 14:1–29

How are Alma and Amulek types of Christ?

ALMA AND AMULEK	SIMILARITIES	JESUS CHRIST
Alma 14:1	Many people followed and believed them	Matthew 4:25
Alma 14:2	The people were angry with and wanted to destroy them	John 7:23; 18:3
Alma 14:3	They testified of the people's wickedness, who in turn wanted to put them away "privily"	Mark 14:1–2

Alma 14:5	They witnessed and testified against the people	Matthew 26:59–60
Alma 14:7	They were innocent of any wrongdoing	John 17:4
Alma 14:7	Someone tried to undo the bad they had done against them	Luke 23:22
Alma 14:7	The people claimed they were possessed with a devil	John 10:20
Alma 14:9	The people took them to the place of martyrdom	Matthew 27:33
Alma 14:10	They felt the pain of others	2 Nephi 9:21; Alma 7:11–13
Alma 14:11	The spirit constrained them not to avoid pain and death	Matthew 26:39
Alma 14:13	They did avoid death before their work was finished	John 7:30
Alma 14:14	They were taken bound before the "chief judge"	Matthew 27:2
Alma 14:14	They were smitten	Matthew 27:30
Alma 14:15	They were asked what they could say for themselves	John 19:10
Alma 14:17	They refused to answer their enemies anything	Luke 23:9
Alma 14:17–18	They went to prison for three days	Matthew 12:40; 1 Peter 4:6
Alma 14:18	They answered their enemies nothing a second time	Matthew 27:12
Alma 14:19	They were asked if they understood they could be put to death for not responding	John 19:10
Alma 14:20, 24	Some chidingly told them to use their power to deliver themselves	Matthew 27:40, 42
Alma 14:21	They were spat upon	Matthew 27:30
Alma 14:22	They were mocked	Matthew 27:29
Alma 14:22	They experienced great thirst	John 19:28
Alma 14:22	Their clothes were taken from them	John 19:23; Matthew 27:28, 35

Alma 14:25	Through the power of God they were raised to their feet	Luke 24:36–39
Alma 14:27	Their enemies fell to the earth	John 18:3–6
Alma 14:27	The earth shook and something nearby was rent in twain	Matthew 27:51
Alma 14:28	They came forth out of prison	Matthew 28:6
Alma 14:28	Bands were loosed	Mosiah 15:8
Alma 14:29	Multitudes saw them afterwards	1 Corinthians 15:6

ALMA 14:6

How is feeling guilt necessary for repentance?
See insights for Alma 36:11–13.

ALMA 14:7–8

The wicked "cast . . . out . . . all those who believed in . . . Alma and Amulek."
See insights for Alma 10:22–23, 27.

ALMA 14:10, 15, 20, 24–25

What must be in place for a servant of God to "exercise the power of God"?

The person must be worthy (see D&C 50:29).

The person must ask for that which is right in the eyes of the Lord (see 3 Nephi 18:20).

The person must ask with complete faith (see James 1:5–6).

ALMA 14:11

Why does the Lord allow bad things to happen to good people?

"Just as Jesus had to endure affliction to prove himself, so must all men endure affliction to prove themselves" (Marion G. Romney, in Conference Report, October 1969, 58).

There are different types of suffering:
"Type I: Some things happen to us because of our own mistakes and our own sins. . . .

"Type II: Still other trials and tribulations come to us merely as a part of living. . . .

"Type III: . . . These come to us because an omniscient Lord deliberately chooses to school us: 'For whom the Lord loveth he chasteneth . . .' (Hebrews 12:6)." (Neal A. Maxwell, *All These Things Shall Give Thee Experience*, 29–30).

"If all the sick for whom we pray were healed, if all the righteous were protected and the wicked destroyed, the whole program of the Father would be annulled. . . . No man would have to live by faith. . . . There would be no test of strength, no development of character, no growth of powers. . . . There would be little or no suffering, sorrow, disappointment, or even death, and if these were not, there would also be no joy, success, resurrection, nor eternal life and godhood. . . . Being human, we would expel from our lives physical pain and mental anguish and assure ourselves of continual ease and comfort, but if we were to close the doors upon sorrow and distress, we might be excluding our greatest friends and benefactors" (Spencer W. Kimball, *Faith Precedes the Miracle*, 97–98).

"When you face adversity, you can be led to ask many questions. Some serve a useful purpose; others do not. To ask, Why does this have to happen to me? Why do I have to suffer this, now? What have I done to cause this? will lead you into blind alleys. It really does no good to ask questions that reflect opposition to the will of God. Rather ask, What am I to do? What am I to learn from this experience? What am I to change? . . . How can I remember my many blessings in times of trial? . . . When you pray with real conviction, 'Please let me know Thy will' and 'May Thy will be done,' you are in the strongest position to receive the maximum help from your loving Father" (Richard G. Scott, *Ensign*, November 1995, 17).

"It is not the function of religion to answer all the questions about God's moral government of the universe, but to give one courage, through faith, to go on in the face of questions he never finds the answer to in his present status" (Harold B. Lee, in Conference Report, October 1963, 108). *See also 1 Nephi 18:11.*

ALMA 14:13

Why don't the wicked prematurely kill the righteous?

"Their bounds are set, they cannot pass. Thy days are known, and thy years shall not be numbered less; therefore, fear not what man can do, for God shall be with you forever and ever" (D&C 122:9).

ALMA 14:14–22

The Lord's servants are often treated poorly.

"The constable who served this second warrant upon me had no sooner arrested me than he began to abuse and insult me; and so unfeeling was he with me, that although I had been kept all the day in court without anything to eat since the morning, yet he hurried me off to Broome county, a distance of about fifteen miles, before he allowed me any kind of food whatever. He took me to a tavern, and gathered in a number of men, who used every means to abuse, ridicule and insult me. They spit upon me, pointed their fingers at me, saying, 'Prophesy, prophesy!'" (Joseph Smith, *History of the Church*, 1:91).

ALMA 15

ALMA 15:3, 5

What causes Zeezrom to "lay sick"?

"There is a *spirit* in man; . . . There are spiritual disorders, too, and spiritual diseases that can cause intense suffering.

"The body and the spirit of man are bound together. Often, very often, when there are disorders, it is very difficult to tell which is which" (Boyd K. Packer, *That All May Be Edified*, 63–64; emphasis in original).

ALMA 15:4-5, 10

"Alma and Amulek . . . went immediately, obeying the message."

"Ye ought to forgive one another; for he that forgiveth not his brother his trespasses standeth condemned before the Lord; for there remaineth in him the greater sin. I, the Lord, will forgive whom I will forgive, but of you it is required to forgive all men" (D&C 64:9–10).

ALMA 15:6-11

"If thou believest in the redemption of Christ thou canst be healed."

"Miracles are the fruit of faith. Signs follow those who believe. If there is faith, there will be miracles; if there are no miracles, there is no faith. The two are inseparably intertwined with each other; they cannot be separated, and there cannot be one without the other. Faith and miracles go together, always and everlastingly. And faith precedes the miracle" (Bruce R. McConkie, *Mortal Messiah*, 2:286–87). *See also Matthew 9:22.*

ALMA 15:13

"Alma . . . consecrated priests and teachers . . . to baptize."

See insights for 2 Nephi 5:26.

ALMA 16

ALMA 16:2-3, 9-10

Why were the people of Ammonihah destroyed?

"We live in a world . . . where we find sadness and destruction in every corner of the world—much of which is brought about by man's failure to listen to the words of the true prophets of God" (Robert D. Hales, *Ensign*, May 1995, 15).

ALMA 16:5

They went to Alma "to know whither the Lord would that they should go."

Going to the prophet for spiritual guidance during times of battle was a common practice for ancient Israel. "The heart of the king of Syria was sore troubled for this thing; and he called his servants, and said unto them, Will ye not shew me which of us is for the king of Israel? And one of his servants said, None, my lord, O king: but Elisha, the prophet that is in Israel, telleth the king of Israel the words that thou speakest in thy bedchamber" (2 Kings 6:11–12).

ALMA 16:14–17, 21

What was the cause of their great success?

"The preaching of the word had a . . . more powerful effect upon the minds of the people than . . . anything else" (Alma 31:5).

ALMA 17

ALMA 17:2

How important is it to search the scriptures diligently?

"We should make daily study of the scriptures a lifetime pursuit. . . . The most important [thing] you can do . . . is to immerse yourselves in the scriptures. Search them diligently. . . . Learn the doctrine. Master the principles" (Ezra Taft Benson, *Ensign*, November 1986, 47). *See also insights for 2 Nephi 32:3; Alma 31:5.*

ALMA 17:9

The sons of Mosiah hoped to be instruments in the hands of God.

"If this were the work of man, it would fail, but it is the work of the Lord, and he does not fail. And we have the assurance that if we keep the commandments and are valiant in the testimony of Jesus and are true to every trust, the Lord will guide and direct us and his church in the paths of righteousness, for the accomplishment of all his purposes" (Joseph Fielding Smith, in Conference Report, April 1970, 113).

ALMA 17:11

What value is there in being "patient in long-suffering"?

"We must have patience in order to withstand pain and grief without complaint or discouragement, which detract from the Spirit. It's necessary to have patience in the face of tribulation and persecution for the cause of truth, which sets an example because the manner in which we bear our cross will be an influence to others to help lighten their load" (Angel Abrea, *Ensign*, May 1992, 25).

Why "show forth good examples"?
See insights for Alma 4:11; 2 Nephi 31:7–10, 12–13, 16.

ALMA 17:13
"Great was the work which they had undertaken."
"One of the *greatest secrets of missionary work is work!* If a missionary *works*, he will get the Spirit; if he gets the Spirit, he will teach by the Spirit; and if he teaches by the Spirit, he will touch the hearts of the people and he will be happy. There will be no homesickness, no worrying about families, for all time and talents and interests are centered on the *work* of the ministry. *Work, work, work*—there is no satisfactory substitute, especially in missionary work" (Ezra Taft Benson, *Teachings*, 200; emphasis in original). *See also Alma 17:5.*

ALMA 17:20–18:17
Ammon is a type of Christ.

AMMON	SIMILARITIES	JESUS CHRIST
Alma 17:20	They were both bound and taken before the king	Matthew 27:2
Alma 17:25	Both took the role of servant	Mark 10:44
Alma 17:25	Both were shepherds	John 10:11
Alma 17:31	Both gathered sheep that had wandered astray	Matthew 18:12–13
Alma 17:37	Both have sharp swords to divide asunder both joints and marrow	D&C 6:2
Alma 17:35; 18:3	No man could slay them before their mission was complete	John 10:17–18
Alma 18:10	Both served faithfully their masters	John 6:38
Alma 18:13	They were called by similar titles "Rabbanah" and "Rabboni"	John 20:16
Alma 18:17	Both were willing to do very difficult things for their master	Luke 22:42

"They knew not that the Lord had promised . . . he would deliver" his servants.

"I saw Elder Brigham Young standing in a strange land, in the far south and west, in a desert place, upon a rock in the midst of about a dozen men of color, who appeared hostile. He was preaching to them in their own tongue, and the angel of God standing above his head, with a drawn sword in his hand, protecting him, but he did not see it" (Joseph Smith, *Teachings*, 108).

"They were angry . . . and they were determined that he should fall."

See insights for Ether 13:27; 15:6, 22, 28.

ALMA 18

Could anyone live in such a Christlike way that they would be mistaken for him?

"This is the record of John, when the Jews sent priests and Levites from Jerusalem to ask him, Who art thou? And he confessed, and denied not; but confessed, I am not the Christ. And they asked him, . . . Art thou that prophet? And he answered, No" (John 1:19–21). *See also insights for 3 Nephi 27:27.*

An unknown author has said, "Live in such a way that people who know you but don't know Christ will want to know Christ because they know you" (quoted in H. David Burton, *Ensign*, May 1994, 68).

"There was a little crippled boy who ran a small newsstand in a crowded railroad station. . . . Every day he would sell papers, candy, gum, and magazines to the thousands of commuters passing through the terminal. One night two men were rushing through the crowded station to catch a train. One was fifteen or twenty yards in front of the other. It was Christmas Eve. Their train was scheduled to depart in a matter of minutes. The first man turned a corner and in his haste . . . plowed right into the little crippled boy. He knocked him off his stool, and candy, newspapers, and gum were scattered everywhere. Without so much as stopping, he cursed the little fellow for being there and rushed on. . . . It was only a matter of seconds before the second commuter arrived on the scene. He stopped, knelt, and gently picked up the boy. After making sure the child was unhurt, the man gathered up the scattered newspapers, sweets, and magazines. Then he . . . gave the boy a five dollar bill. 'Son,' he said, 'I think this will take care of what was lost.' . . . The commuter . . . started to hurry away. As he did, the little crippled boy cupped his hands together and called out, 'Mister, Mister!' The man stopped as the boy asked, 'Are you Jesus Christ?' . . . He smiled and said, 'No, son. I am not Jesus Christ, but I am trying hard to do what He would do if He were here'" (Tom Anderson, in Ezra Taft Benson, *Ensign*, April 1984, 11–12).

ALMA 18:9

Is there evidence of "horses and . . . chariots" in pre-Columbus America?

"Critics have maintained: (1) no horses existed on the American continents before the time of Columbus, and (2) the people who lived on the American continents did not know the principle of the wheel before the coming of Columbus. However, since the publication of the Book of Mormon, considerable archaeological evidence has come forth to reinforce its claims that there were horses on the American continents before the time of Columbus and that these early peoples did know the principle of the wheel" (Daniel H. Ludlow, *Companion*, 206).

ALMA 18:13

What is the meaning of the word "Rabbanah"?

"The Lamanite word 'Rabbanah,' meaning 'powerful or great king,' is strikingly similar to other Semitic words having essentially the same meaning. For example, the New Testament word *rabboni* clearly refers to one who is a leader (John 20:16). Also the word *rabbi*, which is used frequently by Jewish people, designates 'one who teaches or leads.' That the spoken language of both the Nephites and the Lamanites is derived from the Hebrew is made quite clear" (Daniel H. Ludlow, *Companion*, 207; emphasis in original).

ALMA 18:16, 18, 20, 32

"Ammon . . . perceived the thoughts of the king."

See insights for Alma 10:17.

ALMA 18:23

How was the king "caught with guile" by Ammon?

"Although the word *guile* is frequently used to mean 'deceitful cunning' or 'treachery,' it can also denote the use of strategy. It is evidently used in the latter sense in Alma 18:23; in other words, Ammon *planned* or *used strategy* in arranging the questions he asked King Lamoni" (Daniel H. Ludlow, *Companion*, 207; emphasis in original).

ALMA 18:24

"Believest thou that there is a God?"

"It is the first principle of revealed religion to know the nature and kind of being that God is" (Bruce R. McConkie, *Promised Messiah*, 125).

ALMA 18:28-39

How integral to the plan are the Creation, Fall, and Redemption?

"If the earth and man and all living things had not been created in their physical and paradisiacal state, in a state of deathlessness, there could have been no fall. The fall, with its resultant probationary estate, is the child of the original and primeval creation, and the atonement is the child of the fall" (Bruce R. McConkie, *New Witness for the Articles of Faith*, 81–82).

ALMA 18:42

Why did King Lamoni fall "unto the earth, as if he were dead"?

See insights for Alma 19:6, 13–16.

ALMA 19

ALMA 19:6, 13-16

"The power of God . . . had overcome his natural frame."

"From what we can deduce from scriptural writ, it appears that a trance is a state in which the body and its functions become quiescent in order that the full powers of the Spirit may be centered on the revelations of heaven. Freed from the fetters of a mortal body, man's spirit can be ushered into the divine presence; it can hear what otherwise could not be heard and see what otherwise could not be seen" (Joseph Fielding McConkie and Robert L. Millet, *Doctrinal Commentary*, 3:140).

ALMA 19:10

Sometimes those without the gospel have great faith.

"There came unto him [Jesus] a centurion [a Roman] . . . saying, Lord, my servant lieth at home sick. . . . Jesus saith unto him, I will come and heal him. . . . The centurion answered and said, Lord, I am not worthy that thou shouldest come under my roof: but speak the word only, and my servant shall be healed. . . . When Jesus heard it, he marvelled, and said to them that followed, Verily I say unto you, I have not found so great faith, no, not in Israel" (Matthew 8:5–10).

ALMA 19:13

Have others had the great blessing of seeing their Redeemer?

"At one of these meetings . . . when we were all together, Joseph having given instructions, and while engaged in silent prayer, kneeling, . . . a personage walked through the room. . . . I saw him and suppose the others did, and Joseph answered that is Jesus, the Son of God. . . . Afterward Joseph told us to resume our former position in prayer, which we did. Another person came through; He was surrounded as with a flame of fire. . . . The Prophet Joseph said this was the Father of our Lord Jesus Christ. I saw Him. . . . This appearance was so grand and overwhelming that it seemed I should melt down in His presence, and the sensation was so powerful that it thrilled through my whole system and I felt it in the marrow of my bones. The Prophet Joseph said: Brethren now you are prepared to be Apostles of Jesus Christ, for you have seen both the Father and the Son" (Zebedee Coltrin, in Lyndon W. Cook, *Revelations of the Prophet Joseph Smith*, 187–88).

"I was shown a panoramic view of His earthly ministry. . . . My soul was taught over and over again the events of the betrayal, the mock trial, the scourging of the flesh. . . . I witnessed His struggling up the hill in His weakened condition carrying the cross and His being stretched upon it as it lay on the ground, that the crude spikes could be driven with a mallet into His hands and wrists and feet to secure His body as it hung on the cross for public display. . . . I cannot begin to convey to you the deep impact that these scenes have confirmed upon my soul" (David B. Haight, *Ensign*, November 1989, 60). *See also D&C 67:10; 88:67–68; 93:1.*

ALMA 19:33
"Their hearts had been changed."

"Sometimes men are born again miraculously and suddenly, as was Alma. They . . . completely reverse the whole course of their life almost in an instant. But for most members of the Church the spiritual rebirth is a process that goes on gradually. The faithful are sanctified degree by degree as they add to their faith and good works" (Bruce R. McConkie, *Promised Messiah*, 351). *See also insights for Alma 5:14, 26.*

ALMA 20

ALMA 20:2, 5
How did the voice of the Lord come to Ammon?

"I will tell you in your mind and in your heart, by the Holy Ghost, which shall come upon you and which shall dwell in your heart. Now, behold, this is the spirit of revelation" (D&C 8:2–3).

"Dramatic and miraculous answers to prayer may come, but they are the exceptions. Even at the highest levels of responsibility in this kingdom of God, which is being built up upon the earth, *the voice is still small.* . . . My testimony is that the Lord *is* speaking to you! But with the deafening decibels of today's environment, all too often we fail to hear him. . . . Listening is a challenge for us" (Graham W. Doxey, *Ensign*, November 1991, 25; emphasis in original).

ALMA 20:13–17

What is the connection between anger and violence?

"May I suggest that you watch your temper, . . . Discipline yourselves. . . . To flare up in anger and swear and profane . . . is an indication of weakness. Anger is . . . an indication of one's inability to control his thoughts, words, his emotions. . . . When the weakness of anger takes over, the strength of reason leaves" (Gordon B. Hinckley, *Ensign*, November 1991, 51). *See also insights for Alma 2:8–10.*

ALMA 20:29

Aaron and his companions "had suffered hunger, thirst, and all kinds of afflictions."

"There is terrible suffering in our world today. Tragic things happen to good people. God does not cause them, nor does He always prevent them. He does, however, strengthen us and bless us with His peace, through earnest prayer" (Rex D. Pinegar, *Ensign*, May 1993, 67). *See also insights for Alma 14:11.*

ALMA 21

ALMA 21:2–3

Who were the Amalekites and the people of Amulon?

"The Amalekites were a sect of Nephite apostates whose origin is not given. . . .

"The Amulonites were the descendants of Amulon and his associate wicked priests of King Noah. They were Nephites on their father's side, and Lamanites on their mother's. . . .

"Many became followers of Nehor. . . . Not one repented and received the Gospel Message that was preached by the sons of King Mosiah; on the contrary, they became leaders in the persecution carried on against the . . . people of Anti-Nephi-Lehi" (George Reynolds and Janne M. Sjodahl, *Commentary on the Book of Mormon*, 3:290).

ALMA 21:6

"We . . . believe that God will save all men."

See insights for Alma 1:4.

ALMA 21:9

How is Christ the source of resurrection and redemption?

See insights for 2 Nephi 9:7, 11–12.

ALMA 21:12

How do people harden their hearts?

When people harden their hearts they "shut their ears, . . . close their eyes, and are determined to hear nothing that is true" (Brigham Young, *Journal of Discourses*, 4:371).

ALMA 21:16

Why should missionaries be "led by the Spirit of the Lord" when they preach?

"The Spirit is the most important matter in this glorious work" (Ezra Taft Benson, *Teachings*, 198). *See also insights for 2 Nephi 32:5.*

ALMA 21:21–22

How imperative is the freedom to worship?

"Freedom of conscience, the freedom to worship God according to the dictates of one's own conscience, is the greatest of all freedoms" (Bruce R. McConkie, *Mormon Doctrine*, 299).

ALMA 22

ALMA 22:9

"Is God that Great Spirit"?

"According to Lamanite traditions, God is the *Great Spirit*. It is obvious that by this designation the Lamanites had in mind a personal being, for King Lamoni mistakenly supposed that Ammon was the Great Spirit. (Alma 18:2–28; 19:25–27)" (Bruce R. McConkie, *Mormon Doctrine*, 340; emphasis in original). *See insights for Alma 18:24.*

ALMA 22:15, 18

What was the king willing to give up?

Earlier when the king's life was threatened, he was willing to give up "half of [his] kingdom" to save his mortal life (Alma 20:23), but now to save his immortal soul he was willing to give up all that he had.

"Each of us must surrender our sins if we are to really know Christ. For we do not know Him until we become like Him. There are some, like this king, who must pray until they, too, have 'a wicked spirit rooted' from them so they can find the same joy" (Ezra Taft Benson, *Ensign*, November 1983, 43). *See also John 17:3.*

ALMA 22:18

What happened to the king when "he was struck as if he were dead"?

See insights for Alma 19:6, 13–16.

ALMA 22:27–34
"Thus were the Lamanites and the Nephites divided."
See insights for Helaman 4:7.

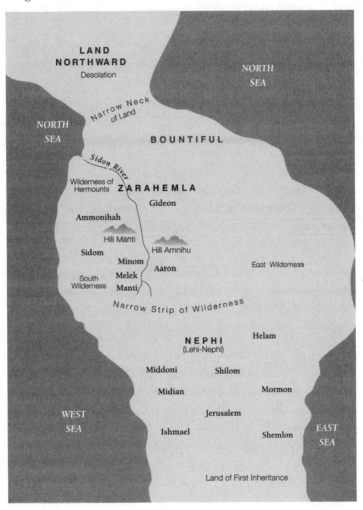

ALMA 23

ALMA 23:1–3
Why would the sons of Mosiah need free access to preach?
See insights for Alma 21:21–22.

ALMA 23:5-6

The converted Lamanites "never did fall away."

"Of these people the record says that thousands were brought to a knowledge of the Lord, and that as many as were brought to a knowledge of the truth never did fall away. . . .

"That is the great message . . . the softening of the hearts that this gospel does to the people who receive it" (Marion G. Romney, in Conference Report, October 1948, 75).

ALMA 23:14

Who were the Amalekites and Amulonites that hardened their hearts?

See insights for Alma 21:2–3.

ALMA 23:18

What was "the curse of God" that "did no more follow them"?

"The curse was the withdrawal of the Spirit of the Lord" (Joseph Fielding Smith, *Answers to Gospel Questions*, 3:122). *See also 2 Nephi 5:20.*

ALMA 24

ALMA 24:1-4

What are the dangers of anger?

See insights for Alma 2:8–10; Alma 20:13–17.

ALMA 24:12-13, 15, 30

Why did this people have such a strong desire to not return to their sins?

"When a righteous man doth turn from his righteousness, and commit iniquity, . . . he shall die in his sin, and his righteousness which he hath done shall not be remembered" (Ezekiel 3:20).

"The miracle of forgiveness is available to all of those who turn from their evil doings and return no more, because the Lord has said in a revelation to us in our day: '. . . go your ways and sin no more; but unto that soul who sinneth [meaning again] shall the former sins return, saith the Lord your God.' (D&C 82:7.)" (Harold B. Lee, *Ensign*, July 1973, 122–23).

ALMA 24:14-15

"God has had mercy on us. . . . Oh, how merciful is our God!"

"The Book of Mormon makes clear that neither the conditional nor unconditional blessings of the Atonement would be available to mankind except through the grace and goodness of Christ. Obviously the unconditional blessings of the Atonement are unearned, but the conditional ones also are not fully merited. . . . Even these greater blessings are freely given of him and are not technically 'earned' by us" (Jeffrey R. Holland, *Christ and the New Covenant*, 236).

ALMA 24:18
How seriously did they take their covenants?
See insights for 1 Nephi 4:32–37.

What are the disadvantages of idleness and the advantages of labor?
See insights for 2 Nephi 5:17, 24.

ALMA 24:24–26
"When the Lamanites saw this" their "hearts had swollen."
See insights for Alma 4:11; 2 Nephi 31:7–10, 12–13, 16.

ALMA 24:27
"The Lord worketh in many ways."
"I have seen, at close range, the manner in which the Lord has turned disasters—war, occupation, and revolution—into blessings" (Ezra Taft Benson, *Teachings*, 168). *See also Isaiah 55:8.*

ALMA 24:30
How could their state be worse than if "they had never known these things"?
See insights for 2 Nephi 10:16; Alma 24:12–13, 15, 30.

ALMA 25

ALMA 25:8–9
"The Lamanites began to hunt the seed of Amulon."
This was in fulfillment of prophecies made by Abinadi in Mosiah 17:18.

ALMA 25:11
Who are some of the many that would "suffer death by fire"?

Abinadi (Mosiah 17:20)

King Noah (Mosiah 19:20)

The righteous Nephites of Ammonihah (Alma 14:8)

The righteous Lamanites in the "east wilderness" (Alma 25:5)

The wicked at the Second Coming (D&C 63:34)

ALMA 25:17

What causes missionaries to "rejoice exceedingly"?
See insights for Alma 26:1–16, 30, 35–37.

ALMA 26

ALMA 26:1–16, 30, 35–37

"How great reason have we to rejoice. . . . My heart is brim with joy."

"I know of no joy on earth that can compare with that which comes to the heart of the man who is an instrument in the hands of God of saving some soul" (Heber J. Grant, in Conference Report, October 1922, 188).

ALMA 26:3, 22

What value is there in going from darkness to light?

"How can the garden grow in darkness? How can the trees blossom and produce their luscious fruit? Or how can the fields grow and ripen into golden harvests, unless the sun shall shine upon them? How can we know or understand the things of God without the light of his Holy Spirit?" (Rulon S. Wells, in Conference Report, October 1927, 57).

ALMA 26:11–12

"I do not boast in my own strength. . . . But I will boast of my God."

"Aaron saw in Ammon's words what he thought was a departure from the path of humility. . . . Aaron thought, also, that Ammon boasted in his own might and wisdom. Boasting is generally associated with pride, and it usually imputes exaggeration, ostentatiousness, or vaingloriousness, to the one who vents his pride . . . [but] Ammon . . . did not boast in [his own strength]" (George Reynolds and Janne M. Sjodahl, *Commentary on the Book of Mormon*, 3:364). *See also Mosiah 4:11.*

ALMA 26:17–20

"Our God . . . did not exercise his justice upon us."

See insights for Alma 34:14–16.

ALMA 26:27

What can we do when we feel depressed and ready "to turn back"?

"There are times when you simply have to righteously hang on and outlast the devil until his depressive spirit leaves you. . . .

"To press on in noble endeavors, even while surrounded by a cloud of depression, will eventually bring you out on top into the sunshine" (Ezra Taft Benson, *Teachings*, 396).

ALMA 26:35

God is omnipotent.

See insights for 2 Nephi 9:20.

God is omniscient.

See insights for 2 Nephi 9:20; 1 Nephi 9:6.

ALMA 27

ALMA 27:8, 10

"If [the Lord] saith unto us go, we will go."

"Obedience is the first law of heaven. . . . There is nothing in all eternity more important than to keep the commandments of God" (Bruce R. McConkie, *Promised Messiah*, 126).

"Now the only safety we have as members of this church is to do exactly what the Lord said to the Church in that day when the Church was organized. We must learn to give heed to the words and commandments that the Lord shall give through his prophet" (Harold B. Lee, in Conference Report, October 1970, 152).

ALMA 27:11

"Ammon went and inquired of the Lord."

"We should let our prayers ascend before the Lord. I have more faith in prayer before the Lord than almost any other principle on earth. . . . We should pray unto the Lord, asking him for what we want . . . and the Lord will not turn them away, but they will be heard and answered" (Wilford Woodruff, *Journal of Discourses*, 17:250). *See also James 1:5.*

ALMA 27:16–19, 26

What is the source of joy?

"Joy is a gift of the Spirit. It comes from the Holy Ghost, is granted to those who gain a remission of their sins (Mosiah 4:3, 20; Alma 22:15), and there is great joy in heaven when sinners repent. (Luke 15:7; D. & C. 18:13–16.) It is in the Lord that the saints rejoice" (Bruce R. McConkie, *Mormon Doctrine*, 397).

ALMA 27:27

What difference does it make to have "zeal towards God"?

"We cannot stand idly by, being merely an interested spectator, rather than a participating member, and still receive the blessing of eternal life" (Delbert L. Stapley, *Ensign*, January 1974, 45). *See also Revelation 3:15–16; D&C 58:27.*

ALMA 27:28

"They never did look upon death with any degree of terror."

"More painful to me are the thoughts of annihilation than death. If I have no expectation of seeing my father, mother, brothers, sisters and friends again, my heart would burst in a moment, and I should go down to my grave.

"The expectation of seeing my friends in the morning of the resurrection cheers my soul and makes me bear up against the evils of life" (Joseph Smith, *Teachings*, 296).

ALMA 28

ALMA 28:8

How long had this "account of Ammon and his brethren" lasted?

"During a fourteen-year mission in the land of Nephi, the Nephite missionaries Ammon and his brothers gained many Lamanite converts (Alma 17–26)" (Daniel H. Ludlow, ed., *Encyclopedia of Mormonism*, 1:194).

ALMA 28:11–12, 14

How can the righteous rejoice at the death of their loved ones?

See insights for Mosiah 13:2–3.

ALMA 29

ALMA 29:1–4

What does our desire have to do with what God will ultimately grant us?

"The prophet and his leaders seek to educate our very desires, for God finally gives to each man the desires of his heart" (Neal A. Maxwell, *Of One Heart*, 3).

ALMA 29:9

What is a primary purpose for missionary work?

See Alma 17:16; insights for Mosiah 28:1–3.

ALMA 29:15

What blessings come to those who have "labored exceedingly" in missionary work?

"By reclaiming an erring brother, we save both him and ourselves. Our sins are hidden (remitted) because we ministered for the salvation and blessing of another member of the kingdom" (Bruce R. McConkie, *Doctrinal New Testament Commentary*, 3:279).

"Each good deed, each testimony, each proselyting effort, each safeguard thrown about others is like a blanket over one's own sins" (Spencer W. Kimball, *Faith Precedes the Miracle*, 184). *See also James 5:20.*

ALMA 30

ALMA 30:6

What is an antichrist?

"An *antichrist* is an opponent of Christ; he is one who is in opposition to the true gospel, the true Church, and the true plan of salvation. (1 John 2:19; 4:4–6.) He is one who offers salvation to men on some other terms than those laid down by Christ. Sherem (Jac. 7:1–23), Nehor (Alma 1:2–16), and Korihor (Alma 30:6–60) were antichrists who spread their delusions among the Nephites" (Bruce R. McConkie, *Mormon Doctrine*, 39).

ALMA 30:10–11

"There was a law that men should be judged according to their crimes."

"Governments were instituted of God for the benefit of man; and that he holds men accountable for their acts in relation to them, both in making laws and administering them, for the good and safety of society" (D&C 134:1).

ALMA 30:12–18, 27

What were the teachings of Korihor the antichrist?

"There should be no Christ" (v. 12).

"No man can know of anything which is to come" (v. 13).

"Prophets . . . are foolish" (v. 14).

"Ye cannot know of things which ye do not see" (v. 15).

"A remission of your sins" is a false idea (v. 16).

"There could be no atonement" (v. 17).

"Man prospered" by his own abilities, not from God's blessings (v. 17).

There is no afterlife (v. 18).

Living the commandments is like living in "bondage" (v. 27).

ALMA 30:24, 27

What do antichrists teach about keeping the commandments?

"One of Satan's most frequently used deceptions is the notion that the commandments of God are meant to restrict freedom and limit happiness. Young people especially sometimes feel that the standards of the Lord are like fences and chains, blocking them from those activities that seem most enjoyable in life. But exactly the opposite is true. . . . The gospel principles are the steps and guidelines which will help us find true happiness and joy" (Ezra Taft Benson, *Teachings*, 357). *See also insights for Mosiah 2:41.*

ALMA 30:30

In what ways can someone blaspheme God?

"Among a great host of impious and sacrilegious speaking that constitute blasphemy are such things as: Taking the name of God in vain; evil-speaking about the Lord's anointed; belittling sacred temple ordinances, or patriarchal blessings, or sacramental administrations; claiming unwarranted divine authority; and promulgating with profane piety a false system of salvation" (Bruce R. McConkie, *Mormon Doctrine*, 90).

ALMA 30:31–34

"We do not receive anything for our labors in the church."

"The Church of Jesus Christ of Latter-day Saints has no paid ministry. As an example: The bishops of the wards throughout the Church are laymen and arrange their time and affairs so that they can provide and care for their families and still shepherd the flocks over which they are placed" (Franklin D. Richards, in Conference Report, April 1964, 66).

ALMA 30:37–39

How did Alma refute Korihor's assertion that there is no God?

"Korihor's arguments sound very contemporary to the modern reader, but Alma used a timeless and ultimately undeniable weapon in response—the power of personal testimony" (Jeffrey R. Holland, *Christ and the New Covenant*, 121).

ALMA 30:40

There is no evidence that there is no God.

"The position of the agnostic is 'I don't know whether or not there is a God, but I don't believe there is; furthermore, I don't believe anyone can *know* that there is a God.' The atheistic position is 'I *know* there is not a God.' This position cannot be defended by reason or logic, for how can a person *know* there is no God? . . . Korihor's position in Alma 30:48 is essentially that of the agnostic: 'I do not deny the existence of a God, but I do not believe that there is a God.'

". . . It is impossible to prove there is *not* a God" (Daniel H. Ludlow, *Companion*, 211–12; emphasis in original).

ALMA 30:44

What evidence is there that there is a God?

"All beauty in the earth bears the fingerprint of the Master Creator" (Gordon B. Hinckley, *Be Thou an Example*, 74).

"As the British scientist Alan Hayward has observed:

"'Clearly, distance from the sun is very critical. Just a bit nearer to the sun, and Planet Earth's seas would soon be boiling; just a little farther out, and the whole world would become a frozen wilderness. . . . If our orbit happened to be the wrong shape . . . we should alternately freeze like Mars and fry like Venus once a year. Fortunately for us, our planet's orbit is very nearly a circle'" (Neal A. Maxwell, *Meek and Lowly*, 59).

ALMA 30:52

"I always knew that there was a God."

"The most powerful opposition to the work of the Savior on this earth comes from those who know the truth and then deliberately turn from it and seek to destroy others" (Chauncey C. Riddle, *Ensign*, September 1977, 18).

ALMA 30:53

To whom does the devil appear?

"Lucifer does not come personally to every false prophet, as he did to Korihor, any more than the Lord comes personally to every true prophet, as he did to Joseph Smith. Such an appearance—either of God on the one hand or of Satan on the other—is, however, the end result of full devotion to the respective causes involved" (Bruce R. McConkie, *Millennial Messiah*, 72).

What can be the end result of teaching falsehoods over and over?

"Nothing is a greater injury to the children of men than to be under the influence of a false spirit when they think they have the Spirit of God" (Joseph Smith, *Teachings*, 205).

ALMA 30:60

"The devil will not support his children."

"Satan does not support those who follow him. He can't! It's the Lord who sustains; the Spirit sustains; righteousness sustains. That sustenance is not Satan's to give" (Janette C. Hales, *1992–93 Devotional and Fireside Speeches*, 89).

ALMA 31

ALMA 31:1–2, 31

Sin and wickedness bring great sorrow.

"Wickedness never was happiness" (Alma 41:10). *See also insights for Mosiah 2:41.*

ALMA 31:5

What has a more powerful effect on people than anything else?

"Often we spend great effort in trying to increase the activity levels in our stakes. We work diligently to raise the percentages of those attending sacrament meetings. We labor to get a higher percentage of our young men on missions. We strive to improve the numbers of those marrying in the temple. All of these are commendable efforts and important to the growth of the kingdom. But when individual members and families immerse themselves in the scriptures regularly and consistently, these other areas of activity will automatically come. Testimonies will increase. Commitment will be strengthened. Families will be fortified. Personal revelation will flow" (Ezra Taft Benson, *Ensign*, May 1986, 81).

"True doctrine . . . changes attitudes and behavior.

"The study of the doctrines of the gospel will improve behavior quicker than a study of behavior will improve behavior" (Boyd K. Packer, *Ensign*, November 1986, 17). *See also Helaman 6:37*.

ALMA 31:13–18, 25–27

How significant is it that the Rameumptom was built "high above the head"?

Consider the following scriptures that speak of "high" things and are connected with pride. The Zoramite prayer indicates five times that they thought they were better than others.

Ephesians 2:2—Satan is "the prince of the power of the *air*"

Genesis 11:4–9—"Let us build a . . . *tower*, whose top may reach unto heaven"

Luke 11:43—"Woe unto you, Pharisees! for ye love the *uppermost seats* in the synagogues"

1 Corinthians 4:6—"No one of you be *puffed up* for one against another"

1 Nephi 8:26—"A great and spacious building . . . stood as it were *in the air, high above* the earth"

1 Nephi 11:36—"the great and spacious building was the *pride* of the world"

Psalm 131:1—"My heart is not haughty, . . . neither do I exercise myself in . . . things *too high*" (emphasis added)

ALMA 31:28

Why should we avoid wearing costly apparel?

See insights for Alma 1:6.

ALMA 31:36

What happened when Alma "clapped his hands upon" them?

"Alma so invoked the power of the Holy Ghost in behalf of his colaborers: 'He clapped his hands upon all them who were with him. And . . . they were filled with the Holy Spirit'" (James E. Talmage, *Articles of Faith*, 166).

ALMA 32

ALMA 32:2-12

How can we be prepared "to hear the word"?

"Just as soil needs preparation for a seed, so does a human heart for the word of God to take root. Before he told the people to plant the seed, Alma told them that . . . the circumstances of their lives, which led them to be humble, had prepared them" (Henry B. Eyring, *Ensign*, November 1995, 38).

ALMA 32:21

What is the relationship between faith and reason?

"The flow of revelation depends on your faith. You exercise faith by causing, or by making, your mind accept or believe as truth that which you cannot, by reason alone, prove for certainty" (Boyd K. Packer, *Ensign*, November 1994, 60).

What need is there for faith today?

"Of all our needs, I think the greatest is an increase in faith" (Gordon B. Hinckley, *Ensign*, November 1987, 54).

ALMA 32:27

How often does faith operate in our lives?

"Faith, and faith only . . . is the moving cause of all action; without it both mind and body would be in a state of inactivity and all . . . exertions would cease, both physical and mental" (Joseph Fielding Smith, *Restoration of All Things*, 186).

What difference can "a particle of faith" make in our actions?

"If ye have faith as a grain of mustard seed, ye shall say unto this mountain, Remove hence to yonder place; and it shall remove; and nothing shall be impossible unto you" (Matthew 17:20).

"If ye can no more than desire to believe . . ."

"Jesus said unto him, If thou canst believe, all things are possible to him that believeth. And straightway the father of the child cried out, and said with tears, Lord, I believe; help thou mine unbelief" (Mark 9:23-24).

What is the difference between faith and belief?

"Belief is in a sense passive, an agreement or acceptance only; faith is active and positive, embracing such reliance and confidence as will lead to works" (James E. Talmage, *Articles of Faith*, 96–97).

ALMA 32:28, 38-39

Faith and doubt cannot exist at the same time.

"Where doubt and uncertainty are there faith is not, nor can it be. For doubt and faith do not exist in the same person at the same time; so that persons whose minds are under doubts . . . cannot have unshaken confidence; and where unshaken confidence is not there faith is weak" (Joseph Smith, *Lectures on Faith*, 6:12). *See also 1 Nephi 5:2.*

ALMA 32:33-36

When "it swelleth and sprouteth, and beginneth to grow," you know it is good.

"If any man will do his will, he shall know of the doctrine, whether it be of God, or whether I speak of myself" (John 7:17).

ALMA 33

ALMA 33:1, 11-23; 34:5-6

What is "the seed, or the word" that is to be planted?

"Adam and Eve . . . refused to worship Satan and chose, rather, to plant the seed of faith in the Lord Jesus Christ" (Bruce C. Hafen, *Broken Heart*, 31).

ALMA 33:3-11

In what different ways does the Lord hear and answer our prayers?

"Just as there are many forms of prayers, so there are many types of revelation. Sometimes the Lord has answered prayers with the spoken word. . . . Sometimes the Lord puts thoughts in our minds in answer to prayers. . . . Sometimes the Lord, and perhaps more frequently in this way than in most other ways, gives us peace in our minds" (Marion G. Romney, in Rulon T. Burton, ed., *We Believe*, 642). *See also D&C 8:2–3; insights for Alma 34:17–27; Alma 37:37.*

ALMA 33:3, 15

Who were Zenos and Zenock?

See insights for 1 Nephi 19:10.

ALMA 33:15-17

Many prophets are killed because they testify of Christ.

See insights for Mosiah 7:26–28.

ALMA 34

ALMA 34:9

Whose idea is the great plan of salvation?

"One of the saddest examples of a misconceived and twisted knowledge of an otherwise glorious concept is the all-too-common heresy that there were two plans of salvation; that the Father (presumptively at a loss to know what to do) asked others for proposals; that Christ offered a plan involving agency and Lucifer proposed a plan denying agency; that the Father chose between them.

". . . All things center in the Father; . . . the plan of salvation which he designed was to save his children" (Bruce R. McConkie, *Mortal Messiah*, 1:48, n. 3).

ALMA 34:10–12

How is the Atonement both an "infinite and eternal sacrifice"?

"'[Our] fathers did eat [the miraculous] manna in the wilderness, and are dead.' They would have remained forever dead, too, except for the blessing of the Atonement, a blessing which in its effects is infinite and endless, not temporary" (Neal A. Maxwell, *Wonderful Flood of Light*, 53). *See also insights for Mosiah 3:7 and Alma 7:11–13.*

ALMA 34:14–16

"Mercy, which overpowereth justice."

"Know this: Truth, glorious truth, proclaims there is . . . a Mediator. . . .

"Through Him mercy can be fully extended to each of us without offending the eternal law of justice.

"This truth is the very root of Christian doctrine" (Boyd K. Packer, *Ensign*, May 1977, 56). *See also insights for Mosiah 26:30; Alma 42:14–15, 21–25, 30.*

ALMA 34:17–27

What three questions about prayer are answered in these verses?

1. When should we pray?

Morning, midday, and evening (see also Alma 37:37)

2. Where can we pray?

In our fields (at our work)

In our homes

In our closets or secret places

3. For what can we pray?

Mercy from Christ

Our fields and flocks (our work)

Our households (family)

Power against our enemies

Power against the devil

Prosperity

Our welfare and others'

ALMA 34:28-30

Don't just pray, also do.

"Not every one that saith unto me, Lord, Lord, shall enter into the kingdom of heaven; but he that doeth the will of my Father which is in heaven" (Matthew 7:21).

ALMA 34:32-35

"Do not procrastinate the day of your repentance."

"Procrastination . . . is the thief of eternal life" (Joseph Fielding Smith, *Way to Perfection*, 202). *See also Helaman 13:38; Mormon 2:15.*

"It is true that the great principle of repentance is always available, but for the wicked and rebellious there are serious reservations to this statement. For instance, sin is intensely habit-forming and sometimes moves men to the tragic point of no return. . . . As the transgressor moves deeper and deeper in his sin, and the error is entrenched more deeply and the will to change is weakened, it becomes increasingly near-hopeless, and he skids down and down until either he does not want to climb back or he has lost the power to do so" (Spencer W. Kimball, *Miracle of Forgiveness*, 117).

ALMA 34:33

Once we are assigned to a kingdom of glory, "there can be no labor performed."

Those who attain "the glory of the telestial . . . shall be servants of the Most High; but where God and Christ dwell they cannot come, worlds without end" (D&C 76:98, 112). *See also D&C 132:17.*

"After a person has been assigned to his place in the kingdom, either in the telestial, the terrestrial, or the celestial, or to his exaltation, he will never advance from his assigned glory to another glory. That is eternal! That is why we must make our decisions early in life and why it is imperative that such decisions be right" (Spencer W. Kimball, *Teachings*, 50).

"It has been asked if it is possible for one who inherits the telestial glory to advance in time to the celestial glory?

"The answer to this question is, *No!*

". . . Those who do not comprehend the word of the Lord argue that . . . in time they will get where God *was*, but he will have gone on to other heights.

"*This is false*" (Joseph Fielding Smith, *Doctrines of Salvation*, 2:31; emphasis in original).

ALMA 34:39

Is prayer a protection against Satan?

"Let us all revive our individual and family prayers. Prayer is an armor of protection against temptation and I promise you that if you will teach your children to pray, fervently and full of faith, many of your problems are solved before they begin" (Spencer W. Kimball, *Teachings*, 117).

ALMA 35

ALMA 35:8–10

What additional problems can anger lead to?

"We may get angry with our parents, or a teacher, or the bishop, and dwarf ourselves into nameless anonymity as we shrivel and shrink under the venom and poison of bitterness and hatred. . . . The hater . . . cheats himself.

". . . To terminate activity in the Church just to spite leaders or to give vent to wounded feelings is to cheat ourselves" (Spencer W. Kimball, *Teachings*, 242–43). *See also insights for Alma 2:8–10; Alma 20:13–17.*

ALMA 35:15–16

"Alma . . . caused that his sons should be gathered" to give them "his charge."

"Take time to have a meaningful weekly home evening. . . . Have your children actively involved. Teach them correct principles. . . . Remember the marvelous promise made by President Joseph F. Smith when home evenings were first introduced to the Church: 'If the Saints obey this counsel, we promise that great blessings will result. Love at home and obedience to parents will increase. Faith will be developed in the hearts of the youth of Israel, and they will gain power to combat the evil influences and temptations which beset them'" (Ezra Taft Benson, *Teachings*, 516).

ALMA 36

ALMA 36:10

Is there a discrepancy between Mosiah 27:23 and Alma 36:10?

"There is no . . . discrepancy because they are not referring to exactly the same thing. In the account . . . of Mosiah the time element clearly refers to the period of fasting by the priests. . . . In the account . . . of Alma, however, the term 'three days and three nights' clearly refers to the *total time* Alma could not open his mouth nor use his limbs. (Alma 36:10)" (Daniel H. Ludlow, *Companion*, 217–18; emphasis in original).

ALMA 36:11–13

How critical are the steps of recognition and sorrow in the process of repentance?

"Alma serves as a pattern. The horror for sin that engulfed him should be felt by every wayward member of the kingdom; then repentance would be forthcoming" (Bruce R. McConkie, *New Witness for the Articles of Faith*, 228–29.) *See also insights for Mormon 2:10–13.*

"We must remember that repentance is more than just saying, 'I am sorry.' It is more than tears in one's eyes. It is more than a half a dozen prayers. Repentance means suffering. If a person hasn't suffered, he hasn't repented. . . . He has got to go through a change in his system whereby he suffers" (Spencer W. Kimball, *Teachings*, 99). *See also Alma 14:6; insights for Mosiah 23:9–10.*

ALMA 36:12

What are the meanings of "harrowed up" and "racked"?

"The prophets chose very graphic words.

"Racked means 'tortured.' Anciently a rack was a framework on which the victim was laid with each ankle and wrist tied to a spindle which could then be turned to cause unbearable pain.

"A harrow is a frame with spikes through it. When pulled across the ground, it rips and tears into the soil" (Boyd K. Packer, *Ensign*, May, 2001, 23).

ALMA 36:13

What are the meanings of "hell"?

See insights for 1 Nephi 15:29–32.

ALMA 36:18–20

What caused Alma to remember his "pains no more"?

"Alma learned the eternal truth that the pain and misery that come from sin can only be erased by repentance. Physical pain ends with death. Spiritual pain, or misery, is everlasting, unless we repent" (Dallin H. Oaks, *Ensign*, November 1991, 74–75).

ALMA 36:22

"I saw, even as our father Lehi saw, God sitting upon his throne."
See insights for 1 Nephi 1:8.

ALMA 36:23–26

What does it mean to be born of God?
See insights for Enos 1:4–7; Alma 5:14, 26; 5:49.

ALMA 36:28

The Lord "will raise me up at the last day."
See insights for Alma 11:41–42, 44.

ALMA 37

ALMA 37:6–7, 41, 44–46

In what ways does the Lord use "small and simple things" to do great things?

"To do well those things which God ordained to be the common lot of all mankind, is the truest greatness. To be a successful father or a successful mother is greater than to be a successful general or a successful statesman" (Joseph F. Smith, *Gospel Doctrine*, 285).

ALMA 37:21–24

What is the meaning of the word "Gazelem"?

"Gazelem is a name given to a servant of God [see verse 23]. The word appears to have its roots in Gaz—a stone, and Aleim, a name of God as a revelator, or the interposer in the affairs of men. If this suggestion is correct, its roots admirably agree with its apparent meaning—a seer" (George Reynolds and Janne M. Sjodahl, *Commentary on the Book of Mormon*, 4:162).

ALMA 37:27–29

What are some things that aren't worth talking about?

"As I have met with many groups of missionaries throughout the mission, I find a tendency for missionaries to tell their faults to their companions, their friends, and sometimes in public. There is no place in the mission field to publicize your weaknesses. When you have something that is disturbing you, you should go to your mission president" (Spencer W. Kimball, *Teachings*, 96).

"Tell to the public that which belongs to the public. If you have sinned against the people, confess to them. If you have sinned against a family or a neighborhood, go to them and confess. If you have sinned against your Ward, confess to your Ward. If you have sinned against one individual, take that person by yourselves and make your confession to him. And if you have sinned against your God, or against yourselves, confess to God, and keep the matter to yourselves, for I do not want to know anything about it" (Brigham Young, *Discourses*, 158).

ALMA 37:29, 32

We ought to "abhor . . . wickedness" and have "an everlasting hatred against sin."

"O Lord, wilt . . . thou make me that I may shake at the appearance of sin?" (2 Nephi 4:31).

ALMA 37:35

What are the benefits of learning to keep the commandments in your youth?

"You may look around today, and who are the leaders among the people but those who early and zealously devoted themselves to the faith? And you may foretell who are to be the leaders by observing the boys who show self-respect and purity and who are earnest in all good works. The Lord will not choose men from any other class of his people. . . . The opposite course, waiting to serve the Lord until the wild oats of youth are sown, is reprehensible. There is always something lacking in the man who spends his youth in wickedness and sin, and then turns to righteousness in later years. . . . The fact is clear that the best part of his life and strength is wasted, and there remains only poor, broken service to offer the Lord. There are regrets and heartburnings in repenting late in life from the follies and sins of youth, but there are consolation and rich reward in serving the Lord in the vigorous days of early manhood" (Joseph F. Smith, *Gospel Doctrine*, 335). *See also Proverbs 8:17; Acts 1:21.*

ALMA 37:36

Why should we let all our "thoughts be directed unto the Lord"?

"How knoweth a man the master whom he has not served, and who is a stranger unto him, and is far from the thoughts and intents of his heart?" (Mosiah 5:13). *See also insights for 2 Nephi 25:26–28.*

ALMA 37:37

What blessings come from praying each morning and night?

"I have little or no fear for the boy or the girl, the young man or the young woman, who honestly and conscientiously supplicate God twice a day for the guidance of His Spirit. I am sure that when temptation comes they will have the strength to overcome it by the inspiration that shall be given to them. Supplicating the Lord for the guidance of His Spirit places around us a safeguard, and if we . . . honestly seek the guidance of the Spirit of the Lord, I can assure you that we will receive it" (Heber J. Grant, *Gospel Standards*, 26).

ALMA 37:38-40

What is the meaning of the word Liahona?

"L is a Hebrew preposition meaning 'to,' . . . Iah is a Hebrew abbreviated form of 'Jehovah,' . . . On is the Hebrew name of the Egyptian 'City of the Sun,' L-iah-on means, therefore, literally, 'To God is Light'; or, 'of God is Light.' That is to say, God gives light" (George Reynolds and Janne M. Sjodahl, *Commentary on the Book of Mormon*, 1:229).

ALMA 37:43, 45

"These things are not without shadow. . . . Is there not a type in this thing?"

"God does nothing by chance, but always by design as a loving father" (Spencer W. Kimball, *Ensign*, December 1974, 5). *See also Ezekiel 14:23.*

"The Lord in ancient times had a meaning for everything" (Orson Pratt, *Journal of Discourses*, 14:9). *See also insights for 1 Nephi 18:10–23.*

ALMA 37:44-45

What is the value of heeding the words of Christ?

"The rod of iron . . . was the word of God, which led to . . . the tree of life; . . . a representation of the love of God" (1 Nephi 11:25).

ALMA 38

ALMA 38:1-5

Throughout time there have been many great brothers like Helaman and Shiblon.

1. Moses and Aaron (Exodus 4:14)

2. Peter and Andrew (Matthew 4:18)

3. James and John (Matthew 4:21)

4. Nephi and Sam (1 Nephi 2:16–17)

5. Jacob and Joseph (Jacob 1:18–19)

6. Ammon and Aaron (Alma 22:1)

7. Nephi and Lehi (Helaman 11:18–19)

8. Nephi and Timothy (3 Nephi 19:4)

9. Jared and Mohonri Moriancumer (Ether 1:33)

10. Joseph and Hyrum (D&C 135:3)

ALMA 38:12

How do we bridle all of our passions?

"What is a bridle for? To kill, to diminish, or even to limit the spirit and power of the steed? Never. . . . We are given our bodies and our emotions not to destroy but to ride" (Truman G. Madsen, *Four Essays on Love*, 36).

ALMA 38:13–14

What attitude will bring the Lord's forgiveness?

"Two men went up into the temple to pray; the one a Pharisee, and the other a publican.

"The Pharisee stood and prayed thus with himself, God, I thank thee, that I am not as other men are, extortioners, unjust, adulterers, or even as this publican.

"I fast twice in the week, I give tithes of all that I possess.

"And the publican, standing afar off, would not lift up so much as his eyes unto heaven, but smote upon his breast, saying, God be merciful to me a sinner.

"I tell you, this man went down to his house justified rather than the other: for every one that exalteth himself shall be abased; and he that humbleth himself shall be exalted" (Luke 18:10–14).

ALMA 39

ALMA 39:2

"Thou didst go on unto boasting."

See insights for Alma 26:11–12.

ALMA 39:2, 11

"When they saw your conduct they would not believe in my words."

"The way we live outweighs any words we may profess to follow" (Delbert L. Stapley, *Ensign*, November 1974, 20).

"I think the greatest crime in all this world is to lead men and women, the children of God, away from the true principles. . . .

"If we labor all our days and save but one soul, how great will be our joy with him; on the other hand how great will be our sorrow and our condemnation if through our acts we have led one soul away from this truth" (Joseph Fielding Smith, *Doctrines of Salvation*, 1:314). *See also insights for 2 Nephi 31:7–10, 12–13, 16.*

ALMA 39:5-6

Which are the most serious sins in the eyes of the Lord?

Sexual sin

"Think of it—unchastity is second only to murder. Perhaps there is a common element in those two things unchastity and murder. Both have to do with life, which touches upon the highest of divine powers. Murder involves the wrongful taking of life; sexual transgression may involve the wrongful giving of life, or the wrongful tampering with the sacred fountains of life-giving power" (Bruce C. Hafen, *New Era*, February 2002, 10).

Murder

"The call to repentance and baptism which includes murderers (3 Ne. 30:2) has reference to those who took life while engaged in unrighteous wars, as did the Lamanites, because they were compelled to do so, and not because they in their hearts sought the blood of their fellow men" (Bruce R. McConkie, *Mormon Doctrine*, 520).

"Behold, I speak unto the church. Thou shalt not kill; and he that kills shall not have forgiveness in this world, nor in the world to come" (D&C 42:18).

"In the final analysis, only God, who can discern the thoughts of the heart, can judge whether a particular killing is an unforgivable murder or not" (Daniel H. Ludlow, ed., *Encyclopedia of Mormonism*, 2:971, s.v. "Murder").

Denying the Holy Ghost

Denying the Holy Ghost is "an *unpardonable* sin because it cannot be paid for (or pardoned) either by the sinner himself or through the atonement of Jesus Christ" (Daniel H. Ludlow, *Companion*, 222; emphasis in original). *See also Matthew 12:31.*

"What must a man do to commit the unpardonable sin? He must receive the Holy Ghost, have the heavens opened unto him, and know God, and then sin against him. After a man has sinned against the Holy Ghost, there is no repentance for him. He has got to say that the sun does not shine while he sees it; he has got to deny Jesus Christ when the heavens have been opened unto him, and to deny the plan of salvation with his eyes open to the truth of it; and from that time he begins to be an enemy. This is the case with many apostates of The Church of Jesus Christ of Latter-day Saints" (Joseph Smith, *Teachings*, 358).

ALMA 39:9

"Forsake . . . the lusts of your eyes."

"Whosoever looketh on a woman to lust after her hath committed adultery with her already in his heart" (Matthew 5:28). *See also D&C 121:45.*

"'The lusts of your eyes.' In our day, what does that expression mean?

"Movies, television programs, and video recordings that are both suggestive and lewd.

"Magazines and books that are obscene and pornographic.

". . . The mind through which this filth passes is never the same afterwards" (Ezra Taft Benson, *Ensign*, May 1986, 45).

"Cross yourself in all these things."

"For a man to take up his cross, is to deny himself of all ungodliness, and every worldly lust, and keep my commandments" (JST, Matthew 16:26).

ALMA 40

ALMA 40:4, 8–9, 16, 18–19

"There is a time appointed . . . for the resurrection."

"Is Joseph glorified? No, he is preaching to the spirits in prison. He will get his resurrection the first of any one in this Kingdom" (Brigham Young, *Discourses*, 468). *See also 1 Corinthians 15:23; D&C 133:52–56; insights for Mosiah 15:21–23.*

"Then angels will come and begin to resurrect the dead, and the Savior will also raise the dead, and they will receive the keys of the resurrection, and will begin to assist in that work" (Brigham Young, *Discourses*, 115).

ALMA 40:11

What does it mean to be "taken home" to God?

"Jesus saith unto her, Touch me not; for I am not yet ascended to my Father: but go to my brethren, and say unto them, I ascend unto my Father, and your Father; and to my God, and your God" (John 20:17).

"These words of Alma . . . do not intend to convey the thought that all spirits go back into the presence of God. . . . 'Taken home to God,' simply means that their mortal existence has come to an end, and they have returned to the world of spirits" (Joseph Fielding Smith, *Answers to Gospel Questions*, 2:85).

ALMA 40:12-13

What are the states called paradise and outer darkness?

"The spirits of those who are righteous are received into a state of happiness which is called paradise, a state of rest, a state of peace, where they expand in wisdom, where they have respite from all their troubles, and where care and sorrow do not annoy. The wicked, on the contrary, have no part nor portion in the Spirit of the Lord, and they are cast into outer darkness, being led captive, because of their own iniquity, by the evil one. And in this space between death and the resurrection of the body, the two classes of souls remain, in happiness or in misery" (Joseph F. Smith, *Gospel Doctrine*, 448).

Where is the spirit world located?

"When you lay down this tabernacle, where are you going? Into the spirit world. . . . Where is the spirit world? It is right here. . . . Do they go beyond the boundaries of the organized earth? No" (Brigham Young, *Discourses*, 376).

"The spirits of the just are . . . not far from us, and know and understand our thoughts, feelings, and motions, and are often pained therewith" (Joseph Smith, *Teachings*, 325).

ALMA 40:13-14

What will the wicked do in outer darkness?

"I once wondered if those who refuse to repent but who then satisfy the law of justice by paying for their own sins are then worthy to enter the celestial kingdom. The answer is no. The entrance requirements for celestial life are simply higher than merely satisfying the law of justice. For that reason, paying for our sins will not bear the same fruit as repenting of our sins" (Bruce C. Hafen, *Broken Heart*, 7-8).

ALMA 40:23

"The soul shall be restored to the body."

See insights for Alma 11:41-42, 44.

ALMA 40:26

"No unclean thing can inherit the kingdom of God."

See insights for Alma 11:37.

ALMA 41

ALMA 41:2, 12

How long will it take for deformities in the flesh to be removed in the resurrection?

"President Joseph F. Smith said that the same person, in the same form and likeness, will come forth 'even to the wounds in the flesh. . . .'

". . . These changes will come naturally, of course, but almost instantly" (Joseph Fielding Smith, *Doctrines of Salvation*, 2:293–4). *See also insights for Alma 11:45.*

ALMA 41:3–6

What is the meaning of good being restored to good and evil being restored to evil?

See insights for Mormon 9:3–5.

ALMA 41:7

How will wicked people feel when "they are their own judges"?

"The great misery of departed spirits in the world of spirits, where they go after death, is to know that they come short of the glory that others enjoy and that they might have enjoyed themselves, and they are their own accusers. . . .

"A man is his own tormenter and his own condemner. . . . The torment of disappointment in the mind of man is as exquisite as a lake burning with fire and brimstone" (Joseph Smith, *Teachings*, 310, 357).

"Though there are specific times and formal occasions designated as days of judgment, in the final analysis every day is a *day of judgment* for every person, and every man is his own judge" (Bruce R. McConkie, *Mormon Doctrine*, 403; emphasis in original). *See also insights for 3 Nephi 27:27.*

ALMA 41:10

"Wickedness never was happiness."

"You cannot do wrong and feel right. It is impossible" (Ezra Taft Benson, *New Era*, June, 1986, 5).

"Wickedness never did, never does, never will bring us happiness. Violation of the laws of God brings only misery, bondage, and darkness" (Ezra Taft Benson, *Teachings*, 71). *See also insights for Mosiah 2:41.*

ALMA 41:15

"That which ye do send out shall return unto you again."

See insight for Moroni 7:18.

ALMA 42

ALMA 42:5, 8, 11, 13, 15

What is "the great plan of salvation"?

"How glorious is the plan of salvation, inaugurated before the foundation of the world for the salvation of men. Adam was sent to start the race, and through doing so, it became necessary for him to transgress a law, to bring death, or mortality, into the world. That made it necessary for the coming of Jesus Christ to redeem us from Adam's transgression, or the mortal death, and through the mercy of our Father in heaven, and His Son Jesus Christ, through that atonement we likewise are granted redemption from our own sins on condition of our repentance" (Joseph Fielding Smith, in Conference Report, April 1944, 49).

ALMA 42:9

How do people experience spiritual death?

See insights for Alma 12:16, 32.

ALMA 42:14–15, 21–25, 30

How do the laws of justice and mercy work together?

"Justice requires that God must be a God of order and that he must be just and impartial. . . .

"The law of mercy agrees entirely with the law of justice. However, the law of mercy introduces the possibility of vicarious payment of the laws that have been transgressed. . . . Whenever a law is transgressed (or broken), a payment (or suffering or atonement) must be made; however, the person who transgressed the law does not need to make payment *if* he will repent and *if* he can find someone else who is both able and willing to make payment" (Daniel H. Ludlow, *Companion*, 176; emphasis in original).

ALMA 42:16, 22

"Repentance could not come . . . except there were a punishment."

"We are punished by our sins, if not for them" (Boyd K. Packer, *Ensign*, November 1995, 19).

"There can be no forgiveness without real and total repentance, and there can be no repentance without punishment. This is as eternal as is the soul. . . .

"It is so easy to let our sympathies carry us out of proportion; and when a man has committed sin, he must suffer. It is an absolute requirement" (Spencer W. Kimball, *Ensign*, May 1975, 78). *See also insights for Alma 36:11–13.*

ALMA 42:29

What should be our attitude toward sins for which we have repented?

"This one thing I do, forgetting those things which are behind, and reaching forth unto those things which are before" (Philippians 3:13).

"Paul's healthy attitude toward his own past in which he had relentlessly persecuted the Christians was his meek realization that he had been forgiven. He did not intend to let his yesterday hold his tomorrow hostage; instead, he pressed forward and forgot that which was past" (Neal A. Maxwell, *Meek and Lowly*, 93–94).

ALMA 43

ALMA 43:9, 26, 30, 45–50; 44:5; 46:12; 48:10, 24

For what reasons are we justified in going to war?

"Is there ever a time when war, or the taking up of arms is justified?

"Yes. . . . When it becomes necessary for a righteous people to take arms against their enemies who are the aggressors, in protection of their lives and in defense of their possessions, the Lord has approved" (Joseph Fielding Smith, *Answers to Gospel Questions*, 3:50). *See also insights for Mosiah 27:2–3.*

ALMA 43:46–47; 47:14

The Lord said to defend and not be "guilty of the first offense."

"Self-defense is as justifiable where war is concerned as where one man seeks to take the life of another. . . . Righteous men are entitled, expected, and obligated to defend themselves; they must engage in battle when there is no other way to preserve their rights and freedoms and to protect their families, homes, land, and the truths of salvation which they have espoused" (Bruce R. McConkie, *Mormon Doctrine*, 826). *See also 3 Nephi 3:20–21; insights for Mormon 3:10, 19; 4:1–4.*

ALMA 43:54–44:2, 6; 47:11

If we are called to war, what should be our attitude?

"We have to be careful as to what spirit we are guided by. If we want to go out to battle, to encroach upon other peoples' liberties and rights, to gain their lands, to destroy their property without any right or reason, that is one thing; but if somebody comes against us to destroy us and our property and our homes and our rights and our privileges, either on land or sea, then we have the right under the divine law to rise for our own protection and take such steps as are necessary. . . . We Latter-day Saints must watch ourselves and not give way to passion and desire to shed blood and to destroy. . . ." (Charles W. Penrose, in Conference Report, April 1917, 21).

ALMA 44

ALMA 44:4
God will support the faithful; Satan will not.
"Thus we see that the devil will not support his children at the last day" (Alma 30:60).

ALMA 44:8, 11, 15, 19–20; 53:11, 13–16
How seriously did the Nephites and Lamanites take promises made to each other?
See insights for 1 Nephi 4:32–37.

ALMA 45

ALMA 45:1
In what ways can we show our thanks to the Lord?
"We should offer unto Him [God] our thanks and honor Him in prayer, in fasting, in singing" (Joseph F. Smith, in Conference Report, April 1911, 86).

ALMA 45:15–16; 46:10, 17; 48:25
For what reasons could the land be cursed or blessed?
See insights for 2 Nephi 1:7, 9–11, 16, 20, 31–32.

ALMA 45:18–19
What ultimately happened to Alma and Moses?
"Moses, Elijah, and Alma the younger, were translated" (Bruce R. McConkie, *Mormon Doctrine*, 805).

ALMA 46

ALMA 46:10
"Amalickiah . . . was . . . a man of many flattering words."
See insights for Jacob 7:2, 4.

ALMA 46:8
"How quick the children of men do forget the Lord their God."
See insights for Helaman 5:5–14.

ALMA 46:12-23

How are renting and covenant making related?

The Hebrew word *qara* (pronouced karà) is to rend or tear clothing. The word *karat* (pronounced carrot) is to cut as in "cutting" a covenant rather than "making" a covenant (Brown, Driver, and Briggs, *Hebrew Lexicon*, 503). These words are similar both in pronunciation and meaning. Genesis 15 is a good example of how cutting and covenanting are connected. "[Abraham] said, Lord God, whereby shall I know that I shall inherit it?

"And he said unto him, Take me an heifer of three years old, and a she goat of three years old, and a ram of three years old, and a turtledove, and a young pigeon.

"And he took unto him all these, and divided them in the midst, and laid each piece one against another: but the birds divided he not. . . .

"When the sun went down, and it was dark, behold a smoking furnace, and a burning lamp that passed between those pieces.

"In the same day the Lord made a covenant with Abram" (Genesis 15:8–10, 17–18).

Interestingly a "broken heart" is the sacrifice the Lord requires of us today (see D&C 59:8). The rent garment was the outward expression of the inner broken heart. All of this brings added meaning and understanding to Moroni's rent coat. Some related scriptures would include:

1. Circumcision was the sign of the covenant (Genesis 17:10–12)

2. Sacrament is broken, or torn (Luke 22:19)

3. "Cleave unto [God]" (Deuteronomy 13:1–4)

4. Cleave unto thy wife (Genesis 2:24; D&C 42:22)

5. Broken heart and contrite spirit (3 Nephi 9:20)

6. Veil of the temple is rent (Matthew 27:51)

7. At the covenants of baptism the water is divided (1 Corinthians 10:1–2)

8. Moses parted the Red Sea (Exodus 14:15–22)

9. Joshua, Elijah, Elisha parted the Jordan River (Joshua 3:14–17; 2 Kings 2:8, 14)

10. The Savior and the cleaved Mount of Olives (D&C 45:48)

11. The cursings and blessings of Joshua (Joshua 8:33; Deutronomy 28)

12. You can be cut into the covenant and cut out of the covenant (Alma 50:20)

ALMA 46:24

"The coat of Joseph . . . had not decayed."

"The Bible does not mention what happened to Joseph's coat after it was smeared with blood . . . and taken to Jacob, but according to the Book of Mormon, the coat was preserved and, miraculously, part of the coat never decayed. [This] account is partially substantiated by . . . the great Moslem historian, Muhammad ibn-Ibrahim ath-Tha'labi: . . .

"'. . . [The] garment . . . *never decayed* or in any way deteriorated. . . . And it was the very one that had belonged to Abraham, having already had a long history'" (Daniel H. Ludlow, *Companion*, 234; emphasis in original).

ALMA 47

ALMA 47:10–12, 18

Satan will entice us to come down in our standards so he can kill us by degrees.

"[The devil] leadeth them by the neck with a flaxen cord [light or thin cord], until he bindeth them with his strong cords forever" (2 Nephi 26:22).

"And others will he pacify, and lull them away . . . and thus the devil cheateth their souls, and leadeth them away carefully down to hell" (2 Nephi 28:21). *See also insights for 2 Nephi 28:21–22; 24–25.*

ALMA 48

ALMA 48:11–17

How did Moroni shake "the very powers of hell"?

"His magnanimous nature as a lover of peace and fair play always prevailed. . . . You cannot ask for a less warlike spirit than that of an army who 'were compelled reluctantly to contend with their brethren . . .' who were 'sorry to take up arms . . . because they did not delight in the shedding of blood' (Alma 48:21–23). In battle Moroni . . . refused to take advantage of an enemy . . . (Alma 55:19). . . . With never a thought of punishing a beaten foe, . . . he was satisfied to take his defeated adversaries at their word and trust them to return to their homes" (Hugh Nibley, *Prophetic Book of Mormon*, 353).

"Men and women who turn their lives over to God will discover that He can make a lot more out of their lives than they can. He will deepen their joys, expand their vision, quicken their minds, strengthen their muscles, lift their spirits, multiply their blessings, increase their opportunities, comfort their souls, raise up friends, and pour out peace" (Ezra Taft Benson, *Teachings*, 361).

ALMA 49

ALMA 49:22

More language evidences point to authenticity of the Book of Mormon.

"One interesting observation was that the Hebrew idiom for 'shooting' an arrow literally also means 'throwing'; thus Alma 49:22 refers to arrows 'thrown' at the Lamanites" (John W. Welch, ed., *Reexploring the Book of Mormon*, 199).

ALMA 49:28

What blessings come from thanking the Lord?

See insights for 1 Nephi 5:7, 9–10.

ALMA 50

ALMA 50:19

"Thus we see how merciful and just are all the dealings of the Lord."

See insights for Alma 42:14–15, 21–25, 30.

ALMA 50:20–21, 25; 51:2, 7, 9, 12, 16; 60:15–16

"The wickedness . . . at our head" is what we must avoid.

"I do not believe the greatest threat to our future is from bombs or guided missiles. I do not think our civilization will die that way. I think it will die when we no longer care—when the spiritual forces that make us wish to be right and noble die in the hearts of men" (Ezra Taft Benson, *Teachings*, 590).

ALMA 51

ALMA 51:2, 4, 7, 9, 12, 16, 22

What role did contention play in the Nephites losing their lands?

See insights for 3 Nephi 11:28–29.

ALMA 51:13–19

What obligation do we have to defend our country?

"Certainly a true American cannot have too much patriotism. Surely Americans who have respect for our traditions, who support our freedoms and are willing to fight to preserve them have been called patriots.

". . . I love America's traditions and its freedoms and I believe they are well worth fighting for" (Ezra Taft Benson, *Teachings*, 591). *See also insights for Alma 43:9, 26, 30, 45–50; 44:5; 46:12; 48:10, 24.*

ALMA 52

ALMA 52:35

Sometimes in war the righteous are "slain on both sides."

"My father hath been slain in battle, and all my kinsfolk" (Mormon 8:5). *See also insights for Mosiah 9:17–19.*

ALMA 54

ALMA 54:16, 24

Why should we try to avoid our own vengeance?

"Man shall not smite, neither shall he judge; for judgment is mine, saith the Lord, and vengeance is mine also, and I will repay" (Mormon 8:20).

ALMA 55

ALMA 55:14, 30–32

What problems can come from drunkenness?

"Over the earth . . . the demon drink is in control. Drunken with strong drink, men have lost their reason; their counsel has been destroyed; their judgment and vision are fled; they reel forward to destruction.

"Drink brings cruelty into the home; it walks arm in arm with poverty; its companions are disease and plague; it puts chastity to flight; it knows neither honesty nor fair dealing; it is a total stranger to truth; it drowns conscience; it is the bodyguard of evil; it curses all who touch it.

"Drink has brought more woe and misery, broken more hearts, wrecked more homes, committed more crimes, filled more coffins, than all the wars the world has suffered" (David O. Mckay, in Conference Report, October 1942, 8). *See also D&C* 89:5, 7.

ALMA 56

ALMA 56:11

"They . . . died in the cause of their country and of their God . . . and they are happy."

First we must be willing to die for the Lord, "whoso is not willing to lay down his life for my sake is not my disciple" (D&C 103:28). Second if the righteous do die in their service they "shall not taste of death, for it shall be sweet unto them" (D&C 42:46).

ALMA 56:47–48; 57:21

How powerful is the influence of righteous mothers?

"Our wives and mothers and daughters are, and when it comes to faith in God and prayer . . . equal to anything that the men may be able to muster" (George Albert Smith, in Conference Report, April 1943, 90).

"If I were asked to name the world's greatest need. I should say unhesitatingly wise mothers" (David O. Mckay, in Jeanette McKay Morrell, *Highlights in the Life of President David O. McKay*, 34).

"The noblest calling in the world is motherhood. True motherhood is the most beautiful of all arts, the greatest of all professions. She who can paint a masterpiece, or who can write a book that will influence millions, deserves the admiration and plaudits of mankind; but she who rears successfully a family of healthy, beautiful sons and daughters, whose immortal souls will exert an influence throughout the ages long after paintings shall have faded, and books and statues shall have decayed or have been destroyed, deserves the highest honor that man can give, and the choicest blessings of God. In her high duty and service to humanity in clothing with mortality eternal spirits, she is co-partner with the Creator Himself" (David O. McKay, *Pathways to Happiness*, 116).

"Your mother is your best friend. Never forget that. She gave you life. She cared for you, nurtured you, nursed you when you were sick, and looked after your every need. Listen to her now. Talk with her candidly and confidentially. You will find that she will keep your confidence and that her wisdom will prove to be wonderful" (Gordon B. Hinckley, *Ensign*, May 1996, 93).

"When the real history of mankind is fully disclosed, will it feature the echoes of gunfire or the shaping sound of lullabies? The great armistices made by military men or the peacemaking of women in homes and in neighborhoods? Will what happened in cradles and kitchens prove to be more controlling than what happened in congresses? When the surf of the centuries has made the great pyramids so much sand, the everlasting family will still be standing, because it is a celestial institution, formed outside telestial time." (Neal A. Maxwell, *Ensign*, May 1978, 10–11.)

ALMA 57

ALMA 57:25–27; 58:33, 37; 61:13

Do "we trust in our God" as we really should?

> Oh, thus be it ever, when free men shall stand
> Between their loved homes and the war's desolation!

Blest with vict'ry and peace, may the heav'n-rescued land
Praise the Pow'r that hath made and preserved us a nation!
Then conquer we must, when our cause it is just,
And this be our motto: "In God is our trust!"
And the star-spangled banner in triumph shall wave
O'er the land of the free and the home of the brave!

("The Star-Spangled Banner," *Hymns*, 340).

ALMA 57:25–27

What wounds should we be afraid of receiving?

"We should look upon this body as something that shall endure in the resurrected state. . . . Be not afraid of soiling its hands; be not afraid of scars that may come to it if won in earnest effort, or in honest fight, but beware of scars that disfigure, that have come to you in places where you ought not have gone, that have befallen you in unworthy undertakings; beware of the wounds of battles in which you have been fighting on the wrong side" (James E. Talmage, in Conference Report, October 1913, 117).

ALMA 58

ALMA 58:3–11

When is it most likely that our God will visit us?

"At midnight! Precisely at the darkest hour, when least expected, the bridegroom came. When the world is full of tribulation and help is needed, but it seems the time must be past and hope is vain, then Christ will come. The midnights of life are the times when heaven comes to offer its joy for man's weariness" (Spencer W. Kimball, *Faith Precedes the Miracle*, 255). *See also insights for Alma 8:14.*

ALMA 59

ALMA 59:3

What is our responsibility toward the government that works to protect us?

"We must pay tribute to sustain the government in the necessary expense incurred in the protection of life, liberty, property, and in promoting the welfare of all persons" (Howard W. Hunter, in Conference Report, April 1968, 65).

ALMA 60

ALMA 60:23-24

How do we cleanse the inner vessel today?

"We have made some wonderful strides in the past. We will be lengthening our stride in the future. To do so, we must first cleanse the inner vessel by awaking and arising, being morally clean, using the Book of Mormon in a manner so that God will lift the condemnation, and finally conquering pride by humbling ourselves" (Ezra Taft Benson, *Witness and a Warning*, 79).

ALMA 61

ALMA 61:3

Why do we sometimes experience trials and difficulties?

"Let us not presume that because the way is at times difficult and challenging, our Heavenly Father is not mindful of us. He is . . . sensitizing us for our great responsibilities ahead" (James E. Faust, *Ensign*, February 1998, 7).

ALMA 62

ALMA 62:9

What happened to those who would not defend their country?

"Someone asked me once how I felt about amnesty for the draft card burner and the deserter. I told him that I thought every one of them should be taken before General Moroni to be judged" (Vaughn J. Featherstone, *Ensign*, November 1975, 7-10). *See also insights for Alma 43:9, 26, 30, 45–50; 44:5; 46:12; 48:10, 24.*

ALMA 62:41

How do the righteous and the wicked react differently to the same afflictions?

"The same testing in troubled times can have quite opposite effects on individuals. . . .

"Surely you know some whose lives have been filled with adversity who have been mellowed and strengthened and refined by it, while others have come away from the same test bitter and blistered and unhappy" (Boyd K. Packer, *Memorable Stories and Parables*, 93–94).

ALMA 62:49-51

How can prayer assist us to possess riches without being lifted up in pride?

"In the hour of trial, temptation, and when we feel the least like praying then is the time for us to go to our secret chamber and kneel before the Lord.

. . . We cannot begin to pray too early. . . . When we neglect this and other duties we do not have the same claim on the blessings of the Lord. . . . The Lord was slow to hearken to the Nephites in their rebellion until they were humbled" (Joseph Fielding Smith, *Church History and Modern Revelation*, 2:135). *See also insights for Alma 34:17–27; Alma 34:39; Alma 37:37.*

ALMA 63

ALMA 63:5

Where are the descendants of the people of Hagoth today?

"The belief that Polynesian ancestry includes Book of Mormon people can be traced back at least to 1851, when George Q. Cannon taught it. . . . President Brigham Young detailed the belief in a letter to King Kamehameha V in 1865. Other Church leaders have since affirmed the belief, some indicating that among Polynesian ancestors were the people of Hagoth, who set sail from Nephite lands in approximately 54 B.C. (cf. Alma 63:5–8). In a statement to the Maoris of New Zealand, for instance, President Joseph F. Smith said, 'I would like to say to you brethren and sisters . . . you are some of Hagoth's people, and there is NO PERHAPS about it!' (Cole and Jensen, p. 388.) In the prayer offered at the dedication of the Hawaii Temple, President Heber J. Grant referred to the 'descendants of Lehi' in Hawaii (*IE* 23 [Feb. 1920]:283)" (Daniel H. Ludlow, ed., *Encyclopedia of Mormonism*, 3:1110).

THE BOOK OF
HELAMAN

HELAMAN 1

HELAMAN 1:2, 18; 3:3, 17, 19

What are the effects of contention?

See insights for 3 Nephi 11:28–29.

HELAMAN 1:11

Why do the wicked prefer to "tell no man" of their deeds?

"When you have the Spirit, . . . you don't mind others seeing what you are doing. . . . When you do not have the Spirit, . . . you may become secretive, evasive" (adapted from John H. Groberg, *Ensign*, April 1986, 70). *See also D&C 121:37.*

HELAMAN 1:11–12; 2:3, 8, 13–14

Do secret combinations exist today?

See insights for Helaman 6:22.

HELAMAN 2

HELAMAN 2:8

What is the purpose of secret combinations?

"Beginning in the days of Cain and continuing through all generations, whenever there have been unrighteous and apostate peoples on earth, Satan has revealed unto them his . . . secret combinations. Cain first took upon himself the secret oaths as they were administered by Satan; then he killed Abel. Murder, plunder, robbery, power, the destruction of freedom, and the persecution of the saints have been the objectives of these societies ever since" (Bruce R. McConkie, *Mormon Doctrine*, 698). *See also Ether 8:16; Moses 5:28–32.*

HELAMAN 2:13–14

What did secret combinations nearly cause?

"Of all the factions that separated themselves from the Nephites none worked so much injury to the people as did the bands of the Gadianton

Robbers. . . . To their abominations can be traced the fall and extinction of both the Jaredite and Nephite races" (George Reynolds and Janne M. Sjodahl, *Commentary on the Book of Mormon*, 5:204). *See also Ether 8:21–22, 25.*

HELAMAN 3

HELAMAN 3:1–36; 4:8, 11–12; 6:1, 7–9, 17, 31, 35
What are the elements of the pride cycle?

Keys to breaking out of the pride cycle are found in Alma 62:49–51 and Helaman 3:35.

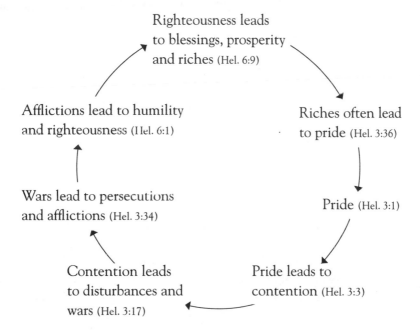

Righteousness leads to blessings, prosperity and riches (Hel. 6:9)

Afflictions lead to humility and righteousness (Hel. 6:1)

Riches often lead to pride (Hel. 3:36)

Wars lead to persecutions and afflictions (Hel. 3:34)

Pride (Hel. 3:1)

Contention leads to disturbances and wars (Hel. 3:17)

Pride leads to contention (Hel. 3:3)

HELAMAN 3:20, 24–35
Some were "lifted up in pride" while others were humble and faithful.

"Since 1960, [in] the U.S. . . . there has been a 560% increase in violent crime; a 419% increase in illegitimate births; a quadrupling in divorce rates; a tripling of the percentage of children living in single-parent homes; more than a 200% increase in the teenage suicide rate" (William J. Bennett, in Gordon B. Hinckley, *Ensign*, November 1993, 59).

Notice what happened in the Church during the same period of time:

	MEMBERS	MISSIONS	STAKES
1960	1,693,180	58	319
1993	8,688,511	295	1,968

(*Deseret News 1995–96 Church Almanac*, 420.)

HELAMAN 3:35

What must I do to experience sanctification?

"To 'yield [our] hearts unto God' is to inquire diligently to know the mind and will of the Almighty; to give way to and follow the impressions of the Spirit; to have no will but God's will" (Joseph Fielding McConkie and Robert L. Millet, *Doctrinal Commentary*, 3:344).

HELAMAN 4

HELAMAN 4:7

What is the narrow neck of land which was "a day's journey for a Nephite"?

"Most would suggest that the 'small neck of land between the land north-ward and the land southward' is describing the mountain pass that provided access to the two lands" (John L. Sorenson, *Ancient American Setting*, 241, 339).

HELAMAN 4:24–25; 6:35

What causes someone to lose the Spirit of the Lord?

The prophets have repeatedly taught that "with transgression we . . . lose the Spirit of God and the Holy Ghost as our comforter (Henry D. Moyle, in Conference Report, April 1963, 46). Heber C. Kimball taught that if we "lightly esteem" the scriptures we "will lose the Spirit" (*Journal of Discourses*, 11:211). Brigham Young explained that "partaking of the sacrament" unworthily will cause us to "lose the Spirit of the Lord" (*Journal of Discourses*, 9:220). Elder Hyrum M. Smith added that the Spirit of the Lord could be lost by "lapsing into indifference, into neglect of duty, into failure to pray, . . . into the spirit of fault-finding. . . . One step leads to another, until by and by the Spirit is grieved and will no longer strive with us. We can go to the extent, in our sinning and neglect, that the Spirit of God will altogether withdraw from us" (Conference Report, October 1912, 58). See also insight for Moroni 8:28.

HELAMAN 5

HELAMAN 5:2

What happens if the wicked outnumber the righteous?

"If distress through the judgments of God comes upon this people, it will be because the majority have turned away from the Lord. Let the majority of the people turn away from the Holy Commandments . . . and cease to hold the balance of power in the Church, and we may expect the judgments of God to come upon us; but while six-tenths or three-fourths of this people will keep the commandments of God, the curse and judgments of the Almighty will never come upon them, though we will have trials of various kinds" (Brigham Young, *Journal of Discourses*, 10:336).

HELAMAN 5:6

How important are our names?

George Albert Smith told of a dream he'd once had. In the dream he had passed to the other side and met his beloved grandfather:

"When Grandfather came within a few feet of me, he stopped. . . . He looked at me very earnestly and said:

"'I would like to know what you have done with my name.'

"Everything I had ever done passed before me as though it were a flying picture on a screen. . . . I smiled and looked at my grandfather and said:

"'I have never done anything with your name of which you need be ashamed.'

"He stepped forward and took me in his arms" (George Albert Smith, *Sharing the Gospel with Others*, 110).

HELAMAN 5:5–14

The word "remember" is used fifteen times in these verses.

"When you look in the dictionary for the most important word, do you know what it is? It could be 'remember.' Because all of you have made covenants . . . our greatest need is to remember. That is why everyone goes to sacrament meeting every Sabbath day, to take the sacrament and listen to the priests pray that they 'may always remember him.' . . . 'Remember' is the word. 'Remember' is the program" (Spencer W. Kimball, in *Book of Mormon Student Study Guide*, 147).

"Some Latter-day Saints remember Him only when adversity overtakes them; in prosperity they forget him. . . . Never forget God" (Joseph F. Smith, in *Collected Discourses*, 2:280).

"What could I ever do to repay Him? The answer is nothing. Nothing I can do could merit what he did for me. But that is only a partial answer.

"[Consider this] article from a medical magazine about 'belaying' in mountain climbing. The belay system is the way a mountain climber protects himself from falls. Someone climbs up first, gets in a firm, secure position, ties the rope tightly around his waist, and calls down to his partner, 'You're on belay,' which means, 'I have you if you fall.' The article reported about Alan Czenkusch, a man who ran a climbing school in Colorado for physicians:

"'Belaying has brought Czenkusch his best and worst moment in climbing. Czenkusch once fell from a high precipice, yanking out three mechanical supports and pulling his belayer off a ledge. He was stopped, upside down, ten feet from the ground when his spread-eagled belayer arrested the fall with the strength of his outstretched arms.'

""'Don saved my life,"" says Czenkusch. "How do you respond to a guy like that? Give him a used climbing rope for a Christmas present? No, *you remember him. You always remember him.*"' (Eric G. Anderson, "The Vertical Wilderness," *Private Practice*, November 1979, p. 17; italics added.)

"What a profound analogy for us. Like the belayer, the Savior stops our traumatic fall toward spiritual destruction and offers us a safe line back to him. And what can we do to repay him? *Always* remember him" (Gerald N. Lund, *Jesus Christ, Key to the Plan of Salvation*, 45).

HELAMAN 5:12

What is the rock upon which we should build?

"Now, the most important principle I can share: Anchor your life in Jesus Christ, your Redeemer. Make your Eternal Father and his Beloved Son the most important priority in your life—more important than life itself, more important than a beloved companion or children or anyone on earth" (Richard G. Scott, *Ensign*, May 1993, 34).

"If our lives are centered in Christ, nothing can go permanently wrong. . . . On the other hand, if our lives are not centered on the Savior and his teachings, no other success can ever be permanently right" (Howard W. Hunter, *Teachings*, 40).

HELAMAN 5:18–11:6

What are the similarities between Nephi and Lehi and the two witnesses mentioned in Revelation 11:2–13?

"The record of the Nephite history just prior to the Savior's visit reveals many parallels to our own day as we anticipate the Savior's second coming" (Ezra Taft Benson, in Conference Report, April 1987, 3).

HELAMAN 5:18, 20–23, 28–31; 11:3–6	COMPARISON	REVELATION 11:2–13
18 And it came to pass that *Nephi and Lehi* did *preach* unto the Lamanites with such great *power* and authority, . . .	Two great prophets	2 . . . *the holy city* shall they tread under foot forty and two months.
20 And it came to pass that Nephi and Lehi did proceed from thence to *go to the land of Nephi.*	Taught the gospel	3 And I will give power unto my *two witnesses;* and they *shall prophesy* a thousand two hundred and threescore days, clothed in sackcloth. . . .
21 And it came to pass that they were taken by an army of *the Lamanites and cast into prison;* . . .	Given power in word	5 And if any man will hurt them, *fire proceedeth out of their mouth,* and devoureth their enemies: and if any man will hurt them, he must in this manner be killed.
22 And after they had been cast into prison many days without food, behold, they went forth into the prison to take them that they *might slay them.*	Sent to a faithless people	6 These have power to *shut heaven, that it rain not* in the days of *their prophecy:* and have power over waters to turn them to blood, and to smite the earth with all plagues, as often as they will.
23 And it came to pass that Nephi and Lehi were *encircled about as if by fire,* even insomuch that they durst not lay their hands upon them. . . .	Stopped the rain, caused a drought	
28 And it came to pass that they were overshadowed with a cloud of darkness, and an awful solemn *fear came upon them.*	They were to be put to death	7 And when they shall have finished their testimony, the beast that ascendeth out of the bottomless pit shall make war against them, and shall overcome them, and *kill them.* . . .
29 And it came to pass that *there came a voice* as if it were above the cloud of darkness, . . .	The Lord raised them from their afflictions	11 And after three days and an half the Spirit of life from God entered into them, and *they stood upon their feet;* and *great fear fell upon them* which saw them.
31 And notwithstanding the mildness of the voice, behold, *the earth shook* exceedingly, and the walls of the prison trembled again, as if it were about to tumble to the earth; . . .	Their enemies heard a voice from heaven	12 And *they heard a great voice from heaven* saying unto them, Come up hither. And *they ascended up to heaven* in a cloud; and their enemies beheld them.
3 . . . Nephi did cry unto the Lord, saying: . . .	An earthquake shook the ground	13 And the same hour was there a *great earthquake,* and the tenth part of the city fell, and in the earthquake were slain of men
4 . . . let there be a famine in the land, . . .		seven thousand: and the remnant were *affrighted,* and gave glory to the God of heaven. (emphasis added)
6 . . . *the earth was smitten that it was dry,* and did not yield forth grain in the season of grain; (emphasis added)	Their enemies felt great fear	

HELAMAN 5:23

"Nephi and Lehi were encircled about as if by fire."

"The scriptures, and even our church history, record miraculous instances when visible flames encircled the humble followers of Christ—literal manifestations of fire and the Holy Ghost—but more often this fire works quietly and unseen in the hearts of those who have received the gift of the Holy Ghost" (Loren C. Dunn, *Ensign*, June 1995, 24).

HELAMAN 5:47

Who spoke the words "my Well Beloved"?

See insights for 3 Nephi 11:7.

"According to the laws of mediation and intercession which the Father himself ordained, he has chosen to reveal himself through the Son, ordaining that all revelation shall come through the Son, though that holy personage frequently speaks in the Father's name by divine investiture of authority; that is, he speaks in the first person as though he were the Father" (Bruce R. McConkie, *Doctrinal New Testament Commentary*, 3:137).

HELAMAN 6

HELAMAN 6:22

Do secret combinations exist today?

"The Book of Mormon teaches that secret combinations engaged in crime present a serious challenge, not just to individuals and families but to entire civilizations. Among today's secret combinations are gangs, drug cartels, and organized crime families. The secret combinations of our day function much like the Gadianton robbers of the Book of Mormon times. They have secret signs and code words. They participate in secret rites and initiation ceremonies" (M. Russell Ballard, *Ensign*, November 1997, 38). *See also Ether 8:14.*

HELAMAN 6:37

How did the word of God destroy the Gadianton robbers?

See insights for Alma 31:5.

HELAMAN 7

HELAMAN 7:7–9

"Oh, that I could have had my days in the days when my father Nephi first came."

This wish serves as a reminder of the way life was for Nephi and his brother Jacob. "The time passed away with us, and also our lives passed away like as it were unto us a dream, we being a lonesome and a solemn people, wanderers, cast out from Jerusalem, born in tribulation, in a wilderness, and hated of our brethren, which caused wars and contentions; wherefore, we did mourn out our days" (Jacob 7:26).

HELAMAN 7:17, 19, 22-24, 28

How are the words "repent" and "turn" related?

The two words "repent" and "turn" come from the same Hebrew word: "shûwb." It means to turn, to go back home, to turn away. (See James Strong, *Exhaustive Concordance of the Bible*, 113.)

HELAMAN 7:24

Why were the Lamanites considered "more righteous" than the Nephites?

See insights for Alma 9:15–23.

HELAMAN 8

HELAMAN 8:14-15

What connection is there between the "serpent" and the "Son of God"?

"Some . . . have wondered if this story of the serpent . . . did not account for the 'serpent motif' in the art and architecture of some of the American Indian cultures. . . . One of the names given . . . to the great white God who appeared out of the eastern sky was . . . *Quetzalcoatl*, which literally means the bird-serpent" (Daniel H. Ludlow, *Companion*, 244; emphasis in original). *See also 1 Nephi 17:41; 2 Nephi 25:20.*

HELAMAN 8:16

Which prophets have testified "of these things"?

See insights for Jacob 7:11.

HELAMAN 9

HELAMAN 9:24-25

By what power did Nephi show the people these things?

See insights for Mosiah 8:13.

HELAMAN 10

HELAMAN 10:2-3

What role did "pondering" have in Nephi's receiving a revelation?

See insights for 1 Nephi 11:1.

HELAMAN 10:5

Why can the Lord trust some servants with this great power?

"The Lord once told me that what I asked for I should have. I have been afraid to ask God to kill my enemies, lest some of them should, peradventure, repent" (Joseph Smith, *Teachings*, 340). *See also Helaman 11:4, 10–16.*

HELAMAN 10:7

What is the power to "seal on earth" and have it "sealed in heaven"?

"Whenever the fulness of the gospel is on earth, the Lord has agents to whom he gives power to bind on earth and seal eternally in the heavens. (Matt. 16:19; 18:18; Hela. 10:3–10; D. & C. 132:46–49.) This *sealing power* [was] restored in this dispensation by Elijah the Prophet (D. & C. 2:1–3; 110:13–16)" (Bruce R. McConkie, *Mormon Doctrine*, 683; emphasis in original).

HELAMAN 10:11–12, 17

How important is prompt obedience?

Abraham "rose up early in the morning, and saddled his ass, and took . . . Isaac his son, and clave the wood for the burnt offering . . . and went unto the place of which God had told him" (Genesis 22:3).

"How often do Church members arise early in the morning to do the will of the Lord? How often do we say, 'Yes, I will have home evening with my family, but the children are so young now; I will start when they are older'? . . . 'Yes, I will obey the commandment to store food and to help others, but just now I have neither the time nor the money to spare; I will obey later'? Oh, foolish people! While we procrastinate, the harvest will be over and we will not be saved. Now is the time to follow Abraham's example; now is the time to repent; now is the time for prompt obedience" (Spencer W. Kimball, *Teachings*, 174).

HELAMAN 11

HELAMAN 11:1–37

How often could the pride cycle revolve completely through its rotation?

Within this one chapter we see the pride cycle completely rotate from wickedness to righteousness at least two and one-half times. The first rotation is in verses 1 through 21, the second in verses 22 through 34, and the third is in verses 36 and 37.

HELAMAN 11:4–5

Can a prophet cause an event that he prophesies?

"A prophet not only prophesies of things that will happen. A prophet, by the exercise of faith, causes things to happen" (A. Theodore Tuttle, *Ensign*, November 1975, 23).

HELAMAN 11:19

"Lehi, his brother, was not one whit behind him."

"If you feel that much of what you do does not make you very famous, take heart. Most of the best people who ever lived weren't very famous, either. Serve and grow, faithfully and quietly" (Howard W. Hunter, *Ensign*, April 1992, 67).

"President Howard W. Hunter is a meek man. He once refused a job he needed as a young man because it would have meant another individual would have lost his job. This is the same lowly man, when I awakened after a weary and dusty day together with him on assignment in Egypt, who was quietly shining my shoes, a task he had hoped to complete unseen" (Neal A. Maxwell, *Ensign*, April 1995, 18).

HELAMAN 11:23

How might we receive "many revelations daily"?

"Many great doctrinal revelations come to those who preach from the scriptures. When they are in tune with the Infinite, the Lord lets them know, first, the full and complete meaning of the scriptures, . . . and then he ofttimes expands their views so that new truths flood in upon them, and they learn added things that those who do not follow such a course can never know" (Bruce R. McConkie, *Promised Messiah*, 515–16).

HELAMAN 11:37

What are the characteristics of pride?

"Pride is essentially competitive in nature. We pit our will against God's. When we direct our pride toward God, it is in the spirit of 'my will and not thine be done.' . . .

". . . The proud wish God would agree with them. They aren't interested in changing their opinions to agree with God's.

". . . The proud stand more in fear of men's judgment than of God's judgment. . . .

". . . The antidote for pride is humility—meekness, submissiveness. (See Alma 7:23.) It is the broken heart and contrite spirit" (Ezra Taft Benson, *Ensign*, May 1989, 4).

HELAMAN 12

HELAMAN 12:3

What will the Lord do to help us remember him?

"Unfortunately, prosperity, abundance, honor, and praise lead some men to the false security of haughty self-assurance and the abandonment of the inclination to pray. Conversely, turmoil, tribulation, sickness, and death crumble the castles of men's pride and bring them to their knees to plead for power from on High" (Thomas S. Monson, *Be Your Best Self*, 26).

"We mortals are so quick to forget the Lord. . . .

"President Young, who knew something about trial and tribulation but also of man's high destiny, said that the Lord lets us pass through these experiences that we might become true friends of God. . . . Then we can, said President Young, learn to be 'righteous in the dark'" (Neal A. Maxwell, *Ensign*, November 1982, 67). *See also Mosiah 3:19; Helaman 15:3; Ether 9:34–35.*

HELAMAN 12:7–18

In what way are men "less than the dust"?

"Now this prophet did not mean to say that the Lord has greater concern for and loves the dust of the earth more than he does his children. . . . The point he is making is that the dust of the earth is obedient. . . . Everything in the universe obeys the law given unto it, so far as I know, except man. . . . Man rebels, and in this thing man is less than the dust of the earth" (Joseph Fielding Smith, in Conference Report, April 1929, 55). *See also Mosiah 4:2, 5, 11.*

HELAMAN 13

HELAMAN 13:2–16:8

How significant were the words of Samuel the Lamanite?

The words of this great prophet were so significant that the Savior himself requested they be added to the gold plates. *See 3 Nephi 23:9–13.*

HELAMAN 13:20–23, 31–36

What are the dangers of riches?

See insights for Jacob 2:12–13; Alma 11:20, 24.

HELAMAN 13:33

"O that we had remembered the Lord our God in the day that he gave us our riches."

"As we pray daily to God for guidance, we should all make the same plea as George Washington did in his prayer for our country: . . .

"'In the time of prosperity, fill our hearts with thankfulness, and in the day of trouble, suffer not our trust in Thee to fail'" (N. Eldon Tanner, *Ensign*, May 1976, 51). *See also Alma 62:49.*

HELAMAN 13:38
"Ye have sought for happiness in doing iniquity."
"Wickedness never was happiness" (Alma 41:10). *See also insights for Mosiah 2:41.*

HELAMAN 14

HELAMAN 14:1–25
What are the prophecies of Samuel the Lamanite about the coming of Christ?

PROPHECY	EVENTS ABOUT THE BIRTH OF CHRIST	FULFILLMENT
Helaman 14:2	Christ to be born in five years	3 Nephi 1:13
Helaman 14:3–4	No darkness for a day, a night, and a day	3 Nephi 1:15
Helaman 14:5	The appearance of a new star	3 Nephi 1:21
Helaman 14:6	Many signs in the heavens	3 Nephi 2:1
Helaman 14:7	People would fall to the earth	3 Nephi 1:16–17

PROPHECY	EVENTS ABOUT THE DEATH OF CHRIST	FULFILLMENT
Helaman 14:20	Sun, moon, and stars to be darkened	3 Nephi 8:19–23
Helaman 14:21	Thunderings and lightnings for many hours	3 Nephi 8:6–7
Helaman 14:21	Earth to shake and be broken up	3 Nephi 8:12, 17–18
Helaman 14:23	Tempests, mountains made low, valleys made high	3 Nephi 8:5–6
Helaman 14:24	Highways to be broken up, cities desolate	3 Nephi 8:8–11, 13
Helaman 14:25	Graves to be opened to a mass resurrection	3 Nephi 23:9–14

HELAMAN 14:8

Do we believe in a God in whose image we are made, or in a God whose image we made?

"Belief brings salvation and belief brings damnation. Men are saved or damned, depending upon what they believe. If they believe in Christ and his saving truths, they are heirs of salvation. If they believe in a false system of salvation, they will be damned. It is one thing to worship the living Lord and quite another to worship dead deities that have been graven by art and man's device" (Bruce R. McConkie, *New Witness for the Articles of Faith*, 23).

HELAMAN 14:16–19

What is the difference between the first death and the second "spiritual death"?

"The term 'first spiritual death' refers to the original transgression of Adam and Eve when they were cast out of the Garden of Eden and to the condition which comes upon a person when he commits his first sin. . . . The 'second spiritual death' . . . is used in the Book of Mormon to refer to a death which takes place after physical death wherein the person is 'cut off again.' . . . The second spiritual death refers essentially to the state or condition of those who become sons of perdition" (Daniel H. Ludlow, *Companion*, 248). *See also insights for Alma 12:16, 32.*

HELAMAN 14:30–31

What are the conditions of our agency?

"Satan . . . tries to create an atmosphere where one unwittingly begins to feel that he can not only choose what to do, but can determine what is right. . . .

"But our Eternal Father defined truth and established what is right and wrong before the creation of this earth. He also fixed the consequences of obedience and disobedience. . . .

"Please understand, no one has the privilege to choose what is right. . . . We are bound to the consequence God has decreed" (Richard G. Scott, *Ensign*, November 1992, 61). *See also insights for 2 Nephi 2:5; 2 Nephi 2:27.*

HELAMAN 15

HELAMAN 15:3

Why does the Lord chasten his children?

"The true purpose of the chastening is that our sins might be forgiven" (Gene R. Cook, *Raising Up a Family to the Lord*, 178). *See also D&C 95:1.*

HELAMAN 15:3-4

"The people of Nephi hath he loved, . . . the Lamanites hath he hated."

See insights for 1 Nephi 17:30–31, 35, 37, 40.

HELAMAN 15:4

Why did the Lord prolong the days of the Lamanites?

The scriptures suggest two reasons the Lamanites were spared:

1. 1 Nephi 2:24—To be a scourge to the Nephites when they forget God, to help them remember him.

2. Helaman 15:4—Many of the Lamanites would join the Church over time.

HELAMAN 15:8, 10

What does it mean to be "steadfast" in the gospel?

"To be firm and steadfast is to be constant, consistent, and vigilant in one's faith and approach to living the gospel" (Joseph Fielding McConkie and Robert L. Millet, *Doctrinal Commentary*, 3:419). *See also 2 Nephi 31:20; Mosiah 5:15.*

HELAMAN 16

HELAMAN 16:2

"They could not hit him with their stones neither with their arrows."

Sometimes the Lord will spare his servants. "And these three men, Shadrach, Meshach, and Abed-nego, fell down bound into the midst of the burning fiery furnace. . . . And the princes, governors, and captains, and the king's counsellors, being gathered together, saw these men, upon whose bodies the fire had no power, nor was an hair of their head singed, neither were their coats changed, nor the smell of fire had passed on them" (Daniel 3:23, 27).

On other occasions he chooses to bring them home to him. "Now, this priest had offered upon this altar three virgins at one time, who were the daughters of Onitah, one of the royal descent directly from the loins of Ham. These virgins were offered up because of their virtue; they would not bow down to worship gods of wood or of stone, therefore they were killed upon this altar, and it was done after the manner of the Egyptians" (Abraham 1:11).

HELAMAN 16:2, 6

The people "were angry with" and rejected the prophet Samuel.

"Why are we mortals so prone to garnish the sepulchers of the dead and stone the living, or give great credence to the past and deny the present?" (Spencer W. Kimball, *Faith Precedes the Miracle*, 28). *See also Mosiah 7:27–28.*

"It is not important that a prophet should say those things with which you and I are in full accord. But it is important that you and I should bring ourselves into full accord with those things which a prophet speaks by virtue of his office and calling" (Richard L. Evans, *Improvement Era*, November 1939, 672).

HELAMAN 16:16–22

How did the wicked explain away the prophecies of the coming of Christ?

1. Prophets "guessed right" in some of their prophecies, but not about Christ's coming (v. 16)

2. Christ's coming is "not reasonable" (v. 18)

3. Prophecies of Christ's coming are only the result of "wicked tradition[s]" (v. 20)

4. We do not believe anything unless we can see it "with our own eyes" (v. 20)

5. The great mysteries the prophets know can only come from "the evil one" (v. 21)

THIRD

NEPHI

"Nowhere in the scriptures do we have a more beautiful or detailed record of God's dealings with man than in the account of this visit as recorded in Third Nephi. I commend to all the reading of this account. Surely we can find nothing there except some warnings and beautiful teachings which, if accepted and lived, will do more than anything else to bring peace and happiness to the world and to the individual. . . . Here we can find explanations for many unanswered questions in the Bible" (N. Eldon Tanner, *Ensign*, May 1975, 34).

3 NEPHI 1

3 NEPHI 1:3; 2:9

Nephi "departed out of the land, and whither he went, no man knoweth."

"The disappearance of Nephi the son of Helaman is somewhat similar to the disappearance seventy-three years earlier of his great-great-grandfather, Alma the younger" (Daniel H. Ludlow, *Companion*, 252). *See also insights for Alma 45:18–19.*

3 NEPHI 1:8

Who continues to "watch steadfastly" for the signs of Christ's coming?

"The righteous that hearken unto the words of the prophets . . . look forward unto Christ with steadfastness for the signs which are given" (2 Nephi 26:8). *See also Hebrews 9:28.*

3 NEPHI 1:13–14

When does the spirit enter the body?

"The Book of Mormon account of Christ speaking to Nephi the grandson of Helaman and saying, 'On the morrow come I into the world' (3 Ne. 1:13), is not intended to infer that the spirit does not enter the body until the moment of the actual birth. Rather this revelation to the Nephites was itself being conveyed in a miraculous and unusual way. Quite probably the one uttering the words was speaking in the first person as though he were Christ, in accordance with the law enabling others to act and speak for Deity on the principal of divine investiture of authority" (Bruce R. McConkie, *Doctrinal New Testament Commentary*, 1:85).

3 NEPHI 1:18

How is the idea of being with God different for the righteous and the wicked?

"So great had been my iniquities, that the very thought of coming into the presence of my God did rack my soul with inexpressible horror" (Alma 36:14).

Alma said after he had repented, "I saw, even as our father Lehi saw, God sitting upon his throne, . . . yea, and my soul did long to be there" (Alma 36:22).

3 NEPHI 1:24

How should we respond to those who want to contend with us over the scriptures?

"There are some of other faiths who do not regard us as Christians. That is not important. . . .

"I hope we do not argue over this matter. There is no reason to debate it. We simply, quietly, and without apology testify that God has revealed Himself and His Beloved Son in opening this full and final dispensation of His work.

"We must not become disagreeable as we talk of doctrinal differences. . . .

"We can respect other religions, and must do so. We must recognize the great good they accomplish. We must teach our children to be tolerant and friendly toward those not of our faith. . . .

"A holier-than-thou attitude is not becoming to us" (Gordon B. Hinckley, *Ensign*, May 1998, 4). *See also Articles of Faith 1:11.*

When was the law of Moses fulfilled?

See insights for 3 Nephi 12:17–19, 46–47; 15:2–9.

3 NEPHI 2

3 NEPHI 2:12

What would justify a people "to take up arms"?

See insights for Alma 43:9, 26, 30, 45–50; 44:5; 46:12; 48:10, 24.

3 NEPHI 2:15

Is dark skin a curse?

One way to tell that the curse and the dark skin of the Lamanites were not the same thing is to note that the conjuction in the verse is "and," not "or." *See also insights for 2 Nephi 5:20–24.*

3 Nephi 3

3 NEPHI 3:2–26

How do Satan's strategies compare with the Lord's strategies?

Satan's Strategy

Reference	What was said or done	Strategy
3 Nephi 3:2, 5	"I . . . give unto you exceedingly great praise. . . . I have written this . . . because of your . . . noble spirit in the field of battle."	Uses flattery
3 Nephi 3:3	I have "so many brave men who are at my command."	Intimidates
3 Nephi 3:4, 5	Our purpose is to right "the many wrongs which ye have done unto" us. . . . "I have written this . . . feeling for your welfare."	Lies
3 Nephi 3:5	"I have written this . . . because of your firmness in that which ye believe to be right."	Creates doubt
3 Nephi 3:6	"Yield up unto this my people, your cities, your lands, and your possessions," or we will destroy you.	Is full of arrogance
3 Nephi 3:6	We will "visit you with the sword" to your "destruction."	Makes threats
3 Nephi 3:7	"Yield yourselves up unto us, and unite with us . . . and become our brethren . . .—not our slaves, but our . . . partners."	Manipulates
3 Nephi 3:7	"Become acquainted with our secret works."	Acts in secret
3 Nephi 3:8	"I swear unto you with an oath, that on the morrow month I will command that my armies shall come down against you, and . . . slay you . . . until ye shall become extinct."	Is boastful
3 Nephi 3:9	"The secret society of Gadianton . . . and the works thereof I know to be good."	Is a hypocrite

The Lord's Strategy

REFERENCE	WHAT WAS SAID OR DONE	STRATEGY
3 Nephi 3:12	"Lachoneus . . . could not be frightened by the demands and the threatenings."	Does not fear
3 Nephi 3:12	"He did not hearken to the epistle of Giddianhi."	Doesn't listen to or give in to evil
3 Nephi 3:12	He "did cause that his people should cry unto the Lord."	Prays
3 Nephi 3:13	He "sent a proclamation among all the people."	Does not act in secret
3 Nephi 3:13	"They should gather together . . . unto one place."	Is surrounded with good people
3 Nephi 3:14	"He caused that fortifications should be built."	Is prepared
3 Nephi 3:14	He "placed . . . guards . . . to guard them from the robbers day and night."	Keeps up guard day and night
3 Nephi 3:15	"Repent of all your iniquities."	Repents
3 Nephi 3:16	"The people . . . did . . . according to the words of Lachoneus."	Follows the prophet
3 Nephi 3:21	"If we should go up against them the Lord would deliver us into their hands; therefore we will prepare ourselves . . . and . . . wait till they shall come against us."	Doesn't start fights or give offense, stands for truth
3 Nephi 3:26	"Gidgiddoni did cause that they should make weapons of war of every kind, and . . . armor, and . . . shields."	Is armed in every way against Satan

3 NEPHI 3:12, 15–16, 25–26

How are our prayers and our works related?

"Here the Lord counsels us on balance. Faith is vital, but it must be accompanied by the personal work appropriate to the task. Only then do we qualify for the blessing. The appropriate approach is to study as if everything depended upon us and then to pray and exercise faith as if everything depended upon the Lord" (Dallin H. Oaks, *Ensign*, October 1994, 11).

3 NEPHI 4

3 NEPHI 4:28

Why was Zemnarihah "taken and hanged upon a tree"?
See Alma 30:10.

3 NEPHI 4:33

"Hearts were swollen with joy, unto the gushing out of many tears."
"We hear the words of the Lord most often by a feeling. If we are humble and sensitive, the Lord will prompt us through our feelings. That is why spiritual promptings move us on occasion to great joy, sometimes to tears. Many times my emotions have been made tender and my feelings very sensitive when touched by the Spirit" (Ezra Taft Benson, *Teachings*, 77). *See also Ether 6:12; insights for 3 Nephi 17:21–22.*

3 NEPHI 5

3 NEPHI 5:4

Why would they preach the word of God to the prisoners?
"The preaching of the word had a great tendency to lead the people to do that which was just—yea, it had had more powerful effect upon the minds of the people than . . . anything else" (Alma 31:5).

3 NEPHI 5:12

What is the meaning of the word "Mormon"?
See insights for Mormon 1:1.

3 NEPHI 5:13

What constitutes "a disciple of Jesus Christ"?
"Discipleship is general; any *follower* of a man or *devotee to a principle* may be called a disciple. The Holy Apostleship is an office and calling . . . comprising as a distinguishing function that of personal and special witness to the divinity of Jesus Christ as the one and only Redeemer and Savior of mankind" (James E. Talmage, *Jesus the Christ*, 212; emphasis in original). *See also D&C 103:28.*

3 NEPHI 5:25

How much of the Lord's gospel is covenant related?
"God's people have been known as a covenant people. The gospel itself

is the new and everlasting covenant. The posterity of Abraham through Isaac and Jacob is the covenant race. We come into the Church by covenant, which we enter into when we go into the waters of baptism. The new and everlasting covenant of celestial marriage is the gate to exaltation in the celestial kingdom. Men receive the Melchizedek Priesthood by an oath and covenant" (Marion G. Romney, in Conference Report, April 1962, 17).

3 NEPHI 6

3 NEPHI 6:10–12, 15

Why do great riches often precede great wickedness?
See insights for Alma 11:20, 24.

3 NEPHI 6:18

What is the difference between sinning ignorantly and rebelling?
"There is a big difference between an honest mistake made in a moment of spiritual weakness and a willful decision to disobey persistently the commandments of God. Those who deliberately choose to violate God's commandments or ignore the standards of the Church, even when promising themselves and others that someday they will be strong enough to repent, are stepping onto a dangerously slippery slope upon which many have lost their spiritual footing" (M. Russell Ballard, *Ensign*, November 1997, 40).

3 NEPHI 6:20, 23; 7:10

What other prophets were put to death for testifying of Christ?
See insights for Mosiah 7:26–28.

3 NEPHI 7

3 NEPHI 7:1–9

What destroyed the government at this time?
See insights for Helaman 2:13–14.

3 NEPHI 7:18

How could Nephi teach so powerfully that his listeners could not "disbelieve"?
"For when a man speaketh by the power of the Holy Ghost the power of the Holy Ghost carrieth it unto the hearts of the children of men" (2 Nephi 33:1).

3 NEPHI 8

3 NEPHI 8:5

How much time passed between Christ's death and his appearance in the Americas?

Christ was crucified "in the thirty and fourth year, in the first month, on the fourth day of the month, [and] there arose a great storm, such an one as never had been known in all the land" (3 Nephi 8:5).

"In the ending of the thirty and fourth year . . . after the ascension of Christ into heaven he did truly manifest himself unto them" (3 Nephi 10:18).

3 NEPHI 8:6

Why was there "a great . . . tempest" at the time of the crucifixion?

"The Lord uses the weather sometimes to discipline his people for the violation of his laws" (Spencer W. Kimball, *Ensign*, May 1977, 4).

"This was earth's God being crucified, this was creation's benefactor, this was 'the God of nature' suffering on the cross, and nature would not receive that injustice passively" (Jeffrey R. Holland, *Christ and the New Covenant*, 43–44). *See also Matthew 27:45, 51.*

3 NEPHI 8:12

Why was there more destruction "in the land northward" among the Nephites?

"The more righteous part of the people had nearly all become wicked; yea, there were but few righteous men among them." There was a secret combinantion organized with Jacob as their leader. "He commanded his people that they should take their flight into the northernmost part of the land" (3 Nephi 7:7, 12). *See also insights for Alma 9:15–23.*

3 NEPHI 9

3 NEPHI 9:5, 7–11

"The blood of the prophets and the saints . . ."

The Lord repeated this message *five times.* While the righteous are usually spared and protected by the Lord, many righteous people were killed by the wicked. Some examples include:

Abinadi (Mosiah 17:20)

Gideon (Alma 1:9)

The righteous people of Ammonihah (Alma 14:8)

The people of Anti-Nephi-Lehi (Alma 24:21–22)

3 NEPHI 9:13

Who survived the storm?

"The time soon cometh that the fulness of the wrath of God shall be poured out upon all the children of men; for he will not suffer that the wicked shall destroy the righteous. . . . He will preserve the righteous by his power, even if it so be that the fulness of his wrath must come, and the righteous be preserved, even unto the destruction of their enemies by fire. Wherefore, the righteous need not fear; for thus saith the prophet, they shall be saved" (1 Nephi 22:16–17). *See also 3 Nephi 10:12; D&C 97:22, 25.*

How does the Lord heal us today?

"The greatest miracles I see today are not necessarily the healing of sick bodies, but the greatest miracles I see are the healing of sick souls" (Harold B. Lee, *Ensign*, July 1973, 123).

3 NEPHI 9:14

How can we fully come unto Christ?

See insights for Omni 1:26.

3 NEPHI 9:15

How are the Father and the Son one?

See insights for Mosiah 15:2–5.

3 NEPHI 9:19–20

When was the law of sacrifice in the law of Moses fulfilled?

See insights for 3 Nephi 12:17–19, 46; 15:2–9.

3 NEPHI 9:22

How can we come unto Christ as a "little child"?

See insights for Mosiah 3:19; 3 Nephi 11:37–38.

3 NEPHI 10

3 NEPHI 10:4–6

"How oft have I gathered you as a hen gathereth her chickens under her wings."

"He shall cover thee with his feathers, and under his wings shalt thou trust" (Psalm 91:4).

3 NEPHI 10:14

What should we do with the scriptures we have?

"These were more noble than those in Thessalonica, in that they received the word with all readiness of mind, and searched the scriptures daily, whether those things were so" (Acts 17:11). *See also insights for 2 Nephi 32:3.*

3 NEPHI 11

3 NEPHI 11

Helaman and 3 Nephi—parallels to our own day.

CHRIST'S COMING TO THE NEPHITES	EVENT OR SIGN	CHRIST'S SECOND COMING
Government		
Helaman 1:5, 13; 2:2; 5:2	Freedom and a democratic form of government in power	2 Nephi 10:11; 3 Nephi 21:4
Helaman 1:11–12; 2:3–13; 3:23; 6:15–30; 11:2, 26–33; 3 Nephi 1:27–29; 2:11, 18; 3:2–10; 6:28; 7:9	Secret combinations (organizations that attempt to get money or power by any means available)	3 Nephi 16:7, 10; D&C 42:64
Helaman 1:2–9; 2:1; 6:37–39; 7:4–5; 3 Nephi 7:1–2, 6	Governmental power struggle and eventual government break down	*Journal of Discourses,* 2:182; 7:15; 23:104
Helaman 2:4, 13	One wicked man's power	Daniel 8:23–25; 11:36–39
Prosperity		
Helaman 3:7, 10–11; 11:20; 3 Nephi 6:5	Advancements, industry, and technological progress	Daniel 12:4; Revelation 9:7–10
Helaman 3:20–21; 5:2–12; 6:3, 21; 16:1, 3, 6, 10, 12; 3 Nephi 7:7	Strong righteous minority	1 Nephi 14:12; Jacob 5:70
Helaman 3:20, 24–26, 31–32; 6:3, 9, 11–13; 3 Nephi 1:22–23	Great growth, prosperity, happiness, and peace within the Church	Daniel 2:44; Jacob 5:72
Helaman 16:13–14; 3 Nephi 1:4; 7:17–20	Spiritual outpourings and miracles	Joel 2:28–30; D&C 45:40
Wars		
Helaman 4:4–10	Civil war between the north and the south	D&C 87:1–3

Helaman 1:14–30; 10:18; 11:1, 24–25; 3 Nephi 2:13–17	Wars and rumors of wars	D&C 45:26; 87:3; JS—M 1:29

Wickedness

Helaman 13:2, 6, 8, 10–11; 14:9, 11; 15:1–3, 17; 3 Nephi 6:20; 7:23	The prophet's constant message of repentance	D&C 11:9; Conference Report, Apr. 1986, 3 (or *Ensign*, May 1986, 4)
Helaman 4:11–12; 6:2, 16, 31–35; 11:36–37; 13:22; 16:12, 22–23; 3 Nephi 2:3, 10	Great wickedness	2 Timothy 3:1–5; D&C 45:27
3 Nephi 1:29–30	Wickedness among the youth	Isaiah 3:5, 12
Helaman 3:14; 4:12	Great immorality	2 Timothy 3:6; 2 Nephi 27:1
Helaman 3:1, 33–34; 3 Nephi 6:10	Much pride	D&C 29:9
3 Nephi 6:12–14	Division of people into class of inequality	Revelation 13:16–17
Helaman 3:26; 13:17–21, 30–31, 35–36	People's hearts set upon riches, followed by their loss of riches	Revelation 17:4; 18:10–14; Ezekiel 16:49–50
Helaman 3:3, 19; 4:1; 11:21–23	Much contention	D&C 10:63; 2 Nephi 28:4
Helaman 11:22–24; 3 Nephi 6:15–18	Personal apostasy	2 Nephi 28:8–11
Helaman 8:3, 5–6; 10:13; 13:24–28; 14:10; 16:2, 6; 3 Nephi 7:14	Wicked reject true prophets and accept false prophets	2 Nephi 27:1, 5; Isaiah 5:20

Missionaries

Helaman 5:4, 18–23, 28–31, 36, 42; 11:3–4, 6, 18–19	Two great prophets with power	Revelation 11:3, 5–6, 11–13; D&C 77:15
Helaman 5:50–52; 6:1, 4, 20, 34–37; 15:4–11	Many Lamanites join the Church and become righteous	Helaman 15:12–16; D&C 49:24

Helaman 6:7–8	A market of commerce, trade, and exchange	Revelation 13:16–17
Helaman 6:20; 7:13–14; 3 Nephi 7:15–16	The righteous sorrow because of great wickedness	Isaiah 14:3; 35:10; D&C 42:45

Signs and Wonders

Helaman 9:7–17; 3 Nephi 6:23; 10:15	Many righteous unjustly imprisoned and killed	Revelation 11:3, 7; 1 Nephi 13:5; D&C 135:4
Helaman 14:3–4; 3 Nephi 1:8	A night with no darkness	Zechariah 14:7
Helaman 14:5–6, 20; 3 Nephi 1:21; 8:19, 22	Signs and wonders in the heavens	Numbers 24:17; Joel 2:30–31; D&C 45:40
Helaman 14:21, 23	Earthquakes in divers places	JS—M 1:29
Helaman 14:11–12; 3 Nephi 10:14–17	Prophets' testimony of the Second Coming	Acts 3:20–21; D&C 133:25
Helaman 16:13–18; 3 Nephi 1:5, 22; 2:1–2	The wicked's denial of signs, wonders, and Christ's coming	2 Peter 3:3–4; D&C 45:26; Isaiah 5:19
3 Nephi 1:16–18	The wicked fear and fall as if dead after seeing some of the signs and wonders	D&C 88:91; Moses 7:66
Helaman 11:4–6	Droughts and famines	Revelation 11:6; 18:8
3 Nephi 10:1–2	A period of silence	Revelation 8:1

Goodness

3 Nephi 2:11–12; 3:13–16, 22, 25	The righteous gathered out from the wicked	D&C 45:64–71; 115:6
3 Nephi 1:8	The righteous watched for the signs	D&C 45:39, 44; Moses 7:62
3 Nephi 1:4–14	Righteous prayed for Christ's coming to hasten	D&C 133:37–40

Wicked Destroyed

3 Nephi 4:7–27	A final terrible battle	Joel 2:2; Revelation 9
Helaman 14:21, 23, 26; 3 Nephi 8:5–7, 12	Storms, tempests, thunders, lightnings	D&C 88:90; Revelation 16:18, 21

Helaman 14:20, 27; 3 Nephi 8:19–23	A period of darkness	Moses 7:61
3 Nephi 8:6, 10–15, 17–18	A major earthquake	Revelation 6:12–14
Helaman 10:12; 11:6; 14:24; 15:1; 3 Nephi 8:14–16; 9:2–12	Complete destruction of the wicked	Isaiah 26:21; Malachi 4:1; D&C 1:9; 133:41
3 Nephi 8:23–25	Great mourning over the destruction of the wicked	D&C 112:24

Appearances

3 Nephi 9:13; 10:12–13	The righteous survived the destructions at Christ's coming	1 Nephi 22:16–22; D&C 97:21–25
3 Nephi 9; 10:3–7; 11:9–12	The voice of the Lord heard by the righteous	D&C 43:23–35; 45:49
3 Nephi 10:10	Great joy felt among the righteous	Moses 7:62–64; D&C 133:44
3 Nephi 10:2	A period of silence	D&C 88:95; Revelation 8:1
3 Nephi 11:8	Jesus descended from the heavens	D&C 88:97; JS—M 1:26
Helaman 14:25	Graves of the dead opened, mass resurrection	D&C 88:96–99; 133:56
3 Nephi 11:14–17	Some personally witnessed the wounds in the hands, feet, and side of the Savior	D&C 45:51–53
3 Nephi 9:17–20; 11:18–22; 12:46–47	Current laws fulfilled and new laws instituted	Revelation 21:5; D&C 101:25

3 NEPHI 11:3

What kind of voice does the Lord use to speak to his children?

The Lord told Elijah to "Go forth, and stand upon the mount before the Lord. And, behold, the Lord passed by, and a great and strong wind rent the mountains, and brake in pieces the rocks before the Lord; but the Lord was not in the wind: and after the wind an earthquake; but the Lord was not in the earthquake: and after the earthquake a fire; but the Lord was not in the fire: and after the fire a still small voice" (1 Kings 19:11–12).

"Dramatic and miraculous answers to prayer may come, but they are the exceptions. Even at the highest levels of responsibility in this kingdom of God, which is being built up upon the earth, the voice is still small. . . . My testimony is that the Lord is speaking to you! But with the deafening decibels of today's environment, all too often we fail to hear him" (Graham W. Doxey, *Ensign*, November 1991, 25).

3 NEPHI 11:7

Who speaks the words "Behold my Beloved Son, in whom I am well pleased"?

One of the conditions of the fall was to be cast out of God's presence, therefore since the fall "no man hath seen God [the Father] at any time, except he hath borne record of the Son" (JST, John 1:19).

"The Father has never dealt with man directly and personally since the fall, and he has never appeared except to introduce and bear record of the Son" (Joseph Fielding Smith, *Doctrines of Salvation*, 1:27).

"A general consideration of scriptural evidence leads to the conclusion that God the Eternal Father has manifested Himself to earthly prophets or revelators on very few occasions, and then principally to attest the divine authority of His Son, Jesus Christ" (James E. Talmage, *Jesus the Christ*, 36). *See also insights for Helaman 5:47.*

Occasions when the Father has spoken directly to man include:

At the baptism of Christ (Matthew 3:17)

At the Mount of Transfiguration (Matthew 17:5)

At the Triumphal Entry (John 12:28)

At the Sacred Grove (JS—H 1:17)

At the visit of Christ to the Americas (3 Nephi 11:7)

To teach repentance and baptism (*see also insights for 2 Nephi 31:11, 15*)

3 NEPHI 11:8, 12, 17, 19

How should we act when we go before the Lord?

While great reverence is appropriate in chapels and temples, specific protocol is necessary in certain circumstances. When the prophet comes into the room the appropriate protocol is to stand, but when we go to the Lord we do so on our knees, with heads bowed low. "God must be approached carefully, respectfully, and with great preparation" (Howard W. Hunter, Ensign, November 1977, 52). See also 3 Nephi 17:10.

3 NEPHI 11:14–15

Are the blemishes of mortality part of a resurrected body?

"It is true that he also showed these wounds to the Nephites when he visited with them . . . to convince them of his identity, and give to them a witness of his suffering. It can hardly be accepted as a fact that these wounds have remained in his hands, side, and feet all through the centuries from the time of his crucifixion and will remain until his Second Coming. But they will appear to the Jews as a witness against their fathers and their stubbornness in following the teachings of their fathers" (Joseph Fielding Smith, Doctrines of Salvation, 2:292).

3 NEPHI 11:15; 17:25

There were 2,500 people, yet the Lord worked with them "one by one."

"Faithful servants nourish by focusing on the individual. God loves us one by one" (Alexander B. Morrison, Ensign, May 1992, 14). See also 3 Nephi 17:21; 18:36.

3 NEPHI 11:17

What is the meaning of the word "Hosanna"?

It is a plea meaning "save now." It was the "cry of the multitude as they joined in our Lord's triumphal procession into Jerusalem" (Merrill F. Unger, New Unger's Bible Dictionary, 589). See also Matthew 21:9, 15; Psalm 118:25.

3 NEPHI 11:27

"The Father, and the Son, and Holy Ghost are one."

"Three glorious persons comprise the Godhead. . . . They are the Father, the Son, and the Holy Ghost. Each one possesses the same divine nature, knows all things, and has all power. Each one has the same character, the same perfections and the same attributes. . . . Because of this perfect unity, they are spoken of as being one God" (Bruce R. McConkie, New Witness for the Articles of Faith, 58). See also insights for Mosiah 15:2–5.

3 NEPHI 11:28–29

"Contention . . . is of the devil."

"I pray that we may be true to our covenants, true to each other; that we will cast out of our hearts all that is evil, that we will not speak evil one of another, or be given to backbiting or contention or strife, for the spirit of wickedness destroys faith and tends to divide and separate instead of uniting and strengthening the people" (Joseph F. Smith, in Conference Report, October 1913, 74).

What is the doctrine of Christ?

See insights for 2 Nephi 31:2–21.

3 NEPHI 11:37–38
"Become as a little child."

"Christ would not have had His chosen representatives become childish; far from it, they had to be men of courage, fortitude, and force; but He would have them become childlike. The distinction is important. Those who belong to Christ must become like little children in obedience, truthfulness, trustfulness, purity, humility, and faith. The child is an artless, natural, trusting believer; the childish one is careless, foolish, and neglectful" (James E. Talmage, *Jesus the Christ*, 360). *See also insights for Mosiah 3:19.*

3 NEPHI 12

3 NEPHI 12:1; 15:12
Were the twelve Nephite leaders called to be apostles?

"While in every instance the Nephite twelve are spoken of as disciples, the fact remains that they had been endowed with divine authority to be special witnesses for Christ among their own people. Therefore, they were . . . apostles" (Joseph Fielding Smith, *Answers to Gospel Questions*, 1:122). *See also Mormon 9:18.*

3 NEPHI 12:5
What relationship is there between "meek" and "weak"?

"If the Lord was meek and lowly and humble, then to become humble one must do what he did in boldly denouncing evil, bravely advancing righteous works, courageously meeting every problem, becoming the master of himself and the situations about him and being near oblivious to personal credit.

"Humility is not pretentious, presumptuous, nor proud. It is not weak, vacillating, nor servile.

"*Humble* and *meek* properly suggest virtues, not weaknesses. . . .

"How does one get humble? To me, one must constantly be reminded of his dependence . . . on the Lord. How remind one's self? By real, constant, worshipful, grateful prayer" (Spencer W. Kimball, *Teachings*, 232–33; emphasis in original).

3 NEPHI 12:7
"Blessed are the merciful, for they shall obtain mercy."

See also 3 Nephi 13:14–15; 14:1.

3 NEPHI 12:13

Who is "the salt of the earth"?

The great value of salt is seen in its use over time. Salt has been used as an antiseptic and cleanser, food flavoring, food preservative, religious offering, and even currency. "When men are called unto mine everlasting gospel, and covenant with an everlasting covenant, they are accounted as the salt of the earth and the savor of men; they are called to be the savor of men; therefore, if that salt of the earth lose its savor, behold, it is thenceforth good for nothing only to be cast out and trodden under the feet of men" (D&C 101:39–40).

3 NEPHI 12:15–16

What is the light that we should hold up?

"Behold I am the light which ye shall hold up" (3 Nephi 18:24).

3 NEPHI 12:17–19, 46–47; 15:2–9

When did Jesus Christ fulfill the law of Moses?

"The Law of Moses . . . continued until the resurrection of Jesus Christ, when this carnal law was fulfilled and was replaced by the fulness of the gospel" (Joseph Fielding Smith, *Doctrines of Salvation*, 3:84).

3 NEPHI 12:21–22

What significant change do the Book of Mormon and Joseph Smith Translation make in Matthew 5:22?

"The phrase 'without a cause' is not found in the inspired Joseph Smith Translation . . . nor in the 3 Nephi 12:22 version. When the Lord eliminates the phrase 'without a cause,' He leaves us without an excuse. . . . We can 'do away' with anger, for He has so taught and commanded us" (Lynn G. Robbins, *Ensign*, May 1998, 80).

3 NEPHI 12:22

What is the meaning of the word "Raca"?

"In the original Semite tongue *raca* means *vain* or *empty*. Thus, the Savior is telling us not to call other people by such derogatory titles" (Daniel H. Ludlow, *Companion*, 265; emphasis in original).

"Profane and vulgar epithets and expressions—for such, in the Jewish culture, were the nature of the words here recited [Raca]—when hurled at our fellowmen lead to damnation. . . . Profane, vulgar, contemptuous, and unholy expressions degrade their author more than they taint the soul of the hearer" (Bruce R. McConkie, *Mortal Messiah*, 2:136).

3 NEPHI 12:27-28

"Whosoever looketh on a woman, to lust after her, hath committed adultery."

"Many years ago a young man came to me . . . and made a confession of a wrong and sinful act. He justified himself by saying that he happened to be in a bookstore at the closing hour, and when the door was locked he yielded to temptation. He rather blamed the circumstances for his fall.

"But I said, 'It wasn't the circumstances; it wasn't the locked door, nor the enticement. You had thought of that before you went to that bookstore. If you had never thought of that act, there would have been no circumstance strong enough to entice or to tempt you, a missionary, to fall. The thought always precedes the act" (David O. McKay, *Man May Know for Himself*, 133).

3 NEPHI 12:30

What does it mean to "take up your cross"?

"For a man to take up his cross, is to deny himself of all ungodliness, and every worldly lust, and keep my commandments" (JST, Matthew 16:26).

3 NEPHI 12:31-32

What is our responsibility concerning this law of divorce?

"Under the law of Moses, divorce came easily. . . . Men were empowered to divorce their wives for any unseemly thing. . . .

"No such low and base standard is acceptable under gospel law. . . . Divorce is totally foreign to celestial standards, a verity that Jesus will one day expound in more detail to the people of Jewry. For now, as far as the record reveals, he merely specifies the high law that his people should live, but that is beyond our capability even today. If husbands and wives lived the law as the Lord would have them live it, they would neither do nor say the things that would even permit the fleeting thought of divorce to enter the mind of their eternal companions. Though we today have the gospel, we have yet to grow into that high state of marital association where marrying a divorced person constitutes adultery. The Lord has not yet given us the high standard he here named as that which ultimately will replace the Mosaic practice of writing a bill of divorcement" (Bruce R. McConkie, *Mortal Messiah*, 2:138–39).

"There may be now and again a legitimate cause for divorce. I am not one to say that it is never justified" (Gordon B. Hinckley, *Teachings of Gordon B. Hinckley*, 162).

3 NEPHI 12:33-37

What does is mean to "not foreswear thyself"?

It shouldn't be necessary to swear an oath in order to tell the truth. Truth ought to be what we say all the time. "Under the perfect law of Christ every man's word is his bond, and all spoken statements are as true as though an oath attended each spoken word" (Bruce R. McConkie, *Mortal Messiah*, 2:140).

3 NEPHI 12:48

"I would that ye should be perfect."

"In both His Old and New World ministries, the Savior commanded, 'Be ye therefore perfect.' A footnote explains that the Greek word translated as *perfect* means 'complete, finished, fully developed.' Our Heavenly Father wants us to use this mortal probation to 'fully develop' ourselves, to make the most of our talents and abilities" (Joseph B. Wirthlin, *Ensign*, May 1998, 14; emphasis in original).

"I am . . . convinced of the fact that the speed with which we head along the straight and narrow path isn't as important as the direction in which we are traveling" (Marvin J. Ashton, *Ensign*, May 1989, 21).

Notice the difference in this verse and Matthew 5:48. Jesus did not include himself as perfect until after he was resurrected. "Begin with the first, and go on until you learn all the principles of exaltation. But it will be a great while after you have passed through the veil before you will have learned them. . . . It will be a great work to learn our salvation and exaltation even beyond the grave" (Joseph Smith, *Teachings*, 348).

"As members of the Church, if we chart a course leading to eternal life; if we begin the process of spiritual rebirth, and are going in the right direction; if we chart a course of sanctifying our souls, and degree by degree are going in that direction; and if we chart a course of becoming perfect, and, step by step and phase by phase, are perfecting our souls by overcoming the world, then it is absolutely guaranteed there is no question whatever about it—we shall gain eternal life. Even though we have spiritual rebirth ahead of us, perfection ahead of us, the full degree of sanctification ahead of us, if we chart a course and follow it to the best of our ability in this life, then when we go out of this life we'll continue in exactly that same course" (Bruce R. McConkie, *Sermons and Writings*, 54). *See also insights for Moroni 10:32–33.*

3 NEPHI 13

3 NEPHI 13:5–13

How should we pray?

"Our prayers should be simple, direct, and sincere.

". . . I am sure that our Heavenly Father, who loves all of his children, hears and answers all prayers, however phrased. If he is offended in connection with prayers, it is likely to be by their absence, not their phraseology" (Dallin H. Oaks, Ensign, May 1993, 17). *See also Ether 2:14; Luke 18:9–14.*

3 NEPHI 13:14–15

"If ye forgive men their trespasses your heavenly Father will also forgive you."

"Ye ought to forgive one another; for he that forgiveth not his brother his trespasses standeth condemned before the Lord; for there remaineth in him the greater sin. . . . Of you it is required to forgive all men" (D&C 64:9–10).

"Remember that we must forgive even if our offender did not repent and ask forgiveness. . . . Reconciliation suggests also forgetting. . . . No bitterness of past frictions can be held in memory if we forgive with all our hearts" (Spencer W. Kimball, in Conference Report, October 1949, 132–33).

3 NEPHI 13:24

How do we sometimes try to "serve two masters"?

"Now there are those among us who are trying to serve the Lord without offending the devil" (Marion G. Romney, in James E. Faust, *Ensign*, September 1995, 2).

"They who love and serve God with all their hearts rejoice evermore, . . . but they who try to serve God and still cling to the spirit of the world, have got on two yokes—the yoke of Jesus and the yoke of the devil. . . . They will have a warfare inside and outside, and the labor will be very galling" (Brigham Young, *Journal of Discourses*, 16:123).

"We cannot survive spiritually with one foot in the Church and the other in the world. We must make the choice. It is either the Church or the world. There is no middle ground. And the Lord loves a courageous man who fights openly and boldly in his army" (Bruce R. McConkie, *Ensign*, November 1974, 34). *See also Revelation 3:16; insights for 2 Nephi 10:16.*

What is "Mammon"?

"['Mammon' is] an Aramaic word for riches or money" (Joseph Fielding McConkie and Robert L. Millet, *Doctrinal Commentary*, 4·88).

3 NEPHI 13:34

"Sufficient is the day unto the evil thereof."

"The men and women, who desire to obtain seats in the celestial king-dom, will find that they must battle with the enemy of all righteousness every day" (Brigham Young, *Journal of Discourses*, 11:15).

3 NEPHI 14

3 NEPHI 14:1

"Judge not, that ye be not judged."

"The more serious the work on our own imperfections, the less we are judgmental of the imperfections in others" (Neal A. Maxwell, *Not My Will, But Thine*, 95).

"Avoid undue concern about others. When you do not worry or concern yourself too much with what other people do and believe and say, there will come to you a new freedom" (Spencer W. Kimball, *Teachings*, 236).

3 NEPHI 14:3

What is the difference between a "mote" and a "beam"?

"*Mote:* A small particle; any thing proverbially small; a spot."

"*Beam:* The largest, or a principal piece in a building, that lies across the walls, and serves to support the principal rafters. Any large piece of timber" (Noah Webster, *American Dictionary of the English Language*, s.v. "Mote"; s.v. "Beam").

3 NEPHI 14:6

What does it mean to "cast . . . your pearls before swine"?

"That which cometh from above is sacred, and must be spoken with care, and by constraint of the Spirit" (D&C 63:64).

"The fact that something is true is not always a justification for communicating it" (Dallin H. Oaks, *Ensign*, February 1987, 68). *See also 1 Corinthians 10:23; insights for Alma 12:9.*

3 NEPHI 14:7–11

How often has the Lord promised to answer our prayers if we will only ask?

"Until now, no divine commandment has been more frequently repeated than the commandment to pray in the name of the Lord Jesus Christ" (Marion G. Romney, *Ensign*, November 1979, 16). *See also insights for 1 Nephi 15:8, 11.*

3 NEPHI 14:12

"All things whatsoever ye would that men should do to you, do ye even so to them."

"The formula for successful relationships with others boils down to that divine code known as the Golden Rule" (Ezra Taft Benson, *Teachings*, 447).

3 NEPHI 14:13

"Wide is the gate, and broad is the way, which leadeth to destruction."

"Most of the adult people who have lived from the day of Adam to the present time will go to the *telestial kingdom*. The inhabitants of this lowest kingdom of glory will be 'as innumerable as the stars in the firmament of heaven, or as the sand upon the seashore'" (Bruce R. McConkie, *Mormon Doctrine*, 778; emphasis in original).

3 NEPHI 14:15–27

"By their fruits ye shall know them."

"There are many people in the Church today who have failed to do, and continue to argue against doing, the things that are requested and suggested. . . .

". . . We talk about it, we listen to it, but sometimes we do not *do* the things which the Lord says" (Spencer W. Kimball, *Ensign*, May 1976, 124; emphasis in original).

3 NEPHI 15

3 NEPHI 15:5, 9

Who gave the law in the first place?

"All revelation since the fall has come through Jesus Christ. . . . He is the God of Israel, the Holy One of Israel; the one who led that nation out of Egyptian bondage, and who gave and fulfilled the Law of Moses" (Joseph Fielding Smith, *Doctrines of Salvation*, 1:27). *See also insights for 3 Nephi 12:17–19, 46–47; 15:2–9.*

3 NEPHI 15:6

Fundamental doctrines of the gospel did not change with the fulfilling of the law of Moses.

The doctrine of the atonement is unchanging, but the procedure for how we remember the atonement changed from sacrifice to sacrament. "Keep in mind that the principles of the gospel of Jesus Christ are divine. Nobody changes the principles and doctrines of the Church. . . . But methods change as the inspired direction comes to those who preside at a given time. If you will analyze all that is being done and the changes that are taking place, you will realize that the fundamental doctrines of the Church are not changing. The only changes are in the methods of teaching that doctrine to meet the circumstances of our time" (Harold B. Lee, *Ensign*, January 1971, 10).

3 NEPHI 15:8

Why does the law of Moses have its end in Christ?

"This [Christ] is the whole meaning of the law, every whit pointing to that great and last sacrifice; and that great and last sacrifice will be the Son of God, yea, infinite and eternal" (Alma 34:14).

3 NEPHI 15:9

What blessings come to those who "endure to the end"?

"Patient endurance is to be distinguished from merely being 'acted upon.' Endurance is more than pacing up and down within the cell of our circumstance; it is not only acceptance of the things allotted to us but also the determination to 'act for ourselves' by magnifying what is allotted to us (Alma 29:3, 6). . . .

"True enduring therefore represents not merely the passage of time but also the passage of the soul—and not merely from A to B, but amid 'mighty change' all the way from A to Z. To endure in faith and do God's will thus involves much more than putting up with a circumstance" (Neal A. Maxwell, Men and Women of Christ, 69–70). *See also D&C 14:7.*

3 NEPHI 15:17, 21

Who are the "other sheep" spoken of by the Lord?

"Other sheep I have, which are not of this fold: them also I must bring, and they shall hear my voice; and there shall be one fold, and one shepherd" (John 10:16). Matthew 15:24 would suggest that the Nephites are part of the scattered or lost tribes of Israel.

3 NEPHI 15:18–19

What causes people to not understand the word of the Lord?

"As far as we degenerate from God, we descend to the devil and lose knowledge, and without knowledge we cannot be saved, and while our hearts are filled with evil, and we are studying evil, there is no room in our hearts for good, or studying good" (Joseph Smith, Teachings, 217). *See also D&C 130:18–19.*

3 NEPHI 16

3 NEPHI 16:1–3; 17:4

Who are these "other sheep"?

"Did not Jesus visit them [the lost tribes of Israel] after he ministered among the Nephites? . . . Of course he did, in one or many places as suited his purposes. He assembled them together then in exactly the same way he gathered the Nephites in the land Bountiful so that they too could hear his voice and feel the prints of the nails in his hands and in his feet. Of this there can be no question. And we suppose that he also called twelve apostles and established his kingdom among them even as he did in Jerusalem and in the Americas" (Bruce R. McConkie, Millennial Messiah, 216).

"He has other worlds or creations and other sons and daughters, perhaps just as good as those dwelling on this planet and they, as well as we, will be visited, and they will be made glad with the countenance of their Lord. Thus he will go, in the time and in the season thereof, from kingdom to kingdom or from world to world" (Orson Pratt, *Journal of Discourses*, 17:332). *See also D&C 88:51–61.*

3 NEPHI 17

3 NEPHI 17:3

What is the role of the family in spiritual learning?

"The family is the basic unit of the kingdom of God on earth. The Church can be no healthier than its families. No government can long endure without strong families.

"It is the duty of parents to so teach by example and precept that the child will fill the measure of his creation and find his way back to the glories of exaltation. Wise parents will see to it that their teaching is orthodox, character-building, and faith-promoting.

"It is the responsibility of the parents to teach their children. The Sunday School, the Primary, the MIA and other organizations of the Church play a secondary role" (Spencer W. Kimball, *Teachings*, 331). *See also 3 Nephi 19:1.*

How can we better ponder the principles of the gospel?

"To ponder is to meditate, to think, to feast, and to treasure. It is more than a mental method, it is a spiritual striving to obtain and to understand truth. We should follow the process taught by the Savior to the Nephites as he taught them sacred principles. He then instructed them to 'Go ye unto your homes, and ponder upon the things which I have said, and ask of the Father, in my name, that ye may understand . . .' (3 Ne. 17:3)" (L. Lionel Kendrick, *Ensign*, May 1993, 14–15). *See also insights for 1 Nephi 11:1.*

3 NEPHI 17:6–9

How many people was the Savior willing to heal?

During His mortal life, Jesus never refused to heal a single person (see Matthew 15:23–28). Elder Richard G. Scott said, "I testify that the Savior will heal you as you choose to obey truth and use your agency according to His counsel" (*Ensign*, November 1992, 62).

3 NEPHI 17:11–24

What can we learn from the Savior's experience with the children?

"Do any of us ever consider serving children to be beneath us? Clearly the Savior felt that the Nephite children were worthy not only to be in his presence, but they were also worthy of his time and his attention. . . .

". . . Consider how much time it must have taken for him to bless and pray over each child. . . .

". . . It's significant to me that later the Savior gave the most sacred teachings only to the children, then loosed their tongues so they could teach the multitude. . . .

"Let us not underestimate the capacity and potential power of today's children" (Michaelene P. Grassli, *Ensign*, November 1992, 93–94).

3 NEPHI 17:21–22

Jesus wept.

This verse show us that Jesus weeps not only from sorrow (see John 11:35; D&C 42:45; Moses 7:28) but also, at times, for joy. *See also insights for 3 Nephi 4:33.*

3 NEPHI 18

3 NEPHI 18:1–29

How important is the sacrament?

The sacrament is the only ordinance of the gospel that we do for ourselves more than once. "No more sacred ordinance is administered in the Church of Christ than the administration of the sacrament" (David O. McKay, in Conference Report, April 1946, 112).

3 NEPHI 18:1

Why are bread and water appropriate symbols for the sacrament?

Bread and water are the two most basic elements to sustain life (see D&C 89:14, 17). In a similar way, Jesus, who is the "bread of life" (John 6:35) and the "living water" (Jeremiah 17:13), is the basic element to sustain our spiritual life.

3 NEPHI 18:4–5, 9

"And they did drink, and they were filled."

By partaking of the sacrament we may be filled with the Holy Ghost. *See also 3 Nephi 12:6.*

3 NEPHI 18:5, 11

Who may appropriately partake of the sacrament?

"Unbaptized children, being without sin, are entitled and expected to partake of the sacrament to prefigure the covenant they will take upon themselves when they arrive at the years of accountability" (Bruce R. McConkie, *Mormon Doctrine*, 660).

3 NEPHI 18:16, 24

How important is Christ's example for us?

"The praying Christ: That is the example to which we are to point others. The Christ of humility. The Christ of spiritual communion. The Christ who is dependent upon his Father. The Christ who asks for blessings upon others. The Christ who calls down the power of heaven. The Christ who submits, yields, and obeys the will of the Father. The Christ who is one with the Father in at least one way that we may be united with him as well—through prayer. That is the light we are to show to the world. It is the image of Christ" (Jeffrey R. Holland, *Ensign*, January 1996, 19). *See also John 13:15; Alma 4:11; 1 Peter 2:21; Alma 39:11; insights for 2 Nephi 31:7–10, 12–13, 16.*

3 NEPHI 18:20

Why should we ask in prayers and blessings for that "which is right"?

"The object of prayer is not to change the will of God, but to secure for ourselves and for others blessings that God is already willing to grant, but that are made conditional on our asking for them" (LDS Bible Dictionary, s.v. "Prayer").

"The Savior reminds us that faith, no matter how strong it is, cannot produce a result contrary to the will of him whose power it is. The exercise of faith in the Lord Jesus Christ is always subject to the order of heaven, to the goodness and will and wisdom and timing of the Lord. That is why we cannot have true faith in the Lord without also having complete trust in the Lord's will" (Dallin H. Oaks, *Ensign*, May 1994, 100).

3 NEPHI 18:26–29

"Ye shall not suffer any one knowingly to partake . . . unworthily."

"If any of the members are not in good standing; if they have in their hearts any feeling of hatred, envy, or sin of any kind, they should not partake of these emblems. If there are any differences or feelings existing between brethren, these differences should be adjusted before the guilty parties partake. . . . We should all see that our hearts and hands are clean and pure" (Joseph Fielding Smith, *Doctrines of Salvation*, 2:343).

"The sacrament is an intensely personal experience, and we are the ones who knowingly are worthy or otherwise" (John H. Groberg, *Ensign*, May 1989, 38). *See also 1 Corinthians 11:27–30.*

3 NEPHI 19

3 NEPHI 19:4-5

What is the value of proper delegation?

"As the Church grows in total membership and regional distribution, wise delegation becomes more and more important—in fact, imperative for continued success" (Ezra Taft Benson, *Teachings*, 378). *See also Exodus 18:13–26.*

3 NEPHI 19:9, 13, 20-22

What difference will the gift of the Holy Ghost make in my salvation?

"The receipt of that member of the Godhead [the Holy Ghost] as a gift, and the enjoyment of the companionship of the Holy Spirit, is essential to salvation" (Bruce R. McConkie, *Promised Messiah*, 560–61). *See also insights for 2 Nephi 32:5.*

3 NEPHI 19:11

Did Nephi baptize himself?

"When Christ appeared to the Nephites on this continent, he commanded them to be baptized, although they had been baptized previously for the remission of their sins. . . . Then we read that the Savior commanded Nephi and the people to be baptized again, because he had organized anew the Church under the gospel. . . .

". . . For the same reason Joseph Smith and those who had been baptized prior to April 6, 1830 [that baptism was for the remission of sins], were again baptized on the day of the organization of the Church. . . .

". . . They had to be in order to come into the Church by the door" (Joseph Fielding Smith, *Doctrines of Salvation*, 2:336).

3 NEPHI 19:18, 22

Why did the people pray to Jesus?

"Jesus was present before them as the symbol of the Father. Seeing him, it was as though they saw the Father; praying to him, it was as though they prayed to the Father. It was a special and unique situation that as far as we know has taken place only once" (Bruce R. McConkie, *Promised Messiah*, 561).

3 NEPHI 19:24

"It was given unto them what they should pray."

"Perfect prayers are those which are inspired, in which the Spirit reveals the words which should be used" (Bruce R. McConkie, *Mormon Doctrine*, 586). *See also D&C 50:30; Romans 8:24.*

3 NEPHI 19:34

"So great and marvelous were the words which he prayed that they cannot be written."

Elder Bruce R. McConkie was present in June 1978 when the First Presidency and the Twelve importuned the Lord for a revelation and subsequently learned that the priesthood would be available to all worthy males. He said: "The Lord in his providences poured out the Holy Ghost upon the First Presidency and the Twelve in a miraculous and marvelous manner." Speaking of this and other revelations, he continued, "There is no way to describe in language what is involved. This cannot be done. . . . I cannot describe in words what happened" (Bruce R. McConkie, *Sermons and Writings*, 167, 168–69). *See also D&C 76:115–116.*

3 NEPHI 20

3 NEPHI 20:3–5

Why did Jesus break bread and bless it two days in a row?

Many that were there had not been there the day before. *See also 3 Nephi 19:2–3.*

3 NEPHI 20:8

What is the symbolism of the bread and water?

The sacrament has beautiful symbolism. As we partake of the bread and water physically, it literally becomes a part of who we are. Symbolically through those emblems the Savior himself also becomes a part of our very being. "We partake of physical food that is, we partake of bread and water etc., to nourish the physical body. It is just as necessary that we partake of the emblems of the body and blood of our risen Lord to increase our spiritual strength" (George Albert Smith, in Conference Report, April 1908, 35).

3 NEPHI 20:11

The Lord commands us to search the words of Isaiah.

See insights for 3 Nephi 23:1–3.

3 NEPHI 20:13, 29; 21:24–26, 28, 33

How are people gathered, both spiritually and geographically?

"The gathering of Israel is first *spiritual and* second *temporal.* It is *spiritual* in that the lost sheep of Israel are first 'restored to the true church and fold of God,' meaning that they come to a true knowledge of the God of Israel, accept the gospel which he has restored in latter-days, and join The Church of Jesus Christ of Latter-day Saints. It is *temporal* in that these converts are *then* 'gathered home to the *lands of their inheritance*, and . . . established in *all their lands of promise*' (2 Ne. 9:2; 25:15–18; Jer. 16:14–21), meaning that the house of Joseph will be established in America, the house of Judah in Palestine, and that the Lost Tribes will come to Ephraim in America to receive their blessings in due course. (D. & C. 133)" (Bruce R. McConkie, *Mormon Doctrine*, 305–6; emphasis in original). *See also 1 Nephi 22:3, 12.*

3 NEPHI 20:13, 15, 27; 21:2, 24

What is one reason the Lord scattered Israel?

"Thus through this scattering the Lord has caused Israel to mix with the nations and bring the Gentiles within the blessings of the seed of Abraham. . . . It is by this scattering that the Gentile nations have been blessed, and if they will truly repent they are entitled to all the blessings promised to Israel" (Joseph Fielding Smith, *Answers to Gospel Questions*, 2:57).

3 NEPHI 20:22, 29; 21:23–25

What do we know about the New and the Old Jerusalem?

New Jerusalem

"The American Zion shall be the capital city, the source whence the law shall go forth to govern all the earth. It shall be the city of the Great King. . . . From there he shall reign gloriously over all the earth" (Bruce R. McConkie, *Millennial Messiah*, 301–2).

"That the remnants of Joseph, found among the descendants of Lehi, will have part in this great work is certainly consistent, and the great work of this restoration, the building of the temple and the City of Zion, or New Jerusalem, will fall to the lot of the descendants of Joseph, but it is Ephraim who will stand at the head and direct the work" (Joseph Fielding Smith, *Doctrines of Salvation*, 2:251). *See also D&C 57:2–3; Mormon 7:1–10; insights for Alma 9:16–17, 24.*

Old Jerusalem

"Judah will gather to old Jerusalem in due course. . . . The present assembling of people of Jewish ancestry into the Palestinian nation of Israel is not the scriptural gathering of Israel or of Judah. It may be prelude thereto, and some of the people so assembled may in due course be gathered into the true church . . . and they may then assist in building the temple that is destined to grace Jerusalem's soil" (Bruce R. McConkie, *New Witness for the Articles of Faith*, 519).

3 NEPHI 20:25; 21:6

Who is part of the house of Israel?

"Every person who embraces the gospel becomes of the house of Israel. . . . The great majority of those who become members of the Church are literal descendants of Abraham through Ephraim, son of Joseph. Those who are not literal descendants of Abraham and Israel must become such, and when they are baptized and confirmed they are grafted into the tree and are entitled to all the rights and privileges as heirs" (Joseph Fielding Smith, *Doctrines of Salvation*, 3:246).

3 NEPHI 20:31

When will the Jews believe in Jesus Christ?

"When the Savior visits [Old] Jerusalem, and the Jews look upon him, and see the wounds in his hands and in his side and in his feet, they will then know that they have persecuted and put to death the true Messiah, and then they will acknowledge him, but not till then" (Brigham Young, *Discourses*, 122). *See also D&C 45:48–52.*

3 NEPHI 20:36

"Awake again, and put on thy strength."

"To put on her strength is to put on the authority of the priesthood" (D&C 113:8).

3 NEPHI 20:43–45

Who is this servant?

"Isaiah's prophecy about the marred servant is clearly Messianic and applies to Jesus who was crucified. . . . But . . . as with many prophecies, the divine word has a dual fulfillment. In this setting we may properly say that Joseph Smith—whose voice declared the word for this dispensation—was marred, as his Lord had been, and yet should be healed" (Bruce R. McConkie, *Mortal Messiah*, 4:354). *See also 3 Nephi 21:10.*

3 NEPHI 21

3 NEPHI 21:9; 22:15–17

How will the gospel become "a great and a marvelous work" in the world?

Count Leo Tolstoi, speaking to Dr. Andrew D. White, said: "The Mormon people teach the American religion; their principles teach the people not only of Heaven and its attendant glories, but how to live so that their social and economic relations with each other are placed on a sound basis. If the people follow the teachings of this Church, nothing can stop their progress—it will be limitless. There have been great movements started in the past but they have died or been modified before they reached maturity. If Mormonism is able to endure, unmodified, until it reaches the third and fourth generation, it is destined to become the greatest power the world has ever known" (in Thomas J. Yates, *Improvement Era*, February 1939, 94.)

"Now, I think we all understand that this great latter-day kingdom has been set up for the last time, never again to be destroyed. . . .

". . . The Church of Jesus Christ of Latter-day Saints [is] to remain among men to prepare a people for the second coming of the Son of man" (Bruce R. McConkie, in Conference Report, October 1958, 115).

3 NEPHI 21:24–26

The ten lost tribes will not be gathered until the Lord dwells in the "New Jerusalem."

"The great day of the return of the Ten Tribes, the day when the assembling hosts shall fulfill the prophetic promises, shall come after our Lord's return" (Bruce R. McConkie, *Millennial Messiah*, 323).

3 NEPHI 22

3 NEPHI 22:1

Who are the "children of the desolate" and "the children of the married wife"?

The "barren" and the "children of the desolate" are "those who for generations have lived without the light of the gospel. . . . The children of the married wife [are] the members of the Church" (Joseph Fielding McConkie and Robert L. Millet, *Doctrinal Commentary*, 4:155).

3 NEPHI 22:2–3

What does the tent represent?

"Isaiah, fifty-fourth chapter, verses one and two, talks about the tent which represents the gospel of Christ. He states that in the last days the cords of the tent would be stretched across the earth and stakes would be planted in every land (see Isa. 54:1–2). We literally are seeing that fulfilled today" (Merrill J. Bateman, *Ensign*, May 1994, 65).

3 NEPHI 22:4–6

Who are the bride and bridegroom?

"Christ (the Bridegroom) shall claim his bride (the Church), celebrate the marriage supper, and become the *Husband* of his wife. (Isa. 54:5; Jer. 31:32; Eph. 5:23; Rev. 19:7–9; 21:2.) As a Husband he shall deal intimately, with tenderness and compassion, toward the remnant of his people who have returned to enjoy millennial rest with him" (Bruce R. McConkie, *Mormon Doctrine*, 370).

3 NEPHI 22:13

How important is it that our children have peace?

"Peace. What a marvelous, desirable blessing to bring to the souls of our children. If they are at peace within themselves and secure in their knowledge of Heavenly Father and His eternal plan for them, they will be able to cope better with the unrest in the world around them and be prepared better for reaching their divine potential" (M. Russell Ballard, *Ensign*, April 1994, 60).

3 NEPHI 22:16

Who is the "smith" that the Lord created?

"Speaking through Isaiah in a passage that was later quoted by the Savior to the Nephites, the Lord said, 'Behold, I have created the smith that bloweth the coals in the fire, and that bringeth forth an instrument for his work' (Isa. 54:16; 3 Ne. 22:16). Joseph was surely the smith who forged the instrument by which the Lord's people continue to prepare individually and collectively for the Savior's return—and that instrument is The Church of Jesus Christ of Latter-day Saints" (Gerald N. Lund, *Ensign*, January 1997, 52).

3 NEPHI 22:17

Will anything stop the progress of the Church in the last days?

"The eternal purposes of the Lord shall roll on" (Mormon 8:22).

"The Standard of Truth has been erected; no unhallowed hand can stop the work from progressing; persecutions may rage, mobs may combine, armies may assemble, calumny may defame, but the truth of God will go forth boldly, nobly, and independent, till it has penetrated every continent, visited every clime, swept every country, and sounded in every ear, till the purposes of God shall be accomplished, and the Great Jehovah shall say the work is done" (Joseph Smith, *History of the Church*, 4:540). *See also Daniel 2:44–45.*

3 NEPHI 23

3 NEPHI 23:1–3

"Great are the words of Isaiah."

"It just may be that my salvation (and yours also!) does in fact depend upon our ability to understand the writings of Isaiah as fully and truly as Nephi understood them" (Bruce R. McConkie, *Ensign*, October 1973, 78).

3 NEPHI 23:9, 11

The resurrection of many saints accompanied the Savior's arrival in the Americas.

"The graves were opened; and many bodies of the saints which slept arose, and came out of the graves . . . and went into the holy city, and appeared unto many" (Matthew 27:52–53).

3 NEPHI 23:11

Are there things we have not written that the Lord might want recorded?

"Do not suppose . . . that your experiences will not be interesting to your posterity.

". . . What could you do better for your children and your children's children than to record the story of your life, your triumphs over adversity, your recovery after a fall, your progress when all seemed black, your rejoicing when you had finally achieved? . . . Maybe the angels may quote from it for eternity" (Spencer W. Kimball, *Teachings*, 350, 351).

3 NEPHI 24

3 NEPHI 24:1

"The Lord . . . shall suddenly come to his temple."

"The Lord, whom we seek, shall suddenly come to his temple. . . . Indeed, he came suddenly to the Kirtland Temple on the 3rd day of April in 1836; he has also appeared in others of his holy houses; and he will come in due course to the temples in Jackson County and in Jerusalem" (Bruce R. McConkie, *Millennial Messiah*, 577).

3 NEPHI 24:2

"He is like a refiner's fire."

"The Savior's return will be a cleansing, refining experience by fire. The righteous will endure and be purified by this flame of truth, while the wicked will be burned as stubble, unable to withstand its unquenchable demands" (Jeffrey R. Holland, *Christ and the New Covenant*, 294).

3 NEPHI 24:3–4

What is the "offering in righteousness" the sons of Levi will make?

"The Lord . . . shall sit as a refiner and purifier of silver, and he shall purify the sons of Levi, and purge them as gold and silver, that they may offer unto the Lord an offering in righteousness. Let us, therefore, as a church and a people, and as Latter-day Saints, offer unto the Lord an offering in righteousness; and let us present in his holy temple, when it is finished, a book containing the records of our dead, which shall be worthy of all acceptation" (D&C 128:24). *See also D&C 13:1*.

"These sacrifices, as well as every ordinance belonging to the Priesthood, will, when the Temple of the Lord shall be built, and the sons of Levi be purified, be fully restored. . . . Those things which existed prior to Moses' day, namely, sacrifice, will be continued" (Joseph Smith, *Teachings*, 172–73).

3 NEPHI 24:8–12

How important is tithing?

"Tithing is paid by faith more than it is by money" (Gordon B. Hinckley, *Ensign*, December 1989, 5).

"By this principle (tithing) the loyalty of the people of this Church shall be put to the test. By this principle it shall be known who is for the kingdom of God and who is against it. By this principle it shall be seen whose hearts are set on doing the will of God and keeping his commandments. . . . There is a great deal of importance connected with this principle, for by it it shall be known whether we are faithful or unfaithful. In this respect it is as essential as faith in God" (Joseph F. Smith, *Gospel Doctrine*, 225).

3 NEPHI 24:16–17

"For them that feared the Lord, and that thought upon his name."

"For how knoweth a man the master whom he has not served, and who is a stranger unto him, and is far from the thoughts and intents of his heart?" (Mosiah 5:13). *See also insights for Helaman 5:5–14*.

3 NEPHI 25

3 NEPHI 25:1

What does it mean to "leave them neither root nor branch"?

"The phrase 'it shall leave them neither root nor branch' means the opposite of turning the 'heart of the fathers to the children, and the heart of the children to their fathers' (3 Nephi 25:6). The righteous will be joined in eternal families while the wicked will be cut off from their fathers and grandfathers (their roots) and also cut off from their children and grandchildren (their branches)" (Thomas R. Valletta, ed., *Book of Mormon for Latter-day Saint Families*, 564).

3 NEPHI 25:2

How will "the Son of Righteousness arise with healing in his wings"?

"The 'Sun of righteousness' (Mal. 4:2; cf. 3 Ne. 25:2) will bring the healing power of the resurrection and redemption (2 Ne. 25:13), and the righteous will be nourished 'as calves of the stall' because of their obedience to the Lord (1 Ne. 22:24)" (Daniel H. Ludlow, ed., *Encyclopedia of Mormonism*, 2:851).

3 NEPHI 25:5-6

What is unique about these verses?

These verses are found in all four standard works. See D&C 2:1–3; Malachi 4:1–6; 3 Nephi 25:1–6; JS—H 1:36–39.

Why was Elijah chosen for this important responsibility?

"Elijah was the last Prophet [in the Old Testament] that held the keys of the Priesthood, and who will, before the last dispensation, restore the authority and deliver the keys of the Priesthood, in order that all the ordinances may be attended to in righteousness" (Joseph Smith, *Teachings*, 172).

When did Elijah come?

Malachi's promise of Elijah's return was in the last chapter of Jewish scripture (Malachi 4:5–6). This prophecy has long been celebrated by the Jews during the feast of the passover. "It is interesting to know that on the third day of April, 1836, the Jews were celebrating the feast of the Passover, and were leaving the doors of their homes open for the coming of Elijah. On that day Elijah came, but not to the Jewish homes, but to the Temple in the village of Kirtland near the banks of Lake Erie, to two humble servants of the Lord who were appointed by divine decree to receive him" (Joseph Fielding Smith, *Church History and Modern Revelation*, 3:84). *See also D&C 110:13–15.*

What did Elijah come to restore?

"By restoring the sealing keys, Elijah revealed the greatest use to which the priesthood may be put by mortals on earth" (Bruce R. McConkie, *New Witness for the Articles of Faith*, 508).

"When the full measure of Elijah's mission is understood . . . it applies just as much on this side of the veil as it does to the other side of the veil (see Malachi 4:5–6). . . . The hearts of you fathers and mothers must be turned to your children right now, if you have the true Spirit of Elijah, and not think that it applies merely to those who are beyond the veil. Let your hearts be turned to your children, and teach your children; but you must do it when they are young enough to be schooled. And if you are neglecting your family home evening, you are neglecting the beginning of the mission of Elijah just as certainly as if you were neglecting your research work of genealogy" (Harold B. Lee, *Teachings*, 281).

3 NEPHI 26

3 NEPHI 26:3

What will happen when "the elements . . . melt with fervent heat"?

"This earth, in its sanctified and immortal state, will be made like unto crystal and will be a Urim and Thummim" (D&C 130:9).

3 NEPHI 26:9–10

"Then shall the greater things be made manifest."

"It shall come to pass that the Jews shall have the words of the Nephites, and the Nephites shall have the words of the Jews; and the Nephites and the Jews shall have the words of the lost tribes of Israel" (2 Nephi 29:13). *See also Alma 37:3–4.*

"Now the Lord has placed us on probation as members of the Church. He has given us the Book of Mormon, which is the lesser part, to build up our faith through our obedience to the counsels which it contains, and when we ourselves, members of the Church, are willing to keep the commandments as they have been given to us and show our faith as the Nephites did for a short period of time, then the Lord is ready to bring forth the other record and give it to us, but we are not ready now to receive it. Why? Because we have not lived up to the requirements in . . . the reading of the record which had been given to us and in following its counsels" (Joseph Fielding Smith, in Conference Report, October 1961, 20).

3 NEPHI 26:14, 16

Do children still communicate great messages?

"Inspired children often show the way through the wilderness. . . .

"It has been a privilege to seal several adopted children to Nan and Dan Barker, now of Arizona. Some time ago *Nate, then just over three*, said: 'Mommy, there is another little girl who is supposed to come to our family. She has dark hair and dark eyes and lives a long way from here.'

"The wise mother asked, 'How do you know this?'

"'*Jesus told me, upstairs.*'

"The mother noted, 'We don't have an upstairs,' but quickly sensed the significance of what had been communicated. After much travail and many prayers, the Barker family were in a sealing room in the Salt Lake Temple in the fall of 1995—where a little girl with dark hair and dark eyes, from Kazakhstan, was sealed to them for time and eternity. Inspired children still tell parents 'great and marvelous things' (3 Ne. 26:14)" (Neal A. Maxwell, *Ensign,* May 1996, 69–70; emphasis in original).

3 NEPHI 26:16, 18

Why were these "marvelous things" forbidden to be written?
    See insights for Alma 12:9.

3 NEPHI 27

3 NEPHI 27:3-8

What is the name of the true church?

Other names the Church of Jesus Christ has had throughout history include:

The Church of Jesus Christ of Latter-day Saints (D&C 115:4)

The church of the Lamb of God (1 Nephi 14:12–14)

Christians (Alma 46:13–14)

The church of the Firstborn (D&C 107:19)

"Let it be understood by all that Jesus Christ stands at the head of this church which bears His sacred name. He is watching over it. He is guiding it" (Gordon B. Hinckley, *Ensign*, May 1994, 59).

"Don't let the Lord down by calling this the *Mormon Church*. He didn't call it the Mormon Church" (George Albert Smith, in Conference Report, April 1948, 160; emphasis in original).

"The name of the Church was not obtained through study or research, but by revelation direct from the Lord. . . . Of all the churches in the world, there was not one that bore his name when the Lord restored his church in this dispensation" (LeGrand Richards, *Marvelous Work and a Wonder*, 131–32).

3 NEPHI 27:8-21

What is the gospel of Jesus Christ?

Consider the following comparison between the "gospel" of Christ from 3 Nephi 27 and the "doctrine" of Christ from 2 Nephi 31:

3 NEPHI 27 (GOSPEL OF CHRIST)	2 NEPHI 31:2–32:6 (DOCTRINE OF CHRIST)
Faith (v. 19)	Faith (vv. 15, 19)
Repentance (vv. 16, 19–20)	Repentance (vv. 11, 13, 14, 17)
Baptism (vv. 16, 20)	Baptism (vv. 4–6, 8, 11–14, 17)
Holy Ghost (v. 20)	Holy Ghost (vv. 8, 12, 13–14, 17–18; 32:2, 5)

Atonement (v. 14)	Atonement (v. 19)
Judgment (vv. 11, 14, 15)	Keep the commandments (vv. 7, 10)
Endure to the end (v. 16)	Scriptures (vv. 19–20; 32:3)
His gospel is to do what he does (v. 21)	Endure to the end (vv. 15–16, 20)

3 NEPHI 27:11

How long will the wicked "have joy in their works"?

"The wicked may prosper for a time, the rebellious may seem to profit by their transgressions, but the time is coming when, at the bar of justice, all men will be judged, 'every man according to their works.' (Rev. 20:13.) No one will 'get [away]' with anything. On that day no one will escape the penalty of his deeds, no one will fail to receive the blessings he has earned. . . . There will be total justice" (Spencer W. Kimball, *Miracle of Forgiveness*, 304–5). *See also 3 Nephi 24:14–15.*

3 NEPHI 27:19

"No unclean thing can enter into his kingdom."

See insights for Alma 11:37.

3 NEPHI 27:21, 27

Whose example are we to follow?

"Christ is God the Son and possesses every virtue in its perfection. Therefore, the only measure of true greatness is how close a man can become like Jesus. That man is greatest who is most like Christ, and those who love him most will be most like him" (Ezra Taft Benson, *New Era*, January 1973, 20).

3 NEPHI 27:24–26

What role will the Book of Mormon play in our judgment?

"No member of this Church can stand approved in the presence of God who has not seriously and carefully read the Book of Mormon" (Joseph Fielding Smith, in Conference Report, October 1961, 18). *See also D&C 128:7–8.*

3 NEPHI 27:27

Who will take part in our judgment?

Ourselves (Alma 41:7; Joseph Smith, *History of the Church*, 6:314; Joseph Smith, *Teachings*, 357)

Our bishops (D&C 41:9; 58:14, 17–20; 64:40; 72:17)

The scriptures (2 Nephi 25:18; 29:11; 33:14; 3 Nephi 27:25–26; Revelation 20:12)

The apostles (D&C 29:12; 1 Nephi 12:9; 3 Nephi 27:27; Mormon 3:18; Matthew 19:27–30)

Christ (John 5:22; 3 Nephi 27:14)

"The reality is that there will be a whole hierarchy of judges who, under Christ, shall judge the righteous. He alone shall issue the decrees of damnation for the wicked" (Bruce R. McConkie, *Millennial Messiah*, 520).

"Christ is at the head. . . . It would seem to be quite reasonable, if the twelve apostles in Jerusalem are to be the judges of the twelve tribes, and the twelve disciples on this continent are to be the judges of the descendants of Nephi, that the brother of Jared and Jared should be the judges of the Jaredites, their descendants; and, further, that the first presidency and twelve who have officiated in our age, should operate in regard to mankind in this dispensation" (John Taylor, *Gospel Kingdom*, 138).

3 NEPHI 28

3 NEPHI 28:1–3

What do our desires have to do with the blessings we receive?

See insights for Alma 29:1–4.

3 NEPHI 28:6

Where is John the Beloved now?

"The Spirit of the Lord fell upon Joseph in an unusual manner, and he prophesied that John the Revelator was then among the Ten Tribes of Israel" (Joseph Smith, *History of the Church*, 1:176, n. 4).

3 NEPHI 28:6, 9

What are the three Nephites doing now?

"The three Nephites . . . are still living upon this continent. He spoke to them of a time when they would perform a great and mighty work among the Gentiles; and that has not yet been fulfilled, but it will be. You will find that many districts where the Elders of Israel cannot reach will be penetrated by these men who have power over death. . . . My testimony is that these men are going abroad in the nations of the earth before the face of your sons, and they are preparing the hearts of the children of men to receive the Gospel. They are administering to those who are heirs of salvation, and preparing their hearts to receive the truth" (John W. Taylor, in Conference Report, October 1902, 75).

3 NEPHI 28:7–10, 15, 18–22, 30, 37–40

What are the characteristics of translated beings?

They will not taste death (vv. 7–8).

They will be changed to a resurrected state at the Second Coming (vv. 7–8, 39–40).

They suffer no pain or sorrow (v. 9).

Their joy is full (v. 10).

They have a change in their bodies equivalent to a long-term "transfiguration"—we usually refer to it as translation (vv. 15, 37–39).

They teach, baptize, and interact with mortals (v. 18).

They can't be incarcerated, they can't be burned, they can't be eaten by wild beasts (vv. 19–22).

They can appear and disappear and travel from place to place like the angels (v. 30).

Satan can't tempt them and has no power over them (v. 39).

"No longer does blood (the life-giving element of our present mortality) flow in their veins. Procreation ceases. . . . They have power to move and live in both a mortal and an unseen sphere. . . . Millennial man will live in a state akin to translation. His body will be changed so that it is no longer subject to disease or death as we know it. . . . He will, however, have children" (Bruce R. McConkie, *Millennial Messiah*, 644).

3 NEPHI 28:11

The primary mission of the Holy Ghost is to bear record of the Father and the Son.

"The Holy Ghost, sometimes called the Comforter, is the third member of the Godhead, and is a personage, distinct from the Holy Spirit. As a personage, the Holy Ghost cannot any more than the Father and Son be everywhere present in person. Little has been revealed as yet concerning the Holy Ghost; but it is evident that His mission is to bear witness to men of the existence of God and the truth of the gospel of Jesus Christ, and also to fill men with knowledge and power and to inspire them to works leading to happiness" (John A. Widtsoe, *Evidences and Reconciliations*, 76–77).

3 NEPHI 28:12–13, 36–38

Why did the Lord touch the nine and not the three?

"The three Nephites . . . wanted to tarry until Jesus came, and that they might He took them into the heavens and endowed them with the power of translation . . . and brought them back to the earth. Thus they received power to live until the coming of the Son of Man" (Franklin D. Richards, *Journal of Discourses*, 25:237).

3 NEPHI 29

3 NEPHI 29:8

What should be our attitude toward the Jews?

"Let us as Latter-day Saints reach out to others not of our faith. Let us never act in a spirit of arrogance or with a holier-than-thou attitude. Rather, may we show love and respect and helpfulness toward them. . . . We can be more tolerant, more neighborly, more friendly, more of an example" (Gordon B. Hinckley, *Ensign*, May 2000, 87).

3 NEPHI 30

3 NEPHI 30:2

How do Gentiles become members of the house of Israel?

"The effect of the Holy Ghost upon a Gentile, is to purge out the old blood, and make him actually of the seed of Abraham. That man that has none of the blood of Abraham (naturally) must have a new creation by the Holy Ghost" (Joseph Smith, *Teachings*, 150).

Fourth
NEPHI

What time period does Fourth Nephi cover?

In fewer than four pages, Fourth Nephi covers one-third of the time of Book of Mormon history.

What are the characteristics of a righteous people who live the law of consecration?

They are all converted to the Lord (v. 2).

They deal justly with one another (v. 2).

They have all things in common or share their wealth equally (v. 3).

They have peace in the land (v. 4).

Great and marvelous miracles are performed (v. 5).

They experience great prosperity (v. 7).

They multiply in number and become strong (v. 10).

They keep the commandments (v. 12).

They fast and pray (v. 12).

They meet together often (v. 12).

The love of God is in their hearts (v. 15).

They are a most happy people (v. 16).

There is no class distinction among them (v. 17).

There is no contention (v. 18).

They become exceedingly rich (v. 23).

What does it mean to have "all things common"?

"The basic principle of all the revelations on the United Order is that everything we have belongs to the Lord; therefore, the Lord may call upon us for any and all of the property which we have, because it belongs to Him. This, I repeat, is the basic principle" (J. Reuben Clark Jr., in Conference Report, October 1942, 55).

"Consecration is the giving of one's own time, talents, and means to care for those in need—whether spiritually or temporally—and in building the Lord's kingdom" (Spencer W. Kimball, *Teachings*, 366).

4 NEPHI 1:4

How were they able to maintain peace for so long?

"He who doeth the works of righteousness shall receive his reward, even peace in this world, and eternal life in the world to come" (D&C 59:23).

"Peace comes from within. . . .

"That makes me responsible for the peace of the world, and makes you individually responsible for the peace of the world. The responsibility cannot be shifted to someone else. It cannot be placed upon the shoulders of Congress or Parliament, or any other organization of men with governing authority" (John A. Widtsoe, in Conference Report, October 1943, 113).

4 NEPHI 1:15, 28, 31, 34

The heart of a person makes all the difference.

"What a glorious time that must have been when everybody was happy, when everybody was at peace, when everyone loved his neighbor as himself, and above all he loved God, because we are informed here that the thing which brought about this condition of happiness was the fact that the love of God was in the hearts of the people. There never will be a time of peace, happiness, justice tempered by mercy, when all men will receive that which is their right and privilege to receive, until they get in their hearts the love of God" (Joseph Fielding Smith, *Doctrines of Salvation*, 3:320). *See also insights for Alma 8:9, 11.*

4 NEPHI 1:16

Why were the people happier than "all the people who had been created"?

See insights for Mosiah 2:41; Alma 41:10.

4 NEPHI 1:20–46

What happens to wicked people who were once righteous?

Rebel against the church (v. 20)

Become prideful (v. 24)

Wear costly apparel (v. 24)

Stop living the law of consecration (v. 25)

Create class distinctions (v. 26)

Organize other churches to make money (v. 26)

Practice all manner of wickedness (v. 27)

Allow Satan to get a hold on their hearts (vv. 28–34)

Fight against the Lord's servants (vv. 30–31)

Willingly follow false prophets (v. 34)

Become divided as a people (v. 35)

Willfully reject the gospel (v. 38)

Learn to hate (v. 39)

Create secret combinations (v. 42)

Have pride in their great riches (v. 43)

4 NEPHI 1:20

The name "Lamanites" becomes a title for the wicked rather than a title for a race.

"It is significant that the name 'Lamanite' here appears to become a generic term. That is, it refers to a general classification of people—those who revolted from the Church. These people may or may not have been the direct descendants of Laman and Lemuel" (Dean L. Larsen, *You and the Destiny of the Indian*, 22).

4 NEPHI 1:38

How serious is the sin of willful rebellion?

"A common sin is rebellion against God. This manifests itself in wilful refusal to obey God's commandments, in rejection of the counsel of his servants, in opposition to the work of the kingdom—that is, in the deliberate word or act of disobedience to God's will. . . .

"Among Church members rebellion frequently takes the form of criticism of authorities and leaders. . . . They complain of the programs, belittle the constituted authorities, and generally set themselves up as judges. After a while they absent themselves from Church meetings for imagined offenses, and fail to pay their tithes and meet their other Church obligations" (Spencer W. Kimball, *Miracle of Forgiveness*, 42–43).

4 NEPHI 1:48

"Ammaron, being constrained by the Holy Ghost, did hide up the records."

Our level of righteousness or wickedness determines how much scripture the Lord will share with us.

REFERENCE	PEOPLE AND THEIR LEVEL OF RIGHTEOUSNESS OR WICKEDNESS	LOST OR GAINED SCRIPTURE
1 Nephi 4:18	Laban was wicked	Lost brass plates
1 Nephi 4:38	Nephi was righteous	Gained brass plates
Alma 14:8	The people of Ammonihah were wicked	Burned scriptures
4 Nephi 1:48	The Nephites became wicked	Lost the records
JS—H 1:59	Joseph Smith was righteous	Gained gold plates
D&C 3:14–15	Joseph temporarily obeyed man rather than the Lord	Lost gold plates
D&C 5:30	Joseph repented	Gained gold plates
Heber C. Kimball, *Journal of Discourses*, 4:105	We as Latter-day Saints if we keep the commandments	Will gain additional scriptures

See also 2 Nephi 29:13; Alma 37:3–4; insights for 3 Nephi 26:9–10.

THE BOOK OF

MORMON

MORMON 1

MORMON 1:1–2:29

What do Mormon and Joseph Smith have in common?

Mormon Scriptures	Similarities	Joseph Scriptures
Mormon 1:1–3 10 years old	A prophet who buried the gold plates in a hill near their home, came to them when they were young and told them that at a future time they were to go to the hill and obtain the plates	JS—H 1:33–35, 42 17 years old
Mormon 1:2	They both started their official work at the age of 24	D&C 20:1
Mormon 1:15 15 years old	They had a glorious vision of the Lord when they were very young	JS—H 1:17 14 years old
Mormon 1:16	After the vision they tried to share part of what they had learned but were rejected by the people	JS—H 1:21–22
Mormon 2:1	Both were physically large and powerful men for their day	Andrus, *Joseph Smith, the Man and the Seer*, 14–15
Mormon 1:5	Both had the same name as their father	JS—H 1:4
Mormon 1:13	Both were born into a state of general apostasy	JS—H 1:18–19
Mormon 2:1	Both led their people as a military leader, prophet, dispensational head, and record	D&C 43:1–5

	keeper (one the abridger, the other the translator of the gold plates)	
Mormon 2:4–6; 4:19–20; 5:6–7	Their enemy's persecutions became so intense that several times they were forced to leave their homes and move with their people from city to city	New York, Pennsylvania, Ohio, Missiouri, Illinois
Mormon 8:3	Their enemy's persecutions continued until they succeeded in murdering them	D&C 135:4
Mormon 2:8, 29	Continued rejection of their message by the general population resulted in a civil war which divided the North from the South in the costliest casualty war of their era	D&C 87:1–3

MORMON 1:1

What is the meaning of the name "Mormon"?

"The word Mormon, means literally, more good" (Joseph Smith, *History of the Church*, 5:400).

MORMON 1:14; 2:26–27

Why did the Holy Ghost "not come upon any"?

See insights for Helaman 4:24–25; 6:35.

MORMON 1:15–16

"I, being fifteen years of age . . . was visited of the Lord."

"You young boys need not wait to be great. You can be superior missionaries, strong young men, great companions, and happy, trusted Church leaders. You need not wait until tomorrow" (Spencer W. Kimball, *Ensign*, May 1976, 47). *See also JS—H 1:7, 17; 1 Samuel 3:4–10.*

MORMON 2

MORMON 2:1–2

What kind of young man was Mormon as the leader of the Nephite armies?

"If you think it an inspiration that a 16 year old boy could win the leadership of a great national army what would you think of a man between the ages of 65 and 74 who was still the best man among his entire people for this top position of leadership, and in those days the general marched at the head and not in the rear of his troops. (Mormon 6:11.) It is one thing to shoot a guided missile at an enemy a thousand miles away, but it is quite another thing to meet the enemy face to face, and with a sword or a battle axe, take on all comers, old and young, on any basis they might choose to elect; and still be in there fighting at age 74. No weakling or coward survives a test like that" (Sterling W. Sill, in Daniel H. Ludlow, *Companion*, 299).

MORMON 2:10–13

"Their sorrowing was not unto repentance."

"It is not uncommon to find men and women in the world who feel remorse for the things they do wrong. Sometimes this is because their actions cause them or loved ones great sorrow and misery. Sometimes their sorrow is caused because they are caught and punished for their actions. Such worldly feelings do not constitute 'godly sorrow' (2 Corinthians 7:10).

"Godly sorrow is a gift of the Spirit. It is a deep realization that our actions have offended our Father and our God. It is the sharp and keen awareness that our behavior caused the Savior, He who knew no sin, even the greatest of all, to endure agony and suffering. Our sins caused Him to bleed at every pore. This very real mental and spiritual anguish is what the scriptures refer to as having 'a broken heart and a contrite spirit' (D&C 20:37). Such a spirit is the absolute prerequisite for true repentance" (Ezra Taft Benson, *Teachings*, 72).

MORMON 2:15

"The day of grace was passed."

"It is possible for people to get so far in the dark through rebellion and wickedness that the spirit of repentance leaves them. It is a gift of God, and they get beyond the power of repentance" (Joseph Fielding Smith, *Doctrines of Salvation*, 2:194). *See also Helaman 13:38; insights for Alma 34:32–35.*

MORMON 2:18–19

How could Mormon have hope for himself when he was "filled with sorrow"?

"A wholesome view of self-worth . . . is best established by a close relationship with God" (Ezra Taft Benson, *Ensign*, May 1986, 6). *See also insights for 4 Nephi 1:4.*

MORMON 2:23

What is worth going to war and fighting for?

See insights for Alma 43:9, 26, 30, 45–50; 44:5; 46:12; 48:10, 24.

MORMON 3

MORMON 3:9, 14-15

Vengeance belongs to the Lord.

See insights for Mormon 8:19–20.

MORMON 3:10, 19; 4:1-4

Offensive wars are not justified in the eyes of the Lord.

"We have to be careful as to what spirit we are guided by. If we *want to go out to battle*, to encroach upon other peoples' liberties and rights, *to gain* their lands, *to destroy* their property without any right or reason, that is one thing; but if somebody comes against us to destroy us and our property and our homes and our rights and our privileges . . . then we have the right under the divine law to rise for our own protection and take such steps as are necessary. . . .

". . . There is a very great difference between arising to go forth for conquest, for blood, for plunder, to gain territory and power in the earth, and in fighting to defend our own possessions in the spirit of justice and righteousness and equity" (Charles W. Penrose, in Conference Report, April 1917, 21–22). *See also insights for Alma 43:46–47; 47:14.*

MORMON 3:12

"*My soul had been poured out in prayer unto my God all the day long for them.*"

See insights for Enos 1:4, 9, 11.

MORMON 3:17-22; 5:12-15

To whom was Mormon writing, and why?

Who	Why
Gentiles (3:17; 5:10)	To issue a warning that we will all be judged some day (3:20)
House of Israel (3:17; 5:12)	
All the ends of the earth (3:18)	So that we might believe in Jesus Christ (3:21; 5:15)
The twelve tribes (3:18)	
Remnant of this people (3:19; 5:15)	So that the Jews will have another witness that Jesus of Nazareth was the Christ (3:21; 5:14)
Everyone (3:20)	
Jews (5:14)	

MORMON 4

MORMON 4:5

Who could the Lord use to punish the wicked?

"The wicked shall slay the wicked, and fear shall come upon every man" (D&C 63:33). *See also Mormon 8:8.*

"Often, very often, we are punished as much by our sins as we are for our sins" (Boyd K. Packer, *Teach Ye Diligently*, 262).

"When souls become wicked they will . . . hurt one another; and this, perhaps, accounts for four-fifths of the suffering of men. It is men, not God, who have produced racks, whips, prisons, slavery, guns, bayonets, and bombs; it is by . . . human stupidity, not by the churlishness of nature, that we have poverty and overwork" (C. S. Lewis, *Problem of Pain*, 89).

MORMON 4:11-12

"There never had been so great wickedness among all the children of Lehi."

How do we compare today? "In 1985 hand guns killed eight people in Great Britain, 48 people in Japan, 34 in Switzerland, 52 in Canada, 58 in Israel, 21 in Sweden, 42 in West Germany, and 10,728 in the United States. There are more murders each year on Manhattan Island which is 3 miles by 12 miles than in the United Kingdom including Ireland" (Victor Cline, in K. Douglas Bassett, comp., *Latter-day Commentary on the Book of Mormon*, 476).

MORMON 5

MORMON 5:1-2

What kind of man was Mormon?

"In this crucible of wickedness the true greatness of Mormon shines like a star . . . no matter how bad things are, we must never stop trying to do what we can to improve matters, 'for if we should cease to labor, we should be brought under condemnation . . .' (Moroni 9:6). In this spirit Mormon took over command of the army even when he knew that all was lost" (Hugh Nibley, *Collected Works*, 7:400–401).

MORMON 5:8-9

"I, Mormon, do not desire to harrow up the souls of men."

"Mormon was torn not only by what he saw but also by what he must—and must not—write" (Jeffrey R. Holland, *Christ and the New Covenant*, 320).

MORMON 5:12-14

One purpose of the Book of Mormon is to persuade the Jews "that Jesus is the Christ."

"The Book of Mormon . . . is . . . to the convincing of the Jew and Gentile that Jesus is the Christ" (Title Page of the Book of Mormon). *See also 2 Nephi 26:12.*

MORMON 5:15, 20

The Gentiles shall drive and kill the Lamanites.

"Both President Spencer W. Kimball and President Ezra Taft Benson taught that this verse had application to the afflictions, deaths, and inequities suffered by the American Indians over the years (see Spencer W. Kimball, *Faith Precedes the Miracle*, 341; Ezra Taft Benson, *This Nation Shall Endure*, 160–61)" (Thomas R. Valletta, ed., *Book of Mormon for Latter-Day Saint Families*, 594).

MORMON 6

MORMON 6:2-6

What is the Hebrew meaning of the word "Cumorah"?

The Hebrew spelling for the word Cumorah would be "kumorah." In Hebrew lexicons, only the root of the word is treated and defined. The Hebrew root of a word usually consists of the three major consonants of the word. The root of "Cumorah" would be (Kmr). (The "h" is often silent or acquiesces to the preceding vowel marking the point of accent or stress.)

As Professor Marcus Jastrow explained, the root (kmr) originally comes from a word that means "shrinking and maturing of fruits by underground storage." The Hiffiel conjugation (the causative tense) is defined as "to hide in the ground" (see Marcus Jastrow, *Dictionary of the Targumim*, 647).

Considering these definitions, the word "Cumorah" was an appropriate name for a hill that was not only the depository of the gold plates but also a general storage space for other sets of plates.

MORMON 6:10-15

How many people died in the final battles of the Book of Mormon?

The number of Nephite soldiers killed adds up to 230,000. This number does not include the women and children, the Lamanites, or those killed in battles immediately leading up to the final battles. There could have easily been between 500,000 and one million killed, and probably more. Compare those numbers with the following numbers of Americans killed in war.

Year	War	United States Casualties
1776	Revolutionary War	4,435
1812	War of 1812	2,260
1848	Mexican War	1,733
1865	Civil War	140,414*
1898	Spanish American War	385
1918	World War I	53,402
1945	World War II	293,986
1953	Korean War	33,629

(Statistics come from Daniel H. Ludlow, *Companion*, 303. *Many other sources suggest this figure is closer to 350,000.)

That considered, there were many more people killed in the battles described at the end of the Book of Mormon than Americans killed in all the wars of her history.

MORMON 6:17–19, 22

"O ye fair ones, how could ye have departed from the ways of the Lord!"

"O Jerusalem, Jerusalem, thou that killest the prophets, and stonest them which are sent unto thee, how often would I have gathered thy children together, even as a hen gathereth her chickens under her wings, and ye would not! Behold, your house is left unto you desolate" (Matthew 23:37–38).

"I hope that we will be able to remain faithful. . . . I hope that we will be able to enjoy the same feeling expressed by Abraham Lincoln during the time of the civil war. A friend was talking with him regarding the condition of the country, and so on, and made the remark, 'I hope that the Lord is on our side.' 'Well,' said President Lincoln, 'I do not worry about that at all; I know that the Lord is always on the side of right. What worries me most is to know if we are on the Lord's side'" (Hugh S. Gowans, in Conference Report, April 1903, 37).

"Great nations do not fall because of external aggression; they first erode and decay inwardly, so that, like rotten fruit, they fall of themselves" (Ezra Taft Benson, *This Nation Shall Endure*, 84).

MORMON 7

MORMON 7:1-10

Many promises are made to the "remnant of this people," the Lamanites.
See insights for Alma 9:16–17, 24.

MORMON 7:5-10

What was the focus of Mormon's last testimony?

Principles of the gospel included in Mormon's last testimony:

Belief in Jesus Christ (faith) (v. 5)

Repentance (v. 5)

Atonement, redemption (vv. 5, 7)

Resurrection (v. 6)

Judgment (v. 6)

Exaltation, never-ending happiness (v. 7)

Nature of the Godhead (v. 7)

Baptism (v. 8)

Scriptures (vv. 8–9)

Covenants (v. 10)

Holy Ghost (v. 10)

MORMON 7:8-9

"If ye believe that ye will believe this also."

"No man can say that this book (laying his hand on the Bible) is true . . . and at the same time say, that the Book of Mormon is untrue; . . . No Latter-day Saint, no man or woman, can say the Book of Mormon is true, and at the same time say that the Bible is untrue. If one be true, both are" (Brigham Young, *Journal of Discourses*, 1:38).

MORMON 8

MORMON 8:2-9

Does righteousness sometimes bring loneliness?

"And he [Elijah] said, I have been very jealous for the Lord God of hosts: for the children of Israel have forsaken thy covenant, thrown down thine altars, and slain thy prophets with the sword; and I, even I only, am left; and they seek my life, to take it away" (1 Kings 19:10).

Jesus was left alone by:

The multitudes (John 6:66)

The apostles (Matthew 26:56)

The Father (Matthew 27:46)

Elder Neal A. Maxwell explained, "Discipleship requires us to be willing to stand alone" (Ensign, November 2001, 79).

"It was one Sarah Ann Meeks who paid what seemed to be her ultimate sacrifice as she stood alone on the doorstep of her home in far-off England nearly a century and a half ago. Her father met her there with a small bundle containing a few of her belongings and with these words, 'You join that church and you must never set foot in my home again.' Unfortunately that was the last she saw of her family. Alone? Very much alone! She could have bowed to that impossible, heart-wrenching rejection. But no—she loved the Lord" (Wm. Rolfe Kerr, Ensign, November 1996, 81).

Are we really as alone as we sometimes feel?
"The Lord will never forsake or abandon anyone. You may abandon him, but he will not abandon you. You never need to feel that you are alone" (Joseph B. Wirthlin, Ensign, November 1989, 75). *See also 2 Kings 6:13–18.*

MORMON 8:3
How do the sins of the wicked affect the righteous?
"In all ages the Lord pours out his *judgments* upon the children of disobedience. Famines, captivity, plagues, floods, lightnings, hailstorms, pestilences, tempests, earthquakes, wars. . . . Obviously these judgments come upon peoples and nations to punish them for their rebellion and to humble them that peradventure they will turn to righteousness. And obviously also a righteous minority group may be called upon to suffer with those who are receiving a just reward for their unholy deeds" (Bruce R. McConkie, Mormon Doctrine, 404). *See also insights for 1 Nephi 22:16–22.*

MORMON 8:10–11
Why did the three Nephite disciples minister to Moroni?
"As a result of his perseverance and righteousness, Moroni was ministered to by the Three Nephites" (Joseph B. Wirthlin, Finding Peace in Our Lives, 156).

MORMON 8:14
"No one shall have them to get gain."
"Again I beheld the same messenger at my bedside, and heard him

rehearse or repeat over again to me the same things as before; and added a caution to me, telling me that Satan would try to tempt me (in consequence of the indigent circumstances of my father's family), to get the plates for the purpose of getting rich. This he forbade me, saying that I must have no other object in view in getting the plates but to glorify God, and must not be influenced by any other motive than that of building his kingdom; otherwise I could not get them" (JS—H 1:46).

MORMON 8:19–20

"For judgment is mine, saith the Lord, and vengeance is mine."

"Men are forbidden to execute vengeance upon their fellow men. . . .

"It is the wicked, not the righteous, who swear vengeance upon their enemies" (Bruce R. McConkie, *Mormon Doctrine*, 821).

MORMON 8:22

"The eternal purposes of the Lord shall roll on."

See insights for 3 Nephi 21:9; 22:15–17; 3 Nephi 22:17.

MORMON 8:24

How were they able to "remove mountains"?

See Ether 12:29–30; Moses 7:13.

MORMON 8:25

Who was prophesied of by many ancient prophets?

"So great was [Joseph Smith's] assigned mission, with reference to the 'restitution of all things' (Acts 3:21), that holy prophets spoke of him, by name, thousands of years before his mortal birth. (2 Ne. 3.) And as to the mighty work to be started by him—there are as many prophecies foretelling it as there are about any other single subject" (Bruce R. McConkie, *Mormon Doctrine*, 396). *See also 3 Nephi 22:4–6.*

MORMON 8:26–41

How can the Book of Mormon help us in our day?

"The Book of Mormon was written for us today. . . . God, who knows the end from the beginning, told [Mormon] what to include in his abridgement that we would need for our day" (Ezra Taft Benson, *Ensign*, May 1975, 63).

"Moroni was shown the last days. . . . [He] saw they would be very much like his own" (Jeffrey R. Holland, *Christ and the New Covenant*, 324).

MORMON 8:31

What are these "great pollutions"?

"I cannot remember when I first heard profane and vulgar expressions in common use. . . . Today, our young people hear such expressions from boys and girls in their grade schools, from actors on stage and in the movies, from popular novels, and even from public officials and sports heroes. Television and videotapes bring profanity and vulgarity into our homes.

". . . Surely this is one fulfillment of the Book of Mormon prophecy that in the last days 'there shall be great pollutions upon the face of the earth.' (Morm. 8:31)" (Dallin H. Oaks, *Ensign*, May 1986, 49).

MORMON 9

MORMON 9:3–5

Will those in the terrestrial and telestial kingdoms be happy there?

"And they who remain shall also be quickened; nevertheless, they shall return again to their own place, to enjoy that which they are willing to receive, because they were not willing to enjoy that which they might have received" (D&C 88:32).

"The prophet and his leaders seek to educate our very desires, for God finally gives to each man the desires of his heart" (Neal A. Maxwell, *Of One Heart*, 30).

"It is his purpose, according to the divine plan, to make all of his creatures as happy as it is possible for them to be under the conditions of their immortal states" (Joseph Fielding Smith, *Church History and Modern Revelation*, 2:68).

MORMON 9:11–12

"By Adam came the fall of man . . . and because of Jesus Christ came the redemption of man."

"Creation is father to the Fall; and by the Fall came mortality and death; and by Christ came immortality and eternal life. If there had been no fall of Adam, by which cometh death, there could have been no atonement of Christ, by which cometh life" (Bruce R. McConkie, *Ensign*, May 1985, 11). *See also insights for Alma 18:28–39.*

MORMON 9:13

How does the Atonement overcome both spiritual and physical death for "all men"?

"In Gethsemane and on Calvary, He worked out *the infinite and eternal atonement.* . . . Thus He became our Redeemer—redeeming all of us from *physical death*, and redeeming those of us from *spiritual death* who will obey the laws and ordinances of the gospel" (Ezra Taft Benson, *Teachings*, 14; emphasis in original).

MORMON 9:20–21, 24–25

What is the role of faith in seeing miracles?

"Without [faith] there is no power" (Joseph Smith, *Lectures on Faith*, 1:24). *See also Ether 12:12.*

MORMON 9:27–28

"Work out your own salvation with fear and trembling before him."

"If ye do not watch yourselves, and your thoughts, and your words, and your deeds, and observe the commandments of God, and continue in the faith of what ye have heard concerning the coming of our Lord, even unto the end of your lives, ye must perish" (Mosiah 4:30).

"We know that it is by grace that we are saved, after all we can do" (2 Nephi 25:23).

MORMON 9:32–33

How did the difficulty of engraving upon metal plates affect the Book of Mormon?

"I, Jacob, . . . cannot write but a little of my words, because of the difficulty of engraving our words upon plates" (Jacob 4:1).

"They saw our day and chose those things which would be of greatest worth to us, is not that how we should study the Book of Mormon? We should constantly ask ourselves, 'Why did the Lord inspire Mormon (or Moroni or Alma) to include that in his record? What lesson can I learn from that to help me live in this day and age?'" (Ezra Taft Benson, *Ensign*, November 1986, 6). *See also Mormon 5:9.*

MORMON 9:34

How did Joseph Smith translate these ancient languages?

"Through the medium of the Urim and Thummim I translated the record by the gift and power of God" (Joseph Smith, *History of the Church*, 4:537).

THE BOOK OF
ETHER

The book of Ether covers 1,500 years of history. One purpose of the book of Ether is to serve as a second witness, along with the Nephite record, that those who live in a land "choice above all other lands" (see 1 Nephi 2:20; Ether 1:38, 42) must either serve God or be destroyed (see Ether 2:8–11). (See Joseph Fielding McConkie and Robert L. Millet, *Doctrinal Commentary*, 4:259). Consider the following comparison between the Jaredites and the people of Lehi:

JAREDITES	SIMILARITY	LEHITES
Ether 1:38, 42	Both peoples were brought by the Lord to a promised land which was "choice above all other lands"	1 Nephi 2:20
Ether 3:13	Both groups were led by mighty prophets who saw the Lord	1 Nephi 1:8
Ether 6:27–28; 7:1	Both peoples experienced prosperity during times of righteousness	4 Nephi 1:2–23
Ether 3:9–19	Both testified of the reality of Jesus Christ	3 Nephi 11–28
Ether 7:20	Both experienced a major division of the people into two groups	2 Nephi 5:5–7
Ether 13:20–21	Both experienced great destruction because of wickedness	Mormon 6:17–18
Ether 13:22	Both destructions are survived by a lone prophet-record keeper who was rejected and hunted by his people	Mormon 8:3

ETHER 1

ETHER 1:2, 5

What history was found on the twenty-four plates?

"Inasmuch as the language of the plates [of Ether] was that of the Jaredite people, it would have been incumbent upon Moroni to translate them by means of the holy 'interpreters' or Urim and Thummim before he could abridge them. This would be a tremendous task, because Moroni says (Ether 15:33) that he had not written the hundredth part of the record" (Sidney B. Sperry, *Book of Mormon Testifies*, 347).

ETHER 1:33

What was the "great tower" spoken of in these verses?

"We come down to the days of the building of the Tower of Babel, soon after the flood. . . . The people being of one language, gathered together to build a tower to reach, as they supposed, the crystalized heavens. They thought that the City of Enoch was caught up a little ways from the earth, and that the city was within the first sphere above the earth; and that if they could get a tower high enough, they might get to heaven, where the City of Enoch and the inhabitants thereof were located" (Orson Pratt, *Journal of Discourses*, 16:51). *See also Genesis 11:4.*

ETHER 1:34

What is the name of the "brother of Jared"?

"While residing in Kirtland, Elder Reynolds Cahoon had a son born to him. One day when President Joseph Smith was passing his door he called the prophet in and asked him to bless and name the baby. Joseph did so and gave the boy the name of Mahonri Moriancumer. When he had finished the blessing, he laid the child on the bed, and turning to Elder Cahoon he said, the name I have given your son is the name of the Brother of Jared; the Lord has just shown [or revealed] it to me. Elder William F. Cahoon, who was standing near, heard the Prophet make this statement to his Father; and this was the first time the name of the Brother of Jared was known in the Church in this dispensation" (George Reynolds, in *Improvement Era* 8 [July 1905], 704–5.)

ETHER 1:34–43; 2:14

How does the Lord respond to those who pray and those who do not pray?

See insights for Ether 2:14–15.

ETHER 1:35

What was "the language of Jared"?

"It is stated in the Book of Ether that Jared and his brother made the request of the Lord that their language be not changed at the time of the confusion of tongues at the Tower of Babel. Their request was granted, and they carried with them the speech of their fathers, the Adamic language, which was powerful even in its written form, so that the things Mahonri wrote 'were mighty even unto the overpowering of man to read them.' That was the kind of language Adam had and this was the language with which Enoch was able to accomplish his mighty work" (Joseph Fielding Smith, *Way to Perfection*, 69).

ETHER 1:38, 42

"A land which is choice above all the earth."

"This last statement is one of the testimonies of the truthfulness of this record, because this is a land choice above all other lands, and God has blessed the people upon this land. He has fulfilled the words recorded in this book time and time again, that those who should come up to fight against the people of this land should not prosper" (Heber J. Grant, in Conference Report, October 1899, 18). *See also insights for 1 Nephi 2:20.*

ETHER 2

ETHER 2:14–15

Why did the Lord chasten the brother of Jared?

"The Lord does answer our prayers. . . . Do you get answers to your prayers? If not, perhaps you did not pay the price. Do you offer a few trite words and worn-out phrases, or do you talk intimately to the Lord? Do you pray occasionally when you should be praying regularly, often, constantly? . . . When you pray, do you just speak, or do you also listen? . . . The Lord stands knocking. . . . But he will never force himself upon us. If we ever move apart, it is we who move and not the Lord" (Spencer W. Kimball, *New Era*, March 1978, 17).

"It seems highly unlikely that a man of the spiritual stature of the brother of Jared . . . would suddenly cease praying to his Maker. It may be that . . . he allowed his prayers to become less fervent, more casual and routine" (Joseph Fielding McConkie and Robert L. Millett, *Doctrinal Commentary*, 4:269). *See also insights for 3 Nephi 13:5–13. See also D&C 68:33.*

ETHER 2:15

"But thou shalt not sin any more."

"If a man repenteth of his sins—behold, he will confess them and forsake them" (D&C 58:43).

"Thou art made whole: sin no more, lest a worse thing come unto thee" (John 5:14).

"We must not be misled into supposing either that forgiveness may be considered lightly or that sin may be repeated with impunity after protestations of repentance. The Lord will indeed forgive, but he will not tolerate repetitions of the sin" (Spencer W. Kimball, *Miracle of Forgiveness*, 357).

ETHER 2:20

What might the Jaredite barges have been like?

In the original Book of Mormon this verse read slightly differently. Hugh Nibley explains: "'And the Lord said . . . thou shalt make a hole in the top thereof, and also in the bottom thereof; and when thou shalt suffer for air, thou shalt unstop the hole thereof, and receive air. And if it so be that the water come in upon thee, behold, ye shall stop the hole thereof, that ye may not perish in the flood' (p. 542, Book of Mormon, 1st ed.) An exacting editor by removing those very significant *thereof's* has made it appear that when Jared wanted air he was to open the top window of the boat and admit fresh air from the outside. But that is *not* what the original edition of the Book of Mormon says. For one thing, the ships had no windows communicating with the outside—'ye cannot have windows' (Ether 2:23); each ship had an air-tight door (Ether 2:17), and that was all. Air was received not by opening and closing doors and windows, but by unplugging air holes. . . .

"This can refer only to a reserve supply of air. . . . So the Lord recommended a device for trapping (compressing) air, with a 'hole in the top thereof and also in the bottom thereof,' not referring to the ship but to the air chamber itself" (Hugh Nibley, *Collected Works*, 6:344).

Another author, speaking of a proposed model he built, suggested, "A tube is built from the bottom to the top of the barge. . . . Now we have a funnel right through the boat. Water can come into the tube as high as the water line of the vessel.

"The model of the barge we have built has a stop hole both in the front and in back of the tube. . . . These stop holes can easily be opened or closed as needed. . . .

"The purpose of the bottom hole is at least two-fold: First, it acted as a stabilizer to keep the barge at an even keel; second, it could be used to get rid of refuse" (A. L. Zobell, *Improvement Era*, April 1941, 211, 252, cited in Daniel H. Ludlow, *Companion*, 315).

ETHER 2:23; 3:1
Is there evidence of the existence of glass in this time period?
"I used to be perplexed by the fact that the reference in Ether 2:33 . . . can only refer to glass windows . . . Moreover, Moroni, in actually referring to 'transparent glass' in Ether 3:1, is probably following Ether. This would make the invention of glass far older than anyone dreamed it was until the recent finding of such objects as Egyptian glass beads from 'the end of the third millennium B.C.' . . . We need not be surprised if the occurrences of glass objects before the sixteenth century B.C. 'are few and far between,' for glass rots, like wood, and it is a wonder that any of it at all survives from remote antiquity" (Hugh Nibley, *Collected Works*, 5:216–17).

ETHER 2:23, 25
What does the Lord expect us to do for ourselves?
"It is contrary to the law of God for the heavens to be opened and messengers to come to do anything for man that man can do for himself" (Joseph Fielding Smith, *Doctrines of Salvation*, 1:196).

"Notice how the Lord dealt with this question. He said to the brother of Jared, 'What will ye that I should do that ye may have light in your vessels?' (Ether 2:23)—as much as to say, 'Well, have you any good ideas? What would you suggest that we should do in order to have light?' . . .

"Then the Lord went away and left him alone. It was as though the Lord were saying to him, 'Look, I gave you a mind to think with, and I gave you agency to use it. Now you do all you can to help yourself with this problem; and then, after you've done all you can, I'll step in to help you'" (Harold B. Lee, *Stand Ye in Holy Places*, 243).

ETHER 3

ETHER 3:6; 6:2
What does this account teach us about the touch of the Savior's hand?
There is interesting symbolism in the account of the Savior touching the stones that lit the way for the Jaredites. "Whatever Jesus lays his hands upon lives. If Jesus lays his hands upon a marriage, it lives. If he is allowed to lay his hands on the family, it lives" (Howard W. Hunter, *Ensign*, November 1979, 65). Jesus is both the rock of our salvation (see Psalm 95:1) and the light of

our lives (see John 8:12). We may rely on him as our rock-solid foundation in life and as the light for our path as we cross the treacherous seas of mortality.

ETHER 3:9, 19

Was it faith or knowledge that allowed the brother of Jared to see the Lord?

"Knowledge and faith are not antithetical, nor are they on opposite ends of a continuum. God possesses all knowledge and God possesses all faith" (Joseph Fielding McConkie and Robert L. Millet, *Doctrinal Commentary*, 4:278).

"Preparatory faith is formed by experiences in the past—by the known, which provides a basis for belief. But redemptive faith must often be exercised toward experiences in the future—the unknown. . . . Exacting faith, mountain-moving faith, faith like that of the brother of Jared, *precedes* the miracle and the knowledge. He had to believe *before* God spoke. He had to act *before* the ability to complete that action was apparent" (Jeffrey R. Holland, *Christ and the New Covenant*, 18; emphasis in original).

ETHER 3:9-15, 19

What was unique about this vision of the Savior?

"[The Lord] was saying to the brother of Jared, 'Never have I showed myself unto man *in this manner, without my volition, driven solely by the faith of the beholder.*' As a rule, prophets are *invited* into the presence of the Lord. . . . The brother of Jared, on the other hand, seems to have thrust himself through the veil, not as an unwelcome guest but perhaps technically as an uninvited one. . . . Obviously the Lord himself was linking unprecedented faith with this unprecedented vision. . . .

"This may be an unprecedented case of a mortal man's desire, will, and purity so closely approaching the heavenly standard that God could not but honor his devotion. What a remarkable doctrinal statement about the power of a mortal's faith!" (Jeffrey R. Holland, *Christ and the New Covenant*, 23–24; emphasis in original).

"President Harold B. Lee suggested that the uniqueness of Moriancumer's experience lay in the fact that he saw the Lord Jesus as he would be. . . . And then he was amazed because he said he saw not only the finger of a spiritual being, but his faith was so great that he saw the kind of body that he would have when he came down to the earth. It was of flesh and blood—flesh, blood, and bones. And the Master said, 'No man has had this kind of faith'" (in Joseph Fielding McConkie and Robert L. Millet, *Doctrinal Commentary*, 4:277). *See also Ether 4:4.*

ETHER 3:13

What does it mean to be "redeemed from the fall"?

With the pronouncement of the redemption of the brother of Jared, "once and for all it was declared that ordinary people with ordinary challenges could rend the veil of unbelief and enter the realms of eternity. And Christ, who was prepared from the foundation of the world to redeem his people, would stand in all his glory at the edge of that veil, ready to receive the believers and show them 'how great things the Father had laid up' for them at the end of faith's journey" (Jeffrey R. Holland, *Christ and the New Covenant*, 29).

ETHER 3:16

How does the appearance of the body compare to that of the spirit?

"The spirit of man in the likeness of his person" (D&C 77:2).

"*Every form of life had a spirit existence in that eternal world . . .* and that prior existence, for all forms of life, was one in which the spirit entity had the exact form and likeness of its present temporal body" (Bruce R. McConkie, *Mormon Doctrine*, 251; emphasis in original).

ETHER 3:21-22, 25-28; 4:1, 4-5, 7; 5:1

What "things" were not allowed "to go forth"?

"And behold the book shall be sealed; and in the book shall be a revelation from God, from the beginning of the world to the ending thereof. . . . The revelation which was sealed shall be kept in the book until the own due time of the Lord, that they may come forth" (2 Nephi 27:7, 10). *See also insights for Alma 12:9.*

ETHER 3:23-24, 28

What were "these two stones"?

See insights for Mormon 9:34.

ETHER 4

ETHER 4:7-15

What could happen if our faith were to win the battle over our unbelief?

"The Book of Mormon is predicated on the willingness of men and women to 'rend the veil of unbelief' in order to behold the revelations—and the Revelation—of God (Ether 4:15). It would seem that the humbling experience of the brother of Jared in his failure to pray and his consternation over the sixteen stones were included in this account to show just how mortal and just how normal he was—so very much like the men and women we know and at least in some ways so much like ourselves. . . . Ordinary individuals with ordinary challenges could rend the veil of unbelief and enter the realms of eternity" (Jeffrey R. Holland, in *Nurturing Faith through the Book of Mormon*, 25).

ETHER 5

ETHER 5:1–6

To whom was Moroni speaking when he said, "Touch them not in order that ye may translate"?

"This appears to be a specific charge to Joseph Smith the modern seer and translater, a directive that he is not to touch or translate the sealed portion of the record" (Joseph Fielding McConkie and Robert L. Millett, *Doctrinal Commentary*, 4:284).

ETHER 5:2–4

Who were the "three witnesses"?

"In the course of the work of translation, we ascertained that three special witnesses . . . should see the plates . . . and that these witnesses should bear record of the same. . . . Almost immediately after we had made this discovery, it occurred to Oliver Cowdery, David Whitmer and the aforementioned Martin Harris . . . that they would have me inquire of the Lord to know if they might not obtain of him the privilege to be these three special witnesses; and finally they became so very solicitous, and urged me so much to inquire that at length I complied" (Joseph Smith, *History of the Church*, 1:51). *See also D&C 17:1.*

ETHER 6

ETHER 6:4

How important is it to be prepared?

"The Lord has urged that his people save for the rainy days, prepare for the difficult times, and put away for emergencies, a year's supply or more of bare necessities so that . . . our families can be sustained through the dark days" (Spencer W. Kimball, *Teachings*, 374).

ETHER 6:9

How much influence can music have in our lives?

Music can bless us

"Some of the greatest sermons are preached by the singing of hymns. Hymns move us to repentance and good works, build testimony and faith, comfort the weary, console the mourning, and inspire us to endure to the end. . . .

"Hymns can also help us withstand the temptations of the adversary. We encourage you to memorize your favorite hymns and study the scriptures that relate to them. Then, if unworthy thoughts enter your mind, sing a hymn to yourself, crowding out the evil with the good" (*Hymns of The Church of Jesus Christ of Latter-day Saints*, ix–x).

Music can hurt us

Elder Gene R. Cook and Mick Jagger of the Rolling Stones were sitting next to each other on a flight. During their conversation, Elder Cook said, "Young people . . . have told me that the kind of music you and others like you sing has no effect on them. . . . Others . . . have told me that it has a real effect on them for evil, and that it affects them in a very bad way. . . . What do you think is the impact of your music on the young people?"

Mick Jagger replied, "Our music is calculated to drive the kids to sex" (Gene R. Cook, *Thirteen Lines of Defense: Living the Law of Chastity*, audiocassette, side 3).

"Don't listen to music that is degrading. 'Music can, by its tempo, by its beat, by its intensity (and I would add by its lyrics) dull the spiritual sensitivity of men (and women)' (Boyd K. Packer, *Ensign*, January 1974, 25)" (Ezra Taft Benson, *Teachings*, 326).

ETHER 6:9, 12

How important is it to remember to thank the Lord?

See insights for 1 Nephi 2:7.

ETHER 6:12

"They . . . shed tears of joy."

See insights for 3 Nephi 4:33; 3 Nephi 17:21–22.

ETHER 6:22–23; 7:5; 8:3

"Surely this thing leadeth into captivity."

See 1 Samuel 8:11; insights for Mosiah 29:7–36.

ETHER 7

ETHER 7:7

Why did Corihor allow Kib to live once he was taken captive?

"Such is the practice . . . of keeping a king prisoner throughout his entire lifetime, allowing him to beget and raise a family in captivity, even though the sons thus brought up would be almost sure to seek vengeance for their parent and power for themselves upon coming of age. . . . It seems to us a perfectly ridiculous system, yet it is in accordance with the immemorial Asiatic usage" (Hugh Nibley, *Collected Works*, 5:207).

ETHER 7:16–17, 21; 8:3, 5

Where does war come from?

"Wars spring from wickedness of unrighteous leaders. Not until freedom triumphs and a just peace comes may we hope for the end of wars and for goodwill among men" (David O. McKay, in Conference Report, April 1969, 5).

ETHER 7:23–25

What is the role of a prophet?

"This is the mission of the prophets of God: to preach repentance. And though it does not make for popularity, it must be done" (N. Eldon Tanner, *Ensign*, May 1975, 34).

"The word, prophet, defined in the Hebrew language, means one who has been called to denounce sin and foretell the consequences and punishment of it. He is to be above all else a preacher of righteousness, to call the people back from idolatry, to faith in the living God, and when moved upon by the Spirit of the Lord to foretell coming events" (Anthony W. Ivins, in Conference Report, October 1933, 84).

ETHER 8

ETHER 8:14

Secret combinations are a prostitution of a sacred truth.

See insights for Helaman 6:22.

ETHER 8:21–22, 25

How did secret combinations afflict both the Jaredites and the Nephites?

"This most correct book on earth [the Book of Mormon] states that the downfall of two great American civilizations came as a result of secret conspiracies whose desire was to overthrow the freedom of the people. . . .

"Now undoubtedly Moroni could have pointed out many factors that led to the destruction of the people, but notice how he singled out the secret combinations" (Ezra Taft Benson, *God, Family, Country*, 321–22).

How can we avoid secret combinations today?

"We can avoid the temptation of being cliquish at school or at church. All of us can refrain from finding fault or alienating anyone by our words or actions. . . . Guard against spreading rumors or saying unkind things or allowing anything to occur that may hurt another. Make friends with your neighbors" (M. Russell Ballard, *Ensign*, November 1997, 39).

ETHER 9

ETHER 9:19

What were "cureloms and cumoms"?

Not much is known about these animals. What we do know is that the verse starts with descriptions of small animals and moves toward larger ones, and that there appears to be a connection between elephants and cureloms and cumoms. Dr. Nibley wrote: "I think it quite significant that the Book of Mormon associates elephants only with the Jaredites, since there is no apparent reason why they should not have been as common in the fifth as in the fifteenth century B.C. All we know is that they became extinct in large parts of Asia somewhere between those dates, as they did likewise in the New World" (Hugh Nibley, *Collected Works*, 5:220).

ETHER 9:34–35

"When the people saw that they must perish they began to repent."

See insights for Helaman 12:3.

ETHER 10

ETHER 10:4–8

Compare the wicked nature of King Riplakish with King Noah

KING RIPLAKISH	SIMILARITY	KING NOAH
Ether 10:5	Very immoral	Mosiah 11:2
Ether 10:5	Taxed the people heavily	Mosiah 11:3
Ether 10:6	Built spacious buildings	Mosiah 11:8
Ether 10:7	Glutted himself on the work of others	Mosiah 11:6
Ether 10:8	Killed by his own people	Mosiah 19:20

ETHER 11

ETHER 11:8; 13:20

How does the Lord respond to those who repent?

See insights for Mosiah 26:30.

ETHER 12

ETHER 12:3

What is the role of faith in the repentance process?

"True repentance is based on and flows from faith in the Lord Jesus Christ" (Ezra Taft Benson, *Teachings*, 71).

ETHER 12:6

How can we deal with those who want to dispute because they can't see?

Often people seem to think they must see in order to believe. On one occasion President Packer was on a plane with just such a man. He refused to believe that President Packer could know of the existence of God without describing exactly how he knew. At one point in the conversation President Packer asked the man if he could describe the taste of salt.

"After several attempts, of course, he could not do it. He could not convey, in words alone, so ordinary an experience as tasting salt. I bore testimony to him once again and said, 'I know there is a God. You ridiculed that testimony and said that if I did know, I would be able to tell you exactly *how* I know. My friend, spiritually speaking, I have tasted salt. I am no more able to convey to you in words how this knowledge has come than you are to tell me what salt tastes like'" (Boyd K. Packer, *That All May Be Edified*, 334; emphasis in original).

ETHER 12:6, 12

"Ye receive no witness until after the trial of your faith."

"Remember that Abraham, Moses, Elijah, and others could not see clearly the end from the beginning. They also walked by faith and without sight.

". . . Remember that there were no clouds in the sky, no evidence of rain, and no precedent for the deluge when Noah [built] the ark according to commandment. There was no ram in the thicket when Isaac and his father left for Moriah for the sacrifice" (Spencer W. Kimball, *Teachings*, 55).

ETHER 12:27

Why does the Lord give us weaknesses and challenges?

"Every trial and experience you have passed through is necessary for your salvation" (Brigham Young, *Discourses*, 345).

"Inadequacy is not the same as being sinful—we have far more control over the choice to sin than we may have over our innate capacity. . . . A sense of falling short or falling down is not only natural but essential to the mortal experience. Still, after all we can do, the Atonement can fill that which is empty, straighten our bent parts, and make strong that which is weak" (Bruce C. Hafen, *Broken Heart*, 19–20).

"Obviously, the personal burdens of life vary from person to person, but every one of us has them. Furthermore, each trial in life is tailored to the individual's capacities and needs as known by a loving Father in Heaven" (Howard W. Hunter, *Ensign*, November 1990, 18).

ETHER 12:39–41

"I have seen Jesus, . . . and now, I would commend you to seek this Jesus."

"And seek the face of the Lord always, that in patience ye may possess your souls, and ye shall have eternal life" (D&C 101:38). *See also Luke 21:19.*

"As something of a concluding, corresponding witness to Nephi, Jacob, and Isaiah's introductory testimonies of the Savior, Moroni closed his second 'final' testimony with an account of his own face-to-face experience with the Lord" (Jeffrey R. Holland, *Christ and the New Covenant*, 331).

ETHER 13

ETHER 13:3–10

What part of the "New Jerusalem" will "come down out of heaven"?

"The Lord said unto Enoch: Then shall thou and all thy city meet them there, and we will receive them into our bosom, and they shall see us; and we will fall upon their necks, . . . and we will kiss each other; And there shall be mine abode, and it shall be Zion" (Moses 7:63–64).

ETHER 13:9

What is meant by "a new heaven and a new earth"?

"This earth was created in a new or paradisiacal state; then, incident to Adam's transgression, it fell to its present telestial state. At the Second Coming of our Lord, it will be renewed, regenerated, refreshed, transfigured, become again a new earth, a paradisiacal earth. Its millennial status will be a return to its pristine state of beauty and glory, the state that existed before the fall" (Bruce R. McConkie, *Mormon Doctrine*, 796).

ETHER 13:13, 22

They rejected Ether "and cast him out."

See insights for Ether 7:23–25.

ETHER 13:27; 15:6, 22, 28

Where does anger lead us?

"Not only does . . . anger affect us physically and mentally, in a negative way, but at the same time it also destroys wisdom and sound judgment. When we become upset, reason is suppressed, and anger rushes in. To make decisions while infuriated is as unwise and foolish as it is for a captain to put out to sea in a raging storm" (ElRay L. Christiansen, *Ensign*, June 1971, 37). *See also insights for 3 Nephi 12:21–22; Moroni 9:3–5.*

ETHER 15

ETHER 15:6, 16, 19

"The people repented not. . . . Satan had full power over the hearts of the people."

"Much adversity is man-made. Men's hearts turn cold and the spirit of Satan controls their actions" (M. Russell Ballard, in Conference Report, April 1995, 30).

ETHER 15:29–30

How could they have "all fallen by the sword, save it were Coriantumr"?

"The insane wars of the Jaredite chiefs ended in the complete annihilation of both sides, with the kings the last to go. . . . This all seems improbable to us, but two circumstances peculiar to Asiatic warfare explain why the phenomenon is by no means without parallel: (1) Since every war is strictly a personal contest between kings, the battle must continue until one of the kings falls or is taken. (2) And yet things are so arranged that the king must be very last to fall, the whole army existing for the sole purpose of defending his person. This is clearly seen in the game of chess, in which all pieces are expendable except the king, who can never be taken. . . . So let no one think the final chapter of Ether is at all fanciful or overdrawn. Wars of extermination are a standard institution in the history of Asia" (Hugh Nibley, *Collected Works*, 5:234).

THE BOOK OF
MORONI

MORONI 1

MORONI 1:1

Moroni's writings add more evidence of multi-authorship within the Book of Mormon.

Moroni translated and edited the book of Ether and wrote the book of Moroni. In a word study comparison between these two books, the phrase "And it came to pass" is used by Moroni 117 times in the book of Ether. Yet in the book of Moroni the phrase does not appear a single time. (See Daniel H. Ludlow, *Companion*, 330–31).

MORONI 1:2-3

"I, Moroni, will not deny the Christ."

"Men changed for Christ will be captained by Christ. . . .

"Not only would they die for the Lord, but more important they want to live for Him" (Ezra Taft Benson, *Ensign*, November 1985, 6).

Moroni was willing to live for Christ thirty-six lonely years (see Mormon 6:5; Moroni 10:1).

MORONI 2

MORONI 2-6

How important are priesthood ordinances?

"Good conduct without the ordinances of the gospel will neither redeem nor exalt mankind; covenants and the ordinances are essential" (Boyd K. Packer, *Let Not Your Heart Be Troubled*, 86). *See also John 3:5; D&C 131:1–3.*

MORONI 3

MORONI 3:4

What does the Holy Ghost have to do with ordinations in the priesthood?

For any ordinance to be effective now and forever, it must be ratified "by the Holy Spirit of Promise," which is a function of the Holy Ghost (see D&C 132:7). The Prophet Joseph Smith explained, "We believe in the gift of the Holy Ghost. . . . We believe that it . . . is necessary to make and to organize the Priesthood, that no man can be called to fill any office in the ministry without it" (Joseph Smith, *Teachings*, 243).

MORONI 4 AND 5

MORONI 4:3

What does it mean to "take upon" us the name of Christ?

    See insights for Mosiah 5:5, 8, 11–12; Helaman 5:5–14.

MORONI 4:3; 5:2

How can we "always remember him"?

    See insights for Mosiah 5:5, 8, 11–12.

MORONI 4–5

How is the ordinance of the sacrament connected to the ordinance of baptism?

    "If we have done wrong; if there is a feeling in our souls that we would like to be forgiven, then the method to obtain forgiveness is not through rebaptism . . . but it is to repent of our sins . . . and then repair to the sacrament table where, if we have sincerely repented and put ourselves in proper condition, we shall be forgiven" (Melvin J. Ballard, *Improvement Era*, October 1919, 1026–27). *See also insights for 3 Nephi 18:1–29.*

MORONI 6

MORONI 6:1–3

What are the requirements for baptism?

    "All those who humble themselves before God, and desire to be baptized, and come forth with broken hearts and contrite spirits, and witness before the church that they have truly repented of all their sins, and are willing to take upon them the name of Jesus Christ, having a determination to serve him to the end, and truly manifest by their works that they have received of the Spirit of Christ unto the remission of their sins, shall be received by baptism into his church" (D&C 20:37).

MORONI 6:4

Why were the names of the members recorded?

    "People are somewhat like the coals of a fire. Should they absent themselves from the warmth and spirit of the active church membership . . . [and]

distance themselves from the intensity of the spirit generated by the active membership, they will lose that warmth and spirit. . . . The visits of home teachers to those who have absented themselves from Church activity can be the key which will eventually open the doors to their return" (Thomas S. Monson, *Ensign*, November 1997, 48).

What benefits come from nourishing members "by the good word of God"?

"With the ever-increasing number of converts, we must make an increasingly substantial effort to assist them as they find their way. Every one of them needs three things: a friend, a responsibility, and nurturing with the 'good word of God' (Moro. 6:4). It is our duty and opportunity to provide these things" (Gordon B. Hinckley, *Teachings*, 539). *See also insights for Alma 31:5.*

MORONI 6:5–6

What problems arise in the lives of those who don't "meet together oft" at church?

"Those members of the Church who habitually absent themselves from the sacrament meeting and who do not enter into the covenants which the sacrament requires of them, are guilty of grievous sin and are under grave condemnation. The Spirit of the Lord cannot dwell in them.

"Willful and protracted absence . . . if persisted in will lead to faultfinding, disagreement with authorities, and misunderstanding and criticism of the doctrines" (Joseph Fielding Smith, *Doctrines of Salvation*, 2:344).

MORONI 6:5, 9

What is the purpose of church meetings?

"We do not go to Sabbath meetings to be entertained or even simply to be instructed. We go to worship the Lord. It is an individual responsibility, and regardless of what is said from the pulpit, if one wishes to worship the Lord in spirit and in truth, he may do so by attending his meetings, partaking of the sacrament, and contemplating the beauties of the gospel. If the service is a failure to you, you have failed. No one can worship for you; you must do your own waiting upon the Lord" (Spencer W. Kimball, *Teachings*, 220).

MORONI 6:7–8

Why are some people's names "blotted out"?

"The most loving action the Church can take at times is to disfellowship or excommunicate a person" (Theodore M. Burton, *Ensign*, May 1983, 70).

MORONI 6:8

How often will the Lord forgive those who repent?

See insights for Mosiah 26:30.

MORONI 7

MORONI 7:1, 21-48

How significant are the three virtues of "faith, hope, and charity"?

"In just the sequence that Mormon taught it, Paul affirmed that faith, hope, and charity are the three great virtues that, as Christians, we must cling to and try to demonstrate" (Jeffrey R. Holland, *Christ and the New Covenant*, 335).

MORONI 7:3

What is this "rest . . . in heaven" and how can we obtain it?

"This is a very significant passage. The rest here referred to is not physical rest, for there is no such thing as physical rest in the Church of Jesus Christ. Reference is made to the spiritual rest and peace which are born from a settled conviction of the truth in the minds of men. We may thus enter into the rest of the Lord today, by coming to an understanding of the truths of the gospel" (Joseph F. Smith, *Gospel Doctrine*, 126).

MORONI 7:6-8

If "a man being evil . . . offereth a gift, . . . except he shall do it with real intent it profiteth him nothing."

"If a person performs a seemingly righteous act but does so for the wrong reasons . . . his hands may be clean but his heart is not 'pure.' His act will not be counted for righteousness. . . . We must not only do what is right. We must act for the right reasons. The modern term is good motive. . . . God understands our motives and will judge our actions accordingly" (Dallin H. Oaks, *Pure in Heart*, 13–14).

MORONI 7:12-13, 16-17

What things are "of God" and what things are of "of the devil"?

"Whenever darkness fills our minds, we may know that we are not possessed of the Spirit of God, and we must get rid of it. When we are filled with the Spirit of God, we are filled with joy, with peace and with happiness no matter what our circumstances may be; for it is a spirit of cheerfulness and of happiness" (George Q. Cannon, *Gospel Truth*, 17).

MORONI 7:16

What is the purpose of "the Spirit of Christ" and who receives it?

"The Holy Ghost . . . is different from the common Spirit of God, which we are told lighteth every man that cometh into the world" (Wilford Woodruff, *Journal of Discourses*, 13:157).

"[The Light of Christ] is the divine power which gives life to all things, and . . . if it were completely withdrawn life would cease" (Bruce R. McConkie, *Promised Messiah*, 209). *See also D&C 88:5–13.*

MORONI 7:18

"With that same judgment which ye judge ye shall also be judged."

"This teaching deserves the most careful consideration, for on judgment day the Lord will mete out to us precisely as we have dealt with our fellowmen, unless we have fully repented. It is a staggering thought, and yet it is an integral factor in the Lord's method of judgment" (Mark E. Petersen, *Ensign*, May 1977, 74).

MORONI 7:21–44

How are faith and power connected?

The Prophet Joseph Smith explained that faith is the moving cause of all action, and "is the first great governing principle which has power. . . . Without it there is no power, and without power there could be no creation nor existence!" (Joseph Smith, *Lectures on Faith*, 12). *See also Moroni 7:33.*

MORONI 7:22

God knows all things.

See insights for 2 Nephi 9:20.

MORONI 7:29, 31

What is the purpose of angels?

"It was made clear to me . . . that angels and missionaries do the very same work—the very same things. They call people to repentance" (Robert E. Wells, in *Doctrines of the Book of Mormon*, 15).

MORONI 7:33

With "faith in me ye shall have power to do whatsoever thing."

"More miracles have been performed in The Church of Jesus Christ of Latter-day Saints than we have any account of in the days of the Savior and His apostles. Today, sickness is cured by spiritual power. . . .

". . . The dead have been raised. My own brother was announced to be dead, but by the prayer of faith he lives" (Heber J. Grant, in Conference Report, October 1910, 119).

MORONI 7:40–42

How is faith connected to hope?

"Whoso believeth in God might with surety hope, . . . which hope cometh of faith" (Ether 12:4).

"Redeeming faith . . . leads to hope, a special, theological kind of hope" (Jeffrey R. Holland, *Christ and the New Covenant*, 334). *See also Alma 13:29.*

MORONI 7:44–45

What is the relationship between "charity" and "faith and hope"?

"Faith in Christ and hope in his promises of resurrected, eternal life can come only to the meek and lowly in heart. . . . Only thorough disciples of Christ . . . come to understand true charity—the pure love of Christ . . . a love born of faith and hope" (Jeffrey R. Holland, *Christ and the New Covenant*, 335).

MORONI 7:44–46

"If ye have not charity, ye are nothing."

"Above all the attributes of godliness and perfection, *charity* is the one most devoutly to be desired. Charity is more than love, far more; it is everlasting love, perfect love, the pure love of Christ which endureth forever" (Bruce R. McConkie, *Mormon Doctrine*, 121; emphasis in original).

MORONI 7:47

What is charity?

"The phrase 'love of Christ' might have meaning in three dimensions:
"1. Love *for* Christ
"2. Love *from* Christ
"3. Love *like* Christ" (C. Max Caldwell, *Ensign*, November 1992, 29).

One example of charity in action happened to Les Goates's family in the fall of 1918. In addition to the terrible flu epidemic spreading through the country, early frosts had frozen the Goates's sugar beat crop into the ground. Les' father, George Goates, and his brother Francis were trying to get the frozen sugar beats to the factory when they received word from another brother, Charles, that his family had been infected with the flu. Over the next six days, George had to drive from his home in Lehi to Ogden, on two occasions to bring home and bury his son and three grandchildren.

As George and Francis returned to their field of frozen sugar beets, they passed wagon after wagon of sugar beats heading to market driven by their neighbors. Les gives the following account:

"On the last wagon was the town comedian, freckled-faced Jasper Rolfe. He waved a cheery greeting and called out: 'That's all of 'em, Uncle George.'

"My dad turned to Francis and said: 'I wish it was all of ours.'

"When they arrived at the farm . . . lo and behold, there wasn't a sugar beet on the whole field. Then it dawned upon him what Jasper Rolfe meant when he called out: 'That's all of 'em, Uncle George!'

"Then dad got down off the wagon, picked up a handful of the rich, brown soil he loved so much, and then in his thumbless left hand a beet top, and he looked for a moment at these symbols of his labor, as if he couldn't believe his eyes.

"Then father sat down on a pile of beet tops . . . this amazing man who never faltered, nor finched, nor wavered throughout this agonizing ordeal—sat down on a pile of beet tops and sobbed like a little child.

"Then he arose, wiped his eyes with his big, red bandanna handkerchief, looked up at the sky, and said: 'Thanks, Father, for the elders of our ward'" (Les Goates, in Vaughn J. Featherstone, *Ensign*, July 1973, 36–37).

MORONI 8

MORONI 8:4–6, 9, 14, 16, 19–22

Why is it wrong to baptize little children under the age of eight?

Some people mistakenly believe "that little children are conceived in sin and enter mortality in a state of natural corruption. That doctrine is false!

"Each time a child is born, the world is renewed in innocence" (Boyd K. Packer, *Ensign*, November 1986, 17).

MORONI 8:8

Why are "little children . . . not capable of committing sin"?

"Little children . . . cannot sin, for power is not given unto Satan to tempt little children, until they begin to become accountable before me" (D&C 29:46–47).

"[Children] are saved through the atonement and because they are free from sin. They come from God in purity; no sin or taint attaches to them in this life; and they return in purity to their Maker. . . . Those who are not accountable for sins never fall spiritually and need not be redeemed from a spiritual fall which they never experienced. Hence the expression that little children are alive in Christ. 'Little children are redeemed from the foundation of the world through mine Only Begotten,' the Lord says" (Bruce R. McConkie, *Ensign*, April 1977, 4–5).

MORONI 8:10

When do children become accountable?

"Children are not accountable before me until they are eight years old" (JST, Genesis 17:11). *See also D&C 68:27.*

MORONI 8:25

What actions, in addition to keeping the commandments, can bring a "remission of sins"?

Having faith (1 Nephi 12:10; Mosiah 3:13; 26:22)

Doing missionary work (James 5:20; D&C 31:5; 60:7; 61:33–34)

Having charity (1 Peter 4:8)

Bearing testimony (D&C 62:3; 84:61)

Performing good works (Luke 3:8)

Being humble (D&C 61:2; 112:3)

Repenting (Alma 5:33)

Obeying (D&C 108:1)

Loving (Luke 7:37–38; 44–47)

Forgiving others (Matthew 6:14)

Giving to the poor (Mosiah 4:26; Alma 4:13–14)

Receiving the scriptures (D&C 84:60–61)

Listening to the words of the Lord through the prophet (D&C 50:36)

MORONI 8:25–26, 28

What blessings come from "fulfilling the commandments"?

These verses suggest a sequence of cause and effect from certain actions. First, "fulfilling the commandments" brings forgiveness, which brings "meekness," which brings the Spirit, which brings hope and perfect love. The Prophet Joseph Smith taught, "Until we have perfect love we are liable to fall and when we have a testimony that our names are sealed in the Lamb's book of life we have perfect love and then it is impossible for false Christs to deceive us" (Joseph Smith, *Teachings*, 9).

MORONI 8:27–28

What proved the destruction of the Nephite nation?

Part of the Book of Mormon warnings to us is that pride destroyed two previous American nations and it could destroy more. The Prophet Joseph Smith warned, "I prophesy, in the name of the Lord God of Israel, anguish and wrath and tribulation and the withdrawing of the Spirit of God from the earth await this generation, until they are visited with utter desolation" (Joseph Smith, *Teachings*, 328).

MORONI 8:28

What becomes of those whose sins cause the Spirit to depart?

"Apostasy comes through the sins of omission as well as through the sins of commission. Immorality is a deadly sin and those who are guilty, if they do not repent, will lose the spirit and deny the faith. Apostasy does not come upon an individual suddenly, but it is a gradual growth in which darkness through sin crowds out the spirit of light from the soul. When a man who was once enlightened loses the Spirit of truth, the darkness which takes its place is overwhelming" (Joseph Fielding Smith, *Church History and Modern Revelation*, 3:150). *See also insights for Helaman 4:24–25; 6:35.*

MORONI 9

MORONI 9:3–5

Why should we avoid being stirred "up continually to anger"?

"Some [husbands] put on a fine face before the world during the day and come home in the evening, set aside their self-discipline, and on the slightest provocation fly into outbursts of anger.

". . . As a servant of the Lord I rebuke you and call you to repentance. Discipline yourselves. Master your temper" (Gordon B. Hinckley, *Teachings*, 2).

"There is another serious thing to which many young men become addicted. This is anger. With the least provocation they explode into tantrums of uncontrolled rage. It is pitiful to see someone so weak. But even worse, they are prone to lose all sense of reason and do things which bring later regret. . . . If you have a temper, now is the time to learn to control it. The more you do so while you are young, the more easily it will happen" (Gordon B. Hinckley, *Ensign*, May 1998, 50). *See also insights for 3 Nephi 12:21–22; Ether 13:27; 15:6, 22, 28.*

MORONI 9:6

How wicked had the Nephites and Lamanites become?

"It is impossible for the tongue to describe . . . the horrible scene of the blood and carnage . . . ; every heart was hardened, so that they delighted in the shedding of blood continually. . . . There never had been so great wickedness among . . . all the house of Israel, according to the words of the Lord" (Mormon 4:11–12). *See also 2 Nephi 10:3.*

"The tragedy of the Nephites . . . was not what became *of* them but what they themselves became" (Hugh Nibley, *Collected Works*, 7:388; emphasis in original).

MORONI 9:7-10

What is "most dear and precious above all things"?

"Chastity and virtue are 'most dear and precious above all things' (Moro. 9:9), more valuable than rubies or diamonds, than herds and flocks, than gold and silver, or than automobiles and land" (Spencer W. Kimball, *Ensign*, November 1979, 5).

"How glorious and near to the angels is youth that is clean; this youth has joy unspeakable here and eternal happiness hereafter. Sexual purity is youth's most precious possession; it is the foundation of all righteousness" (Harold B. Lee, in Conference Report, April 1942, 89).

MORONI 9:20

How do people become "past feeling"?

"Our capacity to feel controls our behavior in many ways, and by inaction when our feelings prompt us to do good, we deaden that capacity to feel" (Neal A. Maxwell, *Time to Choose*, 59–60).

"When we move away from the Lord there seems to grow upon us a film of worldliness, which insulates us from his influence. But when we scrape that film away and humble ourselves with naked soul and sincere supplication and cleansed life, our prayers are answered" (Spencer W. Kimball, *Faith Precedes the Miracle*, 209).

MORONI 10

MORONI 10:4-5

Why is it so important that God "manifest the truth" of the Book of Mormon?

"The Book of Mormon is the keystone of [our] testimony. Just as the arch crumbles if the keystone is removed, so does all the Church stand or fall with the truthfulness of the Book of Mormon. The enemies of the Church understand this clearly. This is why they go to such great lengths to try to disprove the Book of Mormon, for if it can be discredited, the Prophet Joseph Smith goes with it. So does our claim to priesthood keys, and revelation, and the restored Church. But in like manner, if the Book of Mormon be true . . . then one must accept the claims of the Restoration and all that accompanies it" (Ezra Taft Benson, *Witness and a Warning*, 19).

"As soon as Elder Taylor preached the gospel to her family, Mrs. Cannon was ready to be baptized, knowing for herself, as she said, that the principles he taught were the true gospel of the Son of God. Her husband [George Cannon, father of George Q. Cannon] read the Book of Mormon carefully twice before his baptism. After finishing it the second time, he remarked, 'No wicked man could write such a book as this; and no good man would write it, unless it were true and he were commanded of God to do so' (Andrew Jenson, *Historical Record* 6:174)" (quoted in George Q. Cannon, *Gospel Truth*, xii).

MORONI 10:5, 7

How clear and sure are truths manifest "by the power of the Holy Ghost"?

"Unto the Holy Ghost has been given the right and the privilege of manifesting the truth unto men as no other power will. So that when He makes a man see and know a thing he knows it better than he shall ever know anything else; and to sin against that knowledge is to sin against the greatest light there is and consequently commit the greatest sin there is" (Melvin J. Ballard, *Millennial Star*, August 11, 1932, 499–500). *See also 2 Nephi 32:5; D&C 76:31–37; insights for 1 Nephi 17:45, 55; Enos 1:8.*

MORONI 10:8–19

What are gifts of the Spirit?

"Let me mention a few gifts that are not always evident or noteworthy but that are very important. . . . The gift of asking; the gift of listening; the gift of hearing and using a still, small voice; the gift of being able to weep; the gift of avoiding contention; the gift of being agreeable; the gift of avoiding vain repetition; the gift of seeking that which is righteous; the gift of not passing judgment; the gift of looking to God for guidance; the gift of being a disciple; the gift of caring for others; the gift of being able to ponder; the gift of offering prayer; the gift of bearing a mighty testimony; and the gift of receiving the Holy Ghost" (Marvin J. Ashton, *Ensign*, November 1987, 20). *See also D&C 46:10–19; 1 Corinthians 12:1–11.*

MORONI 10:20–23

How important are faith, hope, and charity?

See insights for Moroni 7:1, 21–48; Moroni 7:40–42; Moroni 7:44–45.

MORONI 10:32–33

Perfection comes little by little and only through Christ.

"We can make great strides in the direction of perfection in our personal behavior. We can be perfect in our prayers to our Father in Heaven. There are some things in which it is very difficult to be perfect, but I hope that everyone here, every man and woman and boy and girl, will get on his or her knees night and morning and thank the Lord for His blessings. . . . We can be perfect in our prayers, my brothers and sisters" (Gordon B. Hinckley, *Ensign*, July 1998, 2). *See also insights for 3 Nephi 12:48.*

BIBLIOGRAPHY

1992–93 Devotional and Fireside Speeches. Provo: Brigham Young University, 1993.

Andrus, Hyrum L. *Joseph Smith, the Man and the Seer.* Salt Lake City: Deseret Book, 1960.

Asay, Carlos E. *In the Lord's Service: A Guide to Spiritual Development.* Salt Lake City: Deseret Book, 1990.

Ashton, Marvin J. *What Is Your Destination?* Salt Lake City: Deseret Book, 1978.

Ballard, M. Russell. *Our Search for Happiness: An Invitation to Understand The Church of Jesus Christ of Latter-day Saints.* Salt Lake City: Deseret Book, 1993.

Bassett, K. Douglas, comp. *Latter-day Commentary on the Book of Mormon.* American Fork, Utah: Covenant Communications, 1999.

Benson, Ezra Taft. *God, Family, Country: Our Three Great Loyalties.* Salt Lake City: Deseret Book, 1974.

———. *The Teachings of Ezra Taft Benson.* Salt Lake City: Bookcraft, 1988.

———. *This Nation Shall Endure.* Salt Lake City: Deseret Book, 1977.

———. *A Witness and a Warning: A Modern-Day Prophet Testifies of the Book of Mormon.* Salt Lake City: Deseret Book, 1988.

Bennett, Archibald F. *Saviors on Mount Zion.* Salt Lake City: Deseret Sunday School Union Board, 1950.

Berrett, William E. *The Restored Church: A Brief History of the Growth and Doctrines of The Church of Jesus Christ of Latter-day Saints.* Salt Lake City: Deseret Book, 1973.

Blankenhorn, David. "Life without Father." *USA Weekend,* 26 February 1995.

Book of Mormon Student Study Guide. Salt Lake City: The Church of Jesus Christ of Latter-day Saints, 2000.

Book of Mormon Teacher Resource Manual. Salt Lake City: The Church of Jesus Christ of Latter-day Saints, 2000.

Brewster, Hoyt W., Jr. *Isaiah Plain & Simple: The Message of Isaiah in the Book of Mormon.* Salt Lake City: Deseret Book, 1995.

Brown, Hugh B. *The Abundant Life.* Salt Lake City: Bookcraft, 1965.

Brown, Francis, S. R. Driver, and Charles A. Briggs, eds. *The New Brown, Driver, and Briggs Hebrew and English Lexicon of the Old Testament.* Lafayette, Ind.: Associated Publishers and Authors, 1981.

Burton, Rulon T., ed. *We Believe: Doctrines and Principles of The Church of Jesus Christ of Latter-day Saints.* Salt Lake City: Tabernacle Books, 1994.

Cannon, George Q. *Gospel Truth.* Classics in Mormon Literature Series. Salt Lake City: Deseret Book, 1987.

Church History in the Fulness of Times: The History of The Church of Jesus Christ of Latter-day Saints. Salt Lake City: Church Educational System, 2000.

Clark, J. Reuben, Jr. *Behold the Lamb of God: Selections from the Sermons and Writings, Published and Unpublished, of J. Reuben Clark Jr. on the Life of the Savior.* Salt Lake City: Deseret Book, 1991.

Clark, James R., comp. *Messages of the First Presidency of The Church of Jesus Christ of Latter-day Saints.* 6 vols. Salt Lake City: Bookcraft, 1965–75.

Clarke, Adam. *The Holy Bible.* 6 vols. Nashville: Abingdon, 1977.

Collected Discourses. Ed. Brian Stuy. 5 vols. Burbank, Calif.: B. H. S. Publishing, 1987–1992.

Conference Report. The Church of Jesus Christ of Latter-day Saints, 1897–.

Cook, Gene R. *13 Lines of Defense: Living the Law of Chastity.* Salt Lake City: Deseret Book, 1991, audiocassette.

————. *Raising Up a Family to the Lord.* Salt Lake City: Deseret Book, 1993.

————. *Receiving Answers to Our Prayers.* Salt Lake City: Deseret Book, 1996.

Cook, Lyndon W. *The Revelations of the Prophet Joseph Smith: A Historical and Biographical Commentary of the Doctrine and Covenants.* Salt Lake City: Deseret Book, 1995.

Deseret News 1995–96 Church Almanac. Salt Lake City: Deseret News, 1994.

Dew, Sheri L. *Go Forward with Faith: The Biography of Gordon B. Hinckley.* Salt Lake City: Deseret Book, 1996.

Doctrines of the Book of Mormon: The 1991 Sperry Symposium on the Book of Mormon. Ed. Bruce Van Orden and Brent L. Top. Salt Lake City: Deseret Book, 1992.

Ensign. The Church of Jesus Christ of Latter-day Saints, 1971–.

"The Family: A Proclamation to the World." *Ensign*, November 1995, 102.

Faust, James E. *To Reach Even Unto You*. Salt Lake City: Deseret Book, 1980.

For the Strength of Youth: Fulfilling Our Duty to God. Salt Lake City: The Church of Jesus Christ of Latter-day Saints, 2001.

Grant, Heber J. *Gospel Standards: Selections from the Sermons and Writings of Heber J. Grant, Seventh President of The Church of Jesus Christ of Latter-day Saints*. Comp. G. Homer Durham. Salt Lake City: Improvement Era, 1941.

Hafen, Bruce C. *The Broken Heart: Applying the Atonement to Life's Experiences*. Salt Lake City: Deseret Book, 1989.

Hinckley, Bryant S. *Sermons and Missionary Services of Melvin J. Ballard*. Salt Lake City: Deseret Book, 1949.

Hinckley, Gordon B. *Be Thou an Example*. Salt Lake City: Deseret Book, 1981.

———. *Teachings of Gordon B. Hinckley*. Salt Lake City: Deseret Book, 1997.

Holland, Jeffrey R. *Christ and the New Covenant*. Salt Lake City: Deseret Book, 1997.

———. *However Long and Hard the Road*. Salt Lake City: Deseret Book, 1985.

Hunter, Howard W. *The Teachings of Howard W. Hunter*. Salt Lake City: Bookcraft, 1997.

Hymns of The Church of Jesus Christ of Latter-day Saints. Salt Lake City: The Church of Jesus Christ of Latter-day Saints, 1985.

Improvement Era. The Church of Jesus Christ of Latter-day Saints, 1897–1970.

Jackson, Kent P., ed. *1 Nephi to Alma 29*. Studies in Scripture, vol. 7. Salt Lake City: Deseret Book, 1987.

Jastrow, Marcus. *Dictionary of the Targumim, the Talmud Babli and Yerushalmi, and the Midrashic Literature*. New York: Pardes Publishing House, 1950.

Journal of Discourses. 26 vols. London: Latter-day Saints' Book Depot, 1854–86.

Juvenile Instructor. The Church of Jesus Christ of Latter-day Saints, 1866–1929.

Keil, C. F., and F. Delitzsch, *Commentary on the Old Testament in Ten Volumes*. Grand Rapids, Mich.: William B. Eerdmans, 1976.

Kimball, Spencer W. *Faith Precedes the Miracle*. Salt Lake City: Deseret Book, 1972.

———. *The Miracle of Forgiveness*. Salt Lake City: Bookcraft, 1971.

———. *The Teachings of Spencer W. Kimball*. Edited by Edward L. Kimball. Salt Lake City: Deseret Book, 1982.

Larsen, Dean L. *You and the Destiny of the Indian*. Salt Lake City: Bookcraft, 1966.

LDS Church News. Deseret News, 1981–.

Lee, Harold B. *Decisions for Successful Living*. Salt Lake City: Deseret Book, 1973.

———. *Stand Ye in Holy Places: Selected Sermons and Writings of President Harold B. Lee*. Salt Lake City: Deseret Book, 1976.

———. *The Teachings of Harold B. Lee*. Ed. Clyde J. Williams. Salt Lake City: Bookcraft, 1996.

———. *Ye Are the Light of the World: Selected Sermons and Writings of President Harold B. Lee*. Salt Lake City: Deseret Book, 1974.

Lewis, C. S. *Mere Christianity*. New York: Macmillan, 1960.

———. *The Problem of Pain*. New York: Macmillan, 1962.

———. *The Screwtape Letters*. New York: Macmillan, 1961.

Ludlow, Daniel H. *A Companion to Your Study of the Book of Mormon*. Salt Lake City: Deseret Book, 1976.

———, ed. *Encyclopedia of Mormonism*. New York: Macmillan, 1992.

Ludlow, Victor L. *Isaiah: Prophet, Seer, & Poet*. Salt Lake City: Deseret Book, 1982.

Lund, Gerald N. *Jesus Christ, Key to the Plan of Salvation*. Salt Lake City: Deseret Book, 1991.

Madsen, Truman G. *Four Essays on Love*. Salt Lake City: Bookcraft, 1971.

Maxwell, Neal A. *All These Things Shall Give Thee Experience*. Salt Lake City: Deseret Book, 1979.

———. *Deposition of a Disciple*. Salt Lake City: Deseret Book, 1976.

———. *If Thou Endure It Well*. Salt Lake City: Bookcraft, 1996.

———. *Meek and Lowly*. Salt Lake City: Deseret Book, 1987.

———. *Men and Women of Christ*. Salt Lake City: Bookcraft, 1991.

———. *"A More Excellent Way": Essays on Leadership for Latter-day Saints*. Salt Lake City: Deseret Book, 1967.

———. "Not My Will, But Thine." Salt Lake City: Bookcraft, 1988.

———. Of One Heart. Salt Lake City: Deseret Book, 1990.

———. A Time to Choose. Salt Lake City: Deseret Book, 1974.

———. We Will Prove Them Herewith. Salt Lake City: Deseret Book, 1982.

———. A Wonderful Flood of Light. Salt Lake City: Bookcraft, 1990.

McConkie, Bruce R. Doctrinal New Testament Commentary. 3 vols. Salt Lake City: Bookcraft, 1965–73.

———. The Millennial Messiah: The Second Coming of the Son of Man. Salt Lake City: Deseret Book, 1982.

———. Mormon Doctrine. 2d ed. Salt Lake City: Bookcraft, 1966.

———. The Mortal Messiah: From Bethlehem to Calvary. Salt Lake City: Deseret Book, 1979–81.

———. A New Witness for the Articles of Faith. Salt Lake City: Deseret Book, 1985.

———. The Promised Messiah: The First Coming of Christ. Salt Lake City: Deseret Book, 1978.

———. Sermons and Writings of Bruce R. McConkie. Ed. Mark L. McConkie. Salt Lake City: Bookcraft, 1998.

McConkie, Joseph Fielding, and Robert L. Millet. Doctrinal Commentary on the Book of Mormon. Salt Lake City: Bookcraft, 1987–92.

McKay, David O. Gospel Ideals: Selections from the Discourses of David O. McKay, Ninth President of The Church of Jesus Christ of Latter-day Saints. Salt Lake City: Improvement Era, 1953.

———. Man May Know for Himself: Teachings of President David O. McKay. Compiled by Clare Middlemiss. Salt Lake City: Deseret Book, 1967.

———. Pathways to Happiness. Salt Lake City: Deseret Book, 1957.

Millennial Star. Liverpool: The Church of Jesus Christ of Latter-day Saints, 1840–1970.

Monson, Thomas S. Be Your Best Self. Salt Lake City: Deseret Book, 1979.

———. Live the Good Life. Salt Lake City: Deseret Book, 1988.

Morrell, Jeanett McKay. Highlights in the Life of President David O. McKay. Salt Lake City: Deseret Book, 1971.

Nelson, Russell M. Perfection Pending: And Other Favorite Discourses. Salt Lake City: Deseret Book, 1998.

New Era. The Church of Jesus Christ of Latter-day Saints, 1971–.

Nibley, Hugh. *The Collected Works of Hugh Nibley*. Provo, Utah, and Salt Lake City: Foundation for Ancient Research and Mormon Studies and Deseret Book, 1986–2001.

———. *Prophetic Book of Mormon*. Provo, Utah, and Salt Lake City: Foundation for Ancient Research and Mormon Studies and Deseret Book, 1989.

Nibley, Preston. *Brigham Young, the Man and His Work*. 4th ed. Salt Lake City: Deseret Book, 1960.

Nurturing Faith through the Book of Mormon: The 24th Annual Sidney B. Sperry Symposium. Salt Lake City: Deseret Book, 1995.

Nyman, Monte S. *"Great Are the Words of Isaiah."* Salt Lake City: Bookcraft, 1980.

Nyman, Monte S., and Charles D. Tate Jr., eds. *First Nephi: The Doctrinal Foundation*. Provo, Utah, and Salt Lake City: Brigham Young University Religious Studies Center and Bookcraft, 1988.

———. *Second Nephi, the Doctrinal Structure*. Provo, Utah: Brigham Young University Religious Studies Center, 1989.

Nyman, Monte S., and Robert L. Millet, eds. *Joseph Smith Translation: The Restoration of Plain and Precious Things*. Provo, Utah: Brigham Young University Religious Studies Center, 1985.

Oaks, Dallin H. *Pure in Heart*. Salt Lake City: Bookcraft, 1988.

Packer, Boyd K. *The Holy Temple*. Salt Lake City: Bookcraft, 1982.

———. *Let Not Your Heart Be Troubled*. Salt Lake City: Bookcraft, 1991.

———. *Memorable Stories and Parables*. Salt Lake City: Bookcraft, 1997.

———. *"Teach the Scriptures."* Address to religious educators of the Church Educational System, 14 October 1977.

———. *Teach Ye Diligently*. Salt Lake City: Deseret Book, 1975.

———. *"That All May Be Edified": Talks, Sermons, and Commentary*. Salt Lake City: Bookcraft, 1982.

———. *The Things of the Soul*. Salt Lake City: Bookcraft, 1996.

Parry, Donald W., Jay A. Parry, and Tina M. Peterson. *Understanding Isaiah*. Salt Lake City: Deseret Book, 1998.

Perry, L. Tom. *Living with Enthusiasm*. Salt Lake City: Deseret Book, 1996.

Petersen, Mark E. *1968 BYU Speeches of the Year*. Provo: Brigham Young University, 1969.

————. *The Great Prologue*. Salt Lake City: Deseret Book, 1975.

Pratt, Orson. *Orson Pratt's Works*. Orem, Utah: Grandin Book Company, 1990.

The Quest Study Bible. Grand Rapids, Mich.: Zondervan, 1994.

Reynolds, George, and Janne M. Sjodahl, eds. *Commentary on the Book of Mormon*. 7 vols. Salt Lake City: Deseret Book, 1955–61.

Richards, Franklin D., and James A. Little. *A Compendium of the Doctrines of the Gospel*. Salt Lake City: Deseret Book, 1925.

Richards, LeGrand. *A Marvelous Work and a Wonder*. Rev. ed. Salt Lake City: Deseret Book, 1966.

Roberts, B. H. *Defense of the Faith and the Saints*. 2 vols. Salt Lake City: Deseret News, 1907–1912.

————. *New Witnesses for God*. 3 vols. Salt Lake City: Deseret News, 1950.

Robinson, Stephen E. *Believing Christ: The Parable of the Bicycle and Other Good News*. Salt Lake City: Deseret Book, 1992.

Romney, Marion G. *Learning for the Eternities*. Salt Lake City: Deseret Book, 1977.

Smith, George Albert. *Sharing the Gospel with Others: Excerpts from the Sermons of President Smith*. Comp. Preston Nibley. Salt Lake City: Deseret News, 1948.

Smith, Hyrum M., and Janne M. Sjodahl, eds. *The Doctrine and Covenants, Containing Revelations Given to Joseph Smith, Jr., the Prophet*. Salt Lake City: Deseret News, 1923.

Smith, Joseph. *Discourses of the Prophet Joseph Smith*. Compiled by Alma P. Burton. Salt Lake City: Deseret Book, 1977.

————. *History of The Church of Jesus Christ of Latter-day Saints*. Edited by B. H. Roberts. 7 vols. 2d ed. rev. Salt Lake City: The Church of Jesus Christ of Latter-day Saints, 1932–51.

————. *Lectures on Faith*. Salt Lake City: Deseret Book, 1985.

————. *Teachings of the Prophet Joseph Smith*. Selected by Joseph Fielding Smith. Salt Lake City: Deseret Book, 1938.

Smith, Joseph F. *Gospel Doctrine*. 5th ed. Salt Lake City: Deseret Book Company, 1939.

Smith, Joseph Fielding. *Answers to Gospel Questions*. 5 vols. Compiled by Joseph Fielding Smith Jr. Salt Lake City: Deseret Book Company, 1957–66.

———. *Church History and Modern Revelation*. 4 vols. Salt Lake City: The Church of Jesus Christ of Latter-day Saints, 1946–1949.

———. *Doctrines of Salvation: Sermons and Writings of Joseph Fielding Smith*. Ed. Bruce R. McConkie. Salt Lake City: Bookcraft, 1999.

———. *Man, His Origin and Destiny*. Salt Lake City: Deseret Book, 1973.

———. *The Progess of Man*. Salt Lake City: Deseret Book, 1964.

———. *Restoration of All Things*. Salt Lake City: Deseret Book, 1973.

———. *Seek Ye Earnestly*. Salt Lake City: Deseret Book, 1970.

———. *The Way to Perfection*. Salt Lake City: Deseret Book, 1984.

Sorenson, John L. *An Ancient American Setting for the Book of Mormon*. Salt Lake City: Deseret Book, 1985.

Sperry, Sidney B. *Book of Mormon Compendium*. Salt Lake City: Bookcraft, 1970.

———. *Book of Mormon Testifies*. Salt Lake City: Bookcraft, 1965.

———. *Our Book of Mormon*. Salt Lake City: Bookcraft, 1963.

———. *Paul's Life and Letters*. Salt Lake City: Bookcraft, 1955.

Strong, James. *The Exhaustive Concordance of the Bible*. Nashville, Tenn.: Abingdon, 1981.

Talmage, James E. *The Articles of Faith*. 12th ed. Salt Lake City: The Church of Jesus Christ of Latter-day Saints, 1924.

———. *Jesus the Christ*. Classics in Mormon Literature edition. Salt Lake City: Deseret Book, 1983.

Taylor, John. *The Gospel Kingdom*. Selected by G. Homer Durham. Salt Lake City: Bookcraft, 1943.

———. *The Mediation and Atonement*. Salt Lake City: Deseret News Company, 1882.

Times and Seasons. The Church of Jesus Christ of Latter-day Saints. 1839–1846.

Unger, Merrill F. *The New Unger's Bible Dictionary*. Chicago: Moody Press, 1988.

Valletta, Thomas R., ed. *The Book of Mormon for Latter-day Saint Families*. Salt Lake City: Bookcraft, 1999.

Webster, Noah. *An American Dictionary of the English Language*. New York: S. Converse, 1828.

Welch, John W., ed. *Reexploring the Book of Mormon*. Provo, Utah, and Salt

Lake City: Foundation for Ancient Research and Mormon Studies and Deseret Book, 1991.

Welch, John, and Melvin J. Thorne. *Pressing Forward with the Book of Mormon.* Provo, Utah: Foundation for Ancient Research and Mormon Studies, 1999.

Widtsoe, John A. *Evidences and Reconciliations.* Arr. G. Homer Durham. Salt Lake City: Bookcraft, 1987.

Wirthlin, Joseph B. *Finding Peace in Our Lives.* Salt Lake City: Deseret Book, 1995.

Woodruff, Wilford. *The Discourses of Wilford Woodruff.* Selected by G. Homer Durham. Salt Lake City: Bookcraft, 1946.

Young, Brigham, *Discourses of Brigham Young.* Selected by John A. Widtsoe. Salt Lake City: Deseret Book, 1941.